SHERLOCK HOLMES
on the Screen

SHERLOCK HOLMES
on the Screen

The Motion Picture Adventures
of the World's Most Popular Detective

Robert W. Pohle, Jr. and Douglas C. Hart

SOUTH BRUNSWICK AND NEW YORK: A. S. BARNES AND COMPANY
LONDON: THOMAS YOSELOFF LTD

A. S. Barnes and Co., Inc.
Cranbury, New Jersey 08512

Thomas Yoseloff Ltd
Magdalen House
136-148 Tooley Street
London SE1 2TT, England

Library of Congress Cataloging in Publication Data

Pohle, Robert W   1949-
    Sherlock Holmes on the screen.

    Bibliography: p.
    Includes index.
    1. Sherlock Holmes films. I. Hart, Douglas C.,
joint author. II. Title.
PN1995.9.S5P6   791.43′7   76-10887
ISBN 0-498-01889-X

PRINTED IN THE UNITED STATES OF AMERICA

To our wives, Becky and Nancy,
whose patience, encouragement, understanding,
and love
made this book possible.

Contents

Acknowledgments

Grateful acknowledgment is made to those individuals and institutions who provided time and information to aid us in the preparation of this book:

Mr. Peter Cushing
Mr. William K. Everson
Miss Jennifer Aylmer, Curator of the British Theatrical Museum
National Film Archives of the British Film Institute
The British Museum Reading Room
The New York Public Library
The Lincoln Center Library for the Performing Arts
The London University Library
The Library of Congress
Bryan Williams and Joan and Martin Abrahams for technical assistance
Ed Okie
Robert Pohle wishes to thank his family: his mother Mae Pohle for the loan of her William Gillette collection; his sister Mimi Pohle for her careful research in London; and also his father, sister Terrell, grandparents Pohle and Moore, Aunt Kay, and friend, Aristophanes.

Ms. Susan S. Perry, for her photographic genius

Introduction

Despite the successes he achieved in so many other things, Sir Arthur Conan Doyle was thoroughly unsuccessful when in 1893 he tried to pitch his Great Detective over the Reichenbach Falls; he was met with as little success in 1927 when he attempted to consign both Holmes and Watson to Valhalla with his valedictory incantation, " . . . and so, reader, farewell to Sherlock Holmes!"

For Holmes' immortality has been of an even richer kind than that of his fellow classics of the world of fiction; for the stubborn fellow lives on, not only in our hearts and minds, but palpably before our very eyes!

You feel, perhaps, eerily, that you are indeed in some kind of Valhalla yourself when you spend any great length of time alone in a cubicle of the National Film Archives in London, running some of the old tinted and silent Holmes epics by hand in the glimmering light of a Movieola viewer; but you do not feel that the Holmes you see palely flickering before you in light and shadow is a ghost.

For, unlike most of us, Holmes will never have to make the transition from this world to the next. Rather, he came into this mundane plane itself from another world—the world of the imagination. And far from becoming less-substantial with the passing of time, as his creator seemed to anticipate, he has become more and more earthly, a denizen of this humble material world, until finally there can be only a few left who do not take his flesh-and-blood existence quite for granted—as witnessed by the innumerable letters that are sent to him every year at Baker Street.

During his earthly pilgrimage, Holmes has been incarnated in films alone by a startling succession of some of the finest actors of the last seventy-five years; and like all great dramatic roles, the role of the Great Detective has proven itself capable of a tremendous variety of subtly different interpretations. In this respect, we can follow the progression of styles of acting through these films—and not only of acting, for the history of Sherlock Holmes on the screen spans virtually the entire history of films themselves. Few characters, if any, have exercised so durable a fascination; there have been well over 150 Sherlock Holmes films released since 1903—and this is not even counting the nearly as numerous Sherlock Holmes film parodies.

Accompanying Holmes himself, of course, are all the other inhabitants of his milieu. Foremost, more loved by some even than Holmes himself, is the badly mistreated but unfailingly faithful and steady Dr. John H. Watson, about whom so many changes have been rung by his portrayers—old and young, stupid and clever, military and fuddy-duddy.

Then there is Mrs. Hudson, the long-suffering landlady—Holmes and Watson were both "untidy fellows" as lodgers, and entertained some bizarre guests; the doggedly earnest, if not entirely capable, Inspector Lestrade, who, perhaps, has not done the reputation of Scotland Yard any benefit; Holmes' brother Mycroft, fascinatingly obscure; the unfriendly marksman, Col. Sebastian Moran; and, of course, the obverse side of Holmes himself, his contrary mirror-image—the malevolent Professor Moriarty. This is not to mention the pea-soupers and hansoms, the Hounds and Irregulars, the Persian slippers and hypodermic needles, and all the other animate and inanimate forms and essences that are summoned up with the very sound of the name "Sherlock Holmes."

It is curious how often this milieu has been more fully realized in the more cheaply made Holmes films than in the bigger-budgeted productions—one has only to think of Roy William Neill's astonishingly evocative but economically achieved lighting effects in the Universal series, or George Ridgwell's frequently dynamic camera angles in his two series of Eille Norwood "Adventures"; and, of course, the warmly human playing of Arthur Wontner, Nigel Bruce, and so many others. Next to these, the seemingly more lavishly mounted Barrymore and Brook efforts, for example, somehow seem to have missed the essential atmosphere and feeling, perhaps because Holmes' "country of the mind" is more within reach of the imagination than the well-meaning pocketbook.

The history of Holmes and Watson on the screen is, more than anything else, the history of the multitude of personalities through which these characters have been brought to life. We have tried, therefore, not only to chronicle the films themselves, but, in particular, to paint fairly representative portraits of the actors who have played Holmes and Watson. These many performers, each of a very distinctive individual personality, have successively channeled their own unique characteristics into their interpretations of these same two characters over a period of seventy-five years; and this multitude of interpretations has given these characters, in sum, a richness, variety, and fullness, which few characters other than Shakespeare's have ever had in film, drama, or literature.

The influence of Sherlock Holmes is all-pervading, and you will find his name in the most unexpected contexts: he is mentioned in Basil Davenport's *Roman Reader*; in James Joyce's *Finnegans Wake*; and his tales served as a model for the literary style of the late secretary-general of the United Nations, U Thant.

Recently there has been a renaissance of interest in the character, with several best-selling books on the lists, a long-running Broadway revival, another revival on radio, the television series *Rivals of Sherlock Holmes*; and, announced for the future, an off-Broadway *Hound of the Baskervilles,* a new film with Douglas Wilmer, a new Broadway musical, and a made-for-television movie with Robert Shaw and Donald Pleasance.

The fascination of Holmes for a chaotic world is perhaps his unfailing ability to set things right, in an orderly fashion. And, yet, despite his seemingly materialistic concentration on "facts," he is really the enemy of the everyday and the so-called "rational"; for he delights in proving that things are not what they seem; that everyday things conceal mysteries; and that seemingly insolvable mysteries may be solved.

When we began this project in December of 1971, we were entering largely uncharted seas. During the course of our rather extensive research in Britain and the United States, we were to reaffirm many times over the prudence of going whenever possible to original, contemporary sources for our research, rather than to secondary reference works that have perpetuated so many errors in this particular subject. Since we initiated our own project, several books have been published that dealt with areas of our own concern; but we pressed on with our project when we discovered that each of these new works (no matter how admirable in other respects) conflicted with our own findings in many areas; and also that each seemed to draw, at least in part, from secondary sources in areas where primary sources had in fact been available, thus throwing serious doubt on their own credibility on the points at issue. Further, unfortunately, none of these

rival works has extensively published its sources, which would have helped to clear up many of the controversial points at issue; for example, the question of the casts for the Nordisk series, about which almost every reputable source has given different information. Hopefully, we resolve this particular problem in our Nordisk chapter.

Our book, in addition, is considerably more complete in scope than any of the others that have so far seen print. Unlike any of these others, we have tried to be exhaustive on the subject of Sherlock Holmes in films. It has not, of course, always been entirely within our grasp—due in some cases to the rather incomplete references available, even in the major research centers, for relatively obscure performers and films; and due in others to time-consuming and conflicting commitments of both authors.

We feel very confident, however, that very many of the major areas touched upon in this book have never before been treated in such depth as they have been here.

As an example of the chaotic state in which Holmesian filmography has foundered, we mention here only that we have deleted one entire series of films that has hitherto been listed by several reference works. It develops that the Treville-Moyse series of 1912 was previously counted twice: once as a Franco-British series, and once as by Eclair.

Likewise, the British Samuelson *Study In Scarlet* has been listed twice due to its United States copyright by Pathé Frères; and once again, in 1915, the Pathé's release of the German film *Hund von Baskerville,* of the previous year, also resulted in the same film being counted twice.

Such mistakes as these have abounded; and even where one of the rival books on the subject has been correct on one of these numerous controversial points, it has left the reader without guidance by failing to indicate its sources or reasons for accepting one interpretation and rejecting another. The reader has consequently been left at sea, not knowing which source to believe, and lacking the sort of documentation that would enable him to decide for himself.

However, despite the many controversies that we hope we have cleared up, gray areas remain. In many cases it has seemed impossible to come down firmly on the side of one piece of evidence in preference to another. We have been forced to list as many as three running times for some films, for example. These discrepancies may represent mistakes on the parts of some of our sources, or they may indicate an actual variance in footage due to cutting. A few films we know for certain have been cut after release. Thus, when it has been impossible to verify one single running time, we have thought it best to list the variants.

Who is this character Sherlock Holmes, about whom we propose to treat at such length in the pages to follow? Many names have been suggested as the "originals" of the Great Detective: Dr. Joseph Bell, Wendel Scherer, Poe's Dupin, and Conan Doyle himself, among others. We discuss this question at length in the next chapter, but from wherever this remarkable personage came in 1887, for those of us of this generation of movies, Holmes wears the faces we have seen on the screen. In the following pages we attempt to chronicle each of these myriad faces with which Holmes has looked out upon the darkened theaters throughout this century. Their variety—and quality—is great . . . but all of them are Holmes, and Holmes himself is all the more a living character for being all of them.

Each case has been the prelude to another, and the crisis
once over, the actors have passed forever out of
our busy lives.

Sir Arthur Conan Doyle
The Adventure of the Solitary Cyclist

1

Sir Arthur Conan Doyle and the Origins of Sherlock Holmes

Conan Doyle himself usually intimated that he had based the character of Sherlock Holmes on his old professor at the University of Edinburgh—Dr. Joseph Bell. All those who knew Dr. Bell, and, indeed, even Bell himself, believed this to have been the case, and anyone who inspects Dr. Bell's photograph, or reads of his deductive methods and conversation, finds it very easy to be convinced as well. In fact, it has come to be accepted, almost universally, as the correct explanation, although some writers have made a rather unconvincing case for another of Conan Doyle's professors as having at least a share in the character.

Recently, however, Mr. Michael Harrison made a startling discovery, which was first published a few years ago in "Ellery Queen's Mystery Magazine." It develops that in 1882, five years before Conan Doyle wrote *A Study in Scarlet,* the first Holmes story, a London detective (or private "inquiry agent") named Wendel Scherer received considerable publicity through his connection with the very prominent criminal case of a man named Urban Napoleon Stanger.

Now, any reader of the first Holmes story will immediately recall that a character named Stanger (surely not a common name) plays a very important part in the action. But, even more to the point, in view of the fact that Conan Doyle plainly stated that he drew his detective's surname from Oliver *Wendell* Holmes, the additional coincidence of the 1882 detective's name also being Wendell is rather impressive. Further.

Sidney Paget illustration for "A Case of Identity," as published in the *Strand Magazine* in 1891.

17

if more evidence were needed, Mr. Harrison notes that the German name "Scherer" translates as "Barber" or, in old English usage, "Shear-locks."

It is, of course, possible to read too much into this ·discovery, major though it undoubtly is; the names, after all, may have lain unconsciously in Conan Doyle's mind, so that he was not himself inventing them; and the resemblance of Holmes to Joseph Bell in both appearance and personality is far too close not to be taken into consideration.

There still remains Edgar Allan Poe's detective character (the first detective in fiction, in the sense we use today) who, again, resembles Holmes so closely (even to his "Watson") that it would be too far-fetched to write it off to a merely general influence.

In the long run, though, even though we must credit all of the above gentlemen as having their fingers in the pie, I think that a fair-minded reader will have to admit that the true, original, one-and-only Sherlock Holmes himself was someone quite different in almost all respects:

"I confess that if anyone is Sherlock Holmes, it is myself."

The above ·words were, of course, spoken by Sir Arthur Conan Doyle.

Some have mistakenly identified Conan Doyle with Dr. Watson, due to their similarity in physical appearance and their both being doctor-writers; and others have asserted that Doyle could not be Holmes because the former was so chivalrously polite and the latter so rude. Holmes, however, was in fact equally as passionate in his chivalry as Doyle; we must be wary of judging Holmes by his own self-image of the cooly calculating thinking machine, and remember that few of us are our own best judges; we must judge Holmes, rather, by his *behavior*, which is quite another thing than he says it is. I think no one will find a reference in any of the stories to Holmes being inconsiderate to a

Sidney Paget illustration for "The Boscombe Valley Mystery," as published in the *Strand Magazine* in 1891.

lady (although he surely must have been trying to Dr. Watson!).

But, if we lay the superficialities of physical appearance aside for the moment, we must admit that it was the vivifying personality of Doyle himself that is the largest ingredient in the Holmes we love.

John Dickson Carr, in his biography of Doyle, which had the full cooperation of the surviving members of the Doyle family, notes some of the Holmes-Doyle resemblances: fondness for working in old dressing gowns, for clay pipes, for compiling scrapbooks, for amassing documents, for keeping a magnifying glass on his desk and a pistol in the drawer, and an interest in the works of Winwood Reade—all thoroughly Holmesian, of course. Then there is Conan Doyle's own brilliant detective work in connection with the real-life cases of Oscar Slater and George Edalji, the second of which has been recently dramatized for stage, radio, and TV (the latter featuring Nigel Davenport as Doyle, incidentially; in 1937's *Der Mann, Der Sherlock Holmes War*, Doyle was portrayed by Paul Bildt; and in '71 Josef Patocka played him in *Touha Sherlocka Holmese*).

To return to the Sherlock-Arthur parallels, there is the notably shared trait of Holmes and Doyle of "art in the blood." With Holmes it was the painter Vernet; with Doyle, just about his entire family: his grandfather John Doyle, the first to come from Ireland to England, was an artist, and so, (to varying extents) were all of his sons, including Charles Altamont Doyle, the father of our author. Parenthetically, we may note that "Altamont" was the name Sherlock Holmes chose for his pseudonym in "His Last Bow."

The fact that Conan Doyle tended to make light of his Holmes stories, and regarded them as far less-important achievements than his historical novels and other "serious" works, may quite well have been due to this very closeness of Holmes to himself. His other works were written only after long and painstaking research, while the Holmes stories were written rather quickly: he wrote one of them in the space of a single afternoon, and tossed off the entire full-length play of *The Speckled Band* in two weeks, strictly as a potboiler. It seems plausible that, writing in this haste, he drew more on his own life and subconscious than when he was engaged in one of his other works. G. B. Shaw thought his *Farfetched Fables* produced by something similar to "automatic writing," which phenomenon Doyle himself believed in very sincerely; and I think it may not be too farfetched to suggest that Doyle, in his Holmes stories, perhaps drew unconsciously on deeper spiritual forces than he realized. They have, after all, lasted much longer than his other works. Gavin Lambert's recent book, *The Dangerous Edge*, has suggested that the very reason Doyle became a writer of mysteries and thrillers was that, in common with many other mystery-writers, he had suffered some childhood trauma; and whether or not we are willing to credit Mr. Lambert's entire thesis, he does, at least, lend support to the idea that the Holmes stories

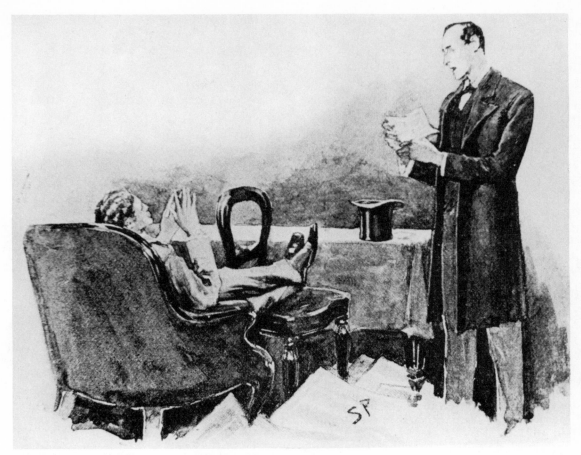

Sidney Paget illustration for "The Adventure of the Noble Bachelor," as published in the *Strand Magazine* in 1892.

sprang from deeper sources than Doyle himself perhaps suspected.

His father, besides being a water-colorist, was an architect and a journalist; and James A. McCash has recently suggested in the London *Times Literary Supplement* that Charles Altamont Doyle may also have been the pseudonymous author of the *James McGovan* detective stories, basing this theory on the rather Holmesian deduction that certain works, which he identifies as that author's, seem to have been written by someone who knew Ediburgh well, but who originally came from London (a later *T.L.S.* writer, however, disputes this identication).

Charles Doyle was overshadowed by his more famous brothers, like the cartoonist "Dickie." Lambert says that Charles was "remote and disconcerting," and that the young Arthur Doyle preferred his mother. Whether or not this was the case, certainly Conan

Sidney Paget illustration for "The Red-Headed League," as published in the *Strand Magazine* in 1891.

Sidney Paget illustration for "The Adventure of the Copper Beeches," as published in the *Strand Magazine* in 1892.

Doyle was very close to his mother, who instilled in him one of the abiding passions of his life: history, and in particular the history of chivalry and adventure. Her name was Mary Foley, and like her husband she came of an ancient Irish family; she was also related, through the Northumberland Percy family (and Shakespeare's Hotspur) to the Royal House of Plantagenet. Her husband's lineage was comparably noble, as his own mother, Marianna Conan, was descended from the Dukes of Brittany of that name. We have happened upon an even earlier and noble Conan—a king (as it happens) of Arthurian Britain, named Aurelius Caninus; but despite the coincidence of our author's two first names, it is not probable that this was a relation. The Doyle family was of Norman descent and was granted their Irish estates in the early fourteenth century, but it was their ruination by the Penal Laws (against Catholics) that led Arthur's grandfather to England. Conan Doyle himself, of course, later was to become a convinced believer in the Spiritualist faith, and also ran for Parliament as a Unionist (hardly a typically Irish Catholic stance.) He was related also to Sir Walter Scott.

He was born at Picardy Place in Edinburgh on 22 May 1859, and, after being educated at Hodder House and Stonyhurst, went on to Edinburgh University (of which he was to make Dr. Watson an alumnus in his story *The Field Bazaar*), where he of course came into contact with the astonishing Dr. Joseph Bell. He had visited London first at the age of fifteen, and was impressed by its damp, foggy atmosphere. After serving briefly as ship's surgeon on an Arctic whaling cruise, he eventually settled down to specialize; but it was his lack of success in medicine that led him to concentrate more fully on his writing career (which he had been pursuing anyway for some time already). Thus, Sherlock Holmes was born. Doyle's non-Holmesian writings were to bring him many well-deserved honors in his lifetime, including a knighthood, and would have even included a peerage had he not been a Spiritualist; but it is for Holmes that he will no doubt be remembered as long as the English language is understood—no doubt longer, since the reader will readily gather from our book what an international (and visual) character the Great Detective has become.

A number of his other writings have also been filmed, however. The first seems to have been *The House of Temperley*, which was made in 1913 by Harold M. Shaw, chief producer of the London Film Company. It was based on Doyle's play of the same story, *Red Stone*, and oddly enough it featured Hubert Willis re-creating his stage role of "Tom Belcher." A few years later, Willis was to become forever associated with the part of Dr. Watson by playing it a total of forty-six times in the Eille Norwood series. Producer

Shaw was to make Doyle's *Firm of Girdlestone* as a five-reeler in 1916.

Next, chronologically, however, came *Brigadier Gerard* (perhaps featuring Eille Norwood), directed in 1915 by Bert Haldane for Barker Films in England—here, too, there is a Holmes link, as two years before, Haldane had worked with G. B. Samuelson on *60 Years a Queen*, and Samuelson looms large in our book as the maker of two classic Holmes silents. *Gerard* was filmed again the following year by Red Feather (Universal) in five reels. There was to be one more silent version, which we shall come to; and recently in '68 yet another version has been shot in Europe in color, by Jerzy Skolimowski, titled *Adventures of Gerard* (United Artists).

In 1923, Pathé released a film dealing with Doyle's Spiritualist beliefs entitled *Is Conan Doyle Right?;* it was credited, coincidentally, to Cullom Holmes Ferrell. 1924 saw *The Tragedy of the Korosko* lensed as, alas, *The Desert Sheik* by Tom Terriss, from a script by Alicia Ramsey for A.C. & R.C. Bromhead. But what was to be by far Doyle's greatest non-Holmesian film success appeared the next year in the shape of Willis O'Brien's classic *The Lost World,* which featured Wallace Beery as Professor Challenger (Claude Rains was to play him in

the inferior remake in '60) and Lewis Stone as Lord John (Stone was later to play Sax Rohmer's imitation-Sherlock Nayland Smith). Footage from this film was reedited into a 1938 one-reeler called *A Lost World,* for use in schools. After the later miraculously improved animation of O'Brien and his disciple Ray Harryhausen, the special effects in this film suffer a bit by comparison, but they are still miles ahead of the live lizards of the '60 version, which were utterly dreadful in all senses of the word.

Still another version of the "Brigadier Gerard" stories was made in 1927—this time by Donald Crisp for DeMille Pictures in nine reels; but it was rechristened *The Fighting Eagle.* Doyle's *Rodney Stone* had been filmed in Britain by Percy Nash in '20, and in '32, Universal in the United States made a twelve-part serial of *The Lost Special.* The latter Doyle tale has long been regarded by devout Holmesians as a Holmes story in every respect save one—Holmes never appears!

In 1929, Sir Arthur himself appeared on film, delightfully accompanied by a weighty tome and a romping canine—two thoroughly apropos props for this adventurous author. He spoke on Sherlock and on Spiritualism—one suspects that he agreed to discuss

Sidney Paget illustration for "The Adventure of the Beryl Coronet," as published in the *Strand Magazine* in 1892.

Sidney Paget illustration for "The Adventure of the Blue Carbuncle," as published in the *Strand Magazine* in 1892.

21

the first subject, of which he was not overfond, in order to be given a platform from which to discuss the second, to which he was devoted. It is a great thrill, in this film, to look upon the face of this rather-upper-class, very gentle man. The next year he cut a phonograph recording on the same two subjects; he had previously been glimpsed in a newsreel in '14.

He died on 7 July 1930, fully convinced that death affected no more than the body.

The subject of Sherlock Holmes on the screen, of course, begins in our next chapter, but this seems a good place to raise the ghost of a Holmes film that might have been. We have inspected several original letters in British Theatre Museum's Sir Henry Irving archive, which established that, firstly, Conan Doyle sent Sir Henry in 1892 a copy of his new book *The Adventures of Sherlock Holmes*, and, secondly, that six years later a gentleman named Charles Arnold was trying to interest Irving in the kinematograph "united with a lantern."

Now although it is true that Arnold was thinking only of using film to provide scenic backgrounds for live plays (thus anticipating mixed-media shows), rather than for the purpose of making "story" films, and also that Doyle never seems to have specifically suggested Holmes as a potential character for Irving to play, one still has food for thought. Suppose Irving had become intrigued with the character? Suppose he had seen the possibilities of the "kinema" as a creative tool—or just a mechanical means of preserving his own performances? It is undoubtedly just an idle dream, but what would we not have given to see the Greatest Actor of the 1890s incarnating the Greatest Detective of those days! Physically as well as temperamentally he would have been just about ideal for the part; some of his great roles were later to become the property of notable Sherlockian performers, and seem to have fitted them as well as they did Irving; Rathbone and Wontner and Saintsbury were all ideally cast as Louis XI, (Rathbone was nominated for an Oscar), and Raymond Massey and Wontner made very fine Richelieus.

But this is only fantasy, and the first screen Holmes was in fact to be a nameless gentleman who was so far from being the greatest actor of his day that he could not even keep a straight face for the few seconds duration of *Sherlock Holmes Baffled*—an inconspicuous beginning for a brilliant film career, as we shall see.

Conan Doyle's total Sherlockian production amounted to four novels, fifty-eight short stories (if we count the self-parodies *The Field Bazaar* and *How Watson Learned the Trick*), the plays *Speckled Band* and *Crown Diamond*, and a few unpublished curiosities such as a play written prior to *Study in Scarlet*, which features Watson without Holmes! Virtually all of these items have been filmed in some form; some of them many times. Many of these films, however, have been "original" stories that were based only on Conan Doyle's characters, while others have been based on bits and pieces of several Doyle stories combined to form something new.

Sidney Paget illustration for "The Adventure of the Blue Carbuncle," as published in the *Strand Magazine* in 1892.

Sidney Paget illustration for "The Man With The Twisted Lip," as published in the *Strand Magazine* in 1891.

22

We will have much more to say about Sir Arthur, his stories, their backgrounds, and how they came to be written, at appropriate places throughout our book, as we discuss the specific film adaptations. For now, we must take our leave of this very remarkable writer. We feel that with all the interest surrounding his creation today, the creator himself has often been badly neglected; but this subject is not entirely within our province, for, as the reader will discover, the films of Sherlock Holmes all too often have had lamentably little in common with the original works of Sir Arthur Conan Doyle—or sometimes with originality of any kind.

2

The Early Silent Films

SHERLOCK HOLMES BAFFLED (United States)

Date of Release: © 24 February 1903; perhaps filmed as early as April 1900.
Running time: 30 seconds
Production Company: American Mutoscope and Biograph Co.
Photography: Arthur Marvin

Holmes makes his screen debut in this film, with the standard image that had been established on the stage by William Gillette, including cigar (rather than pipe)

and dressing gown. The gentleman playing Holmes, whose name we have been unable to find, was certainly not an experienced actor, since he finds it impossible to keep a straight face for the duration of this extremely brief film. He does bear a very marked facial resemblance to a young Walter Huston, but this possibility may safely be ruled out on the score of amateurishness alone.

This is a "trick" film of the Méliès variety, and though the very elementary disappearing and reappearing effects today seem clumsy and obvious, they

A rare sequence of frame enlargements from *Sherlock Holmes Baffled*. Here, in our first sight on the screen of 221B Baker Street, the daring masked burglar has actually invaded Holmes' own premises. (Courtesy Library of Congress)

The first appearance ever of Sherlock Holmes in a film. He courteously taps the interloper on the shoulder to announce his presence. (Courtesy Library of Congress)

24

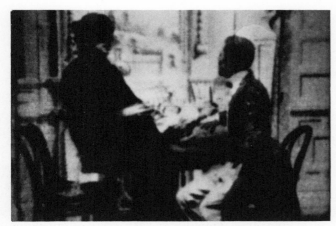

Having disappeared (by Méliès-like stop-motion) as Holmes touched him, the thief reappears seated on the table. (Courtesy Library of Congress)

Revolver drawn, the now-peeved Holmes gives chase. (Courtesy Library of Congress)

were, of course, undoubtedly startling in their own period.

A burglar is seen tossing his booty into a sack on a table; this room in which he is engaged in rifling may, perhaps, afford us with our first glimpse of 221B Baker Street, since the door opens to admit Sherlock Holmes. If this is indeed the place, it is surely a sad comment that Holmes has been so disgracefully remiss as to allow burglars in his home. However, none of the familiar Baker Street paraphernalia is visible—no "VR" on the wall in bullet holes; no Persian slipper for tobacco—so this may not, in fact, be Holmes' own sitting-room at all. If not, however, the situation is nearly as bad, since Holmes has clearly gone visiting while absent-mindedly forgetting to put on his over-coat.

Holmes, in his usual self-confident manner, taps the burglar on the shoulder, and is naturally taken aback when the man vanishes into thin air. Holmes sits down and lights a cigar, apparently preparing to ponder the situation (can this be a "three-cigar" problem?), only to have the cigar explode in his face. Let us hope that it was the burglar who left this trick cigar and not a playful Dr. Watson. (If Holmes is not in his own flat he can surely be forgiven for making free with his host's cigars after the nasty shock he has had.) Through the haze of smoke the burglar materializes, sitting on the edge of the table. Despite Holmes fruitlessly and rather peevishly taking a shot at the burglar with his pistol, the fellow continues to disappear and reappear at ease, at last appearing outside the house with the sack of booty in his hand. Even the great Holmes can surely be forgiven for having been baffled! Let us hope that Mrs. Hudson was not cross with him for allowing so many of her belongings to be stolen; and if he were in someone else's home, let us hope he had quitted the scene of the crime before the owner returned!

The burglar is too elusive for Holmes, who evidently needs to practice his sharp-shooting by shooting another "VR" into Mrs. Hudson's wall. (Courtesy Library of Congress)

Holmes thinks the burglar has forgotten his booty, but the well-filled bag will soon disappear from the detective's hand and materialize in that of the burglar outside the window. (Courtesy Library of Congress)

THE ADVENTURES OF SHERLOCK HOLMES
(United States) (**HELD FOR A RANSOM;** Great Britain: **SHERLOCK HOLMES; HELD TO RANSOM**)

Date of Release: © 6 September 1905; perhaps filmed as early as '03.
Production Company: Vitagraph Co. of America
Running Time: 725 feet
Director: James Stuart Blackton
Screenplay: Theodor Liebler
Based on: *The Sign of the Four*

CAST

Sherlock Holmes   Maurice Costello
                           Kyrle Bellew
                           J. Barney Sherry

Maurice George Washington Costello, the first screen Sherlock who can possibly be identified, was

Frame blowup from 1905 *Adventures of Sherlock Holmes.* **Man with moustache, center, is possibly Maurice Costello as Sherlock Holmes in some disguise. (Courtesy Library of Congress)**

Unidentified players in 1905 *Adventures of Sherlock Holmes.* (Courtesy Library of Congress)

born in Pittsburgh, Pennsylvania on 22 February 1877. At the age of eleven he was working as a printer's devil, but five years later he was an amateur performer, and he made his professional acting debut in 1897 with the Davis Stock Company in the city of his birth. There are many conflicting dates for his debut in films, ranging from 1906 to 1909—all of them obviously after the date on which this film was copyrighted. However, the cast for this film is confirmed by several sources; and since it is said that Costello had made over a thousand films before 1915, it is obviously unwise to generalize too much about his film career. In addition, an article in *Moving Picture Stories,* 2 May 1913, definitely stated that he was free-lancing, or "jobbing," in '06, "rather than playing permanent engagements"; so it is easy to see him doing the same a little earlier. Certainly, however, his famous association with Vitagraph had not yet begun in earnest at the time he was playing Holmes for them.

With Maurice Costello, we observe for the first time a phenomenon that we are to see again and again in this book: often the careers of actors who have played Sherlock Holmes coincide in other areas as well. Costello scored a great success in 1911 with a major version of Dickens' *A Tale of Two Cities,* a vehicle that, in the future, would furnish notable parts for such Holmesian actors as Basil Rathbone, Clive Brook, Reginald Owen, and Christopher Lee.

Another parallel appears in the career of this film's director, who filmed a version of *Raffles* in this same year of 1905. Raffles, as it happens, was created by Conan Doyle's brother-in-law, E.W. Hornung, and was later to be played by such filmic Sherlocks as John Barrymore, Forrest Holger-Madsen, Eille Norwood, and Arthur Wontner, and even to be paired with Holmes in the Nordisk series. Barrymore, by the way, became the son-in-law of Maurice Costello when he married his daughter, the beautiful actress, Dolores.

Dolores, like her sister Helen, began in films as a child while her father was a great star. Her mother was Mae Trensham. Maurice Costello directed as well as acted, and toured the world making films for Vitagraph for a year beginning in December 1915. A film-reference book published that same year credits him with evolving "the 'slow-motion' style of acting" (whatever that may mean) "now used by every pictorial star of importance in the entire world." He was a great amateur athlete, interested in boxing and automobiles, and his long film career stretched well into the era of John Wayne, with whom he appeared in 1941's *Lady From Louisiana.* He played the role of Christ in the silent film *The Battle Hymn of the Republic;* his grandson John Drew Barrymore, curiously enough, played Christ many years later in *Pontius Pilate* with Basil Rathbone. Some of Costello's other films include *A Midsummer Night's Dream,* 1909, (as Orlando, with future professor Moriarty Harry T. Morey); *Night Before Christmas,* 1912; *Human Collateral,* 1920; *Conceit,* 1921 (as a villain); *Glimpses of the Moon,* 1923; *Mad Marriage,* 1925; *Camille,* 1927; and *Holly-*

wood Boulevard (with many other old silent stars) in 1936. Maurice Costello died on 29 October 1950.

Director "Jimmy" Blackton (1868–1941) was an important British-born film pioneer, who co-founded Vitagraph in 1896 in the United States. A former sketcher and performer, he had been working as a journalist when his paper sent him to interview Edison, who interested him in movies. Back in Britain in '21, he made an early experiment in color movies with *Glorious Adventure,* starring Lady Diana Manners, for Sir Oswald Stoll, whose studio was then just beginning their famous Eille Norwood series of Sherlock Holmes adventures.

Kyrle Bellew, noted stage actor, who is also in the cast of this film, appeared years later, in 1922, with another screen Sherlock—Clive Brook—in *Vanity Fair.* Vitagraph may have made another Holmes film during this period, as "Bronco Billy" Anderson (who was later to produce William Gillette's *Sherlock Holmes*) always insisted that he directed a Sherlockian epic for them.

If this is true, the film may well have been *Sherlock Holmes Returns,* about which nothing is known except that it was made in 1906 or 1907, and ran for 250 feet.

J. Barney Sherry, another member of the cast of the *Adventures of Sherlock Holmes.* His exact role is unknown. He also played "Raffles."

Maurice Costello, the first screen Holmes who can positively be identified.

Kyrle Bellew (1855–1911), seen here in a rare illustration from the original Sherlockian *Strand* Magazine of 1892, not only appeared in *Adventures of Sherlock Holmes,* but was also famous on the stage as Conan Doyle's character "Brigadier Gerard," and as Holmes' notorious rival "Raffles."

HOLMES IN ITALY—AMBROSIO AND OTHERS

LE RIVAL DE SHERLOCK HOLMES (Italy) (United States: RIVAL SHERLOCK HOLMES)

Released: 1907
Production Company: Societa Anonima Ambrosio (Torino)
Producer: Arturo Ambrosio
Running Time: 584 feet (6:50 minutes)

REVIEW (*Moving Picture World*, 2 May 1908):

A pictorial detective story of merit, with many lightning changes of disguise by the detective in his pursuit of the lawbreakers. Exciting scenes and physical encounters are numerous. A sensational subject of superb dramatic effect, without any objectionable features.

There is no way, alas, to be sure whether or not Holmes himself actually appears in this film, or whether only one of his rivals does. Ambrosio himself, however, seems to have been very interested in the character, or at least realized his box-office value both in Italy and abroad; for not only did he release this film in the United States in 1908 through his American branch, Ambrosio American Company (in New York City), but he made three more Holmes films over the next six years: the 1913 two-reeler released with the English titles *Griffards Claw* and *In the Grip of the Eagle's Claw*; and the two satires *Tweedledum and the Necklace*, 1911, and *Fricot Als Sherlock Holmes*, '13 (the original Italian title has been lost). *Griffard's Claw* was a kidnapping story that supplied Holmes with an airplane—hardly Victorian, but undoubtedly cinematic.

Arturo Ambrosio (1869–1960) will be remembered in Italy by quite a few films other than the above epics, for he was one of the most significant pioneers of the Italian cinema—having begun his career in 1904 and pioneering, in particular, the sort of pseudo-historical spectacle films for which Italy has been known ever since; in fact, the Steve Reeves-type "muscleman" originated with Maciste in *Cabiria* in 1913. The previous year Ambrosio had become the biggest producer in Italy, making more films than anyone else in the country.

Besides the works of Ambrosio, there were several other Sherlockian films produced in Italy during this period: Itala made *Sherlock Holmes* in 620 feet in 1909 or 1910; Lux filmed the satire *Gaffes* in 1909; *Bloomer Tricks Sherlock Holmes* (surely an indignity for the Great Man) was made by Cines in 1915; and the same year saw the delightfully titled Luna film *The Flea of the Baskervilles*.

SHERLOCK HOLMES IN THE GREAT MURDER MYSTERY (United States)

Released: 1908
Production Company: Crescent Film Manufacturing Co.
Running Time: One reel
Based on: Poe's *Murders in the Rue Morgue* (a Dupin story)

REVIEW and SYNOPSIS (*Moving Picture World*, 28 November 1908):

Our picture relates to a crime committed by a gorilla who escapes from his cage and through circumstantial evidence a young man whom we will call in our story Jim, is accused and is just about to be convicted when, through the aid of our hero, Sherlock Holmes, he is freed just in time.

Our picture opens with a girl and her sweetheart, who are sitting in her room discussing plans for their marriage. The message is brought for Jim, compelling him to leave at once.

Shipyard scene—The Gorilla escapes from his cage on a vessel, with his master, the Captain, in hot pursuit. The frightened animal climbs a porch of this girl's house and into the window of her sitting room, and after a terrific struggle between her and the beast, he kills her before the captain can prevent him. Captain immediately returns to vessel with Gorilla and stays in hiding, fearing the consequences should anyone detect him. The butler discovers the crime, and tells the police about sweetheart's visit, so police accuse Jim of the crime.

Jim, unaware of what has happened, is arrested while boarding a train.

Sherlock Holmes' Study—Sherlock Holmes is reading a book when his old friend and college chum Watson arrives. He has read of the crime in the paper, showing same to Holmes. Holmes, after reading details, decides to lend his aid in unravelling the crime.

Holmes at Work—Arrival at girl's residence. Herein are shown methods employed by Holmes to secure evidence or clue to discover the culprit.

In his study—Holmes returns to his study in deep thought, with his mind concentrating upon the crime. He is trying to unravel the mystery when he takes his old violin down from its peg and begins to play fantastic music which puts him in trance to solve the problem. Herein are shown remarkable visions of the different clues and theories of Holmes' brain. The first vision is of Jim committing the awful crime, but vision fades away before crime is committed. Second vision is of a burglar; that also fades same as the first. Holmes, who has learned of the Gorilla being in port, lends his thought to this and the vision appears of Gorilla escaping from ship, climbing the porch of the house, and into the window and committing the crime that Jim is accused of. Holmes immediately jumps up with a start, and after numerous failures, discovers the ship, Gorilla and master, accusing same of the tragedy.

Court Room—Poor Jim is convicted to be hanged, when our hero Holmes rushes in with sufficient evidence that frees Jim.

This film, unlike most of the early silents, was not content to turn Holmes into an action figure—a kind of cowboy in deerstalker—which all too many, even in the sound era, have been content to do. Rather, it made an effort to visually represent Holmes' deductions, which, of course, are necessarily verbal in the stories themselves, and obviously most easily done with dialogue. However cleverly shot this film may have been, we cannot help but feel that Holmes himself would not like to see the credit for his success taken away from the cold light of deductive reason, and given to a sort of mystic trance, fond though he certainly was of his music and less-beneficial drugs.

It is interesting, also, that this film introduces the notion, foreign to the original stories, that Holmes and Watson were at school together—an idea that was to be elaborated in unfortunate detail in the Barrymore film.

3

The Nordisk (Danish) Series

SHERLOCK HOLMES I; SHERLOCK HOLMES I LIVSFARE (Sherlock Holmes Risks His Life); in United States and Great Britain: **SHERLOCK HOLMES; SHERLOCK HOLMES IN DEATHLY DANGER; SHERLOCK HOLMES CAPTURES MORIARTY;** also known in United States as **SHERLOCK HOLMES CAPTURING MORIARTY**

Date of Release: 20 November 1908 (Great Britain— October, according to one source, though it seems impossible it could have been released there before it was in Denmark; United States—December)
Production Company: Nordisk Films Compagni, Copenhagen (Great Northern Film Company)
Running time: 348m; 1140 feet or 1141 feet (13 minutes), or approximately one and a half reels
Based on: Characters created by Conan Doyle, and the character of Raffles created by his brother-in-law, E. W. Hornung.
Director and Screenplay: Viggo Larsen

CAST

Raffles	Forrest Holger-Madsen
Sherlock Holmes	Viggo Larsen
?	Mr. Brandt
?	Mr. Dethleff
Billy	Elith Plio

(Alwin Neuss perhaps played Dr. Watson)

REVIEWS and SYNOPSES (*Moving Picture World,* 5 December 1908):

COMING HEADLINERS:
Sherlock Holmes, a detective story by the Great Northern Film Co., to be issued next week, is a masterly production in every respect. The plot in itself is interesting and well worked out. The staging is splendid and introduces some novel effects, not claptrap contraptions, but very realistic in all details. The action throughout is natural and spirited in some parts. There is a marked difference [between] the action in the Danish productions and those of other foreign makers. The Danes seem to do everything so seriously that at times their actions seem sluggish; at any rate it differs from the "chic"

Sherlock Holmes in Deathly Danger **(1908), starring Viggo Larsen and Forrest Holger-Madsen (at left). (Courtesy National Film Archives of the British Film Institute.)**

of the French actor. But it is none the worse for this; in fact, it is a pleasing variety, and if their succeeding productions of the *Sherlock Holmes* series equal the first, the series should prove a big success.

From the same magazine of the following week:

Sherlock Holmes Capturing Moriarty. The Great Northern Film Co. (Nordisk) has a notable issue for this week, called *Sherlock Holmes* telling how Holmes overcame Moriarty and Raffles. It does not appear that any of the published tales of Sherlock Holmes are followed in the plot, but the picture story is, nevertheless, it is said, exceedingly thrilling and interesting.

Nordisk ran an ad in that issue that begins to give some idea of what action actually transpired in the film, which seems now to be utterly lost:

Sherlock Holmes—The noted Detective's capture of the King of Criminals—An absorbing subject, the interest of which is enhanced by novel stage effects. The fight in the moving train is the perfection of realism! Photographic quality of our Usual High Standard! Undoubtedly This Season's Biggest Feature Film!

The ad goes on to note that Nordisk was awarded first prize (including a gold medal) at the Cinematograph Exhibition at Hamburg that year; it also mentions that "all purchasers and users of our films will be protected by the American Mutoscope and Biograph Co.," since they were licensed under the Biograph patents.

The following week's issue (19 December) continues the story:

A Notable Danish Film

Sherlock Holmes. . . . This picture had its 1st American presentation at the 14th Street Theatre last week, and offered an excellent opportunity to compare the work of the Danish film pantomimists with that of moving picture actors of other countries. The comparison is not, by any means, to the disadvantage of the Danes. The photography of the film is of a superior quality, and the scenic effects quite ingenious and novel. The plot is also interesting and is developed with considerable skill and with reasonable lucidity, although it might have been made a little more clear in the early scenes. Too much, perhaps, is left to the spectators knowledge regarding the personalities of Sherlock Holmes, Raffles and Moriarty. Nevertheless the story holds the attention strongly. The acting appears oddly stiff compared to that of French and American players, but it is most pleasantly devoid of the ridiculous overacting and contortions resorted to by so many pantomimists. When Raffles is arrested, he does not throw a succession of acrobatic fits, and when Moriarty is taken, he is only reasonably violent in the hands of the officers. In short if we may judge all Copenhagen pictures by this one, the issues of the Great Northern Film Company should prove wel-

Holmes (Viggo Larsen) seems either to have unexpectedly stepped into a room full of policemen, or to be leading the officers back out after some quarry.

come variations to any picture programme. The plot of the Sherlock Holmes picture introduces 3 fictional characters, Sherlock Holmes, Raffles and Professor Moriarty, in connection with a robbery of a pearl necklace. Raffles secures the necklace and is apprehended by the Detective. Raffles then appeals to Moriarty, who plots to kill Sherlock Holmes, but is himself arrested.

That same issue, Nordisk noted in their ad:

We have now started releasing 4 subjects per week. Among the many headliners to go on the market in the very near future are *Sherlock Holmes* Series II and III. Series I released recently is crowding every theatre in which exhibited; irresistible and fascinating pictures!

Nordisk had been founded in '06 (with the usual all-glass studio for natural sunlight) by Ole Olesen; and it was only in March of that year—when his first Holmes film was released—that he opened his American branch.

It has been stated that this film was loosely based on the Sidney Prince portion of William Gillette's Holmes play, but the above synopsis seems to indicate so little resemblance that coincidence seems a better explanation than direct influence; but the circumstances that the first Danish version of the play, by Walter Christmas, was reconstructed from notes written on his shirt-cuffs in the theater (since he could not afford to buy the rights) may perhaps account for the garbling of the plot!

It has also been suggested that this film and the following one may have been based on some Spanish plays that matched Holmes and Raffles, and that also appeared in '08; but it appears more likely to us that Danish films would have been shown in Spain than it does that Spanish plays would have reached Denmark within a few months.

Viggo Larsen, the ex-sergeant who directed and played Holmes, apparently could only think of the Great Detective as a sort of foil for an antihero like Raffles or Arsene Lupin, since he began the Nordisk series on this note; and, when he left the series to go to Germany, he inaugurated an exactly similar concept there. He had a very long and distinguished film career, and had begun with Nordisk at its founding in 1906, as an actor and director, making over one hundred films that year alone—comedies, news, sports and nature subjects (some of them featuring a young Jean Hersholt). In '07 he played the soldier in Hans Christian Andersen's *The Tinder Box*.

Beside his Holmes films, which we cover here, Larsen's later films included: *Scheven Contra Festenberg*, '15; *Die Edelsteinsammlung*, '17; *Bräutigan Auf Aktien*, '18; *Ubo Thomsens Heimkehr*, '19; *Orient*, '20; *Das Madchen Ohne Gewissen*, '22; *Die Elf Schill Schen Offiziere*, '32; *Alle Tage ist Kein Sonntag*, '35; *Stärker als Paragraphen, In Trommelfeuer der Westfront*, '36; *Mordsache Holm, Schatten Über St. Paul*, '38; *Die Geliebte*, '39; *Clarissa*, '41; *G.P.U., Diesel*, '42. At the time when he was playing Holmes, he was one of Nordisk's top directors and, indeed, one of the pioneers of the Danish industry.

Forrest Holger-Madsen, who played Raffles in this first episode, probably took over as Holmes in a later segment. Other actors who have played both Holmes and Raffles include John Barrymore, Eille Norwood, and Arthur Wontner. Like Larsen, Holger-Madsen was also a director and also emigrated to Germany, where he apparently was to direct some silents. Some of his other films included *Dødssejleren* (also known as *Dynamitattentatet Paa Fyrtaarnet*), made for Nordisk in 1911 and released the following year; *Die Herrin der Welt*, '21; *Sei Gegrüsst, du Mein Schönes Sørrent*, '30.

Alwin Karl Heinrich Neuss, though born in Köln-Deutz in 1879, began his notable film career in Denmark with Nordisk, after theater training in Berlin. He studied acting under Josef Kainz, a famous Hamlet of the time. He was eventually to take over the part of Holmes in the Nordisk series, but may perhaps have begun in it with the role of Dr. Watson, thus anticipating Reginald Owen (who also played both parts on the screen) by over twenty years. He later starred in the *Tom Shark* detective series as a sort of imitation Holmes. Neuss's other important films (besides his German Holmes films, which we will cover in this chapter) included the title role in *Hamlet*, '10, filmed by Nordisk in Kronborg (Elsinore) and Fredricksborg castles under the eye of the real Danish king; *Clown Charly*, '19; and *Der Tanz Ins Glück* and *Das Alte Lied*—both from 1930. A director as well as an actor, he died in Berlin on 29 October 1935.

Before we proceed further with our examination of the Nordisk series (and its German continuations), it would be well to say a few words about the great controversies that have seemingly grown up about these films.

IF ONLY HOLMES WERE AVAILABLE FOR CONSULTATION

The Nordisk series presented us with our thorniest problem of all. We consulted a total of ten sources, and found a great deal of totally conflicting information. There is dispute as to the number of films in the series, the titles of the entries, and, most of all, as to the identities of the several actors who portrayed Holmes during the course of the series.

And not one of the ten authors consulted seems to be aware that there is any controversy at all! Rather, each one states his own conclusions without taking any notice of rival opinions or giving his sources in any great detail. The student, then, cannot help being puzzled and unsure as to who to believe. We have, therefore, felt it wise to discuss at some length our own conclusions.

To begin, we will briefly summarize the separate attributions of the writers who have previously tackled this problem.

Mr. Michael Pointer, in his excellent book *The Public Life of Sherlock Holmes*, lists only eleven films for this series. He credits Viggo Larsen as Holmes in the first six entries; Otto Lagoni, Holger Rasmussen, and Alwin Neuss with one film each in the role; and lists no Holmes for the remaining two films he covers. Although his book is generally authoritative, it was not

Alwin Neuss takes a leave of absence from Baker Street to play *Hamlet* **for Nordisk. Here he is seen up to very un-Holmesian behavior, trying to hide the body of the murdered Polonius.**

possible to accept his findings on this series without confirmation from another source, since he lists no sources for his attributions and is flatly contradicted by six other publications that are also usually trustworthy. We will, therefore, return to his book later when more evidence is in.

Of the other seemingly authoritative sources, the National Film Archives of the British Film Institute credits Forrest Holger-Madsen as Holmes in eight of the Nordisk series. William K. Everson's fine book *The Detective in Films,* on the authority (as Mr. Everson personally assured the present writers) of the Danish Film Archives, agrees that Holger-Madsen played Holmes in a "dozen or so" films for Nordisk of Denmark, and adds that Alwin Neuss played Watson, with Lagoni taking over as Holmes in a later Nordisk entry. The magazine *Films in Review* agrees again that Holger-Madsen was Holmes, and Neuss was Watson in twelve films for Nordisk. The late William Baring-Gould, in his *Annotated Sherlock Holmes,* agrees once again that Holger-Madsen played Holmes in a whole series of films for Nordisk; and, although he is silent on whether or not Neuss played the part of Watson, he states that Neuss subsequently replaced Holger-Madsen in the role of Holmes. *The Filmgoer's Companion,* once again, says that Holger-Madsen was Holmes in twelve Nordisk films. And Johan Daisne's valuable Continental European reference work, *Filmographic Dictionary of World Literature,* lists a 1908 Danish film, *The Adventures of Sherlock Holmes,* with Holger-Madsen, Neuss, Einar Zangenberg, and directed by Holger-Madsen. Although Daisne does not list the roles played by Holger-Madsen and Neuss, he lists Holger-Madsen first in a cast of four. In addition, several of the above sources had stated that in his Holmes series Holger-Madsen directed himself, and Daisne appears to be in agreement on this point.

Mr. Pointer *does* list Holger-Madsen as having appeared in the series, but not in the role of Holmes. It was evident, also, from several pieces of internal evidence, that he had not seen the Daisne book when he wrote his own, and was, therefore, perhaps not in possession of all the relevant information.

Since none of the contemporary sources (such as *Moving Picture World* and *New York Dramatic Mirror*) we had thus far been able to consult gave cast lists, we had, at the above point in our research, felt that we had no choice but to accept the verdict of the other six authorities, rather than that of Mr. Pointer.

However, our subsequent examination of the *Danish Film Index 1906–1956* (published by Nordisk themselves) not only added much new information, but also solved some of the controversy—although not all. It proved that the many may be wrong (at least on *some* points) and the one (Pointer) right, no matter how authoritative the many. For although the Nordisk book does not specifically confirm Pointer's casts, it tends to support him by agreeing on many other details. However, the information in the index is sketchy at best, and there remains the somewhat

contradictory information of the Danish Film Archives. Careful study of translations and subtitles enabled us to compile the Nordisk information that we have given in this chapter. In the main, we have agreed with Pointer, but we feel that we have been able to collate all the variant information in such a way so as not to utterly contradict *any* of the previously mentioned sources. We did succeed in finding the twelfth film, not mentioned by Mr. Pointer.

Unfortunately, the Nordisk index lists very few of the actors and directors involved; so this mystery cannot be cleared up once and for all until further sources become available. It is to be regretted that, as none of the above authors, except Everson, listed their sources for different attributions, it has not been entirely possible to weigh their different merits. In the case of the Danish Film Archives, although they seem authoritative, we have not been able to ascertain *their* sources!

We feel, though, as we have said above, that our own attributions do not totally contradict any of the above sources and may therefore come closest to the truth. We are confident, at least, that we have dealt with the films in this Nordisk series at greater length and in greater depth than any of the previously published works. We hope we have done something toward clearing up the controversy.

SHERLOCK HOLMES II; in Great Britain: **RAFFLES ESCAPES FROM PRISON**; known in the United States by combination of both titles.

Released: 1908 (Great Britain—November; in the United States—27 February 1909.)
Production Company: Nordisk Films Compagni, Copenhagen (Great Northern Film Company)
Running Time: 210m; 689 feet. In the U.S.: 680 feet (11½ min.)
Based on: Characters created by Conan Doyle and on character of Raffles created by his brother-in-law, E. W. Hornung. Partly inspired by *The Empty House.*
Director and Screenplay: Viggo Larsen

CAST

Raffles	Forrest Holger-Madsen
Sherlock Holmes	Viggo Larsen
?	Poul Gregaard

(Alwin Neuss perhaps played Dr. Watson)

REVIEWS and SYNOPSES: On 27 February 1909 the New York *Dramatic Mirror* carried Great Northern's announcement of the release of "important subjects for independent service," including this film "in which the detective is again in danger of his life."

The film was reviewed in the issue of March sixth as follows:

Aside from the cavalry picture and *The Last Days of Pompeii,* this was probably the best picture shown. It is a sequel to the Sherlock Holmes picture reviewed some time ago and is done by the same actors.

Raffles escapes from prison and with Moriarty plots to kill Holmes. They entice the detective to a house and throw him into a sewer, but he gets out and they then try to shoot him, but he sets a dummy before his window, and when Raffles is about to fire his rifle at the dummy Holmes slips in behind him and makes him prisoner. The scenes are well managed and the acting is creditable. The picture perhaps would be more clear if subtitles had been more liberally employed, but to all who know their Sherlock Holmes the story is easily understood and exceedingly interesting.

SHERLOCK HOLMES III; SHERLOCK HOLMES I GASKJELDFREN; in Great Britain.: SHERLOCK HOLMES IN THE GAS CELLAR and also THE THEFT OF THE STATE DOCUMENT; SHERLOCK HOLMES IN THE GAS CHAMBER; DET HEMMELIGE DOKUMENT; THE SECRET DOCUMENT; in the United States: SHERLOCK HOLMES III—The Detective's Adventures in the Gas Cellar

Released: 1908 (in Great Britain, December; in the United States, March 1909)
Running Time: 275m; 902 feet; in the United States—890 feet; approximately one and a half reels. (15 min.)
Production Company: Nordisk Films Compagni,

Copenhagen (Great Northern Film Company)
Based on: (perhaps based on a scene in William Gillette's play)
Director and Screenplay: Viggo Larsen

CAST

| ? | Forrest Holger-Madsen |
| *Sherlock Holmes* | Viggo Larsen |

(Alwin Neuss perhaps played Dr. Watson)

The Nordisk book lists only Holger-Madsen in the cast, but he seems not to have played Raffles in this one.

SANGERINDENS DIAMANTER (The Singer's Diamonds); SHERLOCK HOLMES OPLEVELSER IV; in Great Britain: THE THEFT OF THE DIAMONDS

Date of Release: 20 January 1909; in Great Britain, 29 January 1910
Running Time: 180m; 590 feet. (10 min.)

Viggo Larsen's painful predicament in *Sherlock Holmes in the Gas Cellar*. The set (though not the situation) is strikingly reminiscent of that in William Gillette's stage play "Sherlock Holmes." (Courtesy National Film Archives of the British Film Institute)

Production Company: Nordisk Films Compagni, Copenhagen (Great Northern Film Company)
Director and Screenplay: Viggo Larsen

CAST

Sherlock Holmes   Viggo Larsen
    (Alwin Neuss perhaps played Dr. Watson)

SYNOPSIS: Holmes hears a scream over the telephone, and recognizes the voice as belonging to a well-known singer. As the author of *The Polyphonic Motets of Lassus,* he has no doubt deduced the identity by voice quality, etc; however, it is true that before screaming the singer managed to give him her name as well. He drives hurriedly over to her house; and, seeing a rope hanging down, he starts to clamber up it when the thief cuts it; poor Holmes has certainly put up with some bad treatment in these early silents. Holmes gives chase over the roofs of what is no doubt

Copenhagen, and eventually "arrests" him—the Danes seem to have had the same idea as the Germans that Holmes was sort of a police officer.

DROSKE NO. 519; SHERLOCK HOLMES V; in the United States: **CAB NO. 519; CAB 519**

Date of Release: 30 April 1909; in the United States: 2 June 1909
Running Time: 343m; 1125 feet; in the United States: 1105 feet (18½ min.)
Production Company: Nordisk Films Compagni, Copenhagen (Great Northern Film Company)
Director and Screenplay: Viggo Larsen

CAST

?   August Blom
Sherlock Holmes   Viggo Larsen
Billy   Elith Plio
    (Alwin Neuss perhaps played Dr. Watson)

Den Graa Dame: **Viggo Larsen as Holmes seems either to be emerging from the floor or sinking into it. (Courtesy National Film Archives of the British Film Institute.)**

REVIEW (From the New York *Dramatic Mirror*, 12 June 1909:

"A meritorious subject in every respect. One of the finest detective stories, holding the interest continuously from start to finish."

August Blom was an important director with Nordisk. He made such films as *The Vampire Dancer* (with former Holmes Otto Lagoni; *see Nordisk #8*), *Desdemona* (the plot of which was strikingly similar to Ronald Coleman's *A Double Life*), *The Aeroplane Inventor!* (again with Lagoni), *Fru Potifar, Potifars Hustru, Jermbanens Datter*, and *Spaakonens Datter*—all 1911. That same year he made *Dodens Brud* from a story by Baron Palle Rosenkrantz, who is represented in one of the *Rivals of Sherlock Holmes* volumes.

DEN GRAA DAME (The Grey Lady); SHERLOCK HOLMES VI; in the United States: THE GRAY DAME

Date of Release: 27 August 1909; in the United States: 11 September 1909
Running Time: 207m; 1007 feet; in the United States: 975 feet (16½ min.)
Production Company: Nordisk Films Compagni, Copenhagen (Great Northern Film Company)
Based on: *The Hound of the Baskervilles*
Director and Screenplay: Viggo Larsen

CAST

?	Forrest Holger-Madsen
The Uncle	Gustav Lund
Sherlock Holmes	Viggo Larsen

(*Alwin Neuss perhaps played Dr. Watson*)

SYNOPSIS: The plot rather closely followed *The*

Den Graa Dame herself, boding no good to one of the Baskerville family. (Courtesy National Film Archives of the British Film Institute.)

Hound of the Baskervilles, with the exception that a ghostly lady appeared instead of a hound. 1937's *Sherlock Holmes, Oder Graue Dame*, does not seem to have been in any way derived from the same novel, not even from this film, except in its title.

Holger-Madison appears again top-billed, but in an unknown part.

LA FEMME (The Woman); HVEM ER HUN? (Where is She?); MADAME X

Date of Release: 29 September 1910
Running Time: 330m; 1083 ft. (18 min.)
Production Company: Nordisk Films Compagni, Copenhagen (Great Northern Film Company)
Director: Forrest Holger-Madsen
Based on: *La Femme X* by Alexandre Bisson

CAST

?	Oda Nielsen
?	Otto Lagoni
?	Einar Zangenberg

(*Alwin Neuss perhaps played Dr. Watson*)

Although not based on a Doyle story, the film was remade in 1914, still as a Holmes subject, by a rival Danish Company called Filmfabrikken.

The Nordisk book gives no further credits, so it is not possible to say whether Lagoni played Holmes or Holger-Madsen played the part himself; both actors, of course, played the detective for Nordisk at one time or another.

Nielsen, however was surely the title character.

Einar Zangenburg was a very prominent Nordisk actor and director, who made such films as *Hamlet* (as Laertes, with Holmes-Watson Neuss who, by the way, played Dr. Jekyll and Mr. Hyde this same year (1910) for Nordisk.), '10; *The Aeroplane Inventor!* (with Holmes Lagoni) and *Mona Lisa* (both '11); and *Kansleren Kaldet den Sorte Panter, The Two Convicts*, and *The Fisherman and His Sweetheart*, in '12. He also appeared in 1908's *Adventures of Sherlock Holmes* and *Millionobligationen*, '11.

SHERLOCK HOLMES I BONDEFANGERKLOR (Sherlock Holmes in the Claws of the Confidence Men); DEN STJAALNE TEGNEBOG (The Stolen Wallet); in Great Britain: THE CONFIDENCE TRICK. (SHERLOCK HOLMES CAPTURED is perhaps the same film.)

Date of Release: 10 December 1910; Great Britain: the same day
Running Time: 266 m; 872 feet. (14½ min.)
Production Company: Nordisk Films Compagni, Copenhagen (Great Northern Film Company)
(Perhaps directed by Forrest Holger-Madsen)

CAST

Sherlock Holmes	Otto Lagoni
	Axel Boelsen
	Ellen Kornbech

(*Alwin Neuss perhaps played Dr. Watson*)

36

Otto Lagoni appeared in a number of other films for Nordisk: in 1911 he donned a beard to play a moneylender who doubled as a pilot in *The Aeroplane Inventor!*; and that same year he was also in *Love and Friendship* and *The Vampire Dancer*.

He perhaps made at least one other Holmes film, although in all probability it is just an alternate title for this one: *Sherlock Holmes Captured* sounds like the same film. He was also a stage Sherlock.

FORKLAEDTE BARNEPIGE; DEN FORKLAEDTE GUVERNANTE (The Bogus Governess)

Date of Release: 2 January 1911; in Great Britain: 7 January 1911
Running Time: 320 m; 1056 feet. (17½ min.)
Production Company: Nordisk Films Compagni, Copenhagen (Great Northern Film Company)
(Perhaps directed by Forrest Holger-Madsen, with himself as Holmes and Alwin Neuss as Dr. Watson)

MEDLEM AF DEN SORTE HAAND (The Black Hand); MORDET I BAKERSTREET (Murder in Baker Street); DEN SORTE HAAND; in Great

Otto Lagoni takes over the role of the Great Detective in *The Confidence Trick* (also known as *Sherlock Holmes Captured*).

Britain: **THE CONSPIRATORS** (perhaps a separate film)

Date of Release: 2 January 1911; or perhaps before the end of 1910.
Running Time: 292m; 958 feet. (16 min.)
Production Company: Nordisk Films Compagni, Copenhagen (Great Northern Film Company)
Director: Holger Rasmussen

CAST

Sherlock Holmes	Holger Rasmussen
	Ingeborg Rasmussen
	Eric Crone
	Otto Lagoni

(Alwin Neuss perhaps played Dr. Watson, although one source lists him in the part of Holmes for this one.)

MILLIONOBLIGATIONEN; MILLIONTES-TAMENTET, SHERLOCK HOLMES—(The One Million Bond); SHERLOCK HOLMES; SHERLOCK HOLMES MESTERSTYKKE (Sherlock Holmes' Masterpiece); DEN MILLIONOBLIGATION: in Great Britain: THE STOLEN LEGACY; in Germany: EIN MEISTERSTÜCK VON SHERLOCK HOLMES.

(Last three titles perhaps do not refer to this film.)

Date of Release: 14 January 1911 (or perhaps as early as 1909).
Running Time: 310m; 1017 feet. (17 min.)
Production Company: Nordisk Films Compagni, Copenhagen (Great Northern Film Company)
(Perhaps directed by Forrest Holger-Madsen)

CAST

Sherlock Holmes	Alwin Neuss
?	Einar Zangenberg
?	Alfi Zangenberg

HOTELMYSTERIERNE (The Hotel Mystery); SHERLOCK HOLMES SIDSTE BEDRIFT (Sherlock Holmes' Last Exploits); SHERLOCK HOLMES SID-STE BEDRIFTER; HOTELROTTERNE (The Hotel Rats); THE HOTEL THIEVES; SHERLOCK HOLMES' LAST ACHIEVEMENT.

Date of Release: 7 February 1911; in Great Britain: 8 February 1911
Production Company: Nordisk Films Compagni, Copenhagen (Great Northern Film Company)
Running Time: 255 m; 837 ft. (14 min.)
(Perhaps directed by Forrest Holger-Madsen, with himself as Holmes and Alwin Neuss as Dr. Watson; or Neuss may have played Holmes.)

THE ADVENTURES OF SHERLOCK HOLMES

(Danish)
Released: 1908
Director: Forrest Holger-Madsen

Alwin Neuss, a former Watson, is promoted to the
role of Holmes himself. 221B looks rather too neat in
Millionobligation, but it is at least well stocked with
books painted on the backdrop. We presume the boy
is either Billy or one of the original Baker Street
Irregulars. (Courtesy National Film Archives of the
British Film Institute.)

Millionobligation: **Although these films were considered usually naturalistic in their day, this example
of Nordisk humor seems a bit broad. (Courtesy
National Film Archives of the British Film Institute.)**

An unknown Holmes (probably Forrest Holger-Madsen) caught in a tight spot in *Hotel Mysterierne*. The detective's soft-checked cap was often worn in place of a deerstalker in these early silents. (Courtesy National Film Archives of the British Film Institute.)

CAST

Forrest Holger-Madsen (probably as Holmes)
Ellen Rassow
Alwin Neuss (probably as Watson)
Einar Zangenberg

This reference probably refers to one or more films of the Nordisk series, but may perhaps be a separate film. SOURCE: Johan Daisne's *Filmographic Dictionary of World Literature*.

Before we proceed to the German Holmes films, which were derived from the Nordisk series, it seems as well to note the two other Holmes films that were made in Denmark, not by Nordisk, but by Filmfabrikken—both in 1914. The first was *En Raedsom Nat* (A Night of Terror)—a five-reeler released on 6 July 1914, and subsequently released in Germany in January '17 as *Eine Screckensnacht*. Emilie Sannom was in it.

Before the end of the year the studio followed it up with a remake of the Nordisk Holmes film *Hvem er Hun?* (Where is She?) on 7 December, and got this one into Germany as *Wer ist Sie?* after only two years. It was 1827m long, and written and directed by the star, Em Gregers; Nathalie Krause and Jon Iversen were also in it, and the cameraman was Adam Johansen.

By this time the torch had already passed to the Germans, for both Larsen and Neuss had taken the character of Holmes with them when they left Nordisk.

4

The German Series

ARSENE LUPIN CONTRA SHERLOCK HOLMES

Date of Release: first episode—20 August 1910; last episode—22 April 1911.

Running Time: a total of 5518 feet for all five episodes (92 min.)

Based on: *Arsene Lupin contre Herlock Sholmes* (1903) by Maurice Leblanc, variously translated into English as *Arsene Lupin versus Holmlock Shears; Arsene Lupin versus Herlock Sholmes; The Arrest of Arsene Lupin; The Fair-Haired Lady* and *The Blonde Lady;* and Leblanc's *Sherlock Holmes Trop Tard* (1906).

Director: Viggo Larsen

Production Company: Vitascope and Vitascope GmbH (Germany) or Deutsche Vitaskop

CAST

Sherlock Holmes	Viggo Larsen
Arsene Lupin	Paul Otto

The individual segments were:

1. DER ALTE SEKRETAR (The Old Secretaire); in Great Britain: ARSENE LUPIN

Date of Release: 20 August 1910
Running Time: 1133 feet (19 min.)

2. DER BLAUE DIAMANT (The Blue Diamond)

Date of Release: 17 September 1910
Running Time: 1415 feet, (23½ min.)

3. DIE FALSCHEN REMBRANDTS (The Fake Rembrandts); in Great Britain: THE TWO REMBRANDTS

Date of Release: 7 October 1910
Running Time: 968 feet. (16 min.)

4. DIE FLUCHT (The Escape)

Date of Release: 24 December 1910
Running Time: 1122 feet. (19 min.)

5. ARSENE LUPINS ENDE (The End of Arsene Lupin)

Date of Release: 4 March 1911.
Running Time: 880 feet. (14½ min.)

In this series, Lupin usually got the better of poor Holmes, but at least the great man triumphed in the last episode. Lupin, not Holmes, was the master of disguise, appearing as such classically Holmesian alteregos as taxi drivers and elderly porters—all apparently impenetrable to our Baker Street friend. Holmes also disguised himself in these films, though; and with their disguises, sliding panels, gangs of crooks and narrow escapes, they seem to have been more in the vein of such Louis Feuillade serials as *Fantomas* than the works of Conan Doyle. But we have already seen how these early silents have, of necessity, made Holmes more of an action character than the studious eccentric we know from the books.

John Barrymore, curiously, was later to play both Holmes and Lupin in films. The fact, by the way, that Conan Doyle had refused Leblanc permission to call his characters Holmes and Watson (the latter became Wilson) does not seem to have fazed the makers of this series.

After completing this series, Larsen, who seems almost incapable of thinking of Holmes without putting him in tandem with some master criminal or other, at least abandoned Raffles and Arsene Lupin for the more Conanical Moriarty in *Sherlock Holmes Contra Professor Moryarty*—also known as *Der Erbe Von Bloomrod* (The Heir of Bloomrod). Only 65m long, it was released less than two months after the last of the Lupins, on 29 April 1911; as with the Lupins, it was released by Vitascope G.m.b.H.; and Larsen, as always, pulled double duty as both director and detective.

Seven years later Viggo Larsen was still at it with *Rotterdamamsterdam*, released by Mester-Film in February of 1918 in 1145m, with Viggo holding down his usual tasks and a script this time from Richard Hutter.

Film Series Title: **DER HUND VON BASKERVILLE** (Germany)

Released: First Film—June 1914; Last Film—1920
Running Time (All Seven Parts Together): Approx. 7 hours
Directors: Rudolf Meinert, Richard Oswald, Willy Zehn
Screenplays: Richard Oswald, Robert Liebmann
Production Companies: Vitascope GmbH, Union-Vitascope, Greenbaum-Film GmbH, Projections AG Union

CAST

Sherlock Holmes   Alwin Neuss, Eugen Burg,
    perhaps others

The individual segments were:

1. **DER HUND VON BASKERVILLE**; in France as **LE CHIEN DES BASKERVILLE**

Released: June 1914
Running Time: 4385 ft. (73 min.)
Production Company: Vitascope GmbH
Director: Rudolf Meinert
Screenplay: Richard Oswald

CAST

Sherlock Holmes   Alwin Neuss (also in the following 3)
Stapleton   Friedrich Kühne (also following 4)
Barrymore   Andreas von Horn (also following 3)
Miss Lyons   Hanni Weisse (following 1, plus 1 more)
Henry von Baskerville   Erwin Fichter (next 3, plus 1 more)

Released in France and the United States by Pathé Frères

2. **DAS EINSAME HAUS** (The Isolated House)
Date of Release: 30 October 1914
Running Time: 3610 ft. (60 min.)
Production Company: Union-Vitascope
Director and Screenplay: (same as above)
Cast: (same as above)

3. **DAS UNHEIMLICHE ZIMMER** (The Uncanny Room)

Released: April 1915
Running Time: 3 reels (50 min.)
Director and Screenplay: Richard Oswald
Production Company: Greenbaum-Film Gmbh
Scenery: Herman Warm
Cast: Same as above except that Tatjana Irrah, instead of Hanni Weisse, appears as Miss Lyons.

4. **WIE ENTSTAND DER HUND VON BASKERVILLE** (How the Hound of the Baskervilles Arose); **DIE SAGE VOM HUND VON BASKERVILLE**

Released: 1915
Production Company, Director, and Screenplay: (same as above)
Cast: Same as above, except that Hilde Borke appears instead of Tatjana Irrah

5. **DAS DUNKLE SCHLOSS** (The Dark Castle)

Released: August 1915
Running Time: 3 reels (50 min.)
Production Company: Projections AG Union
Director: Willy Zehn

CAST

Sherlock Holmes   Eugen Burg
    Friedrich Zellnik
Stapleton   Friedrich Kühne
Miss Lyons   Hanni Weisse

NOTES: This film was released as a rival version to #3 above.

6. **DR. MACDONALD'S SANATORIUM**

Released: 1920
Running Time: 4967 ft. (83 min.)
Director: Willy Zehn
Production Company: Greenbaum-Film GmbH
Screenplay: Robert Liebmann
Cast: *Sherlock Holmes* (perhaps played by Erich Kaiser-Titz)

NOTES: This episode was counted as #5 in the series, ignoring the rival effort above.

7. DAS HAUS OHNE FENSTER (The House Without Windows)

Released: 1920
Running Time: 5682 ft. (95 min.)
Production Company, Director, and Screenplay:
  (same as above)
Cast: Lu Jurgens, Erwin Fichter, Ludwig Rex

The enormous success of this series is self-evident in the nearly endless sequence of prolongations or sequels it inspired. In the second episode, Stapleton escapes from prison—since nothing at all seems to be able to restrain the villains in these early Holmes films—and repairs to a submersible house. Why the man lusts after Baskerville Hall is indeed hard to fathom when he has such wonders as these for his own already; but it is true, however, that in this series Baskerville Hall is a castle. Holmes, no slouch himself with scientific gadgetry, had a handy pocket radio transmitter on his side—sheer brainpower apparently not being sufficient; or at least, as always, hard to portray on silent film. Stapleton gets drowned and blown to smithereens at the end of this episode, but will, of course, be back for more in episode #3.

When Julius Greenbaum, the president of Vitascope, left to form his own company, he apparently felt that the *Hund* went with him as a sort of hellish mascot, for he turned out a rival episode #3 in direct competition with his old studio, using most of the cast from the first two films. Before he could proceed further than episode #4, Projections AG Union—the successors of Vitascope—released the true, authentic, original, genuine episode #3, or so they claimed. They possessed enough belief in their claim for Greenbaum to have been ordered to cease and desist, but in the chaos following the end of the war, Greenbaum managed to eke out two more episodes; though surely by this time, what was left of Conan Doyle's original conception must have been worn rather thin.

Alwin Neuss left the series in midstream to direct himself as Holmes in a film that displayed a bizarre, Germanic view of the American West—*Ein Schrei in der Nacht* (A Scream in the Night), released by Decla in December 1915. It was a three-reeler with a screenplay by Paul Rosenhayn, and featured Eddie Seefield, Aenne Köhler, Reinhold Pasch, and Adolf Suchanek in the cast.

Rudolf Meinert, the first director of the *Hund* series, also left before it had run its course, being replaced first by his scriptwriter Richard Oswald. Meinert formed his own company and released—in the same month as Neuss' solo effort—a film called *William Voss*. Poor, long-suffering Holmes was bested once again in this one by yet another of those charming master criminals of the Raffles and Lupin stripe. In this film Holmes only had to last for 3300 feet (55 min.). No doubt, though, he was impatient to get back to Baker Street and Professor Moriarty, who, with all his faults, could never be accused of being more charming than Holmes.

Holmes (Alwin Neuss) is closely pursued in *Ein Schrei in Der Nacht.*

Richard Oswald, who wrote all four of the first episodes of the *Hund* series, and directed the second and third episodes, also made about the same time (1914) *Sherlock Holmes Contra Dr. Mors* in three reels, with Ferdinand Bonn as Holmes and Erich Kähne as Dr. Mors. Bonn had played Holmes on the stage as early as 1906 in a play written by himself, and in 1918 he took over the role of Holmes from Hugo Flink in the Kowo Series. This series had begun in 1917 with scripts by Paul Rosenhayn, who had written *Ein Shrei in der Nacht* for Neuss—so all these German and Danish films in this early period seem to be bewilderingly interconnected with those original Nordisks!

The Kowo Series was as follows:

1. DER ERDSTROMMOTOR (The Earthquake Motor)

Production Company: Kowo-Film AG
Running Time: 4787 ft. (80 min.)
Released: 1917
Director: Karl Heinz Wolff
Screenplay: Paul Rosenhayn

CAST

Sherlock Holmes   Hugo Flink

The credits remained the same for the next three entries:

2. DIE KASETTE (The Casket)

Running Time: 3983 ft. (66 min.)
(known during production first as *Der Geheimnisvolle Hut* and then as *Das Ratsel der Ballnacht*)

3. DER SCHLANGENRING (The Snake Ring)

Running Time: 4 reels (67 min.)

4. DIE INDISCHE SPINNE (The Indian Spider)

(This film was in production in 1918, but may never have been released)

At this point Bonn took over the role of Holmes. The company changed its name to Kowo GmbH, but Wolff remained at the helm of the series. All of the following episodes were filmed in '18:

5. WAS ER IM SPIEGEL SAH (What He Saw in the Mirror)

6. DIE GIFTEPLOMBE (The Poisoned Seal)

Running Time: 4 reels (67 min.)

7. DAS SCHICKSAL DER RENATE YONGK (The Fate of Renate Yongk)

Running Time: 4,314 ft. (72 min.)
Screenplay: Werner Bernhardy

8. DIE DOSE DES KARDINALS (The Cardinal's Snuffbox)

Screenplay: Otto Schubert-Stephens

The following year Wolff filmed the last of the durable series, with Bonn dropping out and Kurt Brenkendorff stepping into the Inverness cape.

9. DER MORD IM SPLENDID HOTEL (The Murder in the Hotel Splendid)

There were also a few German Holmes films unconnected with any of the above series: *Verrater Zigarette* (The Treacherous Cigarette) and *Schwarze Kappe* (The Black Hand) were both released in Germany in July '13, but the second one sounds suspiciously like it might be only a print of the 1911 Nordisk film *Medlem af den Sorte Haand; Sherlock Holmes auf Urlaub* (Sherlock Holmes on Leave) was a German opus directed by Karl Schoenfeld in three reels in '16; *Sherlock Holmes Nächtliche Begegnung* was a 1917 four-reeler; and '19's *Drei Tage Tot* (Three Days Dead) was directed by Nils Chrysander for Bioscop Konzern.

And here, for the time being, we will leave our Germanic Holmes—"the shrewd secret policeman"—and turn to the first Sherlockian series in which Sir Arthur Conan Doyle himself had a hand, or even a finger. And although he was later to regret his participation, the fact remains that the Georges Tréville series is the first to attempt filming the stories themselves, rather than trying to turn Holmes into something he is not.

5

The Franco-British Series

THE SPECKLED BAND (Great Britain)

Released: 1912; United States copyright, 1 November 1912; released in Great Britain in October 1913.
Running Time: 1700 feet (28 min.)
Production Company: Franco-British Film Company/Eclair (Fenning); copyrighted by Société Francaise des Filmes et Cinematographes Eclair.
Released in the United States by Union Features
Director: Georges Tréville (or perhaps Adrien Caillard)
Filmed in: Bexhill-on-Sea, England

CAST

Sherlock Holmes   Georges Tréville
Dr. Watson   Mr. Moyse (although he may not have appeared in this initial episode).

Conan Doyle sold the film rights to some of his Holmes stories to Eclair, but he does not in fact appear to have personally supervised these films, as some sources have claimed; they were, however, filmed in England (the interiors at the Kursaal at Bexhill-on-Sea). The cast was all British, with the exception of the French Tréville.

During the course of the film, Holmes disguises himself as "Juanes Rilto," a wealthy foreigner (Treville was halfway there already), and visited the country house of that immortal villain, Dr. Rylott, to ask for the hand of his stepdaughter.

The idea for this story may have been suggested to Conan Doyle by his sister, Mrs. E. W. Hornung (whose husband created "Raffles"). Doyle called it "the grim

Only One Producer in the World Could Obtain It.

Only One Producer in the World Could Perfect It.

Eclair Obtained and Perfected

"SHERLOCK HOLMES"

By Sir Arthur Conan Doyle

The Greatest Detective Tale in the World

The Most Thrilling Character in Literature.

Magnificently Produced in Five Features

TWO REELS

Remember the Success of "Zigomar"! "Sherlock Holmes" is the Sensational Triumph of Eclair's Classic Productions.

Wire and Write at Once for Exclusive State Rights

Universal Features
7 East 14th Street, New York City

An American advertisement for the Treville-Moyse series, which was filmed in England with a French star!

44

snake story," and thought it was his best of all the Holmes tales. When his play *The House of Temperley* (with Hubert Willis, soon to be a film Watson) failed, he turned *Speckled Band* into a highly successful play to replace it—in only two weeks of writing!

SILVER BLAZE

Released: 1912 (copyrighted 29 November 1912)
Running Time: 1300 ft. (22 min.)
Production Company: Franco-British Film Co./Eclair (Fenning), Copyrighted by Société Francaise des Filmes et Cinematographes Eclair. Released in the United States by Union Features.
Director: Georges Tréville (or perhaps Adrien Caillard)
Filmed in: Bexhill-on-Sea, England

CAST

Sherlock Holmes	Georges Tréville
Dr. Watson	Mr. Moyse

SYNOPSIS (From *Moving Picture World,* 8 February 1913):

"Silver Blaze" was the favorite! And a beautiful piece of horseflesh she was. Colonel Ross was expecting a lot from this wonderful animal on Derby Day. And then came despair! Early in the morning the stable-boy is aroused from a deep sleep caused by a drug, to find "Silver Blaze" gone—and the jockey, Shraker, dead, with a crushed skull, in the open field nearby.

Sherlock Holmes had first-hand information of this case since he was at the home of his friend Col. Ross when the beautiful horse disappeared.

An investigation by the great detective gives him a sure clue to the whereabouts of the animal and he acts promptly.

Col. Ross insists that he must withdraw his favorite from the race program, but Holmes says "No!", and his command is emphatic.

Rather bewildered but trusting the wisdom of his old friend, Col. Ross goes to the track on Derby Day, but is dismayed when he can find no trace of good old "Silver Blaze".

But Holmes bids him wait and insists that his horse will come through a sure winner, despite his apparent mysterious absence.

The race is finished and the winner comes to the stables—and here to the nervous and astonished Col. Ross, a little water and a soft cloth remove from the forehead of the winner a dark stain which had covered up the great blazing white mark which had given the beautiful animal the name of "Silver Blaze".

Holmes' investigation had trailed the Derby favorite to the home of trainer Brown and he forced Brown to admit having the horse. The jockey, Shraker, had attempted to steal the animal and had drugged the stable boy, but he was thrown and kicked by the racer and so his villainous plans were suddenly halted.

Brown found 'Silver Blaze' in the open field and

thought to make him unrecognizable by painting over the great white "blaze", but he had not calculated on the genius of Sherlock Holmes.

If we were to believe entirely the above synopsis, "Silver Blaze" was a remarkable horse, indeed—changing from a female in the first paragraph to a male in the last!

With its climactic horse race, this story would seem like a natural for films; often as it has been filmed, one is surprised that it has not been made more often. When Arthur Wontner made his version in 1937, although Colonel Ross was retained as a character, his role as Holmes' host was transferred to Sir Henry Baskerville, thus enabling the film to be released in the United States with the more attractive title *Murder at the Baskervilles.*

Despite the fact that these Franco-British films were by far the most faithful so far on the screen to Doyle's original stories, he was, in a few years, to regret having sold the company the motion-picture rights, for they asked him for ten times the amount they had paid him when he wanted to buy the rights back when the Eille Norwood series was planned.

However, Doyle was so highly pleased with the Norwoods that he considered it all worthwhile.

The credits for the remainder of the Tréville-Moyse series are the same for the next six episodes:

3. THE BERYL CORONET

Released: 1912 (United States, © 1 November 1912)
Running Time: 2300 ft. (38 min.)

4. THE MUSGRAVE RITUAL

Released: 1913 (United States, © 6 January 1913)
Running Time: 1290 ft. (21½ min.)

5. THE REYGATE SQUIRES

Released: 1912 (United States, © 1 November 1912)
Running Time: 1800 ft. (30 min.)

6. THE STOLEN PAPERS

Released: 1912 (United States, © 23 November 1912)
Running Time: 1400 ft. (23 min.)

7. A MYSTERY OF BOSCOMBE VALE

Released: 1912 (United States, © 13 November 1912)
Running Time: 1700 ft. (28 min.) (Cut to 1 reel in the United States)

8. THE COPPER BEECHES

Released: 1912 (United States, © 4 November 1912)
Running Time: 1700 ft. (28 min.)

NOTES: This film survives, although it is difficult to lay hands on it. Watson may again be absent, for although a Watson-like figure appears, he is not identified as such, though titles may of course be missing.

It is evident from the above list that this series was released in a different order in the United States than from the order in which English audiences saw it.

There is, in addition to the above, a title that probably represents either an alternate title for one of the above films in the series, or else an overall title for the series as a whole: *The Adventures of Sherlock Holmes*—listed in some sources as a 1912 production from England, starring Georges Tréville as Holmes. The only thing that makes us suspect that this may, in fact, be a separate production from the main Franco-British series is that all sources we have seen credit Tréville himself as the director for the entire series, whereas this film is said to have been directed by Adrien Caillard. Our assumption, though, is that Caillard was perhaps associated with the main series in some capacity—perhaps producer or screenwriter; thus, causing the confusion.

The French seem to have tried their hands at a Holmes film on only three other occasions. The first was Gaumont's 1909 *The Latest Triumph of Sherlock Holmes*. The film was 566 feet long (9½ minutes). It was produced by Leon Gaumont (1864–1946), also an inventor and exhibitor, who founded both the French and English branches of the film company that bears his name. The film treated Holmes' idiosyncracies with a light and satiric touch, depicting him crawling about on the floor with a magnifying glass and tape measure in search of clues. Holmes finally traces the thief in question by means of a discarded cigar butt.

In 1911, Eclair presaged their Franco-British series when they starred Henri Gouget as Holmes in *Les Aventures de Sherlock Holmes,* a two-reeler that also featured Camille Bardout, Rene d'Auchy, and Josette Andriot. It was written and directed by Victorin Jasset.

The following year, Eclipse ground out an epic whose French title has been lost, but whose title, when released in Germany, was *Schlau, Schlauer, am Schlauesten.* During its length of 1516 feet (25 min.), poor Holmes was bamboozled by Nat Pinkerton, even though the Baker Street sleuth had the assistance of the redoubtable Nick Carter.

6
Harry Benham

SHERLOCK HOLMES SOLVES THE SIGN OF THE FOUR; SHERLOCK HOLMES AND THE SIGN OF THE FOUR; in Great Britain: **THE SIGN OF FOUR**

Date of Release: 25 February 1913; in Great Britain: 29 June 1914
Production Company: Thanhouser
Running Time: 2 reels
Producer: Edwin Thanhouser
Filmed in New Rochelle, New York

CAST

Sherlock Holmes   Harry Benham

SYNOPSIS (From *Moving Picture World*, 22 February 1913):

Major Sholto, a retired British Army officer, who had amassed wealth in India in a mysterious manner, dies suddenly. His two sons were unable to find any trace of the wealth. They searched the house patiently, and at last, in the attic, concealed by a secret panel, they discovered a brass-bound box. It contained jewels of almost fabulous value and a letter telling them that Mary Morstan, orphaned daughter of one of Sholto's brother officers in India, was entitled to an equal share in the treasure. Thaddeus, the younger brother, is willing to carry out his dead father's wishes, but Bartholomew, the elder, insists that they alone should possess the jewels. Finally Thaddeus, unable to persuade his brother to relent, writes Miss Morstan an anonymous letter, telling her that she has been wronged, and naming the place where they can meet.

Miss Morstan, perplexed by the strange communication, consults Sherlock Holmes. Holmes and Dr. Watson, his associate, keep the appointment with Miss Morstan, and are led by Thaddeus Sholto to his home. Thaddeus tells Miss Morstan of her inheritance, and that he intends to force his brother Bartholomew to surrender her share of the treasure.

Harry Benham, who made a rather stocky Holmes in *Sherlock Holmes Solves the Sign of the Four*.

They reach the Sholto mansion, and Thaddeus goes into his brother's room to summon him. But he comes dashing down the stairs, terror stricken. Holmes and Watson dash up the stairs, leading to the room. There, huddled in his chair, is Bartholomew, and on his breast a torn sheet of paper, with five words scrawled upon it, "The Sign of the Four." The treasure is gone!

A quick examination shows that the man has been killed by a poisoned thorn which is lodged in his head.

In the garret Holmes comes upon fresh evidence of intruders. In the heavy dust are impressions of a boot and a wooden leg, and the imprint of two little bare feet. The detective hurries to the roof, where, dangling to the ground below, is a heavy rope.

Securing a blood hound he tracks the fugitive down, the chase finally leading him and his co-worker, Dr. Watson, to a little shipyard, where he learned that a man with a wooden leg, accompanied by a little East Indian, had hired a motor boat and sailed up the river. Holmes, in another boat, pursues.

The fugitives are captured, but not before they throw the treasure overboard. Then Jonathan Small, the man with the wooden leg, and his faithful follower, little Tonga, whose deadly blow-pipe had killed Sholto, are brought to Holmes' rooms and the casket opened. The jewels are not there. The treasure had disappeared forever.

Although the above synopsis seems astonishingly faithful to the novelette for a silent two-reeler, one would wonder if the film itself, like the synopsis, neglected to explicate the meaning of the note or the connection of Small to the Sholtos. Judging by the review that we print next, however, there was indeed a sequence in India that undoubtedly explained things. In addition, of course, there seems to be a complete lack of the Watson-Morstan romance, which would have seemed sure-fire stuff for movies.

In Britain, this film was released as if it were a continuation of the Tréville-Moyse series.

REVIEW (From *Motion Picture World*, 8 March 1913):

This 2-reel film gives us a new kind of Sherlock Holmes, a younger and heavier-built man than we usually see in the part. But once the story gets into action, with its weird, Oriental atmosphere, we forget everything else. The story of the Agra treasure is pictured for us in an intensely fascinating manner. The one-legged man, the East Indian with his blow-pipe, the Sholtos, the Baker Street lodgings, the scenes in India, and the various exciting episodes combine to make this a successful offering. The treasure never comes into the hands of the rightful owner, Mary, as it was cast into the river. A strong production of a famous narrative.

Harry Benham was born in Valparaiso, Indiana, on 26 February 1883. He sang in church choirs, and began his professional career in *Peggy From Paris*, a

Benham as the nasty half of *Dr. Jekyll and Mr. Hyde*.

musical by George Ade and William Lorraine, and produced by Henry Savage. Thereafter, he worked mostly in musical comedy (as a baritone, says one source, though in *Peggy* he played "Len Harvey, the village *tenor*"). Some of his stage plays during this period were *Woodland, Sultan of Sulu, Gay Musician, Marrying Mary*, and *Madam Sherry*. Following this, in 1910, he made his film debut, and spent the next five years in films. His first movie was *David Copperfield*, made in Edwin Thanhouser's studio in New Rochelle, New York. One wonders if he played the same part that his fellow-Holmes Basil Rathbone was to play in the '35 version.

In 1912, Benham played another part that has been shared by other screen Sherlocks (John Barrymore and Christopher Lee) when Thanhouser turned out a one-reel version of *Dr. Jekyll and Mr. Hyde*, with James Cruze cast as Jekyll, and the part of Hyde curiously divided between Cruze and Benham. Lucius Henderson directed; also in the cast was Marguerite Snow (Mrs. Cruze). The film took longer to shoot than the usual three days allotted by Thanhouser for a one-reeler—over a week—due apparently to the delays in changing the "personalities," which makes one wonder if the double-casting sped things up or slowed them down. Perhaps it was helpful for any visual effects, which would have been done "in the camera," rather than optically as they would be done today—meaning that, for instance, Cruze would stand in front of the camera made up as Jekyll, then change into his Hyde makeup while the cameraman was cranking back the film for a dissolve. If Benham were standing by, already made up as Hyde, it probably *was* very time-saving.

Subsequently Benham played nine parts in a single Thanhouser epic, *Harry's Waterloo*, which in some scenes involved quadruple exposures. This took nearly a month to shoot (it was a two-reeler), and the prolonged schedule apparently threw Thanhouser into fits.

Also in 1912 Benham was Bassanio in a version of *The Merchant of Venice*.

One source claims that Benham was in five hundred films by 1915, but another lists the more modest amount of only two hundred by 1916. Some of his other Thanhouser films (beside his Holmes role) were the serial *Zudora, Mother*, with Maude Fealy, *Stronger Than Death*, in two parts (1914), *Mrs. Van Ruyter's Stratagem*, and *Was She Right to Forgive Him?*

Another serial role was in *The Twenty Million Dollar Mystery*. Some "Red Feather" releases (they filmed Conan Doyle's *Brigadier Gerard* in '16) included *The Man Inside, The Path of Happiness*, and *The Sleepers*. At Warner Brothers, he was directed by the prolific William Nigh in *Your Best Friend*. With his costar in that one, Vera Gordon, he also made *Daughter-in-Law*. Before leaving films in 1922 he also made *The Heart of Princess Marsari, Daughter of Kings, The Prey*, with Alice Joyce, and *Polly With a Past*, with Ina Claire. In '22, William Fox cast him in *The Town That Forgot God*.

Around the time *Sherlock Holmes Solves the Sign of the Four* was being released, Thanhouser's studio in New Rochelle had burned down, and a number of current film stars who aquit themselves well on the stage, such as John Bunny, were called upon to perform in a benefit for the Thanhouser employees who had suffered losses. Harry Benham contributed a "pianologue" with Mignon Anderson. Pearl White (of *Perils of Pauline* fame) was also on the bill. The musical stage seems to have been Benham's first love, and in January of 1919 he was back on the stage (as "Lord Wetherell") appearing with Beth Lydy in *The Rainbow Girl*; a few months later, in May, he was appearing with Marion Davies (the original of *Citizen Kane's* "Susan Alexander," of course) in *Cecilia of the Pink Roses*. He also appeared on the stage with Claude Rains, who was a close friend.

In 1912 a five-year-old named *Leland* Benham made his film debut in Thanhouser's New Rochelle studio, and allegedly appeared in as many as one hundred films in the next three years. It seems highly probable that this must have been Harry Benham's son, perhaps by his film-actress wife, Ethyle Cooke Benham, who appeared with him in *The Merchant*.

Harry Benham was still alive in 1963, but we have been unable to locate any further information on him.

7

G. B. Samuelson and George Pearson

A STUDY IN SCARLET (Great Britain)

Released: first shown in October 1914, but not generally released until 28 December 1914. United States, © 25 November 1914

Running Time: 5749 ft. (96 min.)

Production Company: Samuelson Film Mfg. Co. Ltd. (MOSS); released in the United States by Pathé Frères

Producer: G. B. Samuelson

Director: George Pearson

Director of Photography: Walter Buckstone

Screenplay: Harry Engholm

Adaptation: George Pearson

Filmed in: Worton Hall, Isleworth, England

Locations: Cheddar Gorge and Southport Sands

British "U" Certificate

CAST

Jefferson Hope	Fred Paul
Lucy Ferrier	Agnes Glynne
Brigham Young	Harry Paulo*
Sherlock Holmes	James Bragington
John Ferrier	James LeFre*
Lucy Ferrier as a child	Winnifred Pearson

*One source says Paulo played "John Ferrier," and LeFre was "Father."

SYNOPSIS: The film followed Doyle's book very closely in many details, but instead of telling the Mormon sequence in a flashback, as it is in the novel, it is told chronologically, with the result that Holmes did not

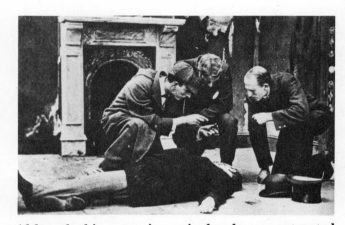

Although this scene is meticulously reconstructed from the original story, the Holmes episode was switched from the position of prologue—which it had in the novel—to epilogue in the film. Watson would seem to be on the extreme right and Inspector Lestrade in the center, unless the pair has exchanged hats.

appear until rather late in the story, and was hardly more than a supporting character. The main interest was centered in the Western sequences.

REVIEWS: *Pictures and the Picturegoer*, 13 March 1915 had this to say:

Those who see the fine Samuelson film of *A Study in Scarlet* cannot help but admire Fred Paul's powerful rendering of Jefferson Hope, the leading character. One is filled with regret when the long film comes to an end, not only because of its ingenious story, but also because Mr. Paul's intense acting succeeds throughout in gripping and fascinating his audience.

Other contemporary reviewers described it as a fairly long film of which not one scene could be discarded as nonessential. The film's realism was also praised.

George Pearson, the director, was making his first film for producer Samuelson, who was himself making his debut as a solo producer. Pearson was one of the major, largely unsung, creative geniuses of the silent British film. He would undoubtedly be remembered today with Griffith and Eisenstein, judging from what one reads of his cinema techniques, except that most of his major films seem to be lost, with little remaining but some of his later "quota quickies." In his fascinating autobiography, *Flashback*, he gives us some revealing behind-the-scenes information on the filming of this particular film.

After Samuelson bought the rights to the novel, Harry Engholm prepared a script with which Pearson was very pleased (apparently he had a hand in it himself), and shooting began on 8 June 1914; on 6 July there were still more scenes to be filmed, and we cannot say with any certainty when filming actually wrapped up. "The film called for ambitious locations," wrote Pearson, "but we hoped to find passable replicas of the Rockies and the Salt Lake Plains in England, for much can be suggested by imaginative camera angles to hide geographical inaccuracies." They chose Cheddar Gorge and Southport Sands.

Pearson felt he had a particularly strong cast in Paul, Paulo, and Glynne. There are a few Holmesian echoes

The young Lucy Ferrier (Winnifred Pearson). She grows up to be Agnes Glynne in the film.

here, as it happens, for Paul was later involved in Samuelson's sequel *Valley of Fear,* and went on to play the imitation-Sherlock character "Nayland Smith" in a long-running series of Fu Manchu adventures, and was also to appear in one of the Norwood Sherlock Holmes films. He also worked with film-Sherlocks Arthur Wontner and Clive Brook in other (non-Holmes) films.

Miss Glynne's sister was married to Dennis Neilson Terry, who was a famous Holmes on the stage.

Pearson's own daughter, four-year-old Winnifred, played Lucy as a child in the sequence when, lost in the desert with her father, she is rescued by the Mormons on their 1850 trek. "Just right for the part, and she played it for me delightfully," continued Pearson.

Sherlock Holmes was a problem; much depended upon physical appearance; build, height, and mannerisms had to be correct. By a remarkable stroke of fortune Samuelson had an employee in his Birmingham office who absolutely fitted these requirements, and as in those days of silent technique, a tactful producer could control every action of an inexperienced actor, I decided to risk his engagement as the shrewd detective. With his long and lean figure, his deer-stalker hat, cape-coat, and curved pipe, he looked the part, and played the part excellently.

We can get some idea of how Pearson managed to get a good performance out of this nonprofessional (James Bragington) by his comments in an interview that appeared a few years later, in 1919:

The art of screen playing is not the art of pantomime; it is a new art—the art of exteriorising thought by action . . . the most difficult thing to attain is repose, yet, paradoxical as it may seem, repose is the very backbone of successful motion picture work.

What Pearson here calls "repose" is undoubtedly the same sort of unactorish quality that DeSica used to seek in *his* nonprofessional actors.

George Pearson's painstaking reconstruction of the Mormon trek—filmed in England before European Westerns moved to Spain. The Mormon sequence occupies about two-thirds of the novel, and apparently rather more of the film version.

51

James Bragington, the nonprofessional who was so irresistably right for the Great Detective in the first film version of *A Study in Scarlet*.

In the long run, Bragington made so little impression in the role that for many years scholars could not even discover what his name had been; and the most successful Holmeses on the screen seem to have been those actors, like Norwood, Wontner, and Rathbone, who had extensive stage backgrounds. The part is perhaps best served by an actor who realizes that it is more than just another detective's part.

George Berthold Samuelson was to follow this film in less than two years with a more Holmesian sequel in *Valley of Fear,* so he seems deserving of some glance at his career—a significant one that has been largely forgotten.

He was born on 6 July 1888 over his father's tobacco shop in Southport, where he was to return twenty-six years later to film *A Study in Scarlet.* He described it as "a marvelous place—if you can find the sea," so it must have seemed well suited to him for a desert standin. His two elder brothers, Julius and Laurie, went into the theater under the name of Wylie. George himself went to school in Southport with two girls who also became very prominent in the theater—Zena and

Phyllis Dare (who he would later star in his films); but at the age of fifteen he left school to enter his father's profession of tobacconist in Liverpool. This did not interest him for long, however, and he soon returned to Southport with "Adler's Concert Party" for a summer season.

He found his life's work quite by chance when, in 1910, he happened to acquire a newsreel print of the recent funeral of King Edward VII. He paid fifteen shillings for it, and promptly sold it to a Southport movie theater for thirty shillings, and had become a distributor!

Three years later he entered production with a film for which he himself had the original idea, *60 Years a Queen,* which he then also released as the first-ever "road-show" attraction. The director, Bert Haldane, later made Doyle's *Brigadier Gerard.* Samuelson's career in films was a highly unusual one in that he reversed the usual sequence of events—he began as a distributor; and became a producer, then a director, and finally a screenwriter!

After hiring Pearson to direct for him, and building within a month a big new glass studio with room for three or four sets in Isleworth on an estate that had been known as Worton Hall, he began shooting *Study,* which was a great success.

He made innumerable other films besides his other Holmes picture, including a few others with Sherlockian echoes. In 1925 he went to Germany to produce *She,* which featured future-Holmes Carlyle Blackwell. Later versions of this story were to star such Sherlocks and Watsons as Nigel Bruce, Peter Cushing, Andre Morell, Gustav von Seyffertiz, and Christopher Lee. Then, in 1931, Samuelson wrote the script for *Should a Doctor Tell?* in collaboration with mystery writer Edgar Wallace, who in the next year scripted Robert Rendel's version of *The Hound of the Baskervilles.* In 1918, Samuelson produced *Hindle Wakes;* the director was Maurice Elvey, who was to direct many of the films in the Eille Norwood series, and in the cast was Norman McKinnell, who was to be the first Moriarty in the Arthur Wontner Holmes series.

Some of Samuelson's films as a director or codirector include *The Admirable Crichton* and *The Way of an Eagle* in 1918; in 1919—*The Bridal Chair;* in 1920—*The Winning Glow;* in 1922—*The Game of Life;* in 1923—*I Pagliacci* and *Afterglow;* in 1927—*Motherland;* in 1928—*Two Little Drummer Boys, For Valour,* and *The Forger;* in 1929—*Valley of the Ghosts* (with future-Watson Ian Hunter); in 1930—*Spanish Eyes* (in Spanish and English; it was the first Spanish-language talkie); in 1931—*The Other Woman, Jealousy, The Wickham Mystery,* and *Inquest;* in 1932—*Collision, Threads,* and *The Callbox Mystery;* and in 1934, his last film, *The Crucifix.*

It is, though, as a producer he will be remembered, and some of the directors who worked for him (with some of the films they made for him) follow: George Pearson—*The Life of Lord Roberts, V.C.,* and *The Great European War,* both in 1914, and from the following year *The Cinema Girl's Romance, Buttons,* and *John Halifax, Gentleman,* among innumerable others; Fred Paul (also a director, as well as the star of *Study in Scarlet)—Dr. Wake's Patient,* in 1916, with Samuelson's old school girlfriend, Phyllis Dare (Paul may also have had a hand in Samuelson's next Holmes film, as we shall see); Alexander Butler (who went with Samuelson to Hollywood when he was producing at Universal in 1919–1920)—*A Fair Imposter* and *The Girl Who Loves a Soldier* in 1916, *Little Women* and *The Sorrows of Satan* (to be remade by D. W. Griffith) in 1917, *Damaged Goods* in 1920, and *Married Love* in 1923, and probably Samuelson's next Holmes film, *Valley of Fear;* Rex Wilson—*Onward, Christian Soldiers* in 1918, *Quinneys* in 1919, and *Tilly of Bloomsbury* in 1921; Percy Nash—*The Elder Miss Blossom* in 1918; Thomas Bentley—*Milestones* in 1916; Albert Ward—*The Last Rose of Summer* in 1921; George A. Cooper—*If Youth But Knew.*

Samuelson also employed such designers as Gordon Craig and Heinrich Richter, and countless more.

More an entire industry in himself than a mere producer in his greatest days, by the early thirties Samuelson was reduced to writing and directing "quota quickies," the worst dregs of the British cinema, which he still approached with great gusto. *Picturegoer Weekly* of 26 December 1931 called him "an old-timer still on the active list," and said " 'fat and happy' describes him, and he has the reputation of being able to make a good film more cheaply than anyone else."

Finally, in 1935, after a very busy quarter of a century in films, Samuelson retired. He died on 17 April 1947. His four sons remained in the industry, building up the Samuelson Film Service into an international technical organization.

8

Harry Arthur Saintsbury

THE VALLEY OF FEAR

Released: May 1916; in the United States, January 1917

Production Company: Samuelson Film Mfg. Co. Ltd.

Running Time: 6500 ft. (108 min.)

Producer: G. B. Samuelson

Director: Alexander Butler (or perhaps Fred Paul)

Screenplay: Harry Engholm

Director of Photography: (perhaps Walter Buckstone)

British "U" Certificate

CAST

Sherlock Holmes	H. A. Saintsbury
Ettie Douglas	Daisy Burrell
Professor Moriarty	Booth Conway
McGinty	Jack Macaulay
John McMurdo	Cecil Mannering
Dr. Watson	Arthur M. Cullin (or Cullen?)
Capt. Marvin	Lionel D'Aragon
Shafter	Bernard Vaughan
Ted Baldwin	Jack Clair

SYNOPSIS: An ex-convict tries to kill a detective who once posed as a member of an American secret society (much like the KKK).

Samuelson probably chose this story because it was similar to his previous success, *A Study in Scarlet*—both having an American background and the bulk of the story in flashback. Arthur Wontner was to remake *Valley of Fear* in 1935.

Seven years later, when Eille Norwood was preparing to film his version of *The Sign of Four*, the decision was made to cast Arthur M. Cullin, who played Watson in this picture, as the Good Doctor, rather than Hubert Willis, who had played the role in every one of Norwood's previous forty-six films. At first glance this may seem very difficult to understand, particularly as Willis' interpretation of the role was as pricelessly brilliant as Nigel Bruce's was to be. The reason for this becomes obvious upon reflection, although this facet of the story was ignored in the Benham version: it is necessary in *Sign of Four* for Watson to romance Mary Morstan, and Willis was rather old for this. The same reason led to Ian Fleming's temporary replacement in the Arthur Wontner series by Ian Hunter. So Cullin, who Eille Norwood described as resembling "a middle-aged provincial butler," and, apparently, who had not made too great an impression in *Valley of Fear*, got the part. Arthur Cullin also appeared with Clive Brook in *Love and a Whirlwind* in 1922.

H. A. Saintsbury (Arthur to his friends) had played the role of Holmes more than one thousand times on the stage at the time he made this film (and in the next four years he was to increase the score to 1400), and in England he was, in fact, more associated with the part than anyone else, including William Gillette (who was, of course, better known in the United States), so he warrants an extended glance here. He is also the first Holmes we have encountered (there will be many more) who stands in the very front rank as a serious actor.

Saintsbury was born in Chelsea on 18 December 1869, the son of Frederic. Young Arthur, after being educated at St. John's College in Hurstpierpoint, was engaged as a clerk at the Bank of England—an occupation similar to youthful Basil Rathbone's first

Royalty Theatre
Glasgow.
27 April 1912

Dear Madam,

It is difficult for me to express my gratitude for your most kind thought in writing to me as you have done. Your generous appreciation of my efforts to amuse you during my all too brief stay at the Repertory Theatre is most flattering. I hardly dared to hope that I had been there long enough to make friends, and believe me, so I'll look forward with eagerness to the possibility of returning.

The Cigarettes I shall smoke, but your most kind letter I shall keep as a memento of a most happy experience.

Yours very truly

H. A. Saintsbury

A very rare original letter from H. A. Saintsbury, who brought his immortal impersonation of Sherlock Holmes to the screen in G. B. Samuelson's *Valley of Fear*. (Private collection of Robert Pohle.)

job in an insurance office. Saintsbury made his first appearance on the stage in March 1887 at the Opéra Comique Theatre, with the lowly status of supernumerary (or "extra") in Kate Vaughan's revival of *Masks & Faces;* his first leading role was that of "Captain Temple" in a tour of *Human Nature*. Like Rathbone's uncle, Sir Frank Benson, Saintsbury spent a great deal of his acting life on tour in England and South Africa; and some of the leads he played "in transit" were in such plays as *Under the Red Robe* (the film version was to star fellow-Holmes Raymond Massey), *The Silver King, In the Ranks, The Harbour Lights, Proof, The Lights O'London,* and *The Notorious Mrs. Ebbsmith.*

A director and playwright as well as an actor, he managed his own tours of his own plays—*D'Artagnan* (fellow-Sherlocks Arthur Wontner and Christopher Lee were also to appear in adaptations of the story) in 1898, *The Eleventh Hour* the previous year, *The Four Just Men* in 1906, and *Anna of the Plains* in 1907.

Among the seemingly countless classical parts he played were Hamlet, Mercutio (both also played by Sherlocks John Barrymore and Basil Rathbone), Charles Surface (Sherlocks Peter Cushing, Eille Norwood, and Douglas Wilmer each played this character's brother), Touchstone, Benedick, Iachimo, Shylock, Macbeth, Triplet, Malvolio, Fagin, Young Marlowe (also played by Eille Norwood), and Jack Absolute. During his long career he appeared in just about all the major London theaters of his day.

To follow his career a little more chronologically, in 1912 he was doing Tiresias in *Oedipus Rex, Zaza,* and producing and starring at the Glasgow Repertory. The next year saw him appearing as Simeon in *Joseph and His Brethren* (Lyn Harding, a brilliant screen Moriarty, was later to tour this play in the role of Jacob); that same year, Saintsbury played Capulet in *Romeo and Juliet,* and the next year saw him as Thomas Percy (a rather distant relation of Sir Arthur Conan Doyle) in *Henry IV, Part I.* Also in 1914 he produced *Much Ado About Nothing.* In 1915 he was Monks in *Oliver Twist,* Lord Robert Ure in *The Christian,* and Atik Ali in *The Right to Kill.* (We will observe how many actors to be cast as Sherlock Holmes have also played Arabs—those aquiline noses, no doubt.) In 1916 he played "Lone Wolf" (not the detective, but an Indian) in *Tiger's Cub,* and was appearing on stage in *Julius Caesar* with Basil Rathbone's uncle, Sir Frank Benson, when the latter was knighted by King George V. That year and the next, Saintsbury toured *Bluff* and also played it in London; in June 1919 he played, for the first time, a historical character who exerted a fascination on him all his life—the great actor Edmund Kean. After filling out the year with *The Mark of a Man,* he again played the role of Kean in 1920. Three years later he was incarnating "Mad Ned" for the third time, although he was surely far too tall for that "little, ill-looking, vagabond." He made so deep an impression as Kean on this occasion that when it was announced to the audience that the play was closing, a wealthy whiskey distiller in the audience rose from his seat and announced that, rather than see the play taken off the stage, he would finance its run himself. Alas, though, he could prolong its life only sixty-one performances. Although the distinguished theatrical historian Macqueen-Pope called Saintsbury "powerful" in the part, the 1920s were not too receptive to the sort of full-blooded acting with which Kean had been associated, and at which, perhaps, no one but Saintsbury could excel in those "modern" days.

A part with which Saintsbury was infinitely more successful, though one which was perhaps a little less close to his heart, was that of Mr. Sherlock Holmes Esq. of Baker Street, which he had played for the first time as long ago as 1902. In 1910, when Doyle's play *The House of Temperley* failed (despite the brilliant performance of future-Watson Hubert Willis in the role of "Tom Belcher"), Doyle recouped his losses many times over by remembering his favorite story, *The Speckled Band,* and turning it into a play in only two weeks' writing. The great Lyn Harding, soon to be Arthur Wontner's film Moriarty, was cast in the lead, which was not Holmes himself, but Dr. Grimesby Rylott. Saintsbury was given the smaller role of the Great Detective, and proceeded to make an absolutely indelible impression with it in the hearts of his audiences. The London *Times* said, "Mr. H. A. Saintsbury seems to have been born to play Sherlock Holmes."

One who had long before been indelibly impressed by Saintsbury's Holmesian interpretation was a small boy named Charles Chaplin, who years later was to say, "I owe more to the tutelage of Mr. Saintsbury . . . than to anybody in the world." Chaplin had in fact appeared on stage with Saintsbury in the role of Holmes' pageboy Billy in one of Saintsbury's earlier Sherlockian ventures, back in 1903, when the future "Tramp" was only twelve and one-half years old. Chaplin had lied about his age and claimed to be all of fourteen when he was taken to see Saintsbury at the Green Room Club (where Saintsbury was to live for the next thirty-six years), and before giving him the role of Billy, H. A. cast him in his own play, *Jim, the Romance of a Cockney.* Charlie was not able to read at this point, so his brother Sydney (who was later to join the Holmes company as "Count von Stahlberg") helped him with his lines. Later, Chaplin was to be cast as Billy by the great William Gillette himself in *The Painful Predicament of Sherlock Holmes,* but even Gillette did not make the impression on Chaplin that had been made by H. A. Saintsbury. Even though Saintsbury's *Valley of Fear* seems to be lost, we may judge his power in the role of Sherlock Holmes by the judgment of Chaplin, if by nothing else.

But there is, of course, very much else. For instance, when he hit his five hundredth performance in the role, he was presented by the producer Charles Frohman with a pipe that had been carved in the likeness of . . . was it Saintsbury or Holmes himself? On his one thousandth performance, Conan Doyle gave him an inscribed gold cigarette case.

It is sad to have to record that Saintsbury, the perfect stage craftsman, was somewhat at sea when confronted with the different acting techniques required for the movies when he made *Valley of Fear,* apparently his one and only film:

> it is very difficult to do it on the spur of the moment. . . . I felt I could have acted the part much better if I had had half-an-hour to think about it. . . . The character of Holmes, with his inscrutable face and passive attitude, was especially difficult to adapt to the (silent) film; I had to do just the things I had left out on the stage.

At least his unsatisfactory experience as Holmes on film did not cramp his stage style, for he was to play the part for many more years.

To resume the recapitulation of Saintsbury's non-Holmes career where we had digressed, in 1920 he was playing the Chevalier O'Shaughnessy in *Daughters of Eve,* Iago (a Rathbone role), and, of course, Kean. The next year he repeated Iago and added Gonzalo in *The Tempest* to his repertoire—also reviving *The Speckled Band* once again for ninety-eight performances, and paired once again with Lyn Harding.

In 1922 he was doing *Decameron Nights,* and in 1924 it was back to Dickens for *Nicholas Nickelby.* A tour in *A Friend of the People* followed, and *Sinners.* The next year he was playing the Messenger in *A Message From Mars,* in the movie version of which Hubert Willis had had a great success in his pre-Watson days. In 1927, Saintsbury played a role that was also to be a great success for fellow-Sherlocks Wontner and Rathbone (the latter receiving an Oscar nomination for his interpretation). It was Sir Henry Irving's old part of King Louis XI of France. One of Saintsbury's own favorite parts was that of another French King, Charles IX, in his own play *King of the Hugenots* (his other favorite was Don Caesar de Bazan), but he was praised highly for his Louis XI; Macqueen-Pope called him "magnificent" in the part, and the run was an outstanding success in its time.

The next year found Saintsbury as a Bishop in *High Treason*, and in 1929 he doubled the parts of Squire Trennion and Lord Wimpole in *Tamaresque*; before the year was out he had done *Captain Banner*, and, hot on the heels of this, he was again out touring in his eternal part of Sherlock Holmes, nearly thirty years and over 1400 performances after he had first played it.

We have mentioned that Saintsbury was a writer as well as an actor, as have been many Holmeses, and it seems as well here to take a look at some of his works so that we might perhaps have a better idea of the personality with which he infused his miraculous incarnation of the Great Detective.

Besides the plays we have mentioned above, he also wrote *The Cardinal's Collation* and many others, and served as a "play doctor" for the less-healthy products of many other author's pens. His monument in literature must undoubtedly be the book that he intended to be a monument to Sir Henry Irving; the book tragically only saw print after Saintsbury's death on 16 June 1939.

The book's title was *We Saw Him Act*, and we quote here from the preface by Cecil Palmer, who completed the book after the death of H. A.:

Throughout the preparation of this book I have always been conscious of the fact that, whereas, for me, it has been a lovely labour, it was for my distinguished colleague, the late Mr. H. A. Saintsbury, a labour of love.... It was obvious to me, as it must have been to others, that Saintsbury's days were numbered. His bodily sufferings were painful to witness, his mental tortures distressing to contemplate. Our numerous editorial conferences will always remain in my memory as occasions when one man's quiet courage epitomized the power of the spirit when the body is broken. I could wish that such a rare spiritual tenacity of purpose prevailed.

We have not been able to learn if Saintsbury's daughter Kathleen survived him.

The book was made up not only of reminiscences and critical comments by Saintsbury and Palmer, but also contained numerous contributions from theatrical notables on the subject of Irving, a few of them also having Sherlockian affiliations, such as Sir Frank Benson, the writer Arthur Machen (who had an occasional word to say about the Great Detective), and Sir Seymour Hicks, who had been the original stage Dr. Watson back in 1893.

We can get a notion of the type of theater Saintsbury favored from this comment, where he laments that the style of Sir Henry Irving is "beyond resuscitation. In that different world the Theatre was loved as an institution; it was a centre of art and gathered a dignity which, alas!, is gone forever, thanks in part to the impertinent familiarity of the gossip-writer and the inquisition of the press photographer." We can also note in Saintsbury's prose style, with its expletives like "Balderdash!", the same affectation that we note in Basil Rathbone's recorded conversations, namely, both men sounded rather like Sherlock Holmes even when they were being themselves.

He reveals, in passing, another trait that he had in common with Rathbone, and also with such other Holmeses as Cushing, Lee, and Granger: he was a very notable swordsman. "I have met three opponents in stage fights, knowing in each case that my life was in my defence."

Although, as in his other book, *Letters of an Unsuccessful Actor* (more about this later), he discusses the old-time actors, like Kean and Irving, with great relish, we can see that he leaned toward "realism" by his comment on Irving's sets: "His sets were not striking, they were inevitably *right*. If squalor was required, we had it—grandeur, dignity, they were there, but never obtrusively, never challenging attention." It seems to have been just this sort of subtlety that characterized his own interpretation of Holmes. Arthur Wontner was a similarly quiet Holmes—a sort of alien concept for modern audiences used to the sometimes "hyper" moments of Rathbone and Cushing.

Basically, though, Saintsbury was a Romantic of the theater; he liked to see actors who "touched common things with spirituality," and often favored a bad play over a good one if the bad one gave an actor scope to embroider his performance—a very unmodern notion. "How dependent is the modern actor on his author," he sniffed.

Plainly referring to the school of Stanislavsky he says: "We hear of the Producer sitting with his cast around him day after day for a year creating the atmosphere of a new play, which suggests a congregation of Buddhas solemnly contemplating their navels." The motto Saintsbury chose for this book perhaps sums up his own feelings for the art of acting, which to him was more than just interpreting the text; he quotes Irving's remark that the theater furthered the education of "the higher kind—the knowledge of the scope and working of human character."

To return to Saintsbury's other book, *Letters of an Unsuccessful Actor*, the reader may well ask how an actor who had the career we have just detailed could have considered himself unsuccessful. The fact is, of course, that Saintsbury's sights were set still higher—he saw himself in the company of Kean and Irving—and although he was held in some esteem as an actor, he was regarded as being somewhat outside the pale of "contemporary fashions" in acting style. Although this very archaism may have helped him achieve the world of Sherlock Holmes—for even in 1910 Holmes' "country of the mind where it is always 1895" was a place of the nostalgic past—it is no wonder that he regarded himself as unsuccessful, for he never really reached the heights. And the heights alone could have satisfied him.

It is curious how many people associated with the creation and interpretation of Sherlock Holmes—Doyle, Saintsbury, and Rathbone, to name a few—have felt that the character of Holmes had "held them back" in some way from their greatest achievements, never realizing that they were engaged in the creation of a classical character who was to rival Hamlet in what was written to try to interpret his character. One is reminded of Hawthorne's story *The Great Stone Face*; greatness always seems to lie elsewhere than right at our feet. And classics never seem to be recognized in their own time.

Saintsbury published his *Letters* anonymously in 1923, but he is accepted as the author. The book is mainly devoted to the great actors of the past such as Burbage, Garrick, etc. He makes the following interesting remarks on his own (and Wontner's and Rathbone's) great character of Louis XI:

Louis required a very full equipment of experience and technique for its adequate portrayal. To the thoroughly accomplished actor the part is a gift, but even he won't excel in it if he lacks some very particular abilities. Indeed I do not know a more exacting part.

Probably to preserve his anonymity, he does not comment directly in this book on the character of Holmes; but he does comment on another of Conan Doyle's memorable characters—Corporal Gregory Brewster in *A Story of Waterloo*, which was written for Sir Henry Irving:

It is an effective little piece of sentiment . . . the thing has no *raison d'être* unless the impersonation of the old Corporal be a *tour de force* . . . a perfect study of plebian senility, but Gregory Brewster is hardly a worthy medium for a great actor's art.

Of Wontner's great screen Moriarty, Norman McKinnel, Saintsbury has the following fascinating comment: "McKinnel in any part that is not, at least, sinister is—well, in my opinion, unsuited."

9
Francis Ford

A STUDY IN SCARLET (United States)

Date of Release: 29 December 1914
Running Time: Two reels (approx. 35 min.)
Production Company: Gold Seal/Universal Film Mfg.
    Co. (Gold Seal was owned by Universal)
Director: Francis Ford
Producer: (probably Francis Ford and Grace Cunard)
Screenplay: Grace Cunard
Filmed in: Los Angeles, California

CAST

Sherlock Holmes	Francis Ford
Doctor Watson	Jack Francis

We can get a notion, but little more, of this now-lost film from the following contemporary trade-paper advertisement, taken out by "Universal Film Mfg. Co., Carl Laemmle, President—Largest Manufacturer of Films in the Universe":

A wonderful detective story that's distinctly different. A *Study in Scarlet* by Sir Arthur Conan Doyle, writer of the world's most fascinating detective stories . . . featuring that popular Universal star, Francis Ford. This is first of a series of fascinating, mysterious, detective stories by the noted author Sir Arthur Conan Doyle, in which Sir Arthur shows himself at his best. It is a story of the supreme cleverness of Sherlock Holmes in which he unravels a tale of human suffering and in which an innocent man nearly suffers for the crime of the guilty one. The masterful style in which this absorbing plot is told in pictures will hold your audience spellbound. It is a picture with a punch, action, dramatic intensity, romance and cleverness. Sir Arthur Conan Doyle's fame as a writer of absorbing detective stories is world-wide. It's a privilege to be able to book such a production. Book it NOW! 1–2–3 sheet posters. Advertize it in a big way. You're bound to play to capacity crowds with this big two-reeler. Wire or write to your exchange immediately!

Besides the above brief glimpse of the plot, the most noteworthy thought this ad provokes is the remembrance that despite the way Laemmle has bandied about the name of Doyle—leading the reader almost to suppose that Sir Arthur had cranked the camera himself—the fact remains that Doyle could not have had any idea that the film was even being made! And there was, of course, excellent reason why he should not: Universal did not own the film rights to this story, or even its title, since they had been sold already to G. B. Samuelson, whose own version had been released just one day before this Ford epic!

Although a series was planned by Ford and Cunard, no other episode was ever made—most probably because of the legal problems arising from the instance of rights infringement begun with this film.

In this film, Francis Ford, though costumed in the regulation dressing gown, sporting sideburns, and smoking a curved pipe, had perched on his head, not a deerstalker, but a sort of oversized street-urchin's cap, similar to the one worn by Otto Lagoni in the Danish series. Ford's appearance was also apparently similar to the imitation-Holmes character "Lambert Chase," who was appearing in American films the previous year, and the same kind of cloth cap apparently was

SIR A. CONAN DOYLE

Although Conan Doyle did not even know that this film was being made (he had sold the rights to another producer), he is heavily invoked in this contemporary ad. Francis Ford was Sherlock Holmes.

worn by Holmes in some of the contemporary German films; certainly King Baggot was wearing a similar one in his own current detective series.

The film was faithful to Doyle's book, at least to the extent of including some sequences involving Mormons. Their inclusion in the book may have been one of the reasons why this story was chosen as a film subject at that time, since the Mormons apparently were popular subjects of topical interest—as witness Evelyn Brent's film *Trapped by the Mormons*.

The more cogent reason for filming, however, was undoubtedly the publicity attendant on the Samuelson version, which, although not released until the day before the Ford version, had, in fact, first been screened for the trade as long ago as the previous October. The delay was due to the war.

Grace Cunard was Francis Ford's wife, and besides this film they made many others together as screenwriter and director. Ford was under contract to Universal also as an actor, and he and Miss Cunard appeared together in most of their films, which were mainly devoted to crime and adventure, and which often took the form of series or serials. She did not evidently appear in *Study,* or the ad would surely have mentioned her, as she was a great drawing card at the time. In an interview of 1916 she noted: "I have written every scenario that Mr. Ford and I produced." One of their films together that particular year was *Peg O' the Ring*. Another of their tandem ventures was the serial *Lucille Love*.

It is problematical where Francis and his more eminent younger brother John were born. Francis was probably born in Portland, Maine, but it may perhaps have been in Ireland. He was born on 15 August 1882, but it is difficult to say just how much older he was than John, since the latter liked to keep his exact age a little mysterious; there may have been as much as thirteen years difference in their ages, but it was probably less.

After fighting in Cuba during the Spanish-American War and spending five years on the stage (where he adopted the name Ford, his own being originally Feeney, O'Fienne, or O'Fearna), Francis made his film debut in 1910 with Edison, then subsequently moved to Vitagraph. He was established earlier and was better known than his brother, and after a prominent career as a leading man he had settled down to mostly directing by the late 1920's, although he still occasionally acted—he was the villain in *Soft Shoes*.

Today, of course, his independent career is largely and unfairly forgotten, but everyone is familiar with his almost countless cameos as an actor in seemingly almost every film his brother directed, right down to *The Sun Shines Bright* and *The Quiet Man*—both in 1952. With his long white beard and priceless comedy in these films and in innumerable Westerns, it is difficult

Francis Ford and his wife Grace Cunard, who wrote the screenplay for *Study in Scarlet*.

to picture him as Sherlock Holmes—unless it is as one of the latter's disguises!

Difficult though it is for most people to dissociate his later career from his brother's, however, he continued to appear in films for other directors all through this period. Some of his non-John Ford films include *So This is Arizona, Wolves of the Air, Thundering Hooves, Sign of the Cactus, Melodies, False Friends, Her Own Story, Charlie Chan's Greatest Case* (1933); *In Old Chicago* (1938, with Rondo Hatton, who later played the homicidal "Creeper" in the Rathbone series); *Lucky Cisco Kid* (1940), *Viva Cisco Kid* and *Diamond Frontier* (1940); *Last of the Duanes* (1941;) *Man Who Wouldn't Die* and *Loves of Edgar Allan Poe* (1942); *The Ox-Bow Incident* (1942, a memorable role, and again with Hatton); and, with Laurel and Hardy (with whom Holmes Peter Cushing also appeared) in 1944's *The Big Noise*.

Francis Ford died in Los Angeles on 5 September 1953. If only through his influence on the style of his brother John, he has made a very great impression on world cinema.

10

William Gillette

SHERLOCK HOLMES; ADVENTURES OF SHER-LOCK HOLMES (United States)

Released: May 1916; United States © 5 May 1916; Released in Great Britain, October 1917

Running Time: 7 reels (approx. 2 hours)

Production Company: Essanay Film Mfg. Co.; Released by V.L.S.E.

Scenery: Arthur Berthelet

Director: Arthur Berthelet (with apparently the participation of William Gillette)

Filmed in: Chicago

Screenplay: H. S. Sheldon

Co-Producers: George K. Spoor & G. M. "Broncho Billy" Anderson (E. T. Lowe, Jr. participated in the film in some unknown capacity)

CAST

Sherlock Holmes	William Gillette
Professor Moriarty	Ernest Maupain
Miss Alice Faulkner	Marjorie Kay
Dr. Watson	Edward Fielding
Billy	Burford Hampden
Sidney Prince	William Postance
James Larrabee	Mario Marjeroni
Madge Larrabee	Grace Reals
Sir Edward Leighton	Hugh Thompson
Count von Stalberg	?

SYNOPSIS: The film is not just a photographed version of Gillette's successful stage play, as the following synopsis from the *Detroit Free Press* of 2 August 1916 makes clear:

Holmes, accompanied by Dr. Watson, meets a beautiful woman while strolling in the streets of London. She so attracts Holmes that he mentions the fact to Dr. Watson. Later he is retained by a representative of one of the noble families of England to recover a package of valuable papers which involve the honor of this family. The package is in the hands of a woman who wishes to use them to create scandal in revenge for a wrong done her. On taking up the case, Holmes discovers the woman he met on the street is the woman who holds the papers. He tricks her out of the package, but is so enamoured in her beauty and personality, he returns the papers, telling her that he believes that she will eventually give them to him of her own accord.

The succeeding incidents develop naturally, showing Holmes falling in love with the woman and their living happily ever after.

The notion of Holmes in love must cause the devout Sherlockian to choke on his (or her) shag tobacco, but, of course, in his day Gillette's interpretation (which had the ambiguous sanction of Conan Doyle) was regarded as the *only* Holmes there was; and in his play version, which has stood the test of time, the "romance" is far more painlessly understated than it seems to have been in the film. One cannot suppose that the more saccharine plot of the film should be blamed on the great Gillette himself.

Since the film seems to be totally lost, we can only suppose from the cast list and the synopsis that the remainder of the film follows, more or less, the incidents of the play: the scheming Larrabees; Mori-

Two scenes from the film, showing an aging Holmes (top), and a romantic interlude between the detective and Alice Faulkner (Marjorie Kay).

We have not been able to find out who played the Count in this film version; it is a pity they could not have contracted Syd Chaplin, who, after all, had Essanay connections, and had played the part on the stage with Saintsbury, with his brother Charlie playing the part of Billy. Later, Charlie Chaplin had played Billy on the stage with Gillette. However, we would surely have heard if Syd Chaplin were in this film.

REVIEWS: We add some more reviews, selected from those excerpted in large ads for this production in *Moving Picture World* for 13 May and 1 October 1916, under the headline:

An Avalanche of Praise for Sherlock Holmes

NEW YORK DRAMATIC MIRROR: Speaking in sporting parlance, which by the way seems particularly appropriate in this instance, the Essanay Company has scored a clean and decisive knockout with this film version of William Gillette's stage success *Sherlock Holmes*. It is not merely a photo drama with a punch—it is a screen triumph with a varied assortment of punches, and veritable trip-hammer punches, all of them. The directing is admirable and the talent supporting the star leaves nothing to be desired, with the result that *Sherlock Holmes* goes forth to the public bearing that stamp of critical approval by all who witnessed its showing. *Sherlock Holmes* is an undoubted super-feature of filmland!

NEW YORK MORNING TELEGRAPH: *Sherlock Holmes* is a picture that can be given unqualified praise, and it is a credit to author, actors, directors, and photographer. There are examples from the spoken drama and fiction which prove exceptionally adaptable to the screen and of these *Sherlock Holmes* is one of the most effective ever undertaken. From the beginning to the end of this seven part feature there is not a dull moment. The fade-in and fade-out process used in this production is positively the best that has been accomplished.

WILLIAM GUNNING'S INDEPENDENT REVIEWS: A big Winner! With the name of William Gillette and the famous *Sherlock Holmes* as a basis for this work, this should be a tremendous box-office attraction. Certainly the film is well enough done to prove a real winner. It should pull big business because of the title and the star's name, and it will certainly more than satisfy. It is quite possible that the offering can be played as a special attraction in many places and it is good enough to justify such handling.

MOTION PICTURE NEWS: The old classic which seems to hold its youth better than most things reaches the screen in excellent form. William Gillette, the only Sherlock Holmes the stage has ever known (NOTE-P&H—Possibly the only stage "Holmes" this reviewer has seen, but certainly not the only stage "Holmes"), appears to unusual advantage in the film version. The direction of the picture by Arthur Berthelet is excellent and uni-

arty brought into the picture by the safecracker Prince; the scene in the gas cellar (which perhaps inspired one of the Nordisk episodes); and the final delivery of the packet to Count von Stalberg.

The early introduction of the romantic interest (much earlier than the play) suggests an attempt at appealing to the broadest possible film audience. It is possible that the makers of the Barrymore Holmes may have screened this film for themselves, and that their version offers clues as to what this one looked like—certainly they follow it in stressing the Holmes-Faulkner romance, and this suggests other links.

form throughout, and the cast is capable. All locations have been well chosen.

MISCELLANEOUS:

Sherlock Holmes is a New York Sensation
The Greatest Super Feature of the Year
William Gillette Stands as a Genius Without Equal
Irresistible Attraction

CHICAGO TRIBUNE (review by Kitty Kelly): The sum of it (*Sherlock Holmes*) is the actor's unexcited conquest of situations; his never-failing meeting of emergencies keenly, shrewdly, unruffledly—just a bit before his opponent; his calm whimsicalness which made him an island of peace forever in a whirlpool of excitement. The incidents where Gillette shines are brilliant spots, and they are many, but one is inclined to feel that there is too much setting between them, in fact the question intermittently pops up—"Aren't seven or more reels too many?" This reviewer votes that they are, except in very exceptional cases, so exceptional in fact that they haven't been seen ... *Sherlock Holmes* is very well staged, and well photographed. In some spots it seems to lack finesse, but in others it was as near perfect as a player of personality and a good director could make it.

Moving Picture World reviewed the film on 6 May 1916. The critic was James McQuade:

William Gillette as Sherlock Holmes in moving pictures, even at the ripe age of 63 years, was a "consummation devoutly to be wished" ... I did not ask whether it had been done or not, but I hope that Essanay took two good negatives of this subject, so that the period of future time during which positive reproductions can be successfully made, shall be prolonged to the classic limit.

Mr. Gillette acts like an old-timer before the camera, and is just as natural and forceful as we have seen him on the stage. The scene in Edelweiss Cottage, where the Larabees hold Alice Faulkner a prisoner, shows Mr. Gillette as the Sherlock Holmes of years ago. The seeming lapses into a sleepiness of manner and action suddenly resolve into a display of imperiousness and overpowering mentality and will. The greatest scene in the photoplay, as it was in the drama, is that showing the test of wit and cunning and masterful resourceful ability between the detective and Professor Moriarty (the Emperor of Crooks), in the home of the former. Mr. Gillette never had a stronger opposite than Ernest Maupain in this great scene. This fine character actor well merits the distinction of being entombed in films for coming years with the master of all detective impersonators.

Miss Marjorie Kay's Alice Faulkner and the Dr. Watson of Edward Fielding are both meritorious. Indeed, the cast is commendable throughout ... all stand out prominently in the action in the film.

The settings are worthy of the acted production, and these and talented direction must be credited to director Arthur Berthelet.

The film's advertisement in that same issue noted: "William Gillette with all-star cast is presented in

Sherlock Holmes in 7 acts ... the character which Mr. Gillette's genius has molded into a virile human being lives and breathes in screen action." The reference to seven "acts" seems to indicate that each reel was somehow divided from the next in the presentation, but may perhaps have only been overblown press-agent's language.

Edward Fielding, who played Watson, was one of several players in the film who were part of Gillette's own company (the rest being regular Essanay performers). Fielding had played the role on the stage with Gillette, but he was not in the original company, and we cannot say whether or not he is the actor illustrated in the role in our accompanying still photograph of Gillette with his stage Watson.

William Postance, who played Prince, was to repeat the role nineteen years later with Gillette on the radio.

The E. T. Lowe, Jr. involved in the production is probably the Edward T. Lowe who later scripted one of the Rathbone series.

At the time he made this film, William Gillette had been playing Sherlock Holmes on the stage for seventeen years, and, although he did not play Holmes again on the screen, he was to continue in the role on

Gillette in a stage role, probably *Secret Service*, also filmed by Essanay with the actor-playwright. The Civil War melodrama was remade with Robert Warwick in 1919, and Richard Dix starred in still another version in 1931 for RKO.

stage for another nineteen years, and also on the radio. He did, however, make a few other films for Essanay in 1916, including another of his stage hits, *Secret Service*. No trace of any of these film classics seems to have survived. Not even Gillette's radio performances as Holmes appear to have been preserved, but there is (apparently recorded separately) a phonograph record of Gillette as Holmes.

In early September of 1916, an exhibitor in Cincinnati who had booked the Holmes film gained an enormous amount of publicity by displaying in his lobby the "actual" old cap, coats, false beards, pistols, and violin that had been used by Sherlock Holmes— not Gillette, but the *real* Sherlock Holmes! *Pictures and the Picturegoer* suggested later in the month that "he might have made his yarn still more complete by stating that Sherlock Holmes had himself sent these articles out to him from Baker Street as a loan!"

Although William Gillette imposed his own physique and personality on the popular image of Sherlock Holmes—almost to the extent that Doyle himself and his illustrator, Sidney Paget, did— Gillette's career as a whole was even wider and more influential than his connection with the Great Detective alone might lead one to believe. Besides writing his two Holmes plays, he was the author, co-author, or adapter of twenty more. His understated style as an actor was one of the chief influences in turning the American theater toward a more naturalistic delivery. On the stage, he originated the device of "fading" in or out of a scene, later to have so decisive an effect in the history of film technique.

Although a brilliant man, Gillette felt no urge to write socially conscious plays; rather, he sought to give his audiences in the theater the same thing he sought for in his own life—escape. "Sometimes I indulge in a dark blue spell," he once said. "It comes on when I think of how things really are. Then I like to look about for the enduring illusions—they are such a solace." He expressed his inner feelings not unlike Sir Arthur Conan Doyle, when the latter was very busily waging a Parliamentary campaign: "Is it not much better—like me—to care for nothing?"

But he cared for a great many other things, most of them connected with the theater. The vehicles he wrote for himself invariably featured the same sort of plot: a man possessed of preternatural calm placed in a desperate situation. It was the sort of escapist fare he would have enjoyed seeing himself—and audiences richly enjoyed seeing him in it. His plays, though, were very astutely constructed, and the longer of his two Holmes plays is not the only one to have stood the test of time without its author to interpret it; for *Secret Service* is, at the time of this writing, being revived on Broadway, and another Gillette play, *Too Much Johnson*, was also revived in New York several years ago, and is currently playing in California. It was also partially filmed in 1938 by a young pre-*Citizen Kane* Orson Welles. In her article on Gillette in the *New York Times* of 22 February 1970, Mae Pohle calls him a "reconciled realist."

An example of the research that he put into his plays can be gleaned from the following anecdote related by Rennold Wolf in the old *Telegraph:*

Returning to his apartments one day (in London), (Gillette) discovered his private papers scattered about the room and under the inspection of two strangers. When they didn't remove their hats, he guessed that they were detectives.

"You live here?" asked one of them.

"Yes," replied Gillette, who is not noted for loquaciousness.

"Are these your private papers?"

"Were," replied Gillette.

"We find among them a complete set of plans of the British Embassy in Paris."

"There are many things among my private papers," replied the actor.

"Would you mind telling us what you intend to do with these plans?"

"Nothing, immediately."

"Then come with us to Scotland Yard."

"Just a moment," said Gillette, "I'm an actor— William Gillette."

"Never heard of you," said one of the men.

"Gee, what rotten press work," exclaimed Gillette. "You must know Conan Doyle. He's a detective. He will identify me."

"But explain about these plans," insisted one of the men.

"It's this way," said Gillette, "I am to appear in a play called *Diplomacy*. The third act is laid at the British Embassy in Paris. In order to get the setting absolutely right on the stage I obtained these plans."

But the detectives decided not to take chances. One of them remained on guard while the other called on Doyle, who vouched for Gillette.

"He's an actor and so, of course, ought to be watched," said Sir Arthur. "But I don't think he's a spy."

Dame Judith Anderson, who appeared on the stage with Gillette in 1918, wrote (in a letter to Mae Pohle) that "he was very learned and remote from the cast," but also noted how impressed she was with his kindness and consideration. Helen Hayes, who also acted with Gillette in her youth, said, "I was never again to see such timing as this man had; it was eerie. There was great simplicity in his style, and style in his simplicity." She compared him with present-day actor Rex Harrison—and how one would love to see Harrison play Holmes someday! Another young actress who was very taken with the man was Ethel Barrymore. Her brother John, of course, and John's father-in-law Maurice Costello, each took a turn at Sherlock Holmes in their time.

Gillette—the son of a United States senator who helped found the Republican Party, descendant of two pioneer New England families, the Hookers as well as the Gillettes, who made his stage debut in Mark Twain's *Guilded Age* through the intervention of Twain himself—does not, at first glance, strike one as an obvious choice for the rather Bohemian English detective.

Apparently the original thought sprang neither from Gillette nor from Doyle, but from some obscure and nameless newspaperman in the American West, who concocted a phony interview with Doyle in which the novelist was made to say that if anybody ever dramatized or played upon the stage the part of Sherlock Holmes, it should be William Gillette. It was apparently this totally unauthorized statement that first put the thought into Gillette's own head; he had not at that time read even one of the Holmes stories. What put the idea into the head of the obscure and forgotten journalist can only be written off as Divine Guidance—or perhaps Doyle, the great spiritualist, unknowingly communicated something from his subconscious to the distant gentleman.

Conan Doyle, meanwhile, had been writing plays for some time. He had, in fact, written an unproduced play featuring Dr. Watson without Holmes even before he was to write *A Study in Scarlet*; and in 1897 he wrote a Holmes play for which he could not find a producer who seemed "suitable." The producer, Charles Frohman, who found Gillette a good study for caricature, eventually got Doyle's permission to give the play to Gillette for revision. As it turned out, after Gillette's four weeks of labor on the play, although it bore Doyle's name as coauthor and contained many elements from various stories of his, all that was really left of original contribution by Sir Arthur was summed up by his telegraphed reply to an urgent request from Gillette. Gillette had asked whether or not he might marry off the detective in the

William Gillette in his stage version of *Sherlock Holmes*, applying the needle under Dr. Watson's scornful gaze. Gillette's screen Watson, Edward Fielding, did indeed play the part with Gillette on the stage, but the actor pictured here may perhaps be Gillette's first stage Watson, Bruce McRae.

play, and Doyle replied laconically that he might marry him or kill him, as he chose. (Conan Doyle himself, as we have seen, was to find that killing Holmes was not so simple as all that.)

In the summer of 1899, Gillette arrived in England, attired in deerstalker and long-caped overcoat, to submit the play for Doyle's approval; the approval of the rest of the human race was soon to follow. The first performance of the play, on 23 October of that year, featured Bruce McRae as Watson—a role later taken by Edward Fielding who plays the part in the film that followed seventeen years later.

The great Holmesian illustrator Frederic Dorr Steele, whose influence on Holmes films was felt, as we shall see, from Barrymore to Rathbone, wrote:

I did not need to be told to make my Sherlock look like Gillette. The thing was inevitable. . . . I can think of no more perfect realization of a fictional character on the stage. . . . Gillette's quiet, but incisive, histrionic method exactly fitted such a part as Sherlock Holmes.

Frederick Dorr Steele's cover portrait for an issue of *Collier's*, was drawn from a photograph of William Gillette on stage.

Another stage photo. Gillette's features did as much as Sidney Paget's illustrations to fix the visage of Sherlock Holmes in the public eye. It was a rather more handsome face than Conan Doyle had originally described.

It was no doubt what Gillette called "the illusion of the first time" in his acting that helped to convince audiences that this was indeed the Sage of Baker Street in the flesh. "I would rather see you play Sherlock Holmes than be a child again on Christmas morning," wrote Booth Tarkington. When the play was premiered, however, the *New York Herald Tribune,* with a truly stunning lack of foresight, said that "the play has no lasting value whatever." Surely if the play has proved that it has any value at all, it is indeed that very ability *to last*!

In 1901, Gillette crossed over to Britain with his play, and, after a stop with it in Liverpool, opened in London at the Lyceum. Gillette was to continue to appear as Holmes on the stage in this play, and *Painful Predicament of Sherlock Holmes*, until 1932, when he said farewell to the detective for the final time—on the stage, that is, for he was to play Holmes on the radio for the last time in 1935, when he was well past eighty.

William Gillette was, in fact, born the year before that in which Holmes himself is generally supposed to have first seen the light. In a story of Doyle's set in 1914, Holmes is stated to be about sixty; Gillette was born on 23 July 1853, the youngest son of six. His non-Sherlockian roles on the stage were in such plays as *Faint Heart*, Barrie's *Dear Brutus*; and among his own works, *Secret Service*, in which he made his London bow. *Held by the Enemy, The Professor, The Dream Maker,* and *She* (film versions of which have involved several screen Holmes and Watsons).

His only wife, Helen Nickles, died tragically young, and his great love afterwards, besides his close-to-life-size miniature railway, was "Seventh Sister," the "castle" he built in Hadlyme, Connecticut, and which is now a great draw for tourists.

William Gillette died on 29 April 1937, just two years after playing Holmes for the last (and probably more than 1300th) time, at the age of eighty-two. He was elected one of the fifty "Immortals" of the National Institute of Arts and Letters. His Sherlockian immortality, to which he was "elected" many times over in the hearts of his audiences, is one that will endure as long as Holmes himself, for there is today nearly as much of Gillette in the image of Holmes as there is of his creator, Sir Arthur Conan Doyle.

Before one of his seemingly interminable (and frequent) "farewell" tours, William Gillette "apologized" (as if that were needed!) by saying: "It all seems to be due to a misunderstanding with God." But perhaps it wasn't.

The only other American-made Holmes film between Gillette and Barrymore was an all-black film, in which the well-known black actor Noble Johnson (of the original *King Kong*, etc.) may have taken a hand as performer or producer. We were unable to find further information on this intriguing entry except that it was made by Ebony Pictures in 1918.

11

The Eille Norwood Series

Like many other great actors in our book, Eille Norwood would be completely forgotten today were it not for his connection with the character of Mr. Sherlock Holmes. Even as an interpreter of Holmes, Norwood does not receive anywhere near his due. He made a total of forty-seven films in the role, covering almost all of the Doyle stories that had been written up to his time; but, today, they are largely lost, and even the few that still exist can only be viewed on a Movieola viewer in the British Film Institute, so that their potential audience is sadly limited. Even those who have written on Holmes in the films do not seem to have taken the trouble to seek out these precious old tinted prints, as one of the authors of this book has been privileged to be able to do. For this reason we have treated those Norwood films that we have screened in unusual depth, so that those less fortunate may be able to get some insight to the very great merits of these films.

The biography of Norwood himself deserves special attention because, whatever the partisans of Wontner and Rathbone may say of their very great merits as individual interpreters of the role of Sherlock Holmes, when it comes to the actual films in which they appeared, no one can deny that Eille Norwood's films, in sum, are by far the most faithful to the original Doyle stories.

EILLE NORWOOD

Eille Norwood was born on 11 October 1861 in York, England. After he had graduated from St. John's College, Cambridge (one source says with a B.A., another with an M.A.), his father wanted him to go into law. But, like his St. John's classmate C. (later Sir) Aubrey Smith, Norwood wanted to go on the stage. His father, though not pleased, acquiesced to the inevitable, and Anthony Edward Brett changed his name (for stage purposes; never legally) to Eille Norwood, inspired by the name of an old girlfriend (Eileen) and his old address (Norwood—the scene of one of the Holmes stories). He made his first professional appearance on the stage in the troupe of Basil Rathbone's lookalike uncle, Sir Frank Benson, in 1884, in the role of Paris in *Romeo and Juliet*.

His career after leaving the Bensonian company was very spotty. He acted in small touring shows and even the humbler "fitups," as they were called. After joining the company of a well-known manageress of the period, he was asked to compose some music for a dance sequence in one of the period pieces she was staging. William Barnes, the company's leading man, resented being called for the necessary dance rehearsals.

"What's the good of a tune like that?" he snarled, and added disdainfully, "It may be good enough for fit-ups or for booths."

Norwood helpfully added, "But not good enough for Barnes."

Some of Norwood's early roles in this period included a promotion from the role of Paris to that of Romeo, opposite Marie de Grey, and tours in *Masks and Faces* and *Fedora*. His father continued to oppose Norwood's theatrical career (perhaps the reason for the name change), but would on rare occasions come

Sherlock Holmes (Eille Norwood) indulges himself in some violin music to aid meditation. Although a master musician when he cared to be, Holmes was liable to just scrape absent-mindedly on the instrument, driving poor Watson to distraction. (Courtesy National Film Archives of the British Film Institute.)

to see his son perform. When he was appearing in *Sweet Lavender* he made a bet with his father that the older man could not penetrate his makeup (which, as always, Norwood had created himself) if he did not look at the program to see what character his son was playing.

"Nonsense!" exclaimed Mr. Brett. "You actors think you are mighty clever, but I should know *you* anywhere, my boy."

"At the end of the first act," Norwood explained, "my father turned to my brother-in-law, and said, with a triumphant chuckle: 'well, he hasn't put in an appearance so far, anyway. I think I shall win the bet!'"

"You've lost it already," was the brother-in-law's rejoinder, for Eille had in fact been on stage for more than half the act. And, in fact, he had actually been wearing very little heavy "character" makeup, something which is, of course, superfluous to the really fine

character actor. This chameleon ability was to serve him well when he was cast as Holmes in years to come.

One of his most important early engagements was in the company of Edward Compton in 1886 and 1887. A few years later Arthur Wontner, also a future Holmes, was to take his turn with Compton. Some of the parts that Eille played with this company included Joseph Surface (later to be played by Peter Cushing and another Sherlock, Douglas Wilmer), Young Marlow (a Saintsbury part), Captain Absolute, and Harry Dornton. On 22 March 1887, at the Grand Theatre in Leeds, Eille made his bow as a writer when Compton produced his play *Hook and Eye*, "hoping it would catch on," as the playwright remarked. It must have done so to some extent because it was revived four years later at the Opera Comique. In the cast, besides Norwood himself, was a Mr. C. Blakiston. This was most probably Clarence Blakiston, who in 1901 was to beat Eille to the Holmes draw by playing a character named "Sheerluck Jones." We have inspected a copy of this play, and it is full of very ripe semi-Shakespearean punning.

Sometime during Eille's early days, he applied to W.

70

W. Kelly for a part that was available in one of his shows.

"What salary are you asking?" demanded Kelly, who was rather fierce.

"Three guineas a week," replied Norwood (a guinea being equal to a pound plus a shilling).

"Guineas are obsolete," retorted Kelly, "you'll have to make it pounds."

"All right then, four pounds a week," suggested Norwood. The flabbergasted Kelly was so tickled by this effrontery that he agreed!

In 1888, Eille appeared at the Globe as Captain Gilchrist in *Bootle's Baby*, then went to Australia for a three-year engagement with an incessant change of parts, one of which was in *A Doll's House*. Norwood was not overfond of Ibsen, so he did not even trouble himself to read the entire play, but only learned his own lines and cues—actually not too uncommon a practice in those days. After the first performance, a member of the audience, who was obviously very agitated, told Eille that he had been "absolutely rank," so the actor was naturally troubled with grave forboding when he was sent for by the manageress. This lady further depressed him by beginning the interview with: "That was an extraordinary performance of yours, young man!"

"I'm sorry," murmured Eille, sure he would be dismissed for his lack of interest in the role.

"Sorry!" she cried in amazement. "What on earth are you sorry about? I tell you it was magnificent."

Norwood stammered that he had just been informed he was "rank."

"So you were!" was the enthusiastic reply. Completely overwhelmed, the actor gradually recalled that the name of the character he had just been playing was "Dr. Rank."

After his return to London, Norwood made his debut as a manager when he took Terry's Theatre and produced his second farce, *The Noble Art,* in 1892. At this point, his career took a similar turn to Peter Cushing's, for both Holmeses had to retire from the stage due to ill health shortly after returning from Australia! Both, of course fortunately for us, returned; in Norwood's case it was after a seven-year hiatus and a successful operation. He reappeared in the same play of his own, now retitled *The Talk of the Town.* The year was 1901 and—a good omen—the theater was the Strand, a name very familiar to devout Holmesians.

The following year he was in *Little French Milliner,* but a few months later there came what Norwood himself always felt was his most important break: he replaced the great Arthur Bourchier in his part of Bramley Burville in Edmond's play *My Lady Virtue.* He also acted *with* Bourchier; but this engagement replacing him led to Norwood's being seen and engaged by Sir Charles Wyndham, with whom he remained for five years playing lead heavies in such plays as *My Lady of Rosedale, Captain Drew on Leave,* and *The Liars.* Before this latter Wyndham play, which was done in 1907, he

Eille Norwood felt that the greatest break of his career occurred when he had the opportunity to be the stage replacement for Arthur Bourchier (pictured here). Reginald Owen, a future screen Holmes *and* Watson, also acted on stage with Bourchier, as did future-Moriartys Norman McKinnel and Lyn Harding.

had left the company to tour America and Canada for ten months with Nat Goodwin and his company; during this tour he appeared at the Waldorf as Lt. Col. Anstruther in *The Second in Command* and played various other leads. Norwood's mentor, Wyndham, had served as a physician in the American Civil War, but he seems not to have passed on his enthusiasm for the United States to Eille; for after the Goodwin tour, when Norwood was sailing for home on the *Minnehaha,* the captain encouraged him to go down to the ship's galley and inspect the spits. "Thanks," retorted the actor with a shudder, "but I've only just left the States."

Back home, he toured with Winifred Emery, created the part of Dick Gascoyne in *Her Son* at Glasgow, and returned to Wyndham for another run before being cast in *Sweet Kitty Bellair* by Louis Calvert, a portly Shavian actor in whose company Arthur

Norwood, on the right, confronts H. B. Irving, who
played the title roles in this stage production of *Dr.
Jekyll and Mr. Hyde*.

Wontner also appeared at one time. In 1908, Eille was
in *Greater Glory,* then returned to his old nonfavorite
Ibsen for the part of "Rosmer." The following year he
was touring in a part that, among fellow Sherlockians,
was also played by Wontner, Barrymore, and
Holger-Madsen; it was none other than that un-
trustworthy creation of Doyle's brother-in-law, *Raffles.*
After playing Gerald Merriam in *Idols,* he joined H. B.
Irving in January of 1910 for a run as Lanyon in *Dr.
Jekyll and Mr. Hyde*—many years later Peter Cushing
was to play a friend of the good doctor's in Christopher
Lee's *I, Monster.*

Norwood remained with Irving for a time, playing
Horatio to H.B.'s Melancholy Dane and other such
supporting characters in *Louis XI, Judge Not,* and
Princess Clementina.

In 1911 he made his film debut, although he apparently liked to forget about the films he had made
before 1920, since it was not until then, at nearly
sixty years of age, that he began to achieve outstanding
success. But it was in 1911 that he appeared in the film
version of *Princess Clementina,* probably in his stage role
of James Stuart. Five years later he did *Frailty,* with
future-Holmes Arthur Wontner, and *The Charletan.*
It is also possible that he appeared in the 1915 version
of Doyle's *Brigadier Gerard.*

In between his film appearances of this period, he
was back on stage in *The Lily, The King's Ransom, Quality
of Mercy,* and his very great success in *A Butterfly on the
Wheel,* which he played in London and New York and
toured in the United States and Canada—he played
George Adamston, MP. In 1913 he was at the Grand
Croydon for a season of repertory, and one of his
parts, Hillary Cutts in *New Sin,* had been played by
Arthur Wontner just the year before. The succeeding
few years saw such plays as *Within the Law, A Working
Man,* and *Peg O' My Heart* come his way, and he also
produced *The Clock Goes Round* and *The Man Who
Stayed At Home,* which ran for over a year; then, in what
must have been a sequel, in 1917 he produced himself
in *The Man Who Went Abroad.* A year later he was doing
Paul Marketel in *The Chinese Puzzle,* which Lyn
Harding, soon to be Professor Moriarty, was to tour
the following year.

In 1920 he produced *French Leave,* written by his
nephew J. E. Harold-Terry. Ten years later Norwood
was to replace Charles Laughton as Brigadier-
General Root in a revival of this play, a long-running
success. This same nephew coauthored the play *Return
of Sherlock Holmes* for Eille in 1923.

1920 was also the year that Eille Norwood joined the
Stoll Film Company to make *The Tavern Knight.* It was
Eille's performance in the title role of this historical
adventure that led to his being cast as the Baker Street
Sleuth in the Stoll series of the following year.

The Tavern Knight was based on the novel by Rafael
Sabatini, whose books have furnished swashbuckling
screen roles for such other screen Sherlocks as Basil
Rathbone and Stewart Granger. In this film, which is
set in the days of Cromwell, Eille played the mysterious elder half of a father-son pair in love with the same
girl. The father is a Royalist who attempts to sacrifice
his own happiness for the sake of his son; but since
Eille is the star, the poor kid has to be killed off to make
way for the big romantic finish, in which the Tavern
Knight also turns out to be a Lord. This was a lavishly
produced picture featuring a re-creation of the Battle
of Worcester.

Some of Norwood's other Stoll pictures include
Gentleman of France (1921) and *Recoil* (1922); the latter

from another Sabatini story, and directed by Geoffrey H. Malins, who was to coscreenwrite the Stoll Holmes series. *Recoil* was remade two years later with Clive Brook in the lead and Fred Paul also in the cast.

Maurice Elvey, who was to be the first director of the series, describes how he cast Eille in the part:

> Down at the studio . . . I suggested that Mr. Norwood should try to make himself as much like the Great Detective in appearance as possible for the purpose of a rough test. Though the suggestion was thus sprung on him, and no special facilities were available, Mr. Norwood went off to his dressing room, and within the space of a very few minutes came back to my room and astonished me. He had done very little in the way of make-up, and he had no accessories, but the transformation was remarkable—it *was* Sherlock Holmes who came in at the door.

Elvey was not the only one to be "astonished" by Norwood's incarnation of the Great Detective, for an almost identical phrase was used by none other than Sir Arthur Conan Doyle: "Mr. Eille Norwood's wonderful impersonation of Holmes has amazed me." It is curious indeed that he says "impersonate" instead of "perform," as if we were concerned with a real person instead of a fictional character. Enjoying such praise from Doyle, who usually tended to deprecate his great creation, was not the least of Norwood's achievements. Conan Doyle further commented:

> Norwood had that rare quality which can only be described as glamour, which compels you to watch an actor eagerly even when he is doing nothing. He has a quite unrivaled power of disguise.

This praise of Eille's "doing nothing" displays the astuteness we would expect of Sir Arthur Conan Doyle, for "nothing" is indeed what Norwood is engaged in doing for long stretches of his films; Norwood's is surely the most understated Holmes ever. It is remarkable that someone who had spent so great a part of his life on the speaking stage could grasp so fully the technique of silent-film acting; that his mime could be at once so subtle and so eloquent. This underplaying was part of Norwood's conception of the character, who he saw as quietly intuitive and unrufflable, taking in facts until he reached his conclusions—then he springs into action "like a cat," as Eille put it.

When first cast as Holmes, Norwood made the following pronouncement, which may sound a trifle pretentious to non-Sherlockians, but the true believer will applaud it:

> It is in no light spirit of bravado that I shoulder my responsibility, he said, but with a very full knowledge of its many difficulties. It is so easy to play the detective in private life, over the breakfast table and in an arm-chair—and so very much the reverse to play Sherlock Holmes on the screen. But I shall set

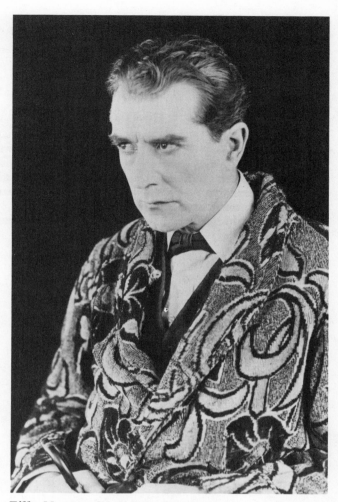

Eille Norwood's Sherlock Holmes was melancholy and intense. The actor shaved his eyebrows to achieve the extra frontal development necessary for the Sage of Baker Street. (Courtesy National Film Archives of the British Film Institute)

about the task with a grim determination to work in all earnestness, for success.

When he was first cast for the part of Holmes, he studied each of the Doyle stories then in print, working well into the wee hours of the morning, absorbing himself into the habits and behavior of Holmes. He learned to handle a violin—for a silent movie! Finally, he shaved the hair from his temples to produce the great Holmesian expanse of forehead, which of all screen Sherlocks perhaps only Robert Rendel has actually possessed.

Norwood made a fine Sherlock because he shared the Great Detective's loves of music, disguises, puzzles, inventions, obscure knowledge, etc.—and he even smoked a pipe. He wrote many plays, of course, but besides these he was the author of many pieces for the piano and songs, and he devised more than two thousand crossword puzzles for the London *Daily*

Express over a period of twelve years. He was credited with the invention of many ingenious stage devices, such as the use of colored ribbons to represent fire (a device used as recently as *Torn Curtain*).

Keenly observant and interested in unusual things, like Peter Cushing he was a bird lover, and Norwood is said to have had an enormous repertoire of bird calls or songs that he could imitate. However, undoubtedly his greatest similarity to Sherlock Holmes, and one that was all to the good for this role, was his own equal measure of Holmes's great vanity and egotism. One really feels, indeed, watching his subtly underplayed Holmes films, that Norwood as Holmes is not an actor acting, but a real person behaving.

Variety called his initial Stoll series of Holmesian *Adventures* "the most exciting mystery detective series thus far to find their way to the screen. Eille Norwood," they continued, "as Sherlock, is an ideal selection."

His disguises and his own makeup were perhaps the highlights of a very good series of films. In the first, *A Scandal in Bohemia*, he assumed four different disguises on top of his initial makeup as the detective himself. As one of the characters, a taxi driver, his disguise was so impenetrable that he was ordered out of the studio on the grounds that he had no business being there. The managing director of Stoll at the time, Jeffrey Bernerd (who had helped cast Norwood as Holmes) said,

I saw a common-looking taxi driver standing there and looking on while a scene was being taken, and I promptly told the stage manager to clear him out . . . in broad cockney the taxi driver whined that he "wasn't doin' no 'arm." He was being escorted off the floor when Maurice Elvey (the director) suddenly called for Mr. Norwood—and the taxi driver turned abruptly and walked straight into the scene.

A journalist from *The Picturegoer* was similarly taken in by the same makeup:

" 'Do you happen to know where Mr. Eille Norwood is?' I asked the taxi driver.

'Blowed if I do,' said, he, 'Kept me waiting two hours, he has. Actors!' . . . I looked at him again . . . and then, and there, under my horrified gaze, he reached up a hand and broke off the end of his nose! 'It tickles,' he said, gruffly, throwing his nose on to the dressing-table, 'And these things are jolly uncomfortable.' Here he withdrew the 'plumpers' from his jaws."

Norwood contrived a new kind of bald pate that did not show any seams, but this makeup was less than successful because it is painfully obvious that it was joined at his eyebrows and nose, the juncture concealed by a pair of spectacles and bushy eyebrows that join to the side whiskers. However, some of his Holmesian disguises are really flawless, as undetectable as Rathbone's music-hall entertainer in *his* second Holmes film.

The Stoll series was so successful that Norwood's name was claimed to be as big an asset on British posters and screens as that of any of the big American names—this is referring to Britain itself, of course; the publicity for the American-produced (if British-shot) Barrymore *Sherlock Holmes* seems to indicate that the Norwoods were not well known in the States. They were, however, well reviewed there, and this seeming ignorance is probably just Goldwynian cupidity.

"The greatest difficulty with my disguises in the Sherlock Holmes stories," Eille observed at the time, "is that I have to remove my makeup before the camera, revealing, not Eille Norwood, but Sherlock Holmes. A disguise within a disguise, you know, and it takes a bit of doing."

The set for Holmes' Baker Street chambers was an astonishingly complex one for the Norwood series. It was a duplicate of the real 144 Baker Street (221B does not actually exist), with the exterior of the street and Holmes' sitting room, bedroom, and hall all actually communicating with each other as in a real house—a thing seldom done in films until recently. Elvey was forced to go to this detail partly because, as he said, "when we started filming in Baker Street, huge crowds collected, making film work impossible."

Elvey also pursued verisimilitude by imitating the story of *The Red-Headed League*, advertising for redheaded men in the newspaper, although whether for actual filmic use (he was shooting in black-and-white, after all), or just for the ensuing publicity when the army of eager redheads descended on the studio, is not clear.

Laurence Hale wrote in *Moving Picture News* on 11 February 1922:

. . . a great deal of the success of the offerings is due to the remarkable impersonation [there's that word again!] of Holmes by Eille Norwood. Really the resemblance to the figure of the imagination is uncanny. It is much more genuine than William Gillette's characterization. . . . Norwood *is* Holmes in countenance, personality, and conduct.

Interestingly enough, the dressing gown that Norwood wore in all his films and stage plays as Holmes had been given to him by Conan Doyle himself—another of those little touches of authenticity that so distinguished this not expensively made series. Doyle had indeed paid (much more than he had sold them for) to buy back the movie rights to his own stories from Franco-British so that the Stoll films could be made at all; he felt it was worthwhile, though, and expressed great satisfaction with the series, regretting only that they were set in current times rather than in the period in which he had originally written them. However, when we see these films today, the London of 1920 seems quite sufficiently in period for us, so that even this objection is met. In the stories themselves, of course, although Doyle continued to write them until 1927, none of them progresses in setting beyond the beginning of World War I, which really saw the finish of the whole Victorian and Edwardian era.

Norwood, incidentally, left the dressing gown to his

Holmes (Eille Norwood) in his classic meditative pose, fingertips pressed together. The dressing gown was a gift from none other than Sir Arther Conan Doyle. (Courtesy National Film Archives of the British Film Institute)

son Gordon Brett in 1948. Many of the touches of authenticity were Norwood's own, not those of the writers of the scripts. He had been horrified to read in one script: "enter Sherlock Holmes in a white beard." "But Holmes would never have done that!" protested the horrified actor, who had much more subtle makeup in mind. The idea, of course, is not just that the audience cannot see beyond the makeup, but that if they can even tell that the character is made up at all the disguise has completely failed.

Fans wrote Eille hundreds of letters, some of them asking him to solve their problems; telling him how to outwit Moriarty; what disguises he should wear; and sometimes writing their letters in invisible ink. These communications were addressed not only to Holmes and Eille Norwood, but also to I. N. Norwood, I. Lee Norwood, Pillo Norwood, and even Elinor Wood.

Once, travelling in a railway carriage full of small boys, he was forced to sustain his characterization of

the Great Detective for the entire journey—no mere actor could have recompensed the children for the loss of the "real" Holmes.

Judging by the evidence of how well they worked together in the series, and by his unkind remarks about his successor, Norwood appears to have had a very good working relationship with his Watson, Hubert Willis. Mrs. Hubert Willis appeared from time to time in the Holmes series, and also appeared with Norwood in *Gwynneth of the Welsh Hills* (1921). *The Hundredth Chance* (1920) and *The Crimson Circle* (1922) complete Norwood's non-Sherlockian filmography.

In 1923, after the completion of the forty-seven Holmes films, Eille returned to the stage to star in his nephew's play, *Return of Sherlock Holmes,* in four acts and produced by Norwood himself. The play had the blessing of Conan Doyle, and ran for 130 performances. The following year, Norwood toured the provinces with this play.

In 1925 he was still on the stage, playing Sir Hugh Symonds in *Yetta Polowski,* and four years later he was impersonating Lord Palmerston in *Lady With a Lamp*—and not with complete success. Dame Edith Evans and other distinguished performers were in the cast, and it ran for 176 performances; but Macqueen-Pope commented that in this play Eille Norwood was "an actor given to inventions which did not work too well."

In 1930, as we have noted, he was replacing Laughton in the *French Leave* revival, and, in December of 1934, Eille Norwood was back on the stage to celebrate his fiftieth anniversary as a performer, playing Sir John Marley in *The Moon is Red.*

Besides the plays that we have already mentioned, he was the author of *Assault and Battery, Chalk and Cheese, A Sacred Promise, One Good Turn,* and *Grey Room*—this latter in collaboration with Sir Max Pemberton, who has a story in one of the *Rivals of Sherlock Holmes* volumes; and he managed a number of theaters and directed many plays.

Norwood was six feet tall and dark in coloring. His wife was the actress Ruth Mackay, and besides his son, Gordon Brett, he had a stepdaughter, Jane Grahame, who was, herself, on the stage.

Earlier in his career he had been living in Farnham, Surrey—first at "Top O' The Hill," then "Corner Cottage"—but when he died on Christmas Eve of 1948, at the age of eighty-seven, he was living in Rawlings Street, Chelsea. His oldest friend, Sir C. Aubrey Smith, had died just a few days previously. Eille Norwood left only £153—and those precious Sherlock Holmes film classics.

Eille Norwood in the rather grubby hat he wore in place of a deerstalker. A similar style was later sported by Clive Brook, Arthur Wontner, and Basil Rathbone in some of the episodes of their respective series.

HUBERT WILLIS

Eille Norwood's Dr. Watson in forty-six of the forty-seven films was Hubert Willis, and anyone who has been able to see any of these fine films knows just how delightful a character-comedian Willis was. His interpretation of Watson was not too dissimilar from Nigel Bruce's; and although Holmesian purists must quibble with a Watson who is not strictly Conanical, anyone who appreciates truly human comedy must praise that interpretation.

Since we have been fortunate enough to find the following 1917 interview with Willis, and since other information is scarce, we print the entire article, with only such parenthetical additions which help fill in the filmographical blanks.

Interview from *Pictures and the Picturegoer,* 22–29 September 1917; interview by "F.D.":

A Film and Footlight Favorite—Hubert Willis Sketches His Busy Life

Are you a playgoer? If so, you will surely know the name Hubert Willis, the owner of which has spent most of his long life on the stage. As picturegoers, of course, you are all familiar with the film work of Hubert Willis, for he has played in nearly every production turned out by the London Film Co.

Mr. Willis, with whom I have just had a most interesting chat, is one of the best all-around actors of the present day. No matter what part has been assigned to him—age, nationality, features, nothing counts—his natural talent, and a positive genius for make-up, have brought him out on top in every instance with flying colours.

One cannot be surprised at his successes for truth to tell, Hubert Willis comes from a fine old theatrical stock. He belongs to the same family as did the late Tom and Sarah Thorne—whose fame was worldwide. His father was an actor-manager and his mother was an actress, and at the age of three little Hubert, a baby in arms, was carried onto the stage of the Theatre Royal, Norwich, in the old farce *Did You Ever Send Your Wife to Camberwell?* He played many children's parts after that, and when school days were done with, he drifted onto the stage for good. .

. . "I have been acting all my life," said Mr. Willis, "and after several years of touring, I made my first appearance in London (the Mecca of all actors) in *The Gay Parisienne* at the Duke of York's, which ran for a year."

"Then I went to the Vaudeville to play in *Never Again* and later, to Terry's to play in *The White Knight* with the late Edward Terry and Kate Rourke. This was the beginning of a happy engagement of 5 years with Edward Terry, and during which I played the second parts to him in all his comedies."

"A season at the Haymarket followed, playing and understudying Cyril Maude; then to the Comedy with Forbes Robertson, after which I played the valet in *Castles in Spain* with the late Harry Fragson at the Royalty, and then I returned to the Duke of York's to play in *Merely Mary Ann,* with Eleanor

Robson, Gerald du Maurier, and Henry Ainley in the cast. I played in *Peter Pan* at the same theatre, and was Harlequin with Pauline Chase in Sir J. M. Barrie's *Pantaloon*. [Screen Sherlock, John Barrymore, played it in the United States.]"

"I went to Australia for two years, appearing in a repertoire of successful plays, and returned to England to play in *Strife* at the Haymarket, with G. P. Huntley in *The Hon. Phil* at the Globe, as Tom Belcher in [Conan Doyle's] *The House of Temperley* at the Adelphi, in the Comedy part in *The Fighting Chance* at the Lyceum, and as the detective in 'Ready Money' at the New Theatre."

"It was *The House of Temperley* that introduced you to filmdom," I suggested, "for that was your first London film, was it not, Mr. Willis?" [*The House Of Temperley*, November 19, 1913, from the story *Red Stone* by Arthur Conan Doyle and his play of the same name. Producer: Harold M. Shaw, Chief of Production at the London Film Co., Ltd.; also featured Ben Webster.]

"Yes," he replied, "but not my first film. I was the tramp, you remember, in *Message From Mars,* with Charles Hawtrey. Then the London Film Co. asked me to appear in my old part of Tom Belcher in *Temperley,* which I did, and fortunately for me, that led to my being engaged in their splendid stock company. I remained with them all the time until it was broken up, and played in nearly all of their productions, the exceptions being the plays which contained no part for me."

"Mention some of the films you appeared in," I urged, "My readers will love the reminder, and will be able to pick you out in them."

"I can't remember them all," he replied, "but the following are not in their right order: *The Man in the Attic, The Third Generation, The Heart of a Child* [1914—these three directed by Harold M. Shaw], *The Middleman, The Christian* [both 1915; both directed by George Loane Tucker], *The Manxman* [1916, Tucker], *Altar Chains* [1916; with Heather Thatcher, directed by Bannister Merwin], *The Greater Need* [1916; with Milton Rosmer, directed by Ralph Dewsbury], *Partners at Last, The Mother, The Man in Motley*—they thought I wouldn't suit in that, but I made up so well as a Jew, they tell me, that I believe they were glad they gave me the part. Then there was *Me an' My Moke* [1916; with Gerald Ames, directed by Shaw]—I was "Me" ["Moke" was a donkey]—and a fine part it was, too. I think I liked it best of all my film parts—and, let me think, I was also in *The Man Without a Soul* [1916; Tucker], *The King's Daughter* [1916; directed by Maurice Elvey, for whom he was to play Watson], *The Old Freck,* and *Bootles Baby* [1914; with Langhorne Buston, who played imitation Holmes "Sexton Blake" in silent films]. That's about all I can remember."

"I guess there are not many picturegoers who have not seen you in some of them at least. With all that experience, you can now tell me which you like best—the stage or the studio?"

"Film work is much more to my liking," replied Mr. Willis, "It's so artistic; though I must confess I am often disappointed with my screen characters. Sometimes I watch a scene and say to myself, 'That's fine, my lad,' but when the next scene is flashed on

it's 'Hubert, my boy, that won't do at all!' "

Mr. Willis tells me he has received flattering letters and requests for photos from every part of the world. His wife, Ann Godfrey, is an actress, and his only daughter, Goodie Willis, is well known on the stage, and an expert in black and white work, as witness the excellent drawing of her father on this page.

With stories and anecdotes Mr. Willis could keep one amused for hours. . . . In conclusion, let me tell you that Mr. Willis who, incidentally, is now on a short tour with his wife in *Helen of the High Hand,* has a very fine part in Broadwest's film *A Gamble For Love* [with Violet Hopson, directed by Frank Wilson, who later directed Fred Paul's "Fu Manchu" series], and I advise you all to watch for the release of this film in December.

MAURICE ELVEY

Maurice Elvey (1887–1967) was the first director of the Norwood Holmes series, and he must get major credit for casting Norwood (after having worked so well with him on *The Tavern Knight*) and for setting up the 221B Baker Street set so lavishly; in general, for the overall planning and supervision of the series. Still, while he has been given his well-deserved due for all these things, it must be admitted that *The Hound of the Baskervilles*, which he directed in 1921, is very stodgy, slow, and dull, while the episodes in the series that were directed by his successor, George W. Ridgwell, are far more carefully crafted from the cinematic point of view, and just plain more exciting to watch. Now this is only to speak of the few films in this long series that we have been able to view, so it is of course quite possible that there are dull episodes by Ridgwell and exciting ones by Elvey. To repeat, though: *we did not see any.* It is possible that Elvey's *Hound* seems slower by comparison with Ridgwell's films because the *Hound* is feature-length and the others only shorts; however, anyone who views them will see that the problem is not length but construction.

Maurice Elvey was born William Folkard in Darlington, and went on the stage in 1905. He became a film director in 1913 with the short *The Fallen Idol*; and before the year was out he had made his feature debut with *The Great Gold Robbery*. In 1913, he also directed an early version of the bloodthirsty melodrama *Maria Marten*. His output was very prolific—over three hundred films—and among many films, the next year he filmed *The Suicide Club*, from a Robert Louis Stevenson story with a very Holmesian atmosphere. Elvey's film of the following year, *London's Yellow Peril*, calls up similar images; and in 1916 he was to direct Hubert Willis in *The King's Daughter*. In 1917 he directed a version of Dickens' *Dombey and Son*, and then in 1918, Elvey was working for G. B. Samuelson on *Hindle Wakes*—in his cast was future-Moriarty Norman McKinnell.

He tackled Dickens' detective character, Bucket, in *Bleak House* the following year; in 1919 he did

Maurice Elvey, the original director of the Stoll series, later moved to Twickenham, although he did not work on any of their Holmes films. In this picture, Elvey is depicted third from the left in the third row from the top among the Twickenham staff, arm in arm with Gracie Fields. (Courtesy National Film Archives of the British Film Institute)

Matheson Lang's stage chiller, *Mr. Wu* (later to be remade by Lon Chaney, Sr.), and then in 1920 he was so impressed with Eille Norwood's work for him in *The Tavern Knight* that he and Stoll chief Jeffrey Bernerd cast the actor in the role of Holmes for their prospective series. Also in 1920 came *At The Villa Rose*, with a "French Sherlock," later remade by Leslie Hiscott. In 1921 he directed Norwood in the non-Holmesian *A Gentleman of France;* that same year he directed Basil Rathbone in his first film appearance, *The Fruitful Vine*, and his second, *Innocent*. The year after that he had another actor in his cast who was destined to play Sherlock Holmes—Clive Brook. The film was *A Debt of Honour*, and he worked with Brook again in 1923's *The Royal Oak*. Both of these were, of

course, for Stoll, where the Norwood Holmes series was as that same time in front of the cameras. In 1923 he also took a crack at Eugene Sue's supernatural classic *The Wandering Jew* (he was to remake it in 1933), and he tried his hand at that other Holmesian pair—*Don Quixote* and his Watson, Sancho Panza; Sir George Robey was playing the latter role, one he was to make peculiarly his own. In 1927, Elvey remade *Hindle Wakes* and another G. B. Samuelson picture, *Quinneys*.

When sound came in, Elvey remained in great demand (he directed in Hollywood and Europe as well as in Britain), and in a *Picturegoer Weekly* interview at the end of 1931 he was characterized as follows:

Maurice Elvey is an actor, and never stops acting. His spectacles, his blue shirt, and his cigar are part of the picture.

When he gives the players their directions he acts every part in turn, and while they are 'doing their stuff,' impulsive movements of his hands and face betray his inclination to do it for them. He is an institution in British Studios, and a valuable one.

In 1932 he followed Hitchcock in attempting to film Marie Belloc Lowndes' "Jack the Ripper" fantasy, *The Lodger*, and in 1938 he was still finding the occasional mystery in his very mixed bag of film fare when he directed *The Return of the Frog*. In 1943, Leslie Howard was trying to make the transition from the front of the camera to the other side, but his was an ethereal sort of genius, and he found the practical expertise of the old-timer Elvey very helpful on *The Lamp Still Burns* and *The Gentle Sex*. The old-timer was destined to outlast the novice, however, and Maurice Elvey continued as busy as ever, making his last film, *Second Fiddle*, in 1957 at the age of seventy.

Even this brief survey should have indicated what a prolific and important career his was.

GEORGE W. RIDGWELL

Although his reputation is far slighter than Elvey's, not to mention his output, Ridgwell directed the better episodes of the Norwood Holmes series.

Born in Woolwich, Ridgwell was a soldier, singer, and playwright before entering films as a script editor. He started directing (for Vitagraph) in 1910. Just before assuming direction of the Holmes series, he had been making *Sword of Damocles, Gamble in Lives* (both in 1920), *The Four Just Men, Greatheart,* and *The Amazing Partnership* (all in 1921); and concurrently with filming him as Holmes in the series, he directed Eille Norwood in *The Crimson Circle* (1922), which also featured Victor McLaglen. The film was remade in 1936.

As it happens, Maurice Elvey, Ridgwell's predecessor in the Holmes series, followed in Ridgwell's footsteps on at least one occasion, when in 1934 he remade Ridgwell's *Lily of Killarney* (1929).

Besides the Holmes films, some of Ridgwell's other films include *The Eleventh Hour, The Pointing Finger, Knight Errant, A Lost Leader, The Missioner* (all 1922); *Becket, One Colombo Night* (1923); *The Notorious Mrs. Carrick* (1924); and a 1923 series, *The Romance of British History*.

EILLE NORWOOD AS SHERLOCK HOLMES

(*All films except* Sign of the Four *have Hubert Willis as Watson. Arthur Cullin is Watson in* Sign of the Four.)

The Adventures of Sherlock Holmes is a series of fifteen films released simultaneously in April of 1921; directed by Maurice Elvey:

The Dying Detective
The Devil's Foot
A Case of Identity
The Yellow Face
The Red-Headed League
The Resident Patient
A Scandal in Bohemia
The Man with the Twisted Lip
The Beryl Coronet
The Noble Bachelor
Copper Beeches
The Empty House
The Tiger of San Pedro
The Priory School
The Solitary Cyclist
Hound of the Baskervilles (released in August of 1921; not part of *Adventures* series)

The Further Adventures of Sherlock Holmes is the second series of films, released simultaneously in March of 1922; directed by George Ridgwell:

Charles Augustus Milverton
The Abbey Grange
The Norwood Builder
The Reigate Squires
The Naval Treaty
The Second Stain
The Red Circle
The Six Napoleons
Black Peter
The Bruce-Partington Plans
The Stockbroker's-Clerk
The Bascombe Valley Mystery
The Musgrave Ritual
The Gold Pince-Nez
The Greek Interpreter

The Last Adventures of Sherlock Holmes is the third and final series of fifteen films, released simultaneously in March of 1923; directed by George Ridgwell:

Silver Blaze
The Speckled Band
The "Gloria Scott"
The Blue Carbuncle
The Engineer's Thumb
His Last Bow
The Cardboard Box
The Disappearance of Lady Frances Carfax
The Three Students
The Missing Three-Quarter
The Mystery of Thor Bridge
The Mazarin Stone
The Mystery of the Dancing Men
The Crooked Man
The Final Problem
The Sign of the Four (released in June of 1923; directed by Maurice Elvey; not part of *Last Adventures* series)

THE EILLE NORWOOD SHERLOCK HOLMES FILMS

The forty-seven films (forty-five shorts and two

feature-lengths) were shot and released between 1921 and 1923. The forty-five shorts, each based very closely on one of Doyle's Sherlock Holmes stories, were released in three groups of fifteen films each, one group each year (1921, 1922, and 1923). Each group had a title: "The Adventures of Sherlock Holmes," "The Further Adventures of Sherlock Holmes," and "The Last Adventures of Sherlock Holmes." The two feature-length films, *Hound of the Baskervilles* and *The Sign of the Four*, were released separately in August 1921 and June 1923, respectively.

Maurice Elvey started off the series, directing the first group of fifteen shorts and both feature-lengths. The remaining two groups, thirty films in all, were directed by George Ridgwell. The production company for the entire series was the Stoll Picture Productions, Ltd.; Jeffrey Bernerd, Chief of Production.

For some reason, only the first nine of the short films and the first feature-length film, *The Hound*, were copyrighted in the United States, although all of them played to American audiences.

THE ADVENTURES OF SHERLOCK HOLMES
(series of fifteen films released simultaneously in April 1921; c. in U.S. by Alex. Film Corp):

Director: Maurice Elvey
Screenplay: William J. Elliott
Based on the Sherlock Holmes stories of Sir Arthur Conan Doyle.
Produced by Stoll Picture Productions, Ltd.; Jeffrey Bernerd, Chief of Production.
Director of Photography: W. Germain Burger
Editor: (probably Leslie Britain)
Art Director: Walter W. Murton

1 **The Dying Detective**   Brit. "A" Cert.
Running Time: 2273 ft. (38 min.)

CAST

Sherlock Holmes	Eille Norwood
Dr. Watson	Hubert Willis
Culverton Smith	Cecil Humphries
Mrs. Hudson	Mme. d'Esterre
Staples	J. R. Tozer

2 **The Devil's Foot**   Brit. "A" Cert.
Running Time: 2514 ft. (42 min.)

CAST

Sherlock Holmes	Eille Norwood
Dr. Watson	Hubert Willis
Mortimer Tregennis	Harvey Braban
Dr. Sterndale	Hugh Buckler

3 **A Case of Identity**   Brit. "U" Cert.
Running Time: 2610 ft. (43½ min.)

CAST

Sherlock Holmes	Eille Norwood
Dr. Watson	Hubert Willis
Mary Sutherland	Edna Flugrath
James Windibank	Nelson Ramsey
Mrs. Hudson	Mme. d'Esterre
Mrs. Windibank	Nessie Blackford

4 **The Yellow Face**   Brit. "A" Cert.
Running Time: 2020 ft. (33½ min.)

CAST

Sherlock Holmes	Eille Norwood
Dr. Watson	Hubert Willis
Grant Munro	Clifford Heatherly
Effie Munro	Norma Whalley
The Negress	L. Allen
The Child	Master Robey

5 **The Red-Headed League**   Brit. "U" Cert.
Running Time: 2140 ft. (35½ min.)

CAST

Sherlock Holmes	Eille Norwood
Dr. Watson	Hubert Willis
Jabez Wilson	Edward "Teddy" Arundell (Arundel)
Vincent Spaulding	H. Townsend
Inspector Lestrade	Arthur Bell

(Edward Arundell thought he was halucinating when he saw the hoard of red-headed men that Elvey had advertised for parading through the studio. "You *can* see them, too, can't you?" he pleaded with a visiting journalist, clutching his arm. The journalist tried to persuade "Teddy" he was drunk, not realizing that Arundell was a teetotaler. Arundell was later to play "Inspector Hopkins" in many of the episodes of the series.)

6 **The Resident Patient**   Brit. "A" Cert.
Running Time: 2404 ft. (40 min.)

CAST

Sherlock Holmes	Eille Norwood
Dr. Watson	Hubert Willis
Inspector Lestrade	Arthur Bell
Dr. Percy Trevelyan	C. Pitt-Chatham
Blessington	Judd Green
Moffatt	Wally Bosco
Maid	Beatrice Templeton
Mrs. Hudson	Mme. d'Esterre

7 **A Scandal in Bohemia**   Brit. "U" Cert.
Running Time: 2100 ft. (35 min.)

CAST

Sherlock Holmes	Eille Norwood

Dr. Watson	Hubert Willis
Irene Adler	Joan Beverly
King of Bohemia	Alfred Drayton
Mrs. Hudson	Mme. d'Esterre
Godfrey Norton	Miles Mander
Maid	Annie Esmond

(Miles Mander was years later to appear in both the Wontner and Rathbone Holmes series.)

8 **The Man with the Twisted Lip** Brit. "A" Cert.
   Running Time: 2412 ft. (40 min.)

CAST

Sherlock Holmes	Eille Norwood
Dr. Watson	Hubert Willis
Neville St. Clair	Robert Vallis
Mrs. St. Clair	Paulette del Baye
Mrs. Hudson	Mme. d'Esterre

(One scene was set in an opium den presided over by a Lascar "of the vilest antecedents" east of London Bridge, where Holmes goes to investigate the disappearance of Neville St. Clair, a respected businessman who apparently has disappeared into thin air. Norwood disguised himself as a bald-headed Japanese addict for the film, and was so sleazily effective that the studio doorman refused to admit him.)

9 **The Beryl Coronet** Brit. "A" Cert.
   Running Time: 2340 ft. (39 min.)
   Screenplay: (one source lists Charles Barnett as the writer for this episode instead of William J. Elliott)

CAST

Sherlock Holmes	Eille Norwood
Dr. Watson	Hubert Willis
Alexander Holder	Henry Vibart
Mary	Molly Adair
Arthur Holder	Lawrence Anderson
Sir George Burnwell	Jack Selfridge
Mrs. Hudson	Mme. d'Esterre

10 **The Noble Bachelor** Brit. "U" Cert.
   Running Time: 2100 ft. (35 min.)

CAST

Sherlock Holmes	Eille Norwood
Dr. Watson	Hubert Willis
Inspector Lestrade	Arthur Bell
Lord Robert St. Simon	Cyril Percival
Hetty Doran	Temple Bell
Francis Hoy Moulton	Fred Earle
Mrs. Hudson	Mme. d'Esterre
Mr. Arlton	Aloysius Doran
Miss Middleton	Flora Millar

11 **Copper Beeches** Brit. "A" Cert.
   Running Time: 2193 ft. (36½ min.)

CAST

Sherlock Holmes	Eille Norwood
Dr. Watson	Hubert Willis
Violet Hunter/Ada Repson	Madge White
Jephro Rucastle	Lyell Johnson
Toller	Fred Raynham
Mrs. Toller	Eve McCarthy
Mrs. Rucastle	Lottie Blackford
Roger Wilson	Bobbie Harwood
Japhat	William J. Elliott, Jr. [son of the screenwriter]
Miss Stoper	C. Nicholls
Inspector Lestrade	Arthur Bell

12 **The Empty House** Brit "A" Cert.
   Running Time: 1800 ft. (30 min.)

CAST

Sherlock Holmes	Eille Norwood
Dr. Watson	Hubert Willis
Hon. Ronald Adair	Austin Fairman
Sir Charles Ridge	Cecil Kerr
Inspector Lestrade	Arthur Bell
Mrs. Hudson	Mme. d'Esterre
Col. Sebastian Moran	Sidney Seaward
Mrs. Adair	J. Gelardi

13 **The Tiger of San Pedro** Brit. "A" Cert.
   Running Time: 2080 ft. (34½ min.)

CAST

Sherlock Holmes	Eille Norwood
Dr. Watson	Hubert Willis
Murillo/The Tiger/ Mr. Henderson	Lewis Gilbert
John Scott Eccles	George Harrington
Garcia	Arthur Walcott
Inspector Lestrade	Arthur Bell
Mrs. Hudson	Mme. d'Esterre
Miss Burnett	Valia Veritskeya

(Holmes disguises himself as a "tough," to spy on Wisteria Lodge, which lay between Esher and Oxshot. It was the home of the patriot Garcia, and in the kitchen are discovered the remains of a voodoo sacrifice, after Garcia has been slain by the exiled Central American dictator known as the "Tiger.")

14 **The Priory School** Brit "A" Cert.
   Running Time: 2100 ft. (35 min.)
   Screenplay: (one source lists Charles Barnett instead of William J. Elliott as the screenwriter)

CAST

Sherlock Holmes	Eille Norwood
Dr. Watson	Hubert Willis
Dr. Thorneycraft Huxtable	Leslie English
Duke of Holderness	C. H. Croker-King
Duchess of Holderness	Irene Rooke

Reuben Haynes	Tom Ronald
Lord Saltire	Patrick Kay
James Wilder	Cecil Kerr
Mrs. Hudson	Mme. d'Esterre
De Castelet	Allen Leamy

15 The Solitary Cyclist Brit. "A" Cert.
Running Time: 2140 ft. (35½ min.)

CAST

Sherlock Holmes	Eille Norwood
Dr. Watson	Hubert Willis
Bob Carruthers	R. D. Sylvester
Violet Relph	Violet Hewitt
Jack Woodley	Allan Jeayes
Mrs. Hudson	Mme. d'Esterre

16 The Hound of the Baskervilles Brit. "A" Cert.
Date of Release: 8 August 1921 in Great Britain; 1
October 1922 in United States
Production Company: Stoll Picture Productions,
Ltd. (released in the United States by Film
Booking Offices of America, and copyrighted
there by R-C Pictures Corp.)
Chief of Production: Jeffrey Bernerd
Running Time: 5500 ft. (92 min.)
Producer: Maurice Elvey
Director: Maurice Elvey
Director of Photography: W. Germaine Burger
Screenplay: Maurice Elvey, William J. Elliott, and
Dorothy Westlake
Editor: Leslie Britain
Art Director: Walter W. Murton
Locations: (probably Dartmoor)

CAST

Sherlock Holmes	Eille Norwood
Beryl Stapleton	Betty (or Catina) Campbell
Sir Henry Baskerville	Rex MacDougal
John Stapleton	Lewis Gilbert
Dr. Watson	Hubert Willis
Sir Charles Baskerville	Robert English

(one source says English played Dr. Mortimer)

| Barrymore (Osborne) | Frederick Raynham |

*(He may have been Barrymore in the English version, but
was definitely renamed Osborne for the American release
for obvious reasons)*

Mrs. Barrymore (Osborne)	Miss Walker
Mrs. Hudson	Mme. d'Esterre
The Convict (Selden)	Robert Vallis
Dr. Mortimer	Allen Jeayes

SYNOPSIS: Since this is one of the films we were able to see at the National Film Archives, we will discuss it at some length.

The film opens with several shots of Baskerville Hall; then we see Dr. Watson at his desk, writing. Holmes is seated, pensively smoking, which is of

Hubert Willis was unquestionably the greatest character comedian among filmic Watsons, with the exception of Nigel Bruce. In this scene from *The Hound of the Baskervilles* (clockwise from top left) are Frederick Raynham as Barrymore, Hubert Willis, Eille Norwood, and Rex MacDougal as Sir Henry Baskerville. (Courtesy National Film Archives of the British Film Institute.)

course the way Holmes is discovered in the novel; but how much more intriguing and even cinematic is the scene when Watson *enters* the chambers at 221B to discover Holmes in a cloud of pipe smoke! To place Watson already in the room, as Elvey has, is to strip the scene of most of its dramatic possibilities. The beginning of the film is generally weaker and more trite than the book.

In this scene we catch a glimpse of Holmes' famous A-B-C scrapbook. Mrs. Hudson now enters; Madame d'Esterre is rather trim and prim in the role—not at all the plump, motherly image of such later famous Mrs. Hudsons as Mary Gordon, Minnie Rayner, or Irene Handl.

There is now a very striking shot of the Hound in silhouette, with light flickering about its outline—this is one of the few Hounds in the film versions of this book which genuinely looks supernatural and even frightening.

Inside Baskerville Hall, Sir Charles and Dr. Mortimer, in what was contemporary dress in the 1920s, observe the Hound through the window in an astonishingly calm manner.

"It never lets me alone," remarks Sir Charles, in a manner so casual that he might be saying, "damned nuisance, really."

When Sir Charles is discovered murdered, there is a very nice effect of lights flickering in the dark, which seem to be related to the Hound. The Hound is just disappearing over the hill as the body is found.

We return to Baker Street, where Holmes is seated at the table in his dressing gown and smoking his pipe. Norwood begins the scene by underplaying gravely;

then suddenly he is alert and full of action as he realizes that he is being watched (a carriage's horse is visible outside the window).

After being retained in the case, Holmes and Watson ride over the moor to Baskerville Hall, when mounted police gallop up and stop the car, looking for the escaped convict, Selden.

Inside the Hall, Watson looks at Holmes before removing his hat, as if to see if it is alright to do so. These character touches seem to have been originated by Norwood and Willis themselves, rather than the director, since they are largely absent in other players, who are frequently poor.

Sir Henry notes that his ancestor was "a great friend of Judge Jeffreys," who would be well known to British moviegoers as the ancient "hanging judge." Dr. Watson collects all the hats of the group and hands them to the butler, Barrymore, then glances back at him twice, double-taking as if he is not sure he should have given him the hats at all.

During a disturbance that night, Watson leaps out of bed, gun in hand and ready for action. Willis is a more "capable" Watson than Nigel Bruce, but is less so than Andre Morell. Barrymore (Osborne) is discovered signaling at the window—this character is particularly overplayed, but he is, after all, meant to be an odd individual. Holmes has left Watson alone at the Hall to watch after Sir Henry—this is, of course, faithful to the book, but it puts the whole burden of carrying the film at this point on the excellent acting of Willis, since the quality of the rest of the film's elements are far poorer than in Ridgwell's shorts.

When Holmes has "returned" (he has, of course, only been in hiding on the moor), costumed in a light-colored suit, Watson has developed a rapport with the other residents of the Hall. This is not typical for Willis in the series, for he is usually just a "shadow" of Holmes—this additional scope for character development may be seen as one of the few advantages found in this longer film. Earlier, Watson has been indeed acting like a very earnest and capable "detective" on his own—this is, of course, always the story for Watson fans.

Norwood has some excellent miming when he

Sherlock Holmes (Eille Norwood) on location in Dartmoor for _The Hound of the Baskervilles_. (Courtesy National Film Archives of the British Film Institute)

stands patiently listening while Sir Henry goes through a tantrum over his romance with Beryl Stapleton; at its conclusion, Holmes gestures eloquently, conveying the silent meaning of "all right, sit down, let's get on with it."

The discussion, however, continues—this is a very "talky" silent film!

Later, ready for the chase, Holmes is dressed nattily in a cape flung behind his shoulders, as if he were planning to go to the opera rather than out on Dartmoor. He is wearing his old reliable shabby modern hat, though—very familiar in this series, and not dissimilar to the one Rathbone wears in the later episodes of his series.

Beryl, tied up and left captive, burns off her bonds with a candle, in a sort of "will-the-cavalry-get-there-in-time" parallel-action climax; eventually she frees herself and goes for help.

Holmes and Stapleton fight in silhouette on the moor, and Stapleton is, surprisingly enough, victorious; but during his escape he falls and sinks into the moor. Holmes staggers up to pursue him, as the action becomes fast and furious, with Beryl sliding down out of the window by a rope made of entwined bed sheets. Then we again see the crackling, electrified outline of the silhouetted Hound (the human characters are also silhouettes at this point, except that their white shirt fronts are luminous).

Holmes, an instant too late, tries to reach for the sinking Stapleton's hand but fails, and as the man sinks, Holmes covers his face with his hand, first partially, then completely as Stapleton goes under completely, off-screen. Dr. Watson shoots and kills the Hound.

The film ends in the cozy atmosphere of the stories, with a request for whiskey and soda. Norwood's appearance is as melancholy as ever, a quality enhanced by his sleepy-looking eyes and slightly protruding upper lip.

REVIEW (From the New York *Times*, 11 September 1922:

At least they haven't rejuvenated Sherlock Holmes and made him a young Romeo.... But neither have they made him particularly impressive as a detective. Eille Norwood ... looks the part all right, and, to a degree, acts it, but he is seldom a compelling figure.... The cold logic, the keen intuition, the sharp and sure perception of the significant ... is missing in this and all other pictorial versions.... Holmes is shown snooping around, spying, and looking wise, but he is not shown really doing anything.... It is possible that motion pictures cannot reveal the real Holmes ... surely, they could more closely approach their original.... Holmes doesn't solve any mystery. It solves itself.... As a story, however, with Holmes in a relatively minor role, the photoplay is not so bad.... The natural settings of the story have been used effectively.... Frederick Raynham is a compelling figure, and Lewis Gilbert ... is villainous enough.

The *Times* also shares our own criticism of the film's visual sense; however, they couple this with carping at the appearance of the Hound, which struck us as not only successful, but as the only successful attempt we have ever seen of illustrating the legendary Hound from Hell.

THE FURTHER ADVENTURES OF SHERLOCK HOLMES (second series of fifteen films released simultaneously in March 1922):

Director: George Ridgwell
Screenplay: Patrick L. Mannock and Geoffrey H. Malins
Based on the Sherlock Holmes stories of Sir Arthur Conan Doyle.
Produced by Stoll Picture Productions, Ltd.; Jeffrey Bernerd, Chief of Production.
Director of Photography: Alfred H. Moise (not "Moses", as was reported in one source)
Editor: (probably Leslie Britain)
Art Director: Walter W. Murton

17 *Charles Augustus Milverton*   Brit. "A" Cert.
   Running Time: 1900 ft. (32 min.)

CAST

Sherlock Holmes	Eille Norwood
Dr. Watson	Hubert Willis
Det. Inspector Stanley Hopkins	Teddy Arundell
Charles Augustus Milverton	George Foley
Butler	Harry J. Worth
Lady Eva Bracknell	Tonie Edgar Bruce
[*the Countess of Eastleigh,* according to one source]	
Mrs. Hudson	Mme d'Esterre
Agatha (the Maid)	Edith Bishop
Cook	Annie Hughes

18 *The Abbey Grange*   Brit. "A" Cert.
   Running Time: 2193 ft. (36½ min.)

CAST

Sherlock Holmes	Eille Norwood
Dr. Watson	Hubert Willis
Inspector Hopkins	Teddy Arundell
Lady Brackenstall	Madeleine Seymour
Sir Eustace Brackenstall	Lawford Davidson
Capt. Jack Croker	Leslie Stiles
Theresa Wright	Madge Tree
Mrs. Hudson	Mme. d'Esterre

19 *The Norwood Builder*   Brit. "U" Cert.
   Running Time: 2067 ft. (34½ min.)

CAST

Sherlock Holmes	Eille Norwood
Dr. Watson	Hubert Willis
Inspector Hopkins	Teddy Arundell

James Oldacre	Fred Wright
John Hector MacFarlane	Cyril Raymond
Miss (Mrs.?) MacFarlane	Laura Walker
Mrs. Hudson	Mme. d'Esterre

20 **The Reigate Squires** Brit. "A" Cert.
Running Time: 1885 ft. (31½ min.)

CAST

Sherlock Holmes	Eille Norwood
Dr. Watson	Hubert Willis
Inspector Hopkins	Teddy Arundell
Alec Cunningham	Richard Atwood
Squire Cunningham	Edward O'Neill
Colonel Hayter	Arthur Lumley
Mrs. Hudson	Mme. d'Esterre
William Kirwan	C. Seguin

21 **The Naval Treaty** Brit. "U" Cert.
Running Time: 1536 ft. (25½ min.)

CAST

Sherlock Holmes	Eille Norwood
Dr. Watson	Hubert Willis
Percy Phelps	Jack Hobbs
Joseph Harrison	Francis Duguid
Miss Annie Harrison	Nancy May

22 **The Second Stain** Brit. "A" Cert.
Running Time: 2179 ft. (36½ min.)

CAST

Sherlock Holmes	Eille Norwood
Dr. Watson	Hubert Willis
Inspector Hopkins	Teddy Arundell
Lord Bellinger	Cecil Ward
Lady Hilda Trelawney Hope	Dorothy Fane
Mrs. Lucas	Maria Minetti
(*Madame Henri Fournaye* in one source)	
Mrs. Hudson	Mme. d'Esterre
Trelawney Hope	A. Scott-Gatty
Edward Lucas	Wally Bosco

23 **The Red Circle** Brit. "A" Cert.
Running Time: 1770 or 1780 ft. (29½ min.)

CAST

Sherlock Holmes	Eille Norwood
Dr. Watson	Hubert Willis
Inspector Hopkins	Teddy Arundell
Gennaro Lucca	Bertram Burleigh
Giuseppe Gorgiano	Maresco Marescini
Amelia Lucca (Emelia)	Sybil Archdale
Leverton	Tom Beaumont
Mrs. Hudson	Mme. d'Esterre
Mrs. Warren	Esme Hubbard

24 **The Six Napoleons** Brit. "A" Cert.

Running Time: 1753 or 1790 ft. (29½ min.)

CAST

Sherlock Holmes	Eille Norwood
Dr. Watson	Hubert Willis
Inspector Hopkins	Teddy Arundell
Beppo	George Bellamy
Pietro Venucci	Jack Raymond
Lucretia Venucci	Alice Moffat
Mrs. Hudson	Mme. d'Esterre

25 **Black Peter** Brit. "A" Cert.
Running Time: 1776 ft. (29½ min.)

CAST

Sherlock Holmes	Eille Norwood
Dr. Watson	Hubert Willis
Inspector Hopkins	Teddy Arundell
Capt. Peter Carey	Fred Paul
Patrick Cairnes	Hugh Buckler
John Hopley Neligan	Jack Jarman
Neligan, Sr.	Fred Raines
Mrs. Carey	Mrs. Hubert Willis
Miss Carey	Miss Goodie Willis
Mrs. Hudson	Mme. d'Esterre

(Holmes disguises himself as a ship's captain during the course of this film. Fred Paul was, of course, associated with Samuelson's two Holmes films, and also played the imitation Holmes character "Nayland Smith" in many *Fu Manchu* episodes. Miss and Mrs. Carey in this film were played by the real-life daughter and wife of Dr. Watson Hubert Willis.)

26 **The Bruce-Partington Plans** Brit. "A" Cert.
Running Time: 2130 or 2196 ft. (35½ or 36½ min.)

CAST

Sherlock Holmes	Eille Norwood
Dr. Watson	Hubert Willis
Inspector Hopkins	Teddy Arundell
Arthur Cadogan West	Malcolm Tod
Mycroft Holmes	Lewis Gilbert
Col. Valentine Walter	Ronald Power
Hugh Oberstein	Edward Sorley
Sidney Johnson	Leslie Britain

(Leslie Britain, who was the editor for many of the films in the series, played a clerk in this film, in the usual shoestring-budget tradition. Lewis Gilbert, who in this film was the first screen Mycroft Holmes, was a familiar figure in other, usually villainous, roles in the series, and also appeared in non-Holmes films in association with Maurice Elvey and Clive Brook.)

27 **The Stockbroker's Clerk** Brit. "A" Cert.
Running Time: 1830 or 1841 ft. (30½ min.)

Sherlock Holmes   Eille Norwood
Dr. Watson   Hubert Willis
Hall Pycroft   Olaf Hytten
Arthur Pinner   Aubrey Fitzgerald
Beddington   George Ridgwell

(The director, George Ridgwell, took a turn in front of the camera in this one.)

**28 The Boscombe (or Bascombe)
Valley Mystery**   Brit. "A" Cert.
Running Time: 2410 or 2450 ft. (40 or 40½ min.)

CAST

Sherlock Holmes   Eille Norwood
Dr. Watson   Hubert Willis
Charles McCarthy   Hal Martin
James McCarthy   Roy (or Ray)
                      Raymond
(one source reverses the casting of Charles and James McCarthy)
John Turner   Fred Raynham
Miss Alice Turner   Thelma Murray
Inspector Hopkins   Teddy Arundell

(Fred Raynham was another familiar figure in the Stoll series. Stoll, like Universal years later, had a virtual stock-company of character actors for their Sherlock Holmes films.)

29 The Musgrave Ritual   Brit. "U" Cert.
Running Time: 1698 or 1750 ft. (28½ or 29 min.)

CAST

Sherlock Holmes   Eille Norwood
Dr. Watson   Hubert Willis
Reginald Musgrave   Geoffrey Wilmer
Richard Brunton   Clifton Boyne
Rachel Howells
  ("The Crazy Maid") Betty Chester

(Geoffrey Wilmer was perhaps a relative of future screen Holmes, Douglas Wilmer, but was definitely not his father.)

30 The Gold (or Golden) Pince-Nez   Brit. "A" Cert.
Running Time: 1630 or 1675 ft. (27 or 28 min.)

CAST

Sherlock Holmes   Eille Norwood
Dr. Watson   Hubert Willis
Inspector Hopkins   Teddy Arundell
Mrs. Anna Coram   Norma Whalley
Prof. Sergius Coram   Cecil Morton York

31 The Greek Interpreter   Brit. "U" Cert.
Running Time: 1796 or 1862 ft. (30 or 31 min.)

Holmes (Eille Norwood) in drag! Holmes is disguised as an old lady for *The Greek Interpreter*.

CAST

Sherlock Holmes   Eille Norwood
Dr. Watson   Hubert Willis
Harold Latimer   J. R. Tozer
Wilson Kemp   Robert Vallis
Melas   Cecil Dane
Sophy Katrides   Edith Saville
Inspector Hopkins   H. Wheeler
Mrs. Hudson   Mme. d'Esterre
Paul Kratides   L. Andre

(Holmes disguises himself as an old lady in this story, in which a wealthy Greek girl and her brother are kidnapped by two Englishmen who then need to kidnap an interpreter to aid them in persuading their two captives to sign away the girl's fortune. Despite the efforts of Holmes, the brother is killed. Arundell was replaced in the role of Hopkins by H. Wheeler; it's curious that Stoll didn't just substitute one of the other detectives from the stories, such as Lestrade, Gregson, or Athelney Jones.)

THE LAST ADVENTURES OF SHERLOCK HOLMES (third and final series of fifteen films, released simultaneously in March 1923):

Director: George Ridgwell
Screenplay: Geoffrey H. Malins and Patrick L. Mannock
Based on the Sherlock Holmes stories of Sir Arthur Conan Doyle.
Produced by Stoll Picture Productions, Ltd.; Jeffrey Bernerd, Chief of Production.

Director of Photography: Alfred H. Moise
Editor: Challis N. Sanderson
Art Director: Walter W. Murton

32 *Silver Blaze*   Brit. "U" Cert.
Running Time: 2077 ft. (34½ min.)

CAST

Sherlock Holmes	Eille Norwood
Dr. Watson	Hubert Willis
Colonel Ross	Knighton Small
Straker	Sam Marsh
Mrs. Straker	Norma Whalley
Silas Brown	Sam Austin
Groom	Bert Barclay
Inspector Gregory	Tom Beaumont

33 *The Speckled Band*   Brit. "U" Cert.
Running Time: 1803 ft. (30 min.)

CAST

Sherlock Holmes	Eille Norwood
Dr. Watson	Hubert Willis
Dr. Grimsby Rylott (or Roylott)	Lewis Gilbert
Helen Stoner (or Stonor)	Cynthia Murtagh
The Baboon	Henry Wilson
Mrs. Hudson	Mme. d'Esterre
Julia Stoner (Stonor)	Jane Graham
?	Celia Bird

34 *The Gloria Scott*   Brit. "U" Cert.
Running Time: 2070 ft. (34½ min.)

CAST

Sherlock Holmes	Eille Norwood
Dr. Watson	Hubert Willis
Victor Trevor	Reginald Fox
James Trevor	Fred Raynham
Jack Prendergast	Roy (or Ray) Raymond
Hudson	Laurie Leslie
Evans	Ernest Shannon
?	Charles Barret

SYNOPSIS: This is another of the films we were able to screen. The story is moved up from Holmes' pre-Watson youth to the present, with Holmes and Watson both guests of Trevor. As all three sit by the fire, drinking, the film is tinted an appropriate and effective amber. Holmes is natty in a collar and dress-shirt front, and gives his usual off-hand but supernaturally accurate deductions about Trevor, after the latter has asked him to do so (in a bantering manner). Trevor faints at Holmes' deductions, in fact, but Holmes, of course, explains that they were "simplicity itself." It seems Trevor has a dark secret to conceal.

Later, Norwood is attired in his usual shoddy but rakish old hat, and Trevor is wearing a white suit, which with his white beard makes for a nice black-and-white composition. These pleasant visual effects are inimitably Ridgwell's, as later episodes in this series will demonstrate. A strange little man arrives to see Trevor and rushes in obviously bursting to speak with him, hurrying through his obligatory handshake with Willis' usual heartily friendly Watson. The little man is engaged as a servant, but rises gradually and mysteriously to become, in fact, the tyrant of the whole household, including his "master" Trevor.

The little fellow is paid overrichly, drinks to excess, and otherwise carries on in a disgraceful manner. Finally he announces: "I've had enough of this place; I'll go see Mr. Beddoes. He'll be *glad* to see me!"

We now get into the explanatory flashback featuring Trevor. It is in fact usual for these short Holmes films to contain a rather lengthy flashback sequence minus Holmes and Watson.

Another nice visual touch lies in the use of handwritten fragments of the letter (which supposedly is narrating the flashback) as subtitles for this sequence. The tinting, too, continues, with amber used for the interiors to suggest fireplace or gaslight; when we go outside, the night scenes are tinted green.

The character contrast between Trevor in the past and the present is also effectively done, with a fine performance by Reginald Fox; these effective supporting performances, which one finds in Ridgwell's entries, are sadly not as numerous or noticeable in the Elvey episodes.

The rather thin Stoll budgets permitted only a few actors and extras for the shipboard revolt sequence, but Ridgwell's sure control results in an effective and exciting treatment, with the camera well placed and the cutting dynamic. When the story returns to the present, the tint vanishes and the film returns to plain black and white, similar to the effect at the end of the 1939 *Wizard of Oz*.

Fred Raynham, another of the Stoll-Holmes stock-company, is back once again in this one.

35 *The Blue Carbuncle*   Brit. "U" Cert.
Running Time: 1866 or 2000 ft. (31 or 33½ min.)

CAST

Sherlock Holmes	Eille Norwood
Dr. Watson	Hubert Willis
Peterson	Douglas Payne
James Ryder	Gordon Hopkirk
Henry Barker	Sebastian Smith
Mrs. Oakshott	Mary Mackintosh
Breckenridge	Archie Hunter
Mrs. Hudson	Mme. d'Esterre
Catherine Cusack	Miss Hanbury

36 *The Engineer's Thumb*   Brit. "U" Cert.
Running Time: 2000 or 2026 ft. (33½ min.)

CAST

Sherlock Holmes	Eille Norwood
Dr. Watson	Hubert Willis
Hatherley	Bertram Burleigh
Ferguson	Ward McAllister
The Girl	Mercy Hatton
Inspector Gregory	Tom Beaumont
Col. Lysander Stark	Henry Latimer

37 *His Last Bow*   Brit. "U" Cert.
Running Time: 1539 or 1600 ft. (25½ or 27 min.)

CAST

Sherlock Holmes	Eille Norwood
Dr. Watson	Hubert Willis
Von Bork	Nelson Ramsey
Baron von Herling	R. van Courtland
Martha	Kate Gurney
Officer	Watts Phillips
Premier	Alec Flood
Foreign Minister	Ralph Forster
Inspector Gregory	Tom Beaumont

Holmes (Eille Norwood) in disguise for *His Last Bow* as an Irish-American spy.

(Madame d'Esterre is replaced as Mrs. Hudson in this episode by Kate Gurney, who was a much plumper "Britannia" and closer to the conventional image of Holmes' landlady. Presumably a new Mrs. Hudson was found for this one, since the character is not supposed to be recognized by the audience at first, as she is masquerading as the villain's housekeeper.)

SYNOPSIS: This is another film we viewed. The film opens with a title card setting the date as August 4, 1914; since Holmes is actually supposed to be about sixty in this story, and the period is only nine years before ths shooting of the film, Norwood and the scenery are for once completely appropriate physically and chronologically.

The first scene is an aqua blue tint of the sea, really more stunning than most conventional color photography. There is a very good working-class atmosphere established in the opening sequence in Von Bork's kitchen, where the domestic staff, including a shabby-looking maidservant, lounge about reading the newspaper, etc. As the story efficiently progresses, we realize again how much crisper the pace of these Ridgwell shorts is than that of Elvey's *Hound of the Baskervilles*. It is established that Von Bork, though a German agent, has a respect for the English people. When we first see his "housekeeper" we should not realize that she has been planted there by Holmes as a spy—unless, of course, we have read the Doyle story, in which case we will also, of course, recognize Holmes when he enters in his disguise. Otherwise it would really be impossible to penetrate, as Norwood's makeup is very effective, but not at all heavy. As a chawing, cocky old Yankee, he strikingly resembles the images of "Uncle Sam"—and, of course, William S. Hart, who posed for the famous "Uncle Sam Wants You" poster. This resemblance is somewhat heightened by a cowboy-type hat tilted on Norwood's head as rakishly as his usual rubbishy old Holmesian head covering.

In the sequence where Holmes overpowers and chloroforms Von Bork, evidence is given of the detective's great physical strength (most notable in *The Speckled Band* when he unbends Rylott's poker).

The film incidentally is the first to incorporate the element of a patriotic Holmes summoned to aid His Majesty's government—a premise so notable in the wartime Rathbone series and even *Study in Terror*.

38 *The Cardboard Box*   Brit. "U" Cert.
Running Time: 1801 ft. (30 min.)

CAST

Sherlock Holmes	Eille Norwood
Dr. Watson	Hubert Willis
Inspector Lestrade (or Inspector Gregory?)	Tom Beaumont
Mary Browner	Hilda Anthony
James Browner	Johnny Butt
Alec Fairbairn	Eric Lugg
Miss Cushing	Maud Wulff

39 *The Disappearance of Lady Frances Carfax*   Brit. "U" Cert.
Running Time: 1818 ft. (30½ min.)
Screenplay: George W. Ridgwell (although some sources credit the screenplay, as usual, to Malins and Mannock, a viewing of the film's original credits reveals that it was done by the director himself).

Sherlock Holmes	Eille Norwood
Dr. Watson	Hubert Willis
Inspector Gregory	Tom Beaumont
Lady Frances Carfax	Evelyn Cecil
Hon. Phillip Green	David Hawthorne
Hily (or Holy) Peters	Cecil Morton York
Mrs. Peters	Madge Tree
?	Joan Beverly
Dorothy Wilkins	Marie Devine

SYNOPSIS: As Roy William Neill did on the Rathbone series, director Ridgwell eventually took over the screenplay chores as well—at least in this episode.

The film opens with Holmes very intently peering into his microscope; his face expresses a silent "oho!" or "eureka!" as he makes some significant discovery—no doubt the subject of a future "trifling monograph." Dr. Watson has popped in for a visit with his old comrade and has been put to work taking notes for the Great Detective. Holmes is surprisingly not in his dressing gown, but clad instead in a dark suit—surely rather formal for him. Norwood is highly animated while giving Watson his instructions, but never overplays; he is just accurately portraying a highly strung and fanatically enthusiastic character.

Hubert Willis does not play Watson with the muttering-under-the-breath of Nigel Bruce or Roland Young, but rather with an eager-to-please quality. He perpetually seems to be saying "oh dear, yes," or something of that nature. His Watson, though small and elderly, is as plucky and bold as Doyle intended him, and as such recent interpreters of the role— Morell and Houston—have made him too.

Holmes, in this one, has occasion to disguise himself as a bald, crotchety old man. Poor Watson is dumbfounded as usual, and Holmes as usual reproves him: "A pretty hash you've made. . . . I *have* done better." It is, of course, these warmly human character touches, these glimpses of the downtrodden Watson and the overbearing and insufferable Holmes, which make these stories so beloved; the actual mystery plots hardly matter when it comes down to it.

Out of his disguise, Norwood is again in his familiar Holmesian togs: cape and cocked gray hat (the latter looking as though it had been sat on, which it no doubt has, Holmes and Watson being the "untidy fellows" they are—poor Mrs. Hudson!).

40 *The Three Students*   Brit. "U" Cert.
Running Time: 2448 or 2500 ft. (41 or 42 min.)

Sherlock Holmes	Eille Norwood
Dr. Watson	Hubert Willis
Hilton Soames	William Lugg
Bannister	A. Harding Steerman
Gilchrist	L. Verne

(A. Harding Steerman had appeared on stage with H. A. Saintsbury, and some of his personal letters from Arthur Wontner will be of biographical interest in our chapter on that future Holmes; he also made a non-Holmes film with Clive Brook.)

A viewing of this film reveals that it opens with Holmes and Watson visiting St. John's College, Cambridge, which is portrayed as Holmes' alma mater in Barrymore's film as well as in this one. This film, however, also makes the very un-Conanical assertion that Holmes actually took his degree—something quite foreign to that brilliant but hardly systematic sleuth—who, of course, adhered to a system all his own, and developed a well-known aversion to many "academic" subjects that could not aid him in his own work.

Holmes is called in to investigate the theft of some papers, and makes one helpful deduction by presuming, as he says to Soames, "You are not in the habit of standing on your desk?"

Watson, as always, follows Holmes like a shadow, totally unobtrusive to the point that he might almost not be there at all, except that Holmes frequently makes comments to him. Willis practically seems to be a worshipful monkey rather than a real help to the detective.

Norwood's characterization is, as usual, under-played, but also melancholy, arrogant, incisive, and highly theatrical, while remaining naturalistic enough for even the standards of our own day. He is not, however, by any means the tallest in the film, and this is rather a disadvantage, as it was to be for Peter Cushing as well.

Holmes' usual abruptness seems, in the case of the Indian, to be bigoted prejudice—or at least it would seem so to an audience that did not realize that the Great Man behaved this rudely to absolutely everyone. Holmes thoughtlessness is again evident when he asks poor Soames to open the door, knowing full well that he will get hit.

There is a great deal of location shooting, which perhaps made the film seem distressingly contemporary when it was released, but today it gives it a fascinating period charm. Very effective advantage is taken of the blowing wind, which seems to be of natural (and, therefore, coincidental) origin, rather than produced by a wind machine.

After all his rude behavior, it carries all the more weight when Holmes, raising his eyebrows, says, "Come, come, it is human to err." As is typical of the series, we see extensive flashbacks as Holmes reconstructs the crime—this is a good attempt at coping with Holmes' deductions in a silent context.

The film has a good deal of human interest stemming from the touching supporting performances, such as when the butler begs the master's son: "Take me with you, please take me with you, sir" (which he does not).

The film ends on a true note with Holmes saying, "I'm afraid we shall be rather late for breakfast,

Watson." Holmes is no ascetic when he is hungry, as any afficionado knows.

41 *The Missing Three-Quarter*   Brit. "U" Cert.
Running Time: 2200 ft. (37 min.)

CAST

Sherlock Holmes	Eille Norwood
Dr. Watson	Hubert Willis
Cyril Overton	Hal Martin
Hotel Porter	Jack Raymond
Dr. Leslie Armstrong	Albert E. Rayner
Godfrey Staunton	Leigh Gabell
Lord Mount-James	Cliff Davies
Mrs. Hudson	Mme. d'Esterre

(one wonders if Albert Rayner was related to the future-Mrs. Hudson Minnie Rayner)

SYNOPSIS (another film we viewed ourselves):

The film opens in 221B where Watson, in a friendly mocking way, applauds a violin recital by Holmes, who, though masterful on the instrument when he cared to be, did not always care. Holmes at the moment is depressed because he is not occupied with a case. As the case at last presents itself, we see another example of Holmes great physical strength as he pushes a man away from him with his fingertip. Although the film begins in bare untinted black and white, the customary flashback sequence is tinted amber; but the effectiveness of this device is somewhat diminished when the film returns to the present and the amber tint remains.

It is noticeably evident in this film that, like many other screen Holmeses, Norwood (despite the appearance of his face) is not all that thin.

A really stunningly effective use of tinting occurs later in the film where a room which is in darkness is tinted green and turns amber as a lamp is switched on, the tint thus enhancing the effect of the lamp's light filling the room in a way that even color film could not equal. Such imaginative use of tinting, though hardly original with Ridgwell, makes us realize how much we miss when silent films are screened without their original coloration.

Norwood's eloquent miming is again evident when he gestures with his hands and wordlessly expresses Holmes' thought, which might be transcribed as, "hmph, a crazy fellow."

Norwood's characteristic rhythm as Holmes is displayed when he listens to the story he is told. He is impassive but keenly attentive, until at last he pounces with great energy on a point in the tale. His dignified melancholy in the role is present in his grave bow of farewell and his pensive walk with one hand in his pocket. "A most interesting personality, Watson," he remarks to his colleague, and the description well fits himself as played by Norwood.

Holmes' energy when his interest has been challenged, in contrast to his lethargy in the beginning of the film, is well shown when he is "on the chase" in a literal sense. Running after the escaping automobile with his dark cape flying behind him, he prepares himself for an effort by clenching his hands behind his back and then unleashes this energy he has gathered with this gesture, by leaping up onto the running-board of the car! Jumping off again, he closely examines the roadway; Watson in true monkey-see, monkey-do fashion gets out of the car to do the same, although when they leave, poor Hubert still does not seem to have the slightest notion what is going on or what clues he is seeking. Holmes in this sequence, with his restless nosing for clues, almost seems to be emulating a bloodhound!

Despite all the evidence of his nervous energy, however, Eille Norwood is a slightly bent and stooped figure here. His own age was, curiously, to set the image for the British audiences of Holmes as a distinctly venerable person—an image that Arthur Wontner's series was so far to augment, that Basil Rathbone at the age of forty-seven was felt by one British reviewer to be "surely too young" in the role!

Holmes in this film shows his rarely seen affection for Watson by rewarding him with a pat on the back; the image is rather that of two old bachelor spinsters. Willis' Watson, as we have noted, is constantly aping Holmes' actions in a hero-worship manner, taking off his own coat when Holmes removes his, and so forth. When Holmes is writing, Watson glances at his pocket watch like a child impatiently waiting for playtime to begin; again, who thinks he can hurry the time on by staring at the clock. Without the evidence of his readiness with a pistol in *Hound of the Baskervilles,* we might have our doubts about the mentality of this Watson; but, of course, the very richness and complexity of Willis' interpretation is due to the length of this very long series of films, in which he is able to ring more changes on the character than an actor can accomplish within the confines of a single picture.

Holmes, his hair a bit gray, paces about nervously, leaps about the room, his arms behind his back, puffing rapidly on his pipe. He nervously rests his hand on his desk, full of impatient energy ready to explode. Where he had been too lethargic without the challenge of a problem, he is now too wound up and intense when presented with one. This is an aspect of Holmes' character that Peter Cushing was later to exploit to good effect, and it reminds us that Holmes is far from a "normal, well-adjusted" sort of character.

This Holmes, in his dark cloak and shabby modern hat, seems to fit very well in the world of 1920's London—halfway between the Victorian era and our own, where survivors of the past jostle precursors of the future. The period is modern enough for us to feel the kinship with our own, but remote enough for Holmes not to seem out of place. The location street photography in this film is particularly good, with the presence of actual sunshine, so different from that of the studio. What is lost by the absence of dramatic artificial lighting effects is amply compensated for by a verisimilitude and airiness, rare in these early motion pictures.

Watson's dog, mentioned in the first Holmes story but subsequently forgotten by Doyle, seems to make an appearance in this film; at least there is *a* dog which Holmes seems to be acquainted with in a friendly fashion.

Ridgwell's workmanlike control of his visual effects is evident in a sequence where a car approaches from the distance. What begins as a long shot pans with the car's motion as the car approaches, fills the frame, and turns away from the camera. The abrupt cut that follows helps the viewer feel the motion of the speeding vehicle. The film's pace as a whole, however, is not set by any visual rhythm from the director, but rather from the rhythm of Norwood's performance with its varying sleepiness and hyperactivity. When Holmes first discovers the body, he whips off his hat from his head, as if to give his overheated brain an opportunity to cool off. He then proceeds to an examination of the corpse in a cool and almost medical fashion. We are reminded that he is a scientist more than a "policeman" as the Germans saw him in their films.

This interest in solving a problem, rather than punishing a wrongdoer, is borne out by Holmes' line: "when a man is lost, it is my job to find him; the facts do not necessarily become public."

The case solved, Holmes is sinking back into his apathy, listening to the explanation with the inscrutible impassivity that Doyle likened to that of a "red Indian."

Watson, although he has contributed exactly nothing to the resolution of the mystery, is anxious—in his usual overhearty fashion—to shake hands with the parties concerned. He ends up this very fine film by fetching along the dog, which has been more of a help to the detective than he has.

Jack Raymond, who has a small role in this episode, was soon to become a director, not only making the Massey-Harding *Speckled Band* in 1931, but also remaking Samuelson's old *Tilly of Bloomsbury* that same year.

42 *The Mystery of Thor Bridge*   Brit. "U" Cert.
Running Time: 2071 or 2200 ft. (34½ or 36½ min.)

CAST

Sherlock Holmes	Eille Norwood
Dr. Watson	Hubert Willis
Mr. Gibson	A. B. Imeson
Miss Dunbar	Violet Graham
Mrs. Gibson	Noel Grahame
Inspector	Harry J. Worth
Mrs. Hudson	Mme. d'Esterre

(The name of the inspector played by Worth is not clear, but Beaumont was to return as Inspector Gregory in the next episode of the series.)

It is interesting to recall that many of these last Norwood films were appearing almost contemporaneously with Doyle's stories, which were not to finish their run in the "Strand" for several more years.

SYNOPSIS: Holmes is in his dressing gown, with his violin and pipe, and is continually being interrupted until at last he looks directly at the camera in exasperation (reminiscent of Oliver Hardy) and unveils a real sneer.

This film, in passing, pokes a little friendly fun at the United States. Tinting is again cleverly used, with the scenes in the woods tinted green, which is more refreshing than any color shot of woods could be, since the effect of the latter would have to be relieved by other colors. Interiors are tinted a red amber, which is all the warmer and cozier by the contrast. The subtitles are perhaps a trifle overblown, one of them reading: "The inexorable grindstone of fate" (which leads us to expect an actual hooded figure perhaps sharpening a scythe).

Holmes has a line, delivered with folded arms, which may be considered either perceptive or chauvinistic: "Women lead an inward life."

The first reel of the film sets the problem, and the second deals with the investigation. Holmes is in a lighter-color hat than his usual shabby number, but one side is turned up as rakishly as ever. There are a number of irises in and out, and also dissolves; and the film makes good use of the huge imposing architecture, which by dwarfing the players helps to aid the sense of "Inexorable Fate" far better than that clumsy subtitle.

Holmes, when trying to comfort a girl, pats her on the arm, but turns his head aside as if even this small display of affection to the opposite sex is a bit much for him.

Although some of the supporting players tend to overact, the performances of Norwood and Willis are as modern as ever and would look quite at home on a contemporary television screen. Another lovely character touch occurs when Holmes, caught without his pipe, sucks on his thumb as a substitute aid to reflection!

Once again, when "on the scent," Holmes is full of almost painful animation, tossing his head and crying, "Come, Watson." Watson has a bit more to contribute actively to this case, as he helps Holmes fish the gun out of the lake to solve the mystery. Basically, though, Willis is a gentle, gentlemanly, and distinguished presence rather than a participant. He is merely a shadow or foil for Holmes, like a good stooge or straight man. But as James Agee wrote in another context, he is a *right* presence.

43 *The Mazarin Stone; The Stone of Mazarin*   Brit. "U" Cert.
Running Time: 1873 or 1878 ft. (31 min.)

CAST

Sherlock Holmes	Eille Norwood

Dr. Watson	Hubert Willis
Inspector Gregory	Tom Beaumont
Count Sylvius	Lionel d'Aragon
Merton	Laurie Leslie
Mrs. Hudson	Mme. d'Esterre

(Although many sources have given the second title, which is of course contrary to Doyle, a view of the credits on the film itself reveals that it was certainly released in at least some areas with the original title.)

The story on which this film was based was itself based by Doyle on his own play "The Crown Diamond." Our sharpshooting friend, Moriarty's lieutenant, Colonel Sebastian Moran, who appeared in the play, is absent here, and the pageboy Billy, who appears in both play and story, is similarly missing in the film.

Laurie Leslie is, of course, yet another Stoll Holmes regular.

SYNOPSIS: Madame d'Esterre is rather reminiscent of Una O'Connor with gray hair in this one, as she expresses to the visiting Dr. Watson her fear for Holmes' safety. The good Dr. is imperturbable and reassuring with the landlady, but when he enters the detective's chambers he finds the dummy of Holmes and fears that Holmes is ill. Holmes explains the situation to Watson and takes him across the street, armed with a gun, to observe the dummy's shadow in the Baker Street window. Norwood is very brisk, full of energy, moving his mouth very little as he speaks, and thus, emphasizing the impression of pent-up nervousness, but tossing his head casually and offhandedly over his shoulder as he explains things to Watson.

When Holmes later reappears in disguise, Norwood achieves one of his greatest makeup triumphs as he is totally unrecognizable as a natty dandy; yet his only real makeup is a little moustache, and the effect is created mainly by his superb character acting.

Norwood's brooding and thoughtful quality as Holmes is enhanced by his very heavy and dark eyebrows. As Watson comprehends the magnitude of what is going on in this case he is bouncing about in agitation, while Holmes agrees with him calmly, and smiles wryly, but then catches his breath when Count Sylvius' card is presented to him for admittance, and then even speaks a little impatiently to Watson. One notes how much more energy there is to these shorts than was present in the Elvey feature.

Holmes dispatches a note to Inspector Gregory and prepares his deception. When the Count sees the real Holmes he pulls the curtain back over the dummy that has tricked him, as if to get the thing out of his sight.

Watson in his excessively gregarious fashion is very confidential and chummy with the Inspector—helping him on with his coat, opening the door for him, leading him to the waiting cab. Willis by his creative acting very often creates a "moment" for himself where the screenwriters have given him almost nothing to work with.

The shots of 1920 London are, as ever, wonderfully charming. Although, of course, they did not have the nostalgic appeal for the film's contemporary audience that they have for us today, it is wise to remember that even Victorian London was contemporary when Doyle began writing stories.

Holmes, on top of the situation, wrings his hands in excess of glee, laughs, and gesticulates, and waggles his fingers as he congratulates Watson and lays his plans with the Inspector. Here, again, we see Holmes as the eccentric of changing moods, perhaps induced to an extent by his narcotics habit.

44 ***The Mystery of the Dancing Men;***
The Dancing Men Brit. "U" Cert.
Running Time: 2387 or 2600 ft. (40 or 43½ min.)

CAST

Sherlock Holmes	Eille Norwood
Dr. Watson	Hubert Willis
Hilton Cubitt	Frank Goldsmith
Slaney	Wally Bosco
Mrs. Cubitt	Dezma du May

45 ***The Crooked Man*** Brit. "U" Cert.
Running Time: 2228 ft. (37 min.)

CAST

Sherlock Holmes	Eille Norwood
Dr. Watson	Hubert Willis
Henry Wood	Jack Hobbs
Mrs. Barclay	Gladys Jennings
Miss Morrison	Dora de Winton
Major Murphy	Richard Lindsay

46 ***The Final Problem*** Brit. "U" Cert.
Running Time: 1686 ft. (28 min.)

CAST

Sherlock Holmes	Eille Norwood
Dr. Watson	Hubert Willis
Professor Moriarty	Percy Standing
Inspector Taylor	Tom Beaumont
Scout	P. Francis

(The Percy Standing who plays Moriarty in this film is probably the Percy Darrell Standing who played Frankenstein's Monster in the 1915 film *Life Without a Soul.*

Colonel Moran is once again conspicuous by his un-Conanical absence.)

47 ***The Sign of Four; The Sign***
of the Four Brit. "U" Cert.
Date of Release: 3 September 1923 (and possibly as early as June 1923)
Production Company: Stoll Picture Productions, Ltd. (released in the United States by Film Booking Offices of America)

Mrs. **John H. Watson, M.D., the former Mary Morstan. Actress Isobel Elsom was actually married to** *Sign of Four* **director Maurice Elvey.**

Chief of Production: Jeffrey Bernerd
Running Time: 6750 ft. (112½ min.)
Director: Maurice Elvey
Director of Photography: John J. Cox

Screenplay: Maurice Elvey
Editor: Challis N. Sanderson
Art Director: Walter W. Murton

CAST

Sherlock Holmes	Eille Norwood
Dr. Watson	Arthur Cullin (or Cullen or Collin)
Mary Morstan	Isobel Elsom
PrinceAbdullah Khan	Fred Raynham
Jonathan Small	Norman Page
Dr. Thaddeus Sholto	Humbertson Wright
Tonga, the Pygmy	Henry Wilson
Mrs. Hudson	Mme. d'Esterre
Insp. Athelney Jones	Arthur Bell

SYNOPSIS: The story revolves around the convict Small's revenge on his former partners (including Major Douglas Sholto) who cheated him of his share in the great Agra treasure.

During the course of the film, Holmes disguises himself as a one-eyed organ grinder, but although he tracks down the blowpipe-wielding villains, they throw the treasure overboard while escaping down the Thames. Watson (who has been cast for the occasion with Cullin, since he looked much younger than Willis) is not deterred by this sad lack of her dowry, and marries Mary Morstan anyway.

Cullin had, of course, previously played the role in the Saintsbury *Valley of Fear*, and was said by Norwood (who no doubt missed Willis with whom he had worked so well) to resemble a "provincial butler."

Elvey had resumed the direction of the series on his return from Hollywood, and in the true Stoll "family" tradition cast his wife Isobel Elsom as Miss Morstan. Arthur Bell, who plays Athelney Jones, had previously been playing Lestrade in the series, and Raynham was yet another familiar face from the Holmesian stock company.

12

John Barrymore

SHERLOCK HOLMES (United States); **MORIARTY** (Great Britain)

Date of Release: (United States) 1 May 1922, and again on 29 October 1922; (Great Britain) 29 January 1923; United States © 3 April 1922
Running Time: 8200 Ft. (136½ min.)
Production Company: Goldwyn Pictures (distributed by Goldwyn Distribution Corp.)
Producer: F. J. Godsol
Director: Albert Parker
Director of Photography: J. Roy Hunt
Screenplay: Marion Fairfax and Earle Browne
Based on: Doyle's Sherlock Holmes stories & Gillette's play
Design: Charles Cadwallader and John Barrymore
Filmed in: United States, England, and Switzerland
Locations: Limehouse; Scotland Yard; St. John's College (Cambridge); the Albert Embankment; Stepney; Lambeth Pier; Hampton Court; and Torrington Square (for Baker Street).

CAST

Sherlock Holmes	John Barrymore
Professor Moriarty	Gustav von Seyffertitz
Alice Faulkner	Carol Dempster
Dr. Watson	Roland Young
Prince Alexis of Arenbeerg	Reginald Denny
Forman Peg (alias Wells)	William H. Powell
Madge Larrabee (or Larraby)	Hedda Hopper
Rose Faulkner	Peggy Bayfield
James Larrabee (Larraby) (alias C. Nevill Chetwood)	Anders Randolf
Craigin (or Craigen)	Louis Wolheim
Sid Jones	Percy Knight
Therese	Margaret Kemp
Alf Bassick	Robert Schable
Count Von Stalberg	David Torrence
Otto	Robert Fischer
Dr. Leighton	Lumsden Hare
Billy	Jerry Devine
Inspector Gregson	John Willard

SYNOPSIS: We were fortunate indeed to have been able to view this film, which had been thought hopelessly lost for half a century. The reconstruction of the film from the original negative was begun by the distinguished film historian (and former instructor to the authors of this book) William K. Everson, who judged from the rough assembly he made that a very great deal of the film was still missing. However, he turned the negative over to Kevin Brownlow, himself a noted film historian, who, with the aid of the film's director, Albert Parker, reassembled *Sherlock Holmes* almost in its entirety. When we remarked to Everson that the film now seemed to lack almost nothing, he qualified his agreement by adding, "except style."

The film opens with an aerial view of London, which is followed by a succession of London location shots, which seem hardly better than stock footage, until at last we arrive in London's Chinatown—Limehouse, the lair of Moriarty. The screen is filled by a spider's web with a huge spider in the center; the spider's image fades out, and we see in its place the face of Moriarty. The Professor, as played by Gustav von Seyffertitz, seems more like a goblin from a fairy-tale than the Napoleon of Crime, but if not a Moriarty, he

John Barrymore on location in London for the film known in the country where it was filmed as *Moriarty* and in the United States as *Sherlock Holmes*. Although Barrymore is depicted here in conference with director Albert Parker, no such scene occurs in the incomplete print of the film that survives. It does, however, serve as the basis for the original newspaper ads. Notice the use of two cameras, surely not a common practice in 1922; and the sunlight reflector in the lower right corner. (Courtesy National Film Archives of the British Film Institute)

is at least a truly splendid film villain, with his grotesque features and stovepipe hat. He also sports the regulation Moriarty scarf. Moriarty lives underground, but enters his office through a trapdoor in its floor, and inside the office we learn that he has his finger in a nasty situation at St. John's College, Cambridge, which is being investigated by Inspector Gregson of Scotland Yard.

At the University, Prince Alexis stands accused of theft by Dr. Leighton. The Prince, insisting he is innocent of appropriating the athletic funds, confides his troubles to his fellow student—Watson (a very boyish-looking Roland Young, sans moustache and with a thick shock of hair hanging in his eyes).

Watson suggests that the Prince consult another one of the students—a chap named Holmes, who is "rather uncanny"; and the scene switches to a country lane, where Holmes is seated on the ground entering notes in his notebook, which the title cards tell us concern "Philosophy," but which seem, alas, more like platitudes hardly worthy of the Great Man. One of them, for instance, is the notably profound question: "What is Love?" But he is also making jottings concerning the "Science of Deduction," measuring the strides of passersby in order to get the ratio for calculating their heights, and listing "My Limitations" (readers of "A Study in Scarlet" will recognize the list as being very similar to the one Watson drew up for the detective); and he seems to be, already, a fiendish pipe-smoker. The problem, alas, is that Holmes and

Watson did not in fact meet until after they had left their respective schools; and Watson's was Edinburgh, not Cambridge.

Holmes climbs up the wall of a nearby tavern to examine a caterpillar, loses his grip, and falls into the pathway where he lies very still, and is nearly run over by a dog-cart driven by Miss Alice Faulkner, played by D. W. Griffith's on (and off) screen leading lady, Carol Dempster. Holmes, when he revives, is so totally smitten by his brief glimpse of the young lady that he cannot forget her for the duration of the picture, and presumably learns the answer to his "Philosophical" question—poor Holmes!

For the Holmes afficianado, this turn of events is very hard to swallow. And the lady is not even Irene Adler! Gillette, of course, created the Faulkner romance in his 1899 play, but it was far more soft-pedalled than it is in this film.

Watson informs Holmes that the young lady is the sister of the girl to whom Prince Alexis is engaged, and so Holmes naturally accepts the Prince's case. Unknown to our youthful sleuth is the fact that Alexis' valet, Otto, is an agent of Moriarty. Indeed at this point Holmes does not even know who Moriarty is. So, when Holmes establishes that the real thief is Forman Wells—a student who was placed in Cambridge by Moriarty to spy on students with influential connections—the detective does not realize that the life of Wells is now in danger from the wrathful Moriarty. Otto, of course, has snitched to Moriarty that Wells had stolen the money to escape from the Professor's clutches, and Moriarty sees the elaborate cover he has built for Wells (in anticipation also of future services) going to waste, and fears that the "weak" Wells will tell all to the police.

Learning of all this from Wells, Holmes decides to face Moriarty in his own den.

This interview gives Holmes his life-long mission: "ridding the world of Moriarty." It is hard to fathom why the Professor does not take care of Holmes when he has him in his grasp, but, of course, Holmes at the time seems to be only a callow stripling, and Moriarty does not suspect the grief he is to get from him. Holmes closes the interview quoting a Chinese proverb.

Earlier, the filmmakers have neatly side-stepped the problem of trying to render Holmes' deductions in silent cinematic terms by giving him the line: "It's easier to know Wells is guilty than to explain how I know it," but now it is not necessary for Holmes to explain it. It develops that Alexis' elder brother has died, putting the Cambridge student in line for the throne. It is now necessary for him to return to his country, and Count Von Stalburg, Alexis' uncle, sent as an emissary from the King, has settled the whole question of the theft by quietly paying the amount missing, so as to avoid any messy scandal.

Another messy scandal that needs to be avoided is poor Rose Faulkner: now that Alexis is the Crown Prince, the girl must be repudiated as too common,

Sherlock Holmes (John Barrymore, right) in his college days pays an unsocial call on Professor Moriarty, who is portrayed here by Gustav von Seyffertitz as an oversized gremlin.

and left in the lurch in Switzerland; eventually she leaves a climbing party by jumping off a mountain.

Holmes has, by this time, settled into Baker Street, where he is devoting his time to three things: the pursuit of Moriarty; the memory of Alice (he has saved the Prince's picture of Rose); and what sounds very like the function of the Statue of Liberty—"helping the weary and mystery-laden."

Dr. Watson is not sharing his chambers, having recently been married, but when he comes to call (with his hair brushed back and the addition of a moustache) Holmes has the opportunity to make his famous deduction about the Dr.'s dressing table obviously having been moved, since his face is badly shaved on a different side than it used to be. The set of 221B, based (with the assistance of Barrymore himself) on the drawings of the classic Holmesian illustrator Frederic Dorr Steele (who later worked on the Rathbone *Hound of the Baskervilles*) is delightfully cluttered. Many of the sets, indeed, and lighting effects in the film are excellent, so far as can be seen from the poor quality print which survives.

The flaw in the film is pace.

Von Stalberg now wants the assistance of Holmes in acquiring the love letters that Prince Alexis had written to Rose, and which are now in the possession of

Alice Faulkner. Holmes at first refuses his aid, even when the Prince himself asks him; but when he learns that Moriarty ("a man—a force—a thing") is in on the matter, he cannot resist the opportunity to combat his old nemesis.

Around this point, as Barrymore blows some excellent smoke rings, Watson utters the classic understatement: "I say, Holmes, you are an odd chap." Barrymore, clad in the regulation dressing gown, makes a melancholy Holmes, like Norwood, Stephens, and Rathbone in his last episodes— Barrymore's Holmes, however, is merely lovelorn.

Miss Faulkner is being held prisoner by the Larrabees, as in Gillette's play (from this point the film sticks pretty closely to the play), so Holmes plants one of his agents in their house to pose as their butler; it is none other than the grateful Forman Wells. The play's thievish Sid Prince is transformed for cinemagoers into Sid Jones, presumably so no one will confuse him with Prince Alexis. Percy Knight, as Jones, performs the miraculous feat of being immediately identifiable as a Cockney in a silent film even before he gets a subtitle. Holmes arrives at the Larrabees' in a silk topper, so we can see where Keaton got his headgear for *Sherlock, Jr.*

The entire sequence that follows is very faithful to the Gillette play; it is a treat—when Holmes sends up the message to Miss Faulkner (telling her that if she does not come down he will come up)—to get another

96

Billy (Jerry Divine) awaits the instructions
of the pensive Holmes (John Barrymore).

look at the scrawling Holmesian handwriting we have first seen in the opening sequences. But if that is a gain over the play, a definite loss is the effect of the mysterious knocking noise which on stage seems to come from nowhere—on silent film if we are to know about the sound at all we must see it being produced, and all the mystery is taken out of it when we see a prosaic hammer in the hand of Wells.

There is, alas, a painfully romantic scene with Miss Faulkner, rather embroidered from the play version. The purist can hardly feel that the Holmes in love is really Holmes, although Carol Dempster is, of course, extremely lovely.

Back at Baker Street, we get another brief glimpse of Dr. Watson (who has little to do in this film, unless scenes have been lost). Roland Young makes a very natty Doctor, indeed—rather like Ian Fleming in the Wontner series; instead of Fleming's pipe, however, he is very "twenties" and smokes cigarettes!

Returning to Moriarty, who has the most screen time of anybody in the film except Holmes, we get a glimpse of one of those curious parallels between the detective and the Professor, as Moriarty whips out his trusty magnifying glass to examine something of moment to him. Not only are Holmes and Moriarty rather similar, but there is also a strong resemblance between Barrymore and von Seyffertitz; and, in their films together, Barrymore liked to work in a sequence where he could distort his features to resemble his friend Gustav. One source says that such a sequence existed in this very film, although if that is so, it is now lost.

The play's sequence that features a visit to Baker Street by the evil Professor is considerably weaker in the film. In the former, Moriarty comes to call very

civilly and politely, and his aura of menace is the more enhanced for it. In the film he comes in with guns blazing—rather unsuitable for the Napoleon of Crime, and a considerable loss in suspense, as there is then nowhere to build to. Holmes' pageboy Billy puts in an appearance in this sequence; he seems to sleep in, and is no doubt maintained by this film's sentimental and socially conscious Holmes in order to give a poor boy a home! Mrs. Hudson is perhaps glimpsed briefly in an earlier moment, but the glimpse is so brief and the print so indistinct that it could perhaps have been a maid instead—somewhat of a luxury for 221B Baker Street, one would have thought, bachelor digs as they were.

Holmes (John Barrymore) discourages the Professor
(von Seyffertitz) from drawing anything suspicious
from his coat pocket.

Moriarty is given a lovely line where he states that since Holmes "drove me into the earth, I drive him off it"; but if this is a reference to his underground lair, we have seen him there (on a higher floor, no doubt) even before he met Holmes.

Holmes arrives for the meeting with Alice in the gas cellar wearing his regulation deerstalker, carrying a Gillettian riding crop, and smoking the cigar he has had on the screen since his first appearance.

221B Baker Street is burned to the ground by the sacrilegious Moriarty; and our suspicions are confirmed that this film is set in "contemporary" (1922) times by our glimpses of automobiles, etc., on the street. This film, like the Norwoods, though filmed in London, refrained from using the actual Baker Street, and no doubt for the same reason: gathering crowds.

For the climactic sequence set in Watson's office (one of our few on-screen glimpses of it), Barrymore's disguise as the elderly clergyman is as delightful as one would expect of this brilliant character actor, and is only recognizable because it is so well played that we are certain it could only be an actor of Barrymore's caliber behind the makeup, and not just some bit player. Disguised as the cabman is our old friend the ubiquitous Forman Wells. Moriarty, too, could apparently think of nothing more impenetrable for his own disguise than a cabman, and, as in the play, one feels that he is captured rather too easily. It is no doubt the penalty for his boldness in walking into the very den of his great nemesis. His vanity is, of course, another thing he shares with Holmes.

The denouement of the film is more romantic than deductive, as poor Von Stalberg and his letters seem to be forgotten completely (unless the sequence is missing from the current print), and, instead, Holmes reveals that he and Alice are about to start out on their honeymoon; can Watson reply anything else to this but "marvelous, Holmes, simply marvelous!" Anyway, that is what he says; but "incredible, Holmes!" might have been more appropriate. The final indignity occurs when the detective asks Watson to leave him alone with his fiancee; surely he would never have tried to shut the good Dr. out of so important an incident for his memoirs?

REVIEWS (From the New York *Times*, 8 May 1922):

No photoplay in which John Barrymore appears can be wholly uninteresting. He is such an expressive pantomimist and is so distinctly an individual that he is bound to vivify many of his scenes. Gustav von Seyffertitz . . . also . . . gives a definite impression. To a lesser degree, the same may be said of Roland Young, Hedda Hopper, Robert Schable and several others. . . . It must be added, too, that many of the scenes in the picture have been persuasively staged, some of them in actual locations . . . others in imaginatively designed settings. And the photography, as a rule, gives them their full value. . . . How stands *Sherlock Holmes?* . . . the answer is, it falls; it falls to pieces. Only its separate pieces remain. The spectator may admire these separately,

Expecting a visit from Moriarty to Baker Street, Holmes (Barrymore) keeps his revolver loaded and handy.

if he pleases, but he cannot take them together as parts of a photoplay which convinces him and holds his interest.

(From the *Mail*, 8 May 1922):

Sherlock Holmes . . . is much less the solver of baffling mystery and much more the relentless nemesis of a great criminal than . . . Doyle pictured . . . (he) is given practically no opportunity to demonstrate these marvels of deductive power. . . . He is rather an energetic, semi-romantic figure, who faithfully clings to his one great purpose in life, that of ridding the world of one of its worst criminals . . . an element of romance (has been) introduced . . . and the detective made to play a leading male role in a love affair that culminates successfully . . . to those who are thoroughly acquainted with him . . . it seems almost a sacrilege.

If there is anyone who can successfully combine the story-book conception of Holmes with the hero of a romance it is John Barrymore, (who) has . . . thoroughly humanized the detective, while retaining some of the characteristics Doyle accorded him.

. . . despite Mr. Barrymore and his co-workers, it is dull.

(From the *Daily News*, 9 May 1922):
  "Direction: Superfine
   Photography: Very Good
   Value: 100%"

(From *Fashionable Dress*, August 1922):

It concerns itself with the student days of Holmes at Oxford [actually Cambridge, of course!] where he first comes in contact with that human octopus Moriarty whose criminal proceedings have for years been the terror of man. . . . The years then advance to a period when Holmes, at the height of his success, but still a failure in ridding London of Moriarty. . . . Needless to say, Holmes succeeds in trapping Moriarty this time, and in addition finds the girl of his dreams, thus ending the first episode of his career.

(From *America*, 8 May 1922, review by Joseph Mulvaney):

Even with Barrymore concentrating until his brow became as corrugated as an accordian, the great detective could not get his stuff across to the spectators, and the subtitles had to be made nearly continuous to let us know what it was all about . . . strange things take place . . . like doors opening and closing, people dashing into telephone booths, peep-holes appearing in solid walls and all that. . . . The thing was so secret that Sherlock refused to let the spectators in on it. . . . Professor Moriarty, a benevolent man who had committed 40 murders, but whenever Holmes got him right, he always let him go in safety to commit more murders. All of which would have been well if they had let the spectators see the murders. But Professor Moriarty murdered in secret, as he did all other things, and it proved a dull day.

(From the *Herald*, 8 May 1922):

There is an unavoidable element of the static. . . . Holmes' greatest feat of analysis . . . occurs when he concludes that his friend Watson has resumed the practice of medicine, that his wife is away, and that he has shifted his dresser from one side of the room to the other, truly a marvelous bit of ratiocination, even if it means nothing in the story. In the final scenes, the pace . . . after having been somewhat tepid at the start develops with a rush . . . hardly time to work in a subtitle while figures scurry about. . . . There is none . . . of the eccentric side of the character except that Barrymore certainly looks a bit extravagant when he runs. Perhaps for this reason the weird personage of the arch-fiend Moriarty stands out more than Holmes. . . . Roland Young makes his silence felt . . . as Dr. Watson, though he hardly fits one's image of that beef and beery blunderbuss.

(From the *American*, 11 May 1922, rhymed review by Rose Pelswick):

Microscopes and tape-lines—all the props that play their part
To denote the sleuthing expert in his pantomimic art;
His hand upon his forehead, as he registers each threat,
With the perfect penetration you'd expect each sleuth to get.
And he gets his information through his piercing concentration,
Which the diabolic villain does the darndest to upset.
For it seemed some crimes were tangled and connected with the scheme
Of a simply horrid villain, whose decisions were supreme.

(and so on, to—)

So the villain was defeated and the papers were restored,
He convinced the stubborn lady, and again his tactics scored.
Some mysterious maneuvers he'd strategically scale
While confiding all to Watson, who was parking on his trail.
Though his system was revealing, still it left me with the feeling
When detectives look like Barrymore—they simply cannot fail.

At the time this film was made, the rights to all the Holmes stories which had then been written were owned by either Stoll or Samuelson, and the only major Holmes property available for Goldwyn to buy was Gillette's play. Barrymore himself participated in the early preproduction stages with the director and

In a re-creation of the gas-chamber scene from Gillette's play, Holmes (Barrymore) prepares to smash the table lamp. Aghast on the far right are Moriarty's henchmen, including James Larabee (Anders Randolf, later a Laurel & Hardy foil) and Craigin (future film star Louis Wolheim).

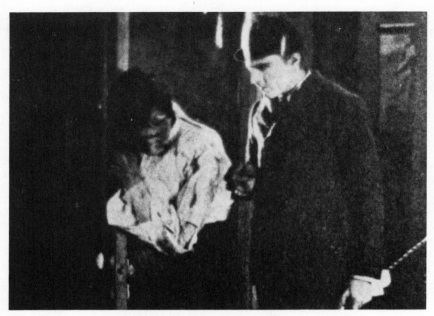

Barrymore, riding crop in hand, interrogates a
villain who seems already quite willing to divulge
any required information.

the designer; in fact, his own sketches were the basis
for the set representing Moriarty's underground lair,
for which the brooding design and ominous lighting is
one of the few highlights of the picture.

Another highlight must be counted: Barrymore's
own performance as Holmes disguised as the clergyman. Perhaps the only other real merits of the film, the
performances of von Seyffertitz and Young, must also
be credited, at least in part, once again to Barrymore,
who indeed dominated the movie in most respects for
good—it is a pity he can also share in the blame for the
romantic interpolations.

In his essay "Sherlock Holmes in Pictures," the
immortal Holmesian illustrator Frederic Dorr Steele
wrote:

"I happened to meet Jack Barrymore, just off the
train from Hollywood. 'There's a film I want you to
see,' he said. 'Just finished it. *Sherlock Holmes*. I dug
up an old German named von Seyffertitz for
Moriarty. Had a lot of fun. Think you'll be
interested.' "
" 'Indeed I will,' I said, hoping the old drawings
were remembered. 'I used to make pictures of
Sherlock.' "
"His eyebrows twisted with the Barrymore grin.
'Why, hell, we had all your old pictures out on the
lot. You're more to blame than Gillette.' "

The 221B set in particular is based on Steele's classic
magazine illustrations for the original Doyle stories.
Barrymore may indeed have dug up von Seyffertitz,
but Gustav had previously been in some Douglas
Fairbanks pictures, so was not a complete newcomer to
the screen. Later, of course, he was to appear in other
films with Barrymore, who loved to distort his own
features to resemble those of the German actor. Some
of von Seyffertitz's other films include *Old Wives for
New* (1918); *Sparrows* (1926); *The Student Prince* (1927);
Barbed Wire (with Clive Brook, 1927); *Yellow Lily* (with
Clive Brook, 1928); *The Bat Whispers* (1931); *Shangai
Express* (1932); *She* (with future Dr. Watson Nigel
Bruce, 1935); *In Old Chicago* (1938); *Nurse Edith Cavell*
(1939); and *Son of Frankenstein* (with Basil Rathbone,
1939).

He was born in 1863 and, during the anti-German
feeling immediately after World War I, used the name
of "G. Butler Clonblough," and appeared so billed in
the role of Kaiser Wilhelm for a Liberty Bond film with
Douglas Fairbanks, Sr.

It is difficult indeed to believe that his Moriarty is an
Irishman, but he is memorable in the role, as indeed he
is in all of his many screen appearances. He died in
1943, one of the uniquely irreplaceables.

Barrymore also had a share in the subtly appealing
performance in this film of Roland Young.

When the modest self-effacing Roland appeared
on my horizon, I took a great liking to him; so much
so that I began to feel sorry for him during our
scenes together. For once in my life, I decided to be
somewhat decent towards a colleague. I suggested a
little stage business now and then, so that such a
charming, agreeable thespian might not be altogether lost in the shuffle. When I saw the
completed film I was flabbergasted, stunned, and
almost became an atheist on the spot. That quiet,
agreeable bastard had stolen not one, but every

One of the Frederick Dorr Steele illustrations on which John Barrymore based his set designs for 221B Baker Street. (Courtesy *Collier's* Magazine)

Moriarty (von Seyffertitz) is prevented from reaching for his own revolver by Holmes' pageboy Billy (Jerry Devine), who has been roused from sleep by the vigilant detective (Barrymore).

damned scene. This consummate artist and myself had been close friends for years, but I wouldn't think of trusting him on any stage. He is such a splendid gentleman in real life, but what a cunning, larcenous demon when on the boards.

Much of the above, however, must be written off as Barrymoresque exaggeration, as (at least in what survives of the print) Young has so little screen time or involvement in the plot that it would be nothing short

of miraculous for him to be able to "steal" much of anything. But he is indeed very notable in the film—a true master of the silent, dominating *presence*. So far from "stealing" the film was Young, however, that ten years later he was surprised that an interviewer even remembered him as Watson. It is quite a pity that he was never cast in the role of Watson in a talkie, as his muttering style of delivering his lines was (though equally inimitable) rather similar to that of that perfect Watson—Nigel Bruce.

In 1968, Catherine Deneuve said that Roland Young's performance as the Earl in *Ruggles of Red Gap* was the best film acting she had ever seen: "quiet, easy comedy." The great cinema critic James Agee wrote in 1944 that Young was "able to make anything he appears in seem much more intelligent, human, and amusing than it has any intrinsic right to."

Young was born in London on 11 November 1887. In private life he was known as something of a ladies' man, a caricaturist, and a wit—once when a producer asked him the age-old question so familiar to beginning actors, "What have you done?" Young replied, "About what?"

The play *Successful Calamity* was written for him by his mother-in-law Clare Kummer, but when it was filmed his part went to George Arliss. In 1926, Young appeared on stage in *The Last of Mrs. Cheyney,* but he missed the opportunity of appearing on the screen with Basil Rathbone, since he was again left out of the movie version. He did appear with Rathbone (and in a detective story, too) in 1930's *Bishop Murder Case,* in which Rathbone was cast not as Holmes, but as his rival, Philo Vance. They appeared together again in *A Woman Commands* (with Reginald Owen, another screen Holmes, 1932), and *David Copperfield* (1935), but never as the Baker Street Duo in the same film. Young was, of course, most famous on the screen as the original Cosmo G. Topper in *Topper* (1937), *Topper Takes a Trip* (1939), and *Topper Returns* (1941); but some of his other films included *The Man Who Could Work Miracles* and *King Solomon's Mines* (both in 1937); *Philadelphia Story* (1940); Agatha Christie's *And Then There Were None* (1945); *The Great Lover* (1949); and many, many more. He was married to Marjorie (or Francis) Kummer in 1921, but divorced from her in 1940, and remarried to Patience DuCroz in 1948.

He died on 5 June 1953, only a few short months before his fellow-Watson Nigel Bruce. As perfectly cast as he was in the role of Dr. Watson, it is a cause of great astonishment to us that he was only cast in it once.

Carol Dempster, who played the role of Alice Faulkner, was specially loaned from D. W. Griffith to Goldwyn for this role. A quote attributed (perhaps doubtfully) to Barrymore alleged at the time that Holmes' romance was his idea:

My feeling is that, for film audiences scattered the world over, it is not sufficient merely to bring on Sherlock and show him at work . . . to explain the conflict in the drama we are presenting, we desire to make it clear why Sherlock Holmes is what he is—to trace, in other words, his development as the Master Sleuth. Our film . . . will bring out the romantic side of Holmes. . . . Gillette, you will remember, had Sir Arthur Conan Doyle's permission to marry him or kill him or do anything he liked with him. We merely avail ourselves rather more generously of that permission.

Barrymore very likely knew William Gillette, as his sister Ethel had appeared with him on the stage in such plays as *The Painful Predicament of Sherlock Holmes*. Ethel, in fact, admitted to having had a crush on the Connecticut Yankee. However, we must doubt that Gillette sanctioned the Barrymore version in any way, since his own play, though introducing the romance element, downplayed it much more; and Gillette did not try, as did Barrymore, to cure Holmes of the eccentricities that are the very secrets of his charm.

Besides his connection with Gillette, John Barrymore was the son-in-law of another screen Holmes, Maurice Costello, by his 1928 marriage to the latter's daughter, Dolores. Barrymore's other wives were Katherine Harris, Michael Strange (a nom de plume), and Elaine Barrie.

Although Barrymore eminently looked the part of Holmes in all other respects, he was not overtall, and so the cast had to be selected carefully so that no one would tower over the detective. Another deviation from Conanical details was noted by the film's director, the late Albert Parker. One scene revolved around a houseboat, and "there was no such episode in the

Roland Young, seen here out of character, played a very subdued Dr. Watson to Barrymore's Holmes.

Gillette play, or in the 'Adventures' so far as I am aware. A houseboat struck us, however, as a picturesque location . . . so we decided on this as the scene of a murder which Holmes investigates." The deviations, of course, as the reader will have noted by this time, hardly stopped there!

David Torrence, who plays Count Von Stalberg in the film, was the Edinburgh-born brother of Ernest Torrence, later a very fine screen Moriarty. David was in films before his brother; two of his other films were *East Lynne* (1931), with Clive Brook, and *Laddie*, which was later remade with Peter Cushing.

John Barrymore himself was, of course, the scion of one of the greatest theatrical families the world has known—his maternal ancestors, the Drews, having been on the stage since the eighteenth century; and the Barrymores and Colts still active in the theater at this writing.

John's real name was Blythe, and he was born in Philadelphia on 15 February 1882, and after the failure of his youthful hopes to be an artist, he found his way to the stage, where his performances in *Richard III* and *Hamlet* were to establish him as the peer of Kean and Booth. There are many Sherlockian echoes in his career.

Like Hubert Willis, he appeared in Barrie's *Pantaloon;* in 1917 and 1925 he made film appearances as Raffles—a part created by Doyle's brother-in-law, and also played by Holger-Madsen, Eille Norwood, and Arthur Wontner. In 1931 he took a turn as that other old nemesis of Holmes, Arsene Lupin, in the picture of that name with his famous brother Lionel. His role in *Peter Ibbetson* was played (with the same leading lady) by a young Basil Rathbone; and he played a very Holmesian master of disguise in *Bulldog Drummond's Revenge* (1937) and *Bulldog Drummond's Peril* (1938).

Like fellow-Holmeses Benham, Norwood, Rathbone, Cushing, and Lee, he has been associated with a version of *Dr. Jekyll and Mr. Hyde,* and he crossed swords with Basil Rathbone in 1936's *Romeo and Juliet.*

Barrymore made his first film in 1912, his last one thirty years later, graduating from light comedy (of the type one associates with his uncle, Sidney Drew) in such films as 1914's *Man From Mexico*, to heavy-breathing romantic items like 1924's *Beau Brummell* (with Gustav von Seyffertitz again); and the early synchronized-sound film, *Don Juan* (1926), to grotesque character parts in *Svengali* (1931) and two versions of *Moby Dick* (the first called *The Sea Beast*); finally, when he was in his tragic decline, caricaturing himself in things with titles like *Hold That Co-Ed* (1938).

In comedy, he was peerless in screen classics like *Twentieth Century* (1934), and his moving performances in such films as 1932's *Bill of Divorcement* are as "modern" today as when they were released. His career was far too notable to be successfully encapsuled here: two of the best books on Barrymore, with many classic anecdotes of his insane Rabelaisian wit, are by his old and dear friend Gene Fowler—*Goodnight, Sweet Prince* and *Minutes of the Last Meeting.*

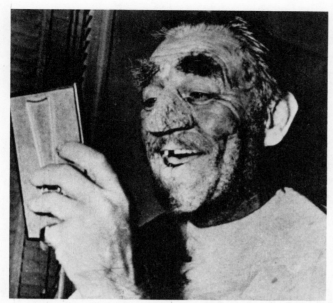

In the *Bulldog Drummond* series, Barrymore played a Scotland Yard inspector with a very Holmesesque flair for bizarre disguises. Here the actor admires himself off-camera.

He died on 29 May 1942, at sixty considered by many at the time a has-been, but remembered today as one of the greatest of them all, a name to conjure with. His daughter Diana had a brief, sad film career, and his son, John Drew Barrymore, is acting at this writing—the son and grandson of portrayers of the role of Sherlock Holmes.

With this film we have arrived at the first Holmesian epic to have been made with a truly "A" budget, like the Clive Brook and Robert Stephens efforts. We find also that Holmes has been considerably changed from his true character to a more romantic and "normal" person, presumably calculated to win him more mass appeal (which obviously is necessary with the larger budgets these films entail).

One would at first think that the evidence of book and magazine sales alone would have given the moviemakers a clue that the original Holmes was appealing enough without cosmetic work. But, on the other hand, all the readers of Holmes or even all the readers of books of any kind are just a drop in the bucket compared to the massive potential movie audience.

One might argue that the more cheaply made and faithful versions like the Norwoods, Wontners, and Rathbones have in fact been more successful, but one would be speaking to deaf ears, for the fact remains that even today the same old tactic of turning Holmes into a more conventional "Pop-hero" still holds sway—in the current best-selling novel, "The Seven-Per-Cent Solution," Holmes is connected firmly with the prevailing fashions of our own day: not a happy and conventional marriage this time around, but a drug habit (never overstressed in the original stories) and psychoanalysis!

13

Carlyle Blackwell

DER HUND VON BASKERVILLE; THE HOUND OF THE BASKERVILLES

Date of Release: 28 August 1929
Running Time: 2382 meters = 7815 feet = 130 min.
Production Company: Sudfilm—Erda Film Produktions GmbH (an English film company also participated)
Director: Richard Oswald
Director of Photography: Frederik Fuglsang
Screenplay: Herbert Juttke and George C. Klaren
Filmed in: Berlin

CAST

Sherlock Holmes	Carlyle Blackwell
Dr. Watson	Georges Seroff
Dr. Stapleton	Fritz Rasp
?	Alexander Murski
?	Lüra Pavanelli
Beryl Stapleton	Betty Bird
?	Valy Arnheim
Mrs. Barrymore	Alma Taylor
?	Carla Bartheel
?	Jaro Fürth
Frankland	Robert Garrison

As a glance at the above cast list will suggest, the film had an international cast—American, British, Russian, German, and Italian.

The director, Richard Oswald, had, of course, been associated with the earlier German *Hund* series, and this film was set in a contemporary 1920s setting, as the earlier *Hunds* had been. Its visual style was characterized by the typically heavy and brooding Germanic sets and lighting, but Holmes himself (for apparently the first time in that country's films) was clad in his classic deerstalker and tweed coat instead of the urchin-type cap of so many previous films. The film also followed the original Doyle story a bit more closely

Dr. Watson (Georges Seroff, left) and his "brilliant friend" Sherlock Holmes (Carlyle Blackwell, right) in a scene from the 1929 *Hund von Baskerville*, which resembles stills from the 1939 and 1959 versions of this famous novel.

than Oswald had in his earlier efforts. Seroff was a rather youngish and chipper Watson, of the company of Roland Young, Ian Hunter, and Donald Houston, rather than the elderly image associated with Hubert Willis or Nigel Bruce.

REVIEW: *Der Kinematograph* noted rather curiously that Fritz Rasp as Stapleton (another source calls him simply "the Murderous Doctor") was playing the role he was born to play; curious because it is hardly one of the great roles of literature or drama, and Rasp (born 1891) was the German equivalent of Lon Chaney (Irving Thalberg, in fact, thought of replacing Chaney with Rasp after Chaney's death, but was stymied by Rasp's heavy German accent); curious also because Rasp was cast in quite another part when *Der Hund* was remade in the 1930s.

Rasp had quite a long film career, surviving to appear with a Holmes of another decade, Christopher Lee, in 1961's *Das Rätsel der Roten Orchidee*. He was also to appear in many of the Edgar Wallace thrillers.

Der Kinematograph went on to note that "since Sherlock Holmes was always portrayed by his creator as an Englishman" an "Anglo-Saxon" had been imported for the part in the shape of Carlyle Blackwell, who, however, "for our taste is not the ideal embodiment of the shrewd secret policeman." The very notion of the Bohemian and democratic Holmes as a sort of CIA or SS man is enough to set the skin crawling!

The London *Daily Worker* of 4 August 1964 underlines the slimness of resemblance that existed between Doyle's conceptions and the legion of Teutonic Holmeses: "In these films . . . London never appears as a big city, with a big working-class population, but more as a polite background atmosphere." Doyle himself, of course, hardly skirts the seamier side—it was his meat as much as it was Dickens'.

Carlyle Blackwell was born on 20 January in either 1888 or 1891; one source says the place was Troy, Pennsylvania; another says Syracuse, New York. Educated at Cornell University, he was first employed as an overland horseback scout-messenger for Wells Fargo, and made his stage debut with a New York stock company in *The Great White Way*. He made his first screen appearance at Vitagraph with Mary Pickford in 1909's *Uncle Tom's Cabin,* remaining at the studio for another year before switching over to Kalem, where he stayed until 1914. He then went to Famous Players to act opposite Miss Pickford again, in such films as *Such a Little Queen* (1914). Leaving Famous Players he and his brother M. H. Blackwell formed a rival company of his own, calling it Favorite Players. Their studios were in Los Angeles, and Carlyle doubled as director-in-chief and star, releasing his product through Alliance.

Some of his films of this period were *The Key to Yesterday* (1914), *The Man Who Could Not Lose,* and *The Lost Chapter.* Another of his early films was *Sealed*

Carlyle Blackwell off-screen. He was the last silent Holmes.

Orders. Later, in London, Carlyle Blackwell was to cofound Piccadilly Pictures with C. M. Woolf and Sir Michael Balcon (who produced the 1932 *Hound of the Baskervilles*).

Much of Blackwell's screen career was, in fact, spent in Britain or on the Continent. As early as 1913 he had been in an English version of *Ivanhoe* for Herbert Brenon. In 1922 he made *Glorious Adventure,* and was working abroad in 1923 in *Beloved Vagabond, Virgin Queen* (for Holmesian director J. Stuart Blackton, with Lady Diana Manners and Ursula Jeans), and *Bulldog Drummond* (a series in which John Barrymore later appeared). In 1925 he was in Germany where for Holmesian producer G. B. Samuelson he played the dual roles of Kallikrates and Leo Vincey (renamed Leon for the film) in Rider Haggard's *She,* which as a film subject has attracted many of the screen Sherlocks and Watsons.

In 1927, Blackwell was back in Britain making *One of the Best* for fellow expatriot T. Hayes Hunter with Elsa Lanchester, and *The Rolling Road.*

Besides this *Der Hund von Baskervilles,* Blackwell is credited by one source with appearing in Barrymore's Holmes film, but this seems very unlikely, and we can find no trace of him in the credits for that film (or for any other film with the same title).

Blackwell did continue to work in the United States, however, appearing in 1920 or 1921 with Marion Davies in *The Restless Sex,* and he was in a few United States talking pictures in the early 1930s. What one source calls his "declamatory style," however, cut his sound career regrettably short.

He was not quite of Sherlockian height, being only 5' 11" tall. His hair and eyes were dark.

A significant figure in his day, he died in Miami on 17 June 1955, largely forgotten. His son Carlyle, Jr., was also a film actor.

With this version of *Der Hund* we reach the end of the silent era, in which Holmes was never truly himself, cut off as he was from the use of his inimitable style of speaking.

Der Hund was not, as it happens, the last film to be released as a silent, for the next film, Clive Brook's *Return of Sherlock Holmes,* was distributed both as a silent and as a sound film, presumably because in many parts of the country, and indeed the world, the theaters had not all completed a changeover to sound-projector systems at the time of its release.

Holmes had at last found his voice, and was to go on to undreamt of success in films. *The Return of Sherlock Holmes,* certainly the first film project designed for synchronous sound, was not the first film to *have* sound—that distinction belongs to a film made as long ago as 1908, in (of all places) Hungary.

14

Clive Brook

THE RETURN OF SHERLOCK HOLMES (United States)

Date of Release: 25 or 26 October 1929 in the United States; 4 August 1930 in Great Britain; United States © 25 October 1929

Running Time: Silent = 6378 ft. (106 min.); Sound = 7102 ft. (79 min.)

Production Company: Paramount/Famous Players/ Lasky Corp.

Executive Producer: David O. Selznick

Director: Basil Dean (and Clive Brook)

Director of Photography: William Steiner, Jr.

Screenplay: Basil Dean and Garrett Fort

Based on: *The Dying Detective* and *His Last Bow* (although one source says $5000 was paid for the rights to the characters alone and not the specific Doyle stories).

Editor: Helene Turner

Filmed in Paramount's Astoria Long Island studios, and on an actual ocean liner; some outdoor filming, surely not common for early-sound 1929.

(This film was simultaneously filmed in at least one foreign-language version, without Reeves-Smith, but perhaps with Brook.)

CAST

Sherlock Holmes	Clive Brook
Col. (or Dr.) Sebastian Moran	Donald Crisp
Dr. Watson	H. Reeves-Smith
Mary Watson	Betty Lawford
?	Charles Hay
?	Phillips Holmes
Professor Moriarty	Harry T. Morey
Roger Longmore	Hubert Druce
?	Arthur Mack

SYNOPSIS: Holmes comes to the wedding of Watson's daughter, Mary, to Roger Longmore. The festivities are somewhat spoiled when the groom's father is poisoned, and Roger himself is kidnapped when he attempts to trace the poisoners. Holmes, Watson, and Mary board an ocean liner at Cherbourg in pursuit, and the bulk of the film takes place on board. Holmes wears several disguises, including those of a violinist in the ship's orchestra, and a cabin steward. The sleuth paints the soles of a suspect's shoes with phosphorescent paint so he can trail the glowing footprints in the darkness. At the climax, Professor Moriarty comes to dine with Holmes and thinks he has poisoned the detective with a thorn concealed in a cigarette case, but his plans have been overheard by Watson through a radio hookup that Holmes has installed in the room. Moriarty then takes poison himself, and vanishes over the side of the ship, and Mary is reunited with Roger.

REVIEWS: In general, the critics liked Brook (although there were dissenters), but found the film itself "diffuse, complicated, unexciting, and lacking in ingenuity."

(From the New York *Times,* 19 October 1929; reviewed by Mordaunt Hall):

Holmes is shorter, healthier-looking, and younger . . . it seems quite absurd for him to refer to

Dr. Watson's daughter Mary (Betty Lawford) seems to think that she is the object of interest for the incognito Moriarty (Harry T. Morey, left), but it is obviously his old nemesis Holmes (Clive Brook, right) who is on the Professor's mind. *Return of Sherlock Holmes*, 1929.

his place in Hampshire and his bees as if he were in the evening of life. [A more precise location of Holmes' bee farm would be the Sussex Downs, of course!] Clive Brook impersonates Holmes with sideburns, a rather old-fashioned lounge suit, and a pipe as formidable in size as his revolver. [It was large-bowled and curved-stemmed.] The familiar double-peaked cap is replaced by a tweed hat; otherwise Sherlock Holmes in this film is much more Brook than Holmes. . . . While the film is far from being a masterpiece, it arouses a certain amount of amusement and interest . . . better entertainment than most murder mystery films. The fun it elicits is not always intended and its thrills fall somewhat flat. . . . Mr. Brook gives a nice easy performance. H. Reeves-Smith flounders about. . . . Betty Lawford is never really natural as the girl in the case. Donald Crisp is excellent. . . . Harry T. Morey is acceptable.

(From *Film Weekly*, 1930, reviewed by Randolph Carroll Burke): "Anyone more alien to the character of Holmes would be difficult to find."

A reader of *Film Weekly* wrote in:

Clive Brook's film was heart-breaking. Sherlock Holmes was left out and Sherlock Brook put in. The story [not by Doyle] was puerile; the setting was modernized [and somewhat Americanized] . . . and worst of all, Watson was given a daughter, so that this film might not lack "love interest."

(From *Picturegoer Weekly,* 21 November 1931):

One of the great mistakes of Clive's career was his appearance on the screen in the part of Sherlock Holmes. Anyone more unlike the great fictional detective would be difficult to find.

It says a lot for Clive's art that while he disappointed Conan Doyle's fans he did at least manage to interest them by his own personality. But he never for one minute convinced us he was Holmes.

(*Masters of Mystery,* 1931, a book by H. Douglas Thompson):

Mr. Clive Brook's performance in the recent talkie was a failure. . . . Even in his make-up he was at no pains to resemble the traditional figure, and there was no need for Mr. Basil Dean to dress this Sherlock Holmes adventure in a contemporary setting. The Sherlock Holmes we know does not grow old, and touring cars are a poor substitute for growlers. Although Sherlock Holmes lived through the war, his period must remain Victorian.

Despite all the obloquies heaped on this unfortunate film, the star (Brook) was to play Holmes twice more on the screen, and the director (Dean) was later to make one of the Arthur Wontner Holmes series, *Sign of Four.* Brook was originally cast in the role because the producer, Selznick, thought he resembled Holmes. Brook, himself, to give this fine actor his due, agreed with the critics in not seeing the resemblance. Brook said that he tried to characterize the detective "larger than life," and thus permit some comedy, stressing the detective's quite Conanical "foibles and eccentricities," which had so often been left out of the earlier versions. He himself completed the direction of the film when Dean left the production.

Clive Brook in a character study from *Return of Sherlock Holmes*, 1929. (Courtesy National Film Archives of the British Film Institute)

Dr. Watson (H. Reeves-Smith) is treated to a Sherlockian serenade by Holmes (Clive Brook). *Return of Sherlock Holmes.*

As we have noted, this was the first Holmes *talkie,* but not the first Holmes *sound* film, for *Sherlock Hochmes,* made in Hungary in 1908 by Projectograph RT with Bauman Karoly as the detective, had been shown with an accompanying synchronized musical score on gramophone records.

Clive Brook was born Clifford Hardman Brook on 1 June in either 1887 or 1891, in London; his mother Charlotte Mary had been in opera.

Brown-haired and blue-eyed, Clive was educated near the birthplace of Boris Karloff, at Dulwich College, but left school at the age of fourteen ("college" not meaning the higher institute it does now). He furthered his education by studying elocution at the Polytechnic in London, also studied the violin, and had a reputation as a "reciter" at the Garrick Amateur Dramatic Club. His profession, however, was that of journalist, until he enlisted in the Artist's Rifles as a private at the outbreak of World War I. When he went to the French Front in 1915, it was as an officer in the machine-gun corps. He eventually rose to the rank of major, but was a victim of shell-shock at the Battle of Messines in June 1918, and was invalided on a pension. Twice after the war he suffered from temporary amnesia, but eventually recovered his health and decided to pursue his acting career as a professional.

As a child he had been very fat, but he was now "matinee-idol" material, and he made his debut in a touring company of *Fair and Warmer* with Fay Compton and Edna Best. Subsequently, he joined the Liverpool Repertory Company of the future director of *The Return of Sherlock Holmes,* Basil Dean, and made his London debut in 1920 with *Just Like Judy.*

Brook made his film debut that same year (although one source places it two years earlier) for Stoll, the company that was just then embarking on its long series of Norwood Holmes films, and the screenwriter of Clive's first film was borrowed from that series—P. L. Mannock. The film was none other than that classic detective story *Trent's Last Case,* an auspicious beginning for the future Sherlock Holmes. Brook, however, played the murder suspect rather than the detective.

Soon after this he moved to Gaumont. Some of his early British films were *Her Penalty* (1921—also known as *The Penalty*), *The Loudwater Mystery, Daniel Deronda, A Sportsman's Wife* (with Brook's future wife Mildred Evelyn), *Christie Johnstone* (with Evelyn again, and filmed in Scotland)—all in 1921.

The following year he appeared (like future Moriarty Lyn Harding) in an episode of the *Tense Moments with Great Authors* series, *Vanity Fair;* also in that segment of the series was a veteran of the 1905 Holmes film, Kyrle Bellew; and in that same year Brook appeared in a film that had previously been made by that same 1905 film's Holmes, Maurice Costello. It was *Tale of Two Cities,* and future versions would feature such fellow Sherlocks as Basil Rathbone, Reginald Owen, and Christopher Lee.

Also in 1922, Brook was in a version of Charlotte Brontë's *Shirley*, in *Married to a Mormon* with Evelyn Brent (who seemed to have specialized in films about Mormons for a time), and in the silent operas *Rigoletto* and *La Traviata*. Before the year was out he was back at Stoll to appear in a film by another of the Holmes series scripters, William J. Elliott, *The Experiment* (again with Brent, his costar for many years) and for Holmesian director Maurice Elvey in *A Debt of Honour;* also in the cast of that one was Lewis Gilbert, a Mycroft Holmes of the Norwood series. That same year Clive acted with that durable screen-Watson Arthur Cullin in the Welsh story *Love and a Whirlwind*.

Brook had an opportunity to show his versatility with a dual role in 1923's *Out to Win,* appeared again for Elvey in *The Royal Oak,* and then was employed by Sir Michael Balcon on a number of pictures scripted by Alfred Hitchcock: 1923's *Woman to Woman* (with A. Harding Steerman from the Norwood series), *The White Shadow,* and *The Passionate Adventure* (both 1924). Balcon's director for all three of these was Graham Cutts, and Brook watched him closely to learn how to direct films—an ambition that Clive was eventually to gratify. Brook was also still a writer, and wrote short stories as well as films. Cutts was to go on to direct one of the Wontner Holmes series, and Balcon to produce the Robert Rendel *Hound of the Baskervilles*.

In 1924, Brook appeared with Fred Paul, a peripheral Holmes figure, in *The Recoil*—a title that had been filmed with Eille Norwood just two years earlier. Before the year was out Brook had settled in Hollywood to work for the pioneer Thomas H. Ince at First National, and most of his subsequent film career was to be in the United States. After years of playing heavies, his career was finally beginning to hit its stride. He appeared with the Nordisk veteran Jean Hersholt in 1925's *If Marriage Fails;* for Holmesian screenwriter Edward T. Lowe, Jr. in *Compromise* that year; for director and former Holmes-imitator King Baggot in *The Home Maker;* director Lewis Milestone in *Seven Sinners;* and had a detective role in *The Pleasure Buyers* (all these in 1925).

In C. B. DeMille's *Three Faces East* the next year, Brook had a spy role, which in future versions was to be played by such dissimilar actors as Erich von Stroheim and Boris Karloff. In 1927 he was working for Holmesian director Rowland V. Lee in *Barbed Wire* with former Moriarty Gustav von Seyffertitz, and had one of the best roles in Josef von Sternberg's *Underworld*. The following year Brook was again appearing with von Seyffertitz in Alexander Korda's *Yellow Lily,* and playing "the world's leading criminologist" (*not* Holmes, however) in *The Perfect Crime,* which for the first time introduced movie audiences to Clive Brook's inimitable vocal style. In 1929 he was in another murder mystery, *Interference,* working for Rowland V. Lee again in *A Dangerous Woman,* and appearing in the second film version of *The Four Feathers*. It was in that year, too, that he made his debut as Holmes, in *Return*.

Brook's Dr. Watson in this film and the next of this series was H. Reeves-Smith, who had been born in 1863, and, thus, continued the Willis-inaugurated image of Watson as rather more elderly than Holmes. Reeves-Smith had been on the stage at least as early as 1892, when he appeared with Mabel Lane in A. C. Fraser-Wood's *In the Eyes of the World*. By 1924, Reeves-Smith was in films, appearing that year in *Three Weeks* and *No More Women*.

He died of heart trouble in Elwell, Surrey, England, on 29 January 1938, but was survived by his daughter Olive Reeves-Smith, who appeared on Broadway years later in *My Fair Lady*. For Brook's third film as Holmes, Reeves-Smith was replaced as Watson by Reginald Owen.

Harry T. Morey, who played Professor Moriarty this time out, had had a very distinguished silent-film career. Born in Michigan, he entered films in 1908 from the legitimate stage, where he had appeared with George M. Cohan and Anna Held. Late the next year Morey joined Vitagraph, where he played both heavies and less-successful leads in such films as *The Deerslayer* (1911), *A Million Bid, The Wreck, Shadows of*

Harry T. Morey in his pre-"Napoleon of Crime" days.

the Past, The Next Generation, 413, Old Lang Syne, The Red Barrier, Fruits of Vengeance, Playing with Fire, The Indian Romeo and Juliet (1912, as Kowa, the Paris of this adaptation), and The Enemies. In The Girl Who Might Have Been, Morey's director was Lionel Belmore, who had acted before the turn of the century with Peter Cushing's grandfather, and was to act in the late 1930s with Basil Rathbone and Clive Brook. In 1912, Vitagraph also cast Morey as Duke Frederick in their As You Like It, with former-Holmes Maurice Costello.

Director Basil Dean (born 1888) was active mainly as a producer for both stage and screen, and, in fact, was the founder of the famous Ealing Studios. His two Sherlockian ventures, despite the presence of Brook and Wontner, were not well liked.

Basil Dean began his theatrical career at Miss Annie Horniman's famous Manchester Repertory—first as an actor; subsequently as a playwright. Like Saintsbury, Harding, and Owen, Dean served a spell as a performer in Sir Herbert Tree's company (Dean in 1912 and 1913). In 1920, Dean produced the play The Blue Lagoon, which twenty-eight years later was to be filmed with future-Watson Donald Houston. The next year Basil offered Just Like Judy, and in the cast was his own future-Holmes Clive Brook, so that the two seem likely to have met for the first time on that occasion.

Dean's partner in production throughout the 1920s in London was Alec L. Rea, and the two billed themselves as the soon-famous joint-pseudonym "Reandean"—Basil Dean, however, was the major creative influence in the partnership.

Theatrical historian W. Macqueen-Pope summed up Dean's indisputedly important stage career by noting that Dean was "not the easiest man in the world to work with," describing him as one who "does not make friends easily" and "cannot brook opposition," but actually a "shy man with a sensitive nature," a "skilled craftsman," and even a "poet."

While unable to deny that a "sense of humor would have saved him so much trouble," Macqueen-Pope continued that "his theatre qualities are beyond reproach . . . worthy of a foremost place in theatre history."

When he entered films, Dean was less critically successful, though his pictures were usually tremendously popular, particularly with the British regional audiences who loved his comedy discoveries, such as Gracie Fields and George Formby. Dean's 1930 film, Escape, featured his future-Watson Ian Hunter, and in 1937 he made 21 Days with former-Watson Fred Lloyd.

Paramount seems to have planned to make a whole series of Holmes films with Brook and Reeves-Smith, for they were featured in the same roles in Paramount on Parade, together with such other Paramount series characters as Philo Vance and Fu Manchu; but as it worked out, Clive Brook played Holmes next not for Paramount, but for William Fox in 1932.

Clive Brook was cast as a Rafflesian gentleman crook in 1930's Slightly Scarlet, and that same year he played a

detective who was also a murderer in Sweethearts and Wives. He appeared with stage-Holmes O. P. Heggie in East Lynne (1931); David Torrence, brother of Brook's future-Moriarty Ernest Torrence, and veteran of the Gillette Holmes film Sherlock Holmes, was also in the cast. Brook had another mystery to unsnarl that year in The Lawyer's Secret, and then displayed his versatility once more by playing a white-haired cockney crook in Silence.

In 1932 he was reunited with von Seyffertitz, "Fu Manchu" Warner Oland, and Josef von Sternberg in Shanghai Express, and of course made his third and last Sherlock Holmes film, with Reginald Owen replacing Reeves-Smith as Watson. In the next Holmes film entry, Owen was to move up to the role of Holmes himself.

Also in 1932 came clear recognition (if any were needed) that Brook had reached the category of "household word" when he played himself in Make Me a Star.

The following year Clive Brook had one of his most memorable screen roles when he played Robert Marryot in Noël Coward's family epic, Cavalcade. Brook was now at the pinnacle of true stardom; according to Picturegoer Weekly he was "England's most

Basil Dean, who followed his direction of Brook's _Return of Sherlock Holmes_ in America in 1929 by producing Arthur Wontner's _Sign of Four_ in Britain three years later.

popular Hollywood star," and he was receiving twelve thousand fan letters a month. He had yet another "crook" role that year in a film with a screenplay by Leslie Charteris (creator of "The Saint")—*Midnight Club,* based on a story by one of the "Rivals of Sherlock Holmes" authors, E. Phillips Oppenheim.

In 1934 he was in *Where Sinners Meet,* adapted from the play, *Dover Road,* by Basil Rathbone's kinsman, A. A. Milne—it was released in Britain under the original play's title, and Reginald Owen was also in the cast.

In 1935, Clive Brook returned to Britain to star in *The Love Affair of the Dictator* for his old studio, Gaumont—perhaps a sign that his Hollywood career was starting downhill. This may seem odd after his recent successes, but an analagous contemporary case would be that of George Arliss. The acting styles of both were felt to be "dated" in the States. After a brief return to Hollywood (or perhaps just the delayed release of an old film), Clive was back in England making *Love in Exile* (1936), which also featured stage-Sherlock Henry Oscar and was directed by future Holmesian director Alfred Werker.

From now on Brook's career was to be confined largely to the British Isles—something for which he was very grateful, for he felt that of all his Hollywood work (and we have enumerated only a small part of it), there was only one project of which he could truly be proud—*Cavalcade.* And yet if his name is remembered today it must be for two other things: his films for von Sternberg and his three portrayals of Sherlock Holmes. Of the Hollywood life style, Brooks' comment was the very Holmesian (and Brooksian): ". . . all the lurid party stuff—I went to one or two—didn't appeal."

Some of Brook's later British films included *The Lonely Road* (1936), with former-Watson Warburton Gamble (released in the United States as *Scotland Yard Commands); Action for Slander* (1937), with another Watson in Athole Stewart, and stage-Holmes Sir Felix Aylmer; *The Ware Case* (1938), which Arthur Wontner did on the stage, as another murderer; *Return to Yesterday* (1940), from the play by future-Mycroft Holmes Robert Morley; and Penrose Tennyson's classic film, *Convoy* (1940), with fellow screen-Holmes Robert Rendel, phonograph-recording-Holmes Sir John Clements, and television-Holmes Stewart Granger—this film was the top British moneymaker of its year.

In 1944, Clive Brook had the opportunity to fulfill an ambition which he had cherished for twenty years: he directed a film from his own screenplay, and coproduced it as well. The picture was *On Approval,* and the star was none other than—Clive Brook!

When the Second World War began, Clive tried unsuccessfully to reenlist in his old regiment. When told by a general whom he had been sent to see, "I understand you are very well known in the theatre but I never read the programmes," Brook characteristically could not resist answering, "I understand you are a very well known general, but I never read a programme."

In 1945, Clive returned to the London stage in *The Years Between,* and in 1946 directed and starred in Molnar's *The Play's the Thing,* which he toured in the provinces for a year until bringing it into London; he was back on the London boards the next year in *The Gioconda Smile,* and in 1951 made his Broadway bow in *Second Threshold,* which he revived later in London. A few other stage appearances followed, and then in 1963 he made his 103rd movie, *The List of Adrian Messenger.* It was, of course, a mystery, and matched him with a fellow Holmes in George C. Scott. It is pleasant to be able to record that Brook was given equal star billing with Scott and Dana Wynter in this film.

Clive Brook died on 17 November 1974. His daughter Faith and his son Clive, Jr. are both in the theater. The London *Times* summed up Brook, Sr.'s, style as an actor very well in their obituary: "He was never a demonstrative or emotional player, but his performance had power, authority, and polish." One may, perhaps, not be able to restrain a laugh the first time one hears him deliver his immortal line in *Shanghai Express,* when he asks Dietrich: "What good is a cigarette lighter without you?"; but if you give the film a well-deserved second viewing you will appreciate the Brook performance, which in itself is not stiff (as many of his performances have been unfairly classified), but is rather a touching interpretation of a rather pathetically stiff human being.

Like most of his screen roles, and despite the critics, there *is,* indeed, some kinship with Holmes—the man of romantic and chivalrous feelings behind the stiff upper lip and eccentric brusqueness.

Brook himself would rather have played intentional comedy, and was grateful for Holmes' eccentricities. Unlike Barrymore he did not try to "normalize" the character, but rather reveled in his rich, unconventional humanity and lovable inhumanity. Clive Brook noted that Holmes was "larger than life," but of course like all such characters—Falstaff, Quixote, Mr. Pickwick—he is rather more durable than most of us who are just "life-size."

PARAMOUNT ON PARADE

Sequence Title: **MURDER WILL OUT (A TRAVESTY OF DETECTIVE MYSTERIES)**

Date of Release: 19 or 26 April 1930 in the United States; 16 March 1931 in Great Britain

Running Time: 9125 feet (101½ min.)

Production Company: Paramount Pictures

Supervising Director: Elsie Janis

Directors (Various Sequences): Dorothy Arzner, Otto Brower, Edmund Goulding, Victor Heerman, Edwin Knopf, Rowland V. Lee, Ernst Lubitsch, Lothar Mendes, Victor Schertzinger, Edward Sutherland, and Frank Tuttle.

Executive Producer: David O. Selznick

Directors of Photography: Harry Fischbeck and Victor Milner

Color: (some sequences): Technicolor

CAST

Sherlock Holmes	Clive Brook
Philo Vance	William Powell
Dr. Fu Manchu	Warner Oland
Dr. Watson	H. Reeves-Smith
Sgt. Heath	Eugene Pallette
The Victim	Jack Oakie

Also in the cast were: Phillips Holmes (from the cast of *The Return*), Richard Arlen, Jean Arthur, William Austin, George Bancroft, Clara Bow, Evelyn Brent, Mary Brian, Virginia Bruce, Nancy Caroll, Ruth Chatterton, Maurice Chevalier, Gary Cooper, Leon Errol, Stuart Erwin, Kay Francis, Skeets Gallagher, Harry Green, James Hall, Helen Kane, Dennis King, Abe Lyman, Frederic March, Nino Martini, Mitzi Mayfair, David Newell, Zelma O'Neill, Joan Peers, Charles Rogers, Lillian Roth, Stanley Smith, and Fay Wray.

SYNOPSIS: Holmes, Watson, and Vance are in pursuit of the archvillain Fu Manchu. This film marks the only occasion when Holmes dies on screen!

This was just a short burlesque sequence in a long revue film. The Holmes segment was originally planned by Selznick in August 1929. William Powell had made his screen debut in Barrymore's *Sherlock Holmes* and was, oddly enough, to be replaced in the Philo Vance series by Basil Rathbone. Warner Oland is, of course, better remembered today as yet another detective, Charlie Chan, but he played Fu Manchu four times on the screen; the Fu Manchu series touches the Holmes series at many points due to the participation of such Holmesian personalities as Fred Paul, Douglas Wilmer, Christopher Lee, H. Marion Crawford, and Thorley Walters, and also due to the fact that author Sax Rohmer's heroes, Nayland Smith and Dr. Petrie, are very thinly disguised editions of Holmes and Watson, and Fu Manchu's evil machinations are topped only by those of the archfiend Moriarty.

We could not determine exactly which of the many directors listed for the various sequences in this film actually directed the Holmes segment, but we cast our vote for Rowland V. Lee, who had directed Oland in a Fu Manchu picture that same year, and who went on to collaborate with Basil Dean in 1932's *Sign of Four,* with Arthur Wontner as Holmes.

Clive Brook played a cameo role as Holmes for *Paramount on Parade.*

Costumes: Rita Kaufman
Editor: Margaret Clancy
Sound: Albert Protzman
Art Director: John Hughes
Screenplay: Bertram Milhauser and Bayard Veiller (some sequences were improvised on the set by Director William K. Howard)
Based on: Gillette's play; *The Red-Headed League;* Doyle's play, *The Speckled Band*
Passed by the National Board of Review (British "A" Certificate)

CAST

Sherlock Holmes	Clive Brook
Alice Faulkner	Miriam Jordan
Professor James Moriarty	Ernest Torrence
George, the Publican	Herbert Mundin
Dr. Watson	Reginald Owen
Little Billy	Howard Leeds
Col. Gore-King	Alan Mowbray
Judge	Montague Shaw
?	Frank Atkinson
Mr. Faulkner	Ivan Simpson
Homer Jones (Tony Ardetti)	Stanley Fields
Chaplain	Arnold Lucy
Hans Dreiaugen (Hans the Hun)	Lucien Prival

SHERLOCK HOLMES; CONAN DOYLE'S MASTER DETECTIVE SHERLOCK HOLMES

Date of Release: 6 or 11 November 1932 in the United States; January 1933 in Great Britain; United States © 18 October 1932
Running Time: variously reported at 6400 ft. (71 min.), 67 min., 65 min., 61 min.
Production Company: Fox Film Corp.
Producer and Director: William K. Howard
Director of Photography: George Barnes
Musical Director: George Lipschultz

Manuel Lopez	Roy D'Arcy
Al, Jones' Henchman	Eddie Dillon
Gaston Roux	Robert Graves
Secretary to Erskine	Brandon Hurst
Sir Albert Hastings	Claude King

SYNOPSIS: The film takes place in London in the 1930s, though on one occasion a horse and carriage is seen to pass by on the street. This is another of the films that we were fortunate enough to screen, so we intend to treat it in some depth, as representative of the Brook Holmes films. The print we saw did lack some scenes that were represented in production still photographs we know of, and was several minutes shorter than the longest recorded running time for this film.

The film opens with a striking silhouette sequence of the captured Professor Moriarty being led into the courtroom for sentencing. As the sentencing begins, veils are lifted away from the faces of each of the principals in turn as they are introduced to the audience. Holmes is not present. Before hearing the sentence, Moriarty sarcastically thanks all those who have brought him to this pass—Prosecutor Erskine, Col. Gore-King of Scotland Yard . . . and Sherlock Holmes.

Moriarty then proceeds to promise that each of them shall die in turn before he himself does (a notable plot point to bear in mind is that only Erskine is actually threatened with hanging, the other two only with death). To Sherlock Holmes, the professor also promises disgrace before death. Having been allowed to speak his piece by the rather tolerant court, Moriarty is then sentenced to hang (the death penalty still existing in England at the time). In another brooding silhouette sequence he is led away.

Ernest Torrence plays the role of Moriarty in a very large fashion, but does not *over*play it. He is like the volcano which merely seethes and bubbles rather than actually erupting, and plays the part with a curious sort of elaborate politeness and understatement that are obviously meant by the Professor to mask his truly ferocious nature only by the thinnest and most transparent veneer. It is one of the classic screen Moriartys, and like the performance of Norman McKinnel the previous year (covered in detail in the Arthur Wontner chapter), it portrays the Professor as a Scotsman; presumably, like Conan Doyle himself, an Irishman born and raised in Scotland!

Holmes is now introduced, seen in what looks like a lab worthy of Dr. Frankenstein—a large room filled with sparking and arcing electrical devices. There is no evidence of stock footage from horror films, as had been stated in one source. Also, the famous scrapbooks

Moriarty (Ernest Torrence) is led to the dock for sentencing in *Sherlock Holmes*.

Holmes (Clive Brook) is interrupted at his electrical experiments by his fiancee Alice Faulkner. The Great Detective seems to have changed a good deal to let the "softer emotions" come before his work!

have been modernized into filing cabinets, an innovation echoing the Raymond Massey Holmes film of the previous year. As we are to see, this film's far-too-neat version of 221B Baker Street is of a veritable mansion, rather than a distinctly untidy walk-up bachelor flat in the house of Mrs. Hudson (completely missing in this film). The wealth of this Holmes is underlined by his sumptuous dressing gown and smoking jacket, far cries from the traditional old "mouse-colored" item the Great Detective has always worn. The pipe, though, is properly curved.

Holmes is so intent over his experiment that he is oblivious to the entrance of Alice Faulkner, his fiancee; but when she presents herself, Holmes claims to have known she was present all along. Alice consequently calls him a "humbug," but this is in fact the only place in the film where Holmes is "shown up," despite reports to the contrary in other sources. Holmes' engagement to Miss Faulkner, and the title, are actually the sole links between this film and the Gillette play. Moriarty is even returned to his original Doyle first name, "James," from Gillette's "Robert." The only reference to the *Red-Headed League* comes later in the film when a bank is tunnelled into from the basement of a nearby shop. There is also an uncredited borrowing from the play of *The Speckled Band*, in which Holmes remarks in an obviously tongue-in-cheek fashion that he may retire to a chicken farm if Watson ever recognizes him in one of his disguises—a notion that this film has regrettably taken seriously, so that we must hear constant references to "Sherlock Holmes—New-Laid Eggs." Actually, as every Holmesophile knows, Holmes retired to a bee farm.

Clive Brook's performance as Holmes is both too effusively romantic (something one would never expect from this usually proper actor, or from this intellectually self-sufficient character) and too foul-tempered. The coolly introspective Holmes did not

tend to either of these extremes with the frequency that Brook does. Brook's handling of Holmes' subtly sarcastic wit, however, is quite good; in this film, that quality is yet another of the Holmes-Moriarty parallels.

The pageboy Billy now enters, and explains to Miss Faulkner and the movie audience Holmes' absurd magnetic automobile-wrecking ray machine, which is to be the farewell gift to Scotland Yard. Billy, who apparently lives elsewhere than at 221B, is said to be Canadian as a means of explaining his painfully American accent, but for some reason the child still attempts a Cockney accent. He is not very successful with it, saying " 'eavy" and "heavy" in the same sentence, so it is probable that the "Canadian" label was attached during shooting to mask this inadequacy.

Dr. Watson now arrives for one of his two brief appearances. As played by Reginald Owen he is such a bumptiously enthusiastic dolt that it is easy to see why he is no longer living with Holmes: the latter must have become weary of his pompous shouting and thrown him out. This Watson would have been far too nerve-wracking for Holmes to have ever contemplated asking him to share his "digs" in the first place.

Herbert Mundin, Brook's costar in *Cavalcade*, was originally slated to play Watson. However, for some reason, he was removed from the part and given another role, and Ivan Simpson was brought in to replace him as the good Doctor. Simpson later appeared with Basil Rathbone in his *Hound of the Baskervilles*, but he was fated never to play Watson either, and he, too, was given something else to do in *Sherlock Holmes*.

The role, of course, finally went to Owen, but all of this confusion about the casting of Watson seems to have resulted in much make-shift improvisation by the director, and the virtual elimination of the Doctor's

Reginald Owen made a boisterous and tiresome Watson in *Sherlock Holmes*, but was subsequently promoted to the deerstalker himself in *Study in Scarlet*. Here Owen as the good doctor is flanked by Holmes (Clive Brook) and Alice (Miriam Jordan).

The jail-breaking Moriarty (Ernest Torrence) crawls up the bank from the water, looking like a beast of prey.

character from the picture, with his normal function of "feed" for Holmes being almost entirely taken over by Billy.

Mundin was apparently compensated for his loss by being billed above Owen, though his sequences are quite extraneous to the main plot and seem obviously added as an afterthought.

When told by Watson of Moriarty's courtroom threat, Holmes remarks that the gesture is "very thoughtful" of the Professor, and underlines the parallel by saying that Moriarty is "the only man to use scientific methods" as Holmes himself does. Before Watson departs, there is the awaited exchange of "Incredible, my dear Holmes; amazing!!" and "Elementary." The reader should not need to be told who speaks which line.

We now see Moriarty's spectacular jailbreak, which is as well executed cinematically as it is by the Professor himself. The nervously roving camera fastens on such details as the naked back of a prisoner, extreme closeups of feet, keys in the hand of a murdered guard, and, finally, the scrawled message on the wall of Moriarty's now-empty cell: "Tell Sherlock Holmes I'm Out—Moriarty." Just *how* the Professor effected his escape is not explained, but this mystery is quite in keeping with the inscrutable character of all his exploits.

There follows a clever sequence done in a single shot. We first see a figure swimming frantically to shore; then the camera swings around to see the police cars whizzing past; and, finally, swings back to the water where Moriarty is pulling himself onto the shore among the bushes, looking rather more like Frankenstein's Monster than the soft-spoken Professor we have just seen.

Another action sequence follows—that of a fox-hunt—for this film is more of a straightforward adventure picture than a faithful rendering of pure Holmesian deduction. The hunt is held on the estate of Alice Faulkner's aristocratic father, who is highly upset that his daughter is marrying such a lowly creature as a detective. Faulkner is an epicure who "hates" milk; when his daughter is unhappy later in

the film he can think of nothing better to cheer her up than to send her a bottle of some of his rarest vintage.

Holmes now has one of his (for this film) rare scenes of deductive reasoning, when he infers that Faulkner has overslept—by his careless shaving, large appetite, etc. In this sequence, Holmes for once has an excuse for his wearing his Gillette-and-Barrymore riding togs around the house! Brook's Holmes is fetishistically attached to his pipe, and is never without it even when later in the film he is impersonating an old woman!

Holmes is called away to investigate the disappearance of Erskine (the prosecutor), as Moriarty's threats seem to be coming true. Holmes silently prowls about Erskine's office, casing it thoroughly, and then tells Billy (who seems to be functioning as his assistant or apprentice) to apply the white powder to the floor to pick up footprints. Holmes, in the meantime, examines Erskine's supposed suicide note, and finds that the Professor has contrived to leave Holmes a clue by adding (after the line when he says he is taking a "dose of his own medicine") the name "Moriarty" in invisible ink.

Holmes enjoys some friendly banter with his Scotland Yard rival, Gore-King ("a delightful day," Holmes says sarcastically), noting that just because Erskine came into the room and is not there now, the inference is not necessarily that he must have gone out; rather, Holmes suggests, if Erskine were not seen to go out, he must still be in the room. He further mentions that it would be rather difficult for a man to commit suicide and then spirit away his own body. Holmes is proved correct when it develops that the footprints suggest that someone carried a heavy burden to an apparently blank wall and then walked away having relinquished the weight. There is a chilling moment when it dawns on Billy what the burden must have been, and as Holmes finds the secret mechanism the wall rolls away to reveal the shadow of Erskine, who has (as Moriarty "promised") been hanged.

Perhaps the most characteristically Holmesian moment in *any* film now ensues, for it is plain from his face that, far from being upset that his friend has been murdered, Holmes is delighted at having been proved right about the disappearance! In this sequence also, however, Holmes curiously identifies his scientific methods of crime detection as the "German School," to which Gore-King quite properly remarks, "Rubbish!" Holmes does redeem himself with a more characteristically Holmesian line: "It is always the obvious which escapes attention."

A fine fairground montage follows, complete with flashing lights, fire-eaters, shimmy dancers, fish-and-chips shops, wild men, and all the usual accoutrements (including the inexplicable glimpse of a supposed ventriloquist who has seated on his lap not a dummy but a live dwarf!). Up to the shooting gallery comes a motley assortment of foreign gangsters, called to a summit meeting by Moriarty. Each hoodlum in turn fires at a target as his ticket of admission to the gathering. The Chicago gangster, Homer Jones, also known as Tony Ardetti, of course, liberally sprays the place with bullets in contrast to the German, Spanish, and French delegates who have fired one, two, and three shots respectively.

The meeting, in a lovely touch, takes place in a wax museum, where Moriarty, disguised as a wax figure, "comes to life" after the four assassins have entered.

Before we learn just what exactly the Professor is up to, our attention is diverted to Scotland Yard, where Holmes and Gore-King are meeting with Sir Albert Hastings. Holmes is very stylish for a visit to the Yard, wearing an old-fashioned tie and gloves, and the same sort of modern, nondeerstalker hat associated with Norwood, Wontner, and the later Rathbone films. He is in good form and deduces the contents of Gore-King's inside pocket, but the Colonel is graceless enough to suggest that "like so many of your *brilliant* deductions, it was merely a lucky guess."

A red herring is introduced in this scene, as a Scotland Yard man is seen eavesdropping at the door, but is never seen again in the picture—unless he was cut out of this shortened print. It seems more likely that he was lost in the shuffle during all the non-Watson improvising that went on during the picture's shooting.

With both of their deaths pending on Moriarty's schedule, Holmes and Gore-King peevishly accuse each other of being nervous, though Holmes is incorrect when he says that the two of them are to *hang*, because Moriarty did not specify method of death in his opening scene, nor is this his plan, as we shall see. Holmes, with sardonic glee, explains that he believes Moriarty to be planning to introduce American gangster methods into London, and we immediately cut back to the Professor, who is holding a meeting with his new allies in a moving truck, in front of a poorly done process-screen of London streets. The plan, it develops, is exactly as Holmes has theorized: to force the city's pubkeepers to pay "protection" (Chicago-style) for the privilege of not having their shops blown up with "pineapples."

"A fruit can do that?!?" asks Gaston the Frenchman, and it is explained to him that "pineapple" is slang for a handgrenade. Homer is anxious to help the Professor dispose of Holmes, who is somehow responsible for sending the former to Sing Sing; but Moriarty tells him, "you're like a child" (compared to Holmes). Jones insists that Holmes is only "flesh and blood," but Moriarty qualified his agreement by adding, ". . . and brains." Moriarty's own plan is to make use of the quarrel between Holmes and Gore-King in order to frame the Baker Street sleuth for the murder of the Colonel. Jones still insists that his revolver, "Li'l Sophie," would do just as well.

In this sequence we gain another insight into the personality of Torrence's Moriarty, who, despite all his theatrics, is a private, melancholy, and unfathomable personality with as much secret admiration for his nemesis Holmes, as Holmes has for him.

Col. Gore-King receives a message, supposedly from Holmes, asking him to call at 221B by the back door that night, and the stage is set.

While Holmes sits absorbed in his violin playing, Dr. Watson is talking to him; one does not know if Holmes is being rude for playing while Watson speaks, or vice-versa. Watson believes that the floral wreath Holmes has received must be from his bachelor friends on the eve of his impending marriage, but Holmes explains that among American gangsters the wreath is meant to be the harbinger of another kind of impending fate, and attributes it to that "interesting but rather dull character Homer Jones."

Holmes sends Billy home and delegates Watson to phone Alice to warn her away from the house, while he himself draws the shades. Miss Faulkner having already left, Watson asks Holmes for the loan of a gun, intending to stay and defend his friend, but, "My dear Watson, your life is of value to me if not for yourself," says the detective, sending Watson out to try and stop Alice on her way. He tells the Doctor that he intends to "shoot first," as is the American custom.

"But is it sporting, old chap?" asks Watson, as he dons his topper and departs. Of course, his attempts at disuading the lady only make her more curious and more determined, and she soon arrives; an explosion overheard in the lab leads Holmes to discover that Billy has not gone home as told, but stayed to perform a little experiment. "Why all the mystery?" asks Alice, but the fact of the matter is that there is no particular mystery in the film (at least from the audience's point of view). Her pleading with him does not persuade him to leave with her, and he gives her a very abrupt kiss in true Clive Brook tradition, sending her away.

There is a splendid fog effect as Gore-King arrives at the back door. He is apparently shot by Holmes, who has been led to expect a visit from Homer Jones, but after Holmes is taken away handcuffed by the men from the Yard, the "dead" Gore-King turns out to be unharmed and in on the plot with Holmes, to make Moriarty think they are both out of the way.

The question raised here is how on earth Holmes found out about the plan to frame him. Hopefully the

Herbert Mundin, left, was cast as Watson before either Simpson *or* Owen, and apparently given this wholly superfluous cockney role as a consolation prize.

Faulkner (Ivan Simpson) discusses the kidnapping of his daughter with his "aunt" (Clive Brook in disguise).

explanation was included in one of the cut sequences, but if so, it seems an odd thing to have cut out.

We now have a prolonged sequence with Herbert Mundin being offered "protection" by Homer Jones. The sequence is treated at considerably more length than is warranted by its importance to the central plot, however funny Mundin happens to be. The publican's insistence to Jones that his premises could never be blown up since they are in the middle of London does not seem so funny today, after the Blitz and the IRA have passed this 1932 film by.

Meanwhile Faulkner is attempting to console his daughter, who is trying hard not to believe her fiancee is a murderer. He supposes that she would love Holmes even if he were "ten times a detective, a hundred times a murderer"—thus seeming to rank detectives as ten times worse than murderers. Alice herself tries to console Billy, and they wind up crying on each other's shoulders.

Another and even more extraneous sequence with Mundin follows, wherein he and a friend engage in some cockney crosstalk, while in intercut scenes pubs all over London are being shot up and blown up by Jones and his men. When Mundin's place has also been hit, with them inside, a truly funny scene of black comedy takes place in the hospital. His friend suggests that perhaps Jones should have been paid off after all, and regrets that he was unable to finish his beer. Mundin reminds him that the beer in question was not yet paid for, and regrets that his wife has seen fit to bring him a pineapple as a gift.

Holmes now pays a call on his prospective father-in-law. Brook's disguise as an old woman in this scene is really splendid, although another voice is unfortunately dubbed in for his own. He is totally unrecognizable until he pulls out his pipe, and, more importantly, he looks like an old lady and not like an actor in a disguise. Holmes explains that Faulkner's bank is due to be robbed by Moriarty; that all the American gangster tactics were just meant to serve as diversions. It is

The Professor (Ernest Torrence) makes a helpful suggestion to Alice Faulkner's father. In the latter role is Ivan Simpson (right), originally cast as Watson in this film before being shifted to the character of the aristocratic banker in order to make way for Owen, who seems to have been rather a last-minute choice.

not satisfactorily explained how Holmes arrived at this conclusion, despite his talk of "threads leading vaguely" in that direction.

At this juncture, Moriarty himself pays a rather coincidental call, unctuously genial and obsequious as ever; and Holmes listens to Moriarty's whole conversation with Faulkner, who describes the detective to his visitor as his deaf and senile aunt: "She's deaf as a post," he tells Moriarty. "Time for toast?" asks Holmes.

The Professor has kidnapped both Alice and Billy, and holds them prisoner in order to secure the cooperation of Faulkner. When the "aunt" hears this she makes a hasty exit, the courteous Moriarty holding the door open for her.

It develops that Holmes has earlier paid a visit to the bird shop that stands next to Faulkner's bank, a sequence cut from the print we saw, though there are still photographs of this scene. The professor and his gang are tunnelling through the cellar into the bank next door. Holmes is convinced that Moriarty would want to keep his eye on both the gold and his hostages, so he proceeds at once to the shop.

"Sorry to inconvenience you," says Moriarty to Alice, when he has returned to the shop where she is bound and gagged. Billy is in a similar condition— "Holmes' favorite pupil" the Professor calls him. Holmes in the meantime has just had a knockdown dragout fight with the Professor's henchman, Hans—a great pity that fisticuffs were substituted for deductive reasoning. Disguised in the German's welding mask, Holmes enters the tunnel to help open the vault with acetelene torches. The lighting of these tunnel scenes is pleasantly gloomy and evocative, as well as the dimly lit bank and the pet shop where the goldfish tank is filled with an eerie light.

When the police arrive, summoned of course by Holmes, Moriarty sends his men up to meet them and prudently waits down in the cellar himself. A very American and un-Holmesian shootout occurs in the bank, while, below, Sherlock foolishly gets his back against the open stairway just as he is confronting Moriarty. One of the gang comes down the stairs and tackles Holmes, giving Moriarty the opportunity to escape temporarily to the room where he holds his two captives; and he gives Billy a well-deserved slap, which

This elderly lady being so gallantly shown the door by Moriarty (Ernest Torrence) is actually Sherlock Holmes (Clive Brook).

all Conanical purists must applaud. In the desperate frustration of his situation, the towering intellect of the Professor falls away and he is reduced to a growling beast (one wonders, though, if the presence of Billy is not at least partly to blame, for Holmes himself has earlier growled at the wretched child).

Moriarty is, of course, outgunned by Holmes, and one is truly sorry to see the end of him, since he has been by far the most fascinating character in the film. Holmes, too, has ambiguous feelings about the Professor, for he turns back to take one last look at his old enemy, and there are in his glance traces of regret for the loss of so fine an adversary—the world must surely be a little dull without Moriarty to match wits with, he seems to be thinking. Holmes delivers a very respectable eulogy for the Napoleon of Crime when he says that Moriarty possessed "the ability to stimulate genius in others."

More than one reader of the original Doyle stories, in fact, has suggested that after the death of Moriarty in Reichenbach the genius seemed to have gone out of Holmes.

Sherlock Holmes ends with an off-screen Dr. Watson sending word that he cannot attend Holmes' wedding, so the latter asks Col. Gore-King to be his Best Man (one is glad that Lestrade was spared such an ordeal!). The last scene must be very trying to the purist who likes his Holmes straight, for it closes with the line,

"Elementary, my dear Billy, elementary," topped off with a big kiss for Alice.

Clive Brook was loaned to Fox by Paramount for this film, the latter studio having of course made the first two in the Clive Brook Sherlock Holmes series. Reginald Owen, the third choice for Watson in the film, as it happened, was to take over the role of Holmes himself in the next film in the series, which made a final studio change to World-Wide for *A Study in Scarlet.*

REVIEW (From *Picturegoer Weekly,* 25 March 1933):

Everyone has different ideas of the personality of Conan Doyle's famous detective. This is Hollywood's; go and see what you think of it.

Clive Brook is cast as the famous detective, and the story has been brought up to date, both of which facts, to my mind, militate against a convincing rendering of the atmosphere and the character of the book.

Instead of incisive deduction and clever detail, there is all the paraphernalia of melodrama, with thrills of a popular order.

Clive Brook presents a bumptious, obstinate character rather than a brilliant one.

Ernest Torrence, on the other hand, is well cast as

Two studies of Ernest Torrence as one of the finest Moriartys on the screen—a restrained volcano of hatred and violence behind a mask of obsequious innocence.

the detective's arch enemy, Moriarty, and gives the best performance. The rest of the cast is adequate.

The screenwriter, Milhauser, was later to be notably associated with the Rathbone series. Some of Milhauser's other screenplays, in the meantime, included those for *An Angel From Texas* and *River's End* of 1940, and *Pierre of the Plains* and Bogart's *Big Shot* in 1942.

Director William K. Howard (1899–1954) was an American, but in England in 1936 he directed former-Holmes Raymond Massey and Moriarty Lyn Harding in the Elizabethan story *Fire Over England*. Some of Howard's other films include the classic *White Gold* (1927), with Jetta Goudal, *The Power and the Glory* (1933, an undoubted influence on Orson Welles' *Citizen Kane*), *Transatlantic* (1931), and *When the Lights*

Go on Again (1944). Brook was not happy with Howard's interpretation of Holmes, but most critics found the film well paced, at least.

Ernest Torrence was born in Edinburgh in 1876 or 1878, and educated at the Edinburgh Academy and in Stuttgart, Germany, where he trained for a musical career. As a pianist he won a Westminster Scholarship in London, but edged into the acting profession by going into comic opera (he was a baritone in *Emerald Isle*), and, from there, on to the musical-comedy stage.

Torrence came to New York to play a Scottish comedian in "The Only Girl," and acted in that city for the next nine years before making his film debut in 1921 in that classic, *Tol'able David*. This film gave him a very American role, and then he was to be associated mainly with such parts until sound came and revealed him as a Scot. In 1923 came his famous Western scout (paired with Tully Marshall as another grizzled cowboy) in *The Covered Wagon*, but that same year he had a change of pace when he appeared as a medieval Frenchman in Lon Chaney, Sr.'s *Hunchback of Notre Dame*, playing the Beggar King of Paris.

The next year Torrence was cast in a role that had been played by fellow-Moriarty Lyn Harding on the stage, as well as by screen-Holmes Arthur Wontner, namely, Captain Hook in *Peter Pan*, stunningly photographed by a young James Howe before he restored the "Wong" to his name.

In 1925, Torrence was cast in the original *Captain Blood*; Basil Rathbone had one of the greatest successes in his career in the remake ten years later. In 1927, Ernest was playing St. Peter in C. B. DeMille's *King of Kings*, and like radio-Watson and fellow-Scotsman Finlay Currie he made a notably rustic and human Big Fisherman.

Some of Torrence's other films were *The Cossacks* (1928); *The Bridge of San Luis Rey* (1929); *The New Adventures of Get-Rich-Quick Wallingford* (1931); *Cuban Love Song* (1932); *The Blind Goddess, Pony Express, American Venus*, and *Lady of the Harem*. As late as 1959, Torrence was visible in the film *The Tingler*, if only via a clip from his 1921 *Tol'able David*.

Ernest Torrence was an inch over six feet tall, with black hair and hazel eyes; he was married and had a son, born about 1909.

"Moriarty" was the brother of "Count von Stalberg," it seems, as Ernest's brother David had played the latter role in the Barrymore version of *Sherlock Holmes* just ten years before this film.

Alan Mowbray, who played an un-Conanical Scotland Yard Colonel in this last film of Brook's Holmes, was to return in the next (Owen) film as a more legitimate Inspector Lestrade; some years later, he was to join his good friend Basil Rathbone as that highly Conanical (if not exactly *legitimate*) Colonel, Sebastian Moran.

15
Reginald Owen

A STUDY IN SCARLET

Date of Release: April 1933 in the United States (copyright 2 April 1933) 29 January 1934 in Great Britain.

Running Time: (various times reported) 6972 feet (77½ min.); 75 min.; 70 min.; 62 min.

Production Company: distributed by World Wide, and copyrighted in the United States by K.B.S. Productions, Inc.; Great Britain distributor Gaumont Ideal.

Producer: E. W. Hammons

Director: Edwin L. Marin

Photography: Arthur Edelson

Screenplay: adaptation by Robert Florey; continuity and dialogue by Reginald Owen.

Based on: The novel by Arthur Conan Doyle (at least according to the credits) and "The Red-Headed League"

Editor: Rose Loewinger

Sound: Hans Weeren

CAST

Sherlock Holmes	Reginald Owen
Eileen Forrester	June Clyde
Mrs. Pike (or Pyke)	Anna May Wong
Merrydew	Alan Dinehart
John Stanford	John Warburton
Dr. Watson	Warburton Gamble
Jabez Wilson	J. M. Kerrigan
Insp. Lestrade (or Lastrade)	
Mrs. Murphy	Alan Mowbray
?	Doris Lloyd
	Billy Bevan
Baker	Cecil Reynolds
Mrs. Hudson	Tempe Pigott
Dearing	Halliwell Hobbes
Ah Yet (or Ay Yet)	Tetsu Komai
?	Leila Bennett
Captain Pike (or Pyke)	Wyndham Standing

SYNOPSIS: A suave but crooked solicitor named Merrydew is the brains of a gang of jewel thieves known as the "Scarlet Ring." The members of the gang are all sworn to leave their estates (in the event of their own deaths) to the surviving members, and Merrydew (with the assistance of Captain and Mrs. Pike and Ah Yet) plans to kill the other members to inherit everything himself. Eileen Forrester is the daughter of a recently deceased gang member, and Merrydew involves her in his shady activities. Her fiancee John Stanford becomes suspicious and calls in the aid of Holmes and Watson. Holmes manages to save Eileen from harm by unmasking the remaining members of the gang, although Merrydew proves a worthy foil to the Great Detective.

Although this film bore precious little resemblance to the Doyle novel from which it took its title, it did borrow Jabez Wilson as a character from another Holmes tale—"The Red-Headed League"—and bits and pieces from other Doyle stories.

REVIEW: *The Kinematograph Weekly* of 10 August 1933 called the adaptation "artless" and "free yet entertaining," noting that the characterizations were "artificial," but the "situations devised on safe lines." It went on:

Reginald Owen, kicked upstairs as Sherlock Holmes in *A Study in Scarlet*.

. . . only the barest skeleton of the original story is recognizable, and although the situations which evolve from the developments are obvious, there are thrills galore and a great deal of high-speed action. It cannot be said that Reginald Owen conforms ideally to the popular conception of Sherlock Holmes, but his performance is not unsatisfactory. . . . (He) will probably not appeal to Holmes' fans, for he fails to suggest the physical and facial conceptions. . . . Warburton Gamble, a feeble Watson. . . . The neatness and originality in construction displayed in the author's story has been almost completely lost . . . what remains is just commonplace mystery melodrama. The producer has failed to avoid the obvious, and . . . slow development tends to prevent the situations from building up good suspense and rather takes the edge off the thrills. . . . London and country interiors and exteriors are fairly good . . . obvious humor.

The trade publication went on, however, to say that there was potentially strong audience appeal in the title and author, especially for the youth market, and there was even a small dash of romantic interest supplied by Miss Clyde. As for the other players, they found nothing to quarrel with in the smiling menace of Dinehart, and liked Anna May Wong too, but chided Gamble, Kerrigan, Lloyd, Mowbray, and Bevan alike with overacting.

Warburton Gamble has proved an elusive quarry for our research, and we have been able to unearth only two other film credits for him. Later the same year he was playing Owen's Watson, or early the next, he was featured in James Whale's *By Candlelight*. Then in 1936, Gamble had left Hollywood for England, where he appeared with Clive Brook as "Fedden" in *The Lonely Road* (known in the United States as *Scotland Yard Commands*), based on a Nevil Shute novel. By 1938 the elusive Gamble seems to have vanished from the reference books, and so there we must leave him.

Director Edwin L. Marin (1901–1951) was to work with Owen again on 1940's *Florian*, and also worked on such films as *The Casino Murder Case*, a Philo Vance mystery of 1935; *Maisie Was A Lady*, 1941; *Nocturne*, 1946; and *Sugarfoot*, 1951, with former screen-Holmes Raymond Massey.

Halliwell Hobbes, who appeared in this film as Dearing, was later to appear in the Rathbone series; like Rathbone and Norwood, Hobbes had been a member of the acting troupe of Sir Frank Benson.

It is possible that this film's Wyndham Standing and the Percy Standing who appeared as Moriarty for Norwood may have been related, since the Standing theatrical family certainly seems to be a large one.

Reginald Owen had been hopeful of inaugurating a new series of low-budget Holmes films, starring and written by himself, but it was not to be. The career of Owen himself went on to new strengths anyway, but there was not to be another American attempt at a Holmes film until the advent of Rathbone and Bruce at the end of the decade.

Meanwhile, the Sherlockian torch had already returned to England, where Arthur Wontner's highly cinematic impersonations of Holmes had begun (two years after the commencement of the Brook-Owen series) in 1931 and were to continue until 1937 (and indeed on radio and television for an additional twenty years).

Reginald Owen (he dropped his first name John) was born 5 August 1887 in Wheathampstead, England. He was on the stage by 1905, and ten years later rated a caricature by Haselden in *Punch* for his performance at the Savoy with H. B. Irving, in *Searchlights*. Owen played "Harry Blaine," the typical young wastrel complete with slicked black hair, cigarette drooping from a weak mouth, and hands crammed petulantly in the pockets of his evening-dress suit. A photo in the British film magazine *Pictures and the Picturegoer's* 8 July 1916 edition clearly proves that Owen was in films no later than that date, despite those sources that have claimed that he did not make his movie debut before 1929. Owen in fact played Cromwell in Will Barker's 1911 *Henry VIII*, with Arthur Bourchier repeating his stage success in the title role, and also featuring Sir Herbert Tree.

Certainly the major phase of Owen's career began in 1929, however, with his arrival in Hollywood. This ubiquitous character seems to be in almost every second film made in Hollywood over the following twenty years. He made literally hundreds of films in his entire career. A very few of the more notable ones include *The Letter*—1929; *Platinum Blonde*—1931–32; *Lovers Courageous, A Woman Commands* (with Roland Young), *Downstairs,* and *Man Called Back*—1932; *Robbers' Roost, Voltaire,* and *Queen Christina*—1933; *Nana, The House of Rothschild, Of Human Bondage,* and *Where Sinners Meet* (with Clive Brook)—1934; *Anna Karenina, A Tale of Two Cities* (both with Basil Rathbone), and *Call of the Wild*—1935; *Suicide Club, Rose Marie,* and *The Great Ziegfeld*—1936; *Conquest, Rosalie,* and *Dangerous*—1937; *A Christmas Carol* (replacing an ailing Lionel Barrymore as Scrooge at the last minute) and *Everybody Sing*—1938; *The Earl of Chicago*—1939 or 1940; *Pride and Prejudice* and *Florian*—1940 (for his *Study in Scarlet* director, Malin); *Free and Easy, Tarzan's Secret Treasure,* and *Charlie's Aunt*—1941; *White Cargo, Random Harvest, Woman of the Year,* and *Mrs. Miniver*—1942; *Madame Curie* and *Lassie Come Home* (with Nigel Bruce)—1943; *Frenchman's Creek* (with Rathbone and Bruce) and *Canterville Ghost*—1944; *Diary of a Chambermaid, The Valley of Decision* (with radio-Holmes Sir Cedric Hardwicke), and *Kitty*—1945; *Monsieur Beaucaire* and *Cluny Brown*—1946; *The Pirate* and *Green Dolphin Street*—

1947; *Piccadilly Incident* and *The Three Musketeers*—1948; *The Secret Garden*—1949; *Kim* and *The Miniver Story*—1950; *The Great Diamond Robbery*—1953; *Red Garters*—1954; *The Young Invaders*—1958; *Five Weeks in a Balloon* (with Hardwicke again and that perfect Moriarty Henry Daniell)—1962; *The Thrill of It All*—1963; *The Voice of the Hurricane* and *Mary Poppins*—1964.

Married three times, for the first time in 1908 and the last in 1956 (to Lydia Bilbrook, Mrs. Harold Austin, and Barbara Haveman, successively), Reginald Owen died in 1972. To the legions of movie viewers who have seen him countless times as rather pompous "Boobus Brittanicus" types, it must be very difficult to visualize him as the keen and incisive Sherlock Holmes, however well suited he was for Watson. Holmes, of course, however egotistic, was totally unpretentious and not at all pompous. But Owen had a very strong interest in the Baker Street Savant, working himself on the script of his single venture in the role, and he must have been greatly disappointed when his plans for prolonging the series fell through.

Reginald Owen's Holmes epic was followed by *The Radio Murder-Mystery* the same year, with Richard Gordon and Leigh Lovell unsuccessfully attempting to transfer their popular radio interpretations of the Baker Street Duo onto the screen.

16

Raymond Massey

THE SPECKLED BAND (British)

Date of Release: March or 3 November 1931; United States copyright 6 November

Running Time: 7 reels; 90 minutes; 66 min.

Production Company: British and Dominions Studios/First Division Pictures Inc./AmerAnglo Corporation

Producer: Herbert Wilcox

Director: Jack Raymond

Screenplay: W. P. Lipscomb

Based on: The story and play by Doyle

Photography: Frederick A. ("Freddie") Young

Editor: P. M. Rogers

Sound: L. M. O'Dell

(British "A" Certificate)

CAST

Dr. Grimesby Rylott	Lyn Harding
Sherlock Holmes	Raymond Massey
Dr. Watson	Athole Stewart (or Steward)
Helen Stonor (or Stoner)	Angela Baddeley (she may perhaps have been billed second, above Massey)
Mrs. Staunton	Nancy Price
Mrs. Hudson	Marie Ault
Rodgers	Stanley Lathbury
Builder	Charles Paton
Violet Stonor (or Stoner)	Joyce Moore

SYNOPSIS: Aside from the fact that the period of the story was modernized, with stenographers, dictaphones, typewriters and a filing cabinet system installed in 221B (Holmes, that untidy Bohemian, would surely rather have died first!), the film seems to have followed Doyle's play rather closely. The starring part in the play (as in the film) is not Holmes himself, but the villainous Rylott: Sherlock does not appear onstage until about halfway through the play. Watson,

Watson (Athole Stewart) looks on while Dr. Grimesby Rylott (Lyn Harding) lays down the law to a wryly amused Sherlock Holmes (Raymond Massey). (Courtesy National Film Archives of the British Film Institute)

however, is visible in the play's very first scene in his capacity of family friend to the Stonors at the inquest into Violet's death. (Her murder in the film occurs on screen, of course, as witness Violet's name in the credits.) Watson's extensive share in the action is undoubtedly the reason that he gets better billing in this film that he has in the films we have been most recently covering. It is curious that although the play's "Enid" Stonor reverts in the film to the name she bore in the original story—Helen—her sister Violet is not rechristened Julia, nor is Dr. Rylott returned to his original appellation of Roylott. The play's "Mrs. Soames" also appears to be missing in the film, but Doyle himself had removed that lady when he published the playscript in 1912, two years after it was first produced.

The pageboy Billy is also absent from the cast lists we have been able to find, which is curious as he is so important as a "feed" to Holmes in the stage version. Presumably his functions were largely distributed in the film among Watson, Mrs. Hudson, and one of the "stenographers." We do not know if the short story's gypsies appeared in the screen version, though they would have made good cinematic material.

The fundamental story of the play appears to have remained intact, however, with Rylott still rejoicing in his pet baboon and cheetah, poisoning his stepdaughter Violet for her inheritance, and attempting to do the same for her sister Helen. When the villainous Doctor visits Holmes at Baker Street, there is the famous scene where Rylott attempts to frighten the detective by bending a fireplace poker nearly double with his bare hands. Sherlock, however, magnificently nonplussed, merely affords us a rare glimpse of his own superhuman strength by calmly bending the thing back into shape!

Holmes appears at Rylott's Stoke Moran house disguised as the new butler, "Peter," and at one point is threatened by the Doctor with a horse whip when he catches the latter mistreating Helen. "Peter" has, of course, not neglected to pack a concealed pistol, however, thus averting further mischief for the time being.

The instrument of Rylott's most nefarious plans is of course the "Speckled Band" itself—Doyle himself thought that "the grim snake story" was the best Holmes tale he ever wrote. The snake, of course, which was the vehicle for the murder of Violet, eventually "does for" its villainous master as well.

REVIEW (*Picturegoer Weekly*, 31 October 1931):

To try and modernise a famous character of fiction like Sherlock Holmes is asking for trouble. You cannot divorce Holmes from the period of hansoms and a Baker Street that is long past.

Nor can you hope to succeed unless the actor who plays this hero of detective fiction does not (sic) resemble the Holmes of our imagination.

On the credit side I must say that the director has used his camera very skillfully and does achieve

The formidable Dr. Rylott (Lyn Harding) confers with his "friend" Mrs. Staunton (Nancy Price). (Courtesy National Film Archives of the British Film Institute)

moments of suspense and plenty of movement.

Lyn Harding, who has played the villainous Dr. Rylott in the stage version of *The Speckled Band* since it was adapted, is excellent.

In this case, at least, one feels that tradition has been followed.

We have already seen how Conan Doyle, when his Hubert Willis play *The House of Temperley* failed and he had the Royal Adelphi Theatre on his hands, wrote the play of *The Speckled Band* in two weeks; and we have seen in our Saintsbury biography how the play was revived again and again over the years with Saintsbury and Lyn Harding, the original stars; we shall look at Harding's career in a little more depth later on in this book, as he was later to join the Wontner series as Moriarty and is, thus, a filmic Sherlockian figure of some importance. First, however, we shall take a look at Raymond Massey, who as Holmes in this film was making his screen debut.

Raymond Hart Massey was born in Toronto, Canada on 30 August 1896, and was, thus, one of the youngest screen Sherlocks, in marked contrast to such sexagenarians as Norwood and Wontner. Massey's Canadian birth was to enable him to play successfully both Britons in Britain and Americans in the United States—his versatility helped, too, of course. He made

In Rylott's lair of Stoke Moran, Holmes (Raymond Massey, right) has infiltrated himself in the guise of a butler. Seen as Helen Stonor is Angela Baddeley, more recently seen on TV in *Upstairs, Downstairs*; and the interloper who seems to have startled her is Dr. Watson (Athole Stewart). (Courtesy National Film Archives of the British Film Institute)

his stage debut in 1922 in Britain, and his next English film after *Speckled Band* was another detective picture, *The Face at the Window*, 1931, for Wontner's studio and director, Twickenham and Leslie Hiscott. Also in the cast was Mrs. John H. Watson from the Wontner *Sign of Four*, Isla Bevan.

Massey, however, was not cast as Holmes this time, but as the French detective Paul le Gros, although he was teamed with a "silly-ass" English friend introduced in obvious imitation of Dr. Watson. The *Picturegoer* review taxed the film with being "unsophisticated and broad," but the same magazine said that Massey himself had a "terrific personality, which 'comes over' from the screen as few others do in this country." They noted that Miss Bevan must be "quite used to being questioned by detectives" by this time.

In between *Speckled Band* and this film, however, Massey had already made his first film jaunt to Hollywood, where he was to spend much of his career. His Hollywood films in this early period included the original *Old Dark House,* 1932 (future-Mycroft Robert Morley was in the remake), the *Scarlet Pimpernel,* 1934, and the *Prisoner of Zenda,* 1937 (both swashbucklers of the type in which such fellow Holmeses as Norwood, Rathbone, Granger, Cushing, Lee, and Wilmer have also cavorted), and *The Hurricane,* '37 (in which Massey replaced Basil Rathbone.) With '39's *Abe Lincoln in Illinois,* Massey was to become forever identified with the role of the sixteenth president, which he was to re-create in *How The West Was Won* (only a cameo) in '62.

In the meantime he had been continuing his British career and had an outstanding dual role as John and Oswald Cabal in *Things to Come* in 1936, with fellow screen-Holmes Robert Rendel, radio-Holmes Cedric

Hardwicke, and radio-Watson Ralph Richardson as Cabal's nemesis. In *Fire Over England* the next year, Holmes was rematched with Dr. Rylott, as Massey appeared with Lyn Harding in this Tudor costumer; in that same year's *Under the Red Robe* with Conrad Veidt, Massey stepped into the role of Cardinal Richelieu, which among his fellow Holmeses has been incarnated by both Saintsbury and Wontner. He was a Subcontinental Indian in *Drums* in '38 with Sabu, and before the year was out he joined stage-Holmes Henry Oscar in *Black Limelight*. From then on, though, he was mainly associated with American roles, even playing one in his next British picture *49th Parallel* in '41. In '61 he returned to England to make *The Queen's Guards* for *Parallel* director Michael Powell.

Some of his notable roles back in Hollywood were as the abolitionist John Brown in *Santa Fe Trail* in '40; in *Reap the Wild Wind*, '42, as a merchant marine skipper; in *Action in the North Atlantic*, '43 (on the set of which Massey and Humphrey Bogart laid bets as to which of them had the braver stunt-man!); the Fritz Lang mystery *Woman in the Window*, '44; Eugene O'Neill's *Mourning Becomes Electra*, '47; Ayn Rand's *The Fountainhead*, '48; *Roseanna McCoy*, '49 (in which he became involved in the Hatfield-McCoy squabbles); *Sugarfoot*, '51 (for Holmesian director Edwin Marin); *Prince of Players*, '55 (as the great tragedian Junius Brutus Booth, father of Lincoln's assassin); John Steinbeck's *East of Eden*, '55; Norman Mailer's *The Naked and the Dead*, '58; and *MacKenna's Gold* in 1968. Massey had a notable relief from Americana in '44's *Arsenic and Old Lace* with his adequate Boris Karloff imitation, and another as the sympathetic Nazi General (of all things!) in *Hotel Berlin* the following year. He was transported to Biblical times for *David and Bathsheba* in '51, and to the court of the Abbassid Caliph in *Omar Khayyam*, '57. On United States television in the early sixties, Massey stepped into Lionel Barrymore's old role of Dr. Gillespie and dispensed irascible advice to young *Dr. Kildare*. A recent TV role was in *All My Darling Daughters* in which Massey stole the show with his subtly played heart-attack sequence.

Married for the first time to Peggy Fremantle in 1923, subsequently to Adrienne Allen, and finally (in '39) to Dorothy Whitney, Raymond Massey is the father of three children, of whom Daniel and Anna have recently been notably on the screen. His other son is Geoffrey.

In Raymond Massey's long and distinguished career he has displayed the highly uncommon ability to portray equally well characters who are either coldly aristocratic or warmly "folksy," chillingly evil or believably heroic. It is pity that he was never again cast as Sherlock Holmes (no doubt Wontner was too strong a rival in the role) or that no one had the bright idea to give him a shot at Moriarty, at whom he would have been excellent. Massey's career though, has certainly not been diminished in any way by these omissions, let us hasten to add!

About Athole Stewart, his Dr. Watson in *Speckled*

Watson (Athole Stewart) seems very jolly in his topper and boutonniere. Note the uncurved pipe Holmes (Raymond Massey) is smoking in *Speckled Band.*

Band, we have been able to find little information. In 1937, Stewart did appear with Clive Brook in *Action for Slander,* as well as in the British *Dr. Syn,* based on Russell Thorndike's *Scarecrow* series. This outing was directed by Roy William Neill who was later to take over the direction of the Rathbone Holmes series in Hollywood. When this smuggling tale was refilmed years later with Peter Cushing, the leading character was for some obscure reason renamed Dr. Blyss for a distinct contrast! (Walt Disney, too, of course, tried his hand at a version.) In the '37 *Dr. Syn,* Stewart was cast as Sir Anthony Cobtree, and two years later he was playing the Reverend Hector Matthews in *The Spy in Black,* with former-Holmes Robert Rendel.

Angela Baddeley, the leading lady in *Speckled Band,* has been more recently familiarly seen on both British and American TV as the cook on the highly popular series *Upstairs, Downstairs.*

Director Jack Raymond, who began working on *Speckled Band* late in 1930, was born in Wimborne in 1886 as John Caines, and was an engineer before he went into the music halls as a performer. He became a film actor for Hepworth in 1908, and after serving as assistant director on the 1920 *Grand Guignol* series he became a director in 1926 with *The Greater War,* a short. Noted in particular for his comedy work, Raymond's *Guignol* experience probably stood him in better stead for directing Lyn Harding, whose Rylott was famous for its melodramatic excess. In '31, Raymond remade G. B. Samuelson's old hit *Tilly of Bloomsbury,* and in '37 he returned to mystery with Edgar Wallace's *The Frog,* for *Speckled Band* producer Wilcox, with stage-Holmes Felix Aylmer in the cast. Another detective story was *The Mind of Mr. Reeder* in '39, and in the following year he directed future-Mycroft Robert Morley in the charming musical-biography *You Will Remember.* Raymond's last film was 1952's *Little Big Shot* and he died in '53.

Herbert Wilcox, who produced *Speckled Band,* was one of the most notable (if not critically praised) figures in the British industry. Born in Cork, Ireland in 1892, he was eventually awarded a C.B.E. and was the cofounder of the Elstree studio. As a director, Wilcox made Wilkie Collins' mystery *Woman in White* in '29; *Nell Gwynn,* '34 (with his wife Anna Nagle and radio-Holmes Cedric Hardwicke); *Victoria the Great,* '37; *Lady with the Lamp,* '51 (Eille Norwood was in the play version); the classic mystery *Trents Last Case,* '52 (Clive Brook had been in an earlier edition); *Trouble in the Glen,* '54 (with radio-Holmes *and* -Moriarty Orson Welles); and *Heart of a Man in* '59.

If *Speckled Band* is remembered for its technical side at all, though, it will hardly be for the efforts of Raymond or Wilcox, but rather due to the fact that it was shot by one of the greatest of all movie cameramen, Freddie Young (1902–), who also shot *Nell Gwynn* and other films for Wilcox, and *49th Parallel* with Massey. Young, however, is better remembered for his stunning visuals in such David Lean classics as *Lawrence of Arabia,* '62; *Doctor Zhivago,* '65; and the really breathtaking work he did on *Ryan's Daughter*— for all three of these films Young won best-cinematography Oscars.

For Sherlockian purposes, however, the most important figure in *The Speckled Band* is Lyn Harding, who had been starring in it on the stage since 1910, and was to go on to play Professor Moriarty in Wontner's '35 *Triumph of Sherlock Holmes* and '37 *Silver Blaze* (*Murder at the Baskervilles*), and he deserves to be treated here in some depth.

Born David Llewellyn Harding in Newport, Wales on Monday, 12 October 1867, Lyn made his first acting appearance on the stage of the Theatre Royal, Bristol on 25 August 1890 in the role on M. Guerin in *The Grip of Iron,* before graduating to the role of Jago in the same play, which he played on the subsequent tour. He spent most of his early career touring the provinces or playing in stock companies, and cut his teeth on such Shakespearean parts as Camillo and, later, Leontes in *The Winter's Tale,* Don Pedro in *Much Ado,* and Gratiano and Shylock in *The Merchant of Venice.* A more contemporary role was as Wilfred Denver in *The Silver King.* In October of 1893, Harding embarked on a theatrical tour that was to take him out of the provinces and through India, Burma, China, and Japan, during which he played such leading roles as that of the great actor Garrick in a play based on his life. He also essayed the character of Rob Roy and appeared in *Jim the Penman* and the melodrama *The Corsican Brothers,* as well as *School for Scandal* (in which play have also appeared such fellow Holmesian actors as Saintsbury, Rathbone, Gielgud, Cushing, and Wilmer.)

Two years later Harding was back in the British provinces touring as Lord Dunmasy (a fictional character and not the similarly named fantasist) in *The Egyptian Idol,* and also playing Captain Starlight in

A very early picture of Lyn Harding, looking very unvillainous indeed.

Robbery Under Arms. Some of the parts with which Lyn was busy over the next several years included Ned Drayton (for the second time) in *In The Ranks,* and roles in *A Life of Pleasure* and *The Indian Mutiny.*

Harding's London debut came on 19 July 1897 in *The Silence of the Night,* followed the next year by his third appearance as Drayton in *In The Ranks.* We will notice again in his career how fond Lyn was of reviving favorite parts. He did not, however, have a really outstanding success on the London boards until 1903 when he did Ganthony's *Prophecy,* followed the same year by another hit in *A Snug Little Kingdom,* after which he was engaged for Sir H. Beerbohm Tree's company.

Harding appeared with Tree in *Richard II* and *The Darling of the Gods* and then made his film debut in *The Tempest,* a 1905 film that Charles Urban made in London by photographing the elaborate storm scene from Tree's production of Shakespeare's play. (His cinematographer was probably F. Martin Duncan.) Harding played Antonio, his stage role. The film was less than two minutes long, but Tree's stunningly mounted special stage effects of the foundering ship were far in advance of anything else on the screen at the time, even if not truly cinematic in nature.

Harding was to appear in many other films on both sides of the Atlantic and made his United States film debut before World War I, but we will not be able to supply any more specific titles until we reach 1920.

Some of Harding's other roles with Sir Herbert were Prospero, Pistol (in *The Merry Wives Of Windsor*), Bill Sykes and Owen Glendower, the Ghost in *Hamlet*, and others; most of which we can easily visualize him in when we consider his later notoriety as a practitioner of full-bodied melodrama. It is rather surprising, though, to read that he played that innocent dolt Sir Andrew Aguecheek, who seems more suited for Stan Laurel than a fireeater like Lyn Harding was to become. The answer, of course, is that Harding could always play it "straight" when he wanted to, and was a far more subtle actor than he was often given credit for.

A few of his other pre-Sherlockian roles were the title characters in *The Admirable Crichton* and *The Devil*. In April of 1910 he was once again with Tree in *Julius Caesar,* exchanging his old part of Cassius for that of

Lyn Harding coaxes the title character (a snake) out of its basket in the original stage version of *Speckled Band*. Grimesby Rylott was his most famous role, but he subsequently donned Professor Moriarty's outrageous scarf for two episodes of the Wontner series.

Brutus. Then, two months later, Lyn made his bow in the part for which he will be most remembered—Dr. Grimesby Rylott in the original production of *The Speckled Band.*

Harding, who also directed the production, persuaded Doyle to let him emphasize the "neurotic" aspects of the character, which he then proceeded to emphasize almost to the point of chewing the scenery, to the intense delight of the audiences and even some of the critics. Macqueen-Pope, for one, wrote that Harding was "always amazing" in his performance of the part, "a magnificent actor." The Holmes of this first production was of course our old friend H. A. Saintsbury, and Claude King was Watson who, in the play, is stated to have just become engaged to Mary Morstan.

Harding, with chin-beard and twitching eye, petted his snake in its wicker basket while his Indian servant played a reed pipe (presumably to soothe the two-legged beast as well as the limbless one). Rylott, however, and his scaly friend, were not the only menaces with which Holmes had to contend in this play, for the wretched pageboy Billy goes so far as to smash the poor detective's bottle of cocaine when he asks for it—surely a rather priggish way to handle the Great Man's drug problem (and, one would think, none too effective).

Rylott, of course, gets his comeuppance in the end, as he is discovered by Holmes with his own snake coiled about his throat and forehead. Harding here had the opportunity to cry out hoarsely and stagger two paces forward before dropping dead on stage—surely a scene that an actor of his style must have relished. The snake thereupon crawls away to be bludgeoned by Dr. Watson. Harding maintained that a good actor could hold his audience spellbound by reciting the multiplication table, so it is little wonder that he was able to cast the spell he did with rich melodrama like this! He played it until September, then went on tour as Sir Walter Raleigh for a change of pace while two other companies toured in *Speckled Band.* Harding himself then revived "the grim snake story" in February of 1911, with O. P. Heggie stepping in for Saintsbury as Holmes (remember Heggie as the blind man in *Bride of Frankenstein*); Lyn revived it once more (in the United States this time, in 1914, and then again with Saintsbury returning) in 1921 when it ran for ninety-eight performances at the St. James in London and another twenty-six at the Royalty, not closing there until '22. The film version, of course, began shooting in '30.

Harding kept busy with other projects, too, over these years, however, appearing with another future-Moriarty, Norman McKinnel, in 1911's *Money,* playing in music-hall sketches, then reviving his Bill Sykes in the United States and Britain, and, for a change of pace, essaying the romantic and witty Benedick in *Much Ado About Nothing* (previously he had played that character in it who was more up his alley, the "fantastical" Don Pedro). He played Sir Francis

Drake and then toured the United States as Jacob in *Joseph and His Brethren*. (Saintsbury had played Simeon in it for the London run.) Also in the United States, Harding made the acquaintance of Svengali, a role that he would re-create before the cameras in 1922 as part of the *Tense Moments with Great Authors* series (in another episode of which Clive Brook appeared). John Barrymore was, of course, another fine screen Svengali. Still in America in 1916, Harding stepped into another part which he was to do for films, when he rejoined Tree to play *Henry VIII*. Lyn first played the Tudor King in films in 1921's *When Knighthood Was in Flower*, rendered him again in *Fire Over England* (with Rendel and Massey) and finally in Sacha Guitry's *Pearls of the Crown* in '39.

Yet another of Harding's New York parts was in *The Case of Lady Camber*—this one was to be filmed in 1932 with Nigel Bruce (and without Harding) as *Lord Camber's Ladies*.

Lyn was back in London before the end of '17, playing in *Wild Heather*, following which he did *L'Aiglon*. In 1919 he toured as Marquis Chi-Lung in *A Chinese Puzzle*, a play that Eille Norwood had just done the year before. In *Bird of Paradise*, Harding was the Beachcomber. In 1920 he made two films—*A Bachelor Husband* and *The Barton Mystery*.

Returning to the stage in 1921 he had a rather unfortunate season when he tried to become an actor-manager at the St. James. He produced three failures in a row there, and only saved his season by the previously mentioned *Speckled Band* revival. When that play finally closed in '22 he took another turn as Svengali and then played Captain Hook in the annual Christmas run of *Peter Pan*. (He was in it again in 1925.) That pirate has also been played not only by Harding's fellow-Moriarty Ernest Torrence, but also by none other than Holmes himself (Arthur Wontner).

In 1924, Harding was associated with a dreadful flop—*Conchita*. Tallulah Bankhead was also in the cast and Macqueen-Pope wrote that her fans "were distraught and in tears, and would have wreaked violence on the malcontents if they could have got at them."

Some of Harding's other parts during this period were in *White Cargo* (filmed with Reginald Owen), *Pollyana* (of all unlikely shows for him!), and *The Mayor of Casterbridge*. Another film role was in '27's *Land of Hope and Glory;* then in '28 he was back in New York as the mad Czar Paul in *The Patriot*. (Emil Jennings got the role when it was filmed.) Before returning to Britain he took a turn as Macbeth, among other things (one wonders how Duncan ever could have trusted him).

He was very active in films during the thirties; some of his titles that we have not yet mentioned were *Yolanda; Spy of Napolean*, '36; *Knight Without Armour*, '37; and *Goodbye Mr. Chips*, '39 (as Dr. Wetherby, with former-Holmes Robert Rendel and future-Watson Nigel Stock). Then of course there are his two outings as Professor Moriarty: *Triumph of Sherlock Holmes* and *Silver Blaze*—both of which we will cover in some depth in our Wontner section.

Like his old stage-foil H. A. Saintsbury, Lyn Harding belonged to the Green Room Club (Harding also belonged to the Garrick). Like Saintsbury again, he was a masterful actor of the "old school," who, had he lived a hundred years earlier, would undoubtedly have been counted among the truly greats. Both of them, of course, *do* live in that company, as far as devout Sherlockians are concerned—and is there any other scale of measurement?

Six feet tall and dark of complexion, Lyn Harding died in London on 26 December 1952.

17

Robert Rendel

THE HOUND OF THE BASKERVILLES (British)

Date of Release: July 1931 or 22 February 1932; copyright: 2 January 1932 or 15 April '32 (apparently rereleased in 1936).

Running Time: 75 minutes; 72 min.; 6761 feet; 7 reels

Production Company: A Gainsborough Picture/ Ideal/Gaumont-British (copyrighted in the United States by First Anglo Corp., released there by First Division)

Producer: Sir Michael Balcon

Director: V. Gareth Gundrey

Scenario: V. Gareth Gundrey

Dialog: Edgar Wallace

Photography: Bernard Knowles

Editor: Ian Dalrymple

Recorded on RCA Photophone

Locations: Lustleigh Hall, near Hound Tor; Dartmoor

(British "U" Certificate, Passed by the National Board of Review)

CAST

Sherlock Holmes	Robert Rendel (or Rendell)
Dr. Watson	Fred Lloyd
Sir Henry Baskerville	John Stuart
Stapleton	Reginald Bach
Beryl Stapleton	Heather Angel
Dr. Mortimer	Wilfred Shine
Sir Hugo Baskerville	Sam Livesey
Mrs. Laura Lyons	Elizabeth Vaughan
Barrymore	Henry Hallatt
Mrs. Barrymore	Sybil Jane
Cartwright	Leonard Hayes

SYNOPSIS: With the exception, of course, of the Hugo Baskerville prologue, the film was set in current (1930s) times. A very large dose of authenticity, however, was added by actually filming the story in the real locations that inspired Doyle to write *The Hound of the Baskervilles*. The actual Lustleigh Hall is generally accepted as the basis for Baskerville Hall, and is so used in the film. A few miles away is Hound Tor, and then of course there is the real Dartmoor, a far cry from the lushly vegetated backlots that Hollywood has usually tried to foist off on non-British audiences when a moor was required (for example, as in the '39 *Wuthering Heights*). The original of the wicked Sir Hugo is thought to have been Sir Richard Cabell, Lord of the Manor of Brook, who died in 1677. Doyle got the cursed family's "fictitious" name from the groom who drove the author around Dartmoor to obtain local color for his novel—the fellow's name turns out to have been Mr. Henry Baskerville! (Still living at the age of ninety as recently as 1961, Baskerville has since died.)

All of this film was allegedly shot on the actual locations, but this seems hard to believe at so early a date as 1931. There surely must have been *some* studio work involved. Despite all this care taken with authenticity, the film was still taxed with poor production values in some quarters.

Other than modernizing the setting, the film seems to have followed the book rather closely, but, since the surviving negative is of the picture alone, without a

131

Sherlock Holmes (Robert Rendel, left) discusses a suspicious boot with Beryl Stapleton (Heather Angel), Dr. Watson (Fred Lloyd), and Sir Henry Baskerville (John Stuart). Most of the film was made on location in the actual sites that inspired Doyle's novel. (Courtesy National Film Archives of the British Film Institute)

soundtrack, it is difficult to judge. This lack is especially regrettable as the film's musical score was critically praised at the time.

The makers of the 1939 Rathbone version evidently screened the earlier Norwood silent edition for themselves, since its influence is felt in a few sequences, so it is probable that the '39 version also reflects that of '32, as well.

The only part of the film that it was possible for us to screen was the opening few minutes, but even silent these were so outstanding that it is all the more regrettable that this film has been allowed to virtually vanish. We can only hope that some day the rest of the picture negative, and perhaps even the sound nega-

tive, may resurface so that the film can be properly assessed and enjoyed.

This version of *The Hound* opens immediately with the Hugo Baskerville sequence, and tells the legend very crisply indeed with many setups and tracking shots (such as that up the long table past his roistering cronies to Sir Hugo himself.) The film in fact moves so well that it plays quite well even without sound—always the acid test. The vigorous construction is especially unusual for British films of this period, and is all the more notable by contrast with the highly static and unimaginative camerawork and editing of the first Wontner film, made this same year. It is hard to see why the Wontner series was so exalted at the time at the expense of this film, for, although Wontner himself was of course a flawless Holmes, this film is far better made, and Rendel does not seem at all objectionable in the role—a bit heavyset perhaps, but so was Norwood. One might suspect that the film's pace was good at the beginning but later flagged, but this can hardly have been the case when we see that, even after switching to 221B after concluding the initial flashback, the camera work remains lively and thoughtful when Gundrey could in fact have gotten away with one or two purely expository setups, as was done all too often by Hiscott in the Wontner films.

The seventeenth-century costumes in the prologue seem fairly authentic, and the real-life Lustleigh Hall and its environs are moodily lit to achieve the maximum in atmosphere. Sam Livesey's Hell-Bound Baronet seems perhaps to be played in a somewhat broad style, and one fears that the addition of sound to this already overexplicit characterization might have been a bit much.

The storyline follows the familiar pattern, with the poor victimized girl skulking fearfully about in the shadows, as Baskerville and his boon companions search for her. The rowdy crew are soon quarrelling among themselves like a pack of ravenous hounds, and one of them is pitched off the balcony even as the pursued girl slips out a window.

The exterior night scenes are nicely achieved as much by lighting as by more conventional filters, so that the visual quality retains some dramatic contrast in place of the bland gray that could have ensued and taken the edge off the suspense. Sir Hugo tracks the girl by means of a handkerchief she has dropped, and there is a fine sequence when he calls for his horse and the white animal emerges from the surrounding darkness surrounded by Baskerville's yapping hunting dogs and men with flaming torches. The camera moves along with the chase, until finally the poor girl faints.

At this point, before her enemies can reach her, the Hound materializes over her helpless prone form. The supernatural beast is, for once on the screen, larger than life as called for in the novel, and though its transparency is perhaps disappointing at first, there is an effective shock when the seemingly insubstantial creature moves out of the frame, and we see that it has left fiery footprints behind it upon the ground.

The Hound in this film seems to be portrayed as a force of Good, not Evil, for it materializes to protect the girl and to prevent evil rather than merely to punish evil after it has been committed, as in more orthodox versions. This notion lends an additional clue to those members of the audience who are perhaps unfamiliar with all the ramifications of the plot, since it should occur to them that such a Hound would not punish the innocent such as Sir Henry, and that, therefore, it is some force other than that of the legend which is seeking his life.

Before we actually see what the Hound does to Sir Hugo, the screen is filled with the old manuscript from which Dr. Mortimer is narrating the legend in "modern" times. Mortimer looks off-camera in the direction of Holmes, and Gundrey makes the most of the audience's anticipation of their first sight of the Great Detective by slowly panning over Holmes' classically littered table (on which his violin reposes); then slowly up to Holmes' hands as he taps his fingers together in that familiar way which signifies intense

intellectual activity; and then, at last, continues its way up to his face. Rendel is smoking a long straight pipe, and clad in a pleasantly well-worn-looking dressing gown. Under his eyes are very distinct circles, which lend him the brooding appearance of Norwood, but we can see quite clearly from his expressions (even without the benefit of his voice) that he is playing Holmes in a delightfully peevish and sarcastic vein. As he rises and goes to the window, we see regrettably few books on the room's shelves, and, indeed, the walls of the apartment seem entirely too bare; but as the camera follows him to the window, the telescope that is sitting on the windowsill is a reassuring touch that echoes the detective's restlessly scientific mind. A fine high-angle shot follows from Holmes' point of view as he observes a suspicious character standing in the street below.

A touch that may have seemed too modern in 1932 is the fact that Holmes lights his pipe not with the live coal from the fire used in the stories and by Wontner,

Holmes (Robert Rendel) is on the receiving end of a great deal of trouble from the villainous Stapleton (Reginald Bach, top).

but with ordinary matches, and Holmes' necktie is a bit jarring as well. All in all, though, Rendel seems to make quite a splendid Holmes, and his Watson, Lloyd, seems absolutely right for the part. Lloyd projects upper-class distinction even silent and in repose, and though he may be a bit too much in the Nigel Bruce "Boobus Britannicus" vein for devout Sherlockians, he does convey a very strong sense of military trustworthiness that any Watson must display in order to justify the confidence Holmes places in him (in this story particularly), but which too few screen Watsons have actually had.

Here, alas, we must take our leave of this tantalizingly "lost" film, though we have found surprises even in this tiny fragment.

REVIEW (*Picturegoer Weekly*, 20 February 1932, reviewed by Lionel Collier): (average entertainment)

This picture fails to do justice to Conan Doyle's thrilling Sherlock Holmes story.

While production qualities are good, there is an absence of suspense or thrill, and it is very pedestrian in the unfolding of its rather vague plot.

Once again a type that fails to look like the original has been chosen for Sherlock Holmes. Robert Rendel acts well, but he is not at all the conception of fiction's most famous detective.

John Stuart makes a personable and likeable hero, but I found Reginald Bach much too obvious a villain.

It seems to me that a great chance has been missed in the filming of this story.

Robert Rendel was having a rare moment of glory when he played Holmes in this film, for a large number of his other film roles were unbilled cameos. He received a great deal of publicity for *Hound*, since the production was chronicled in a series of *Film Weekly* articles stretching over a period of nine weeks (the readers had voted *Hound* the story they most wanted to see filmed).

Due to the rather fleeting nature of so many of his appearances, it has been difficult to fully cover Rendel's film career. In 1934 he had another mystery role in *Death at Broadcasting House* as Sir Herbert Farquharson. Also in the cast, as Inspector Gregory (a familiar name from the Norwood series) was former-Dr. Watson Ian Hunter. Two years later Rendel was cast with former-Holmes Raymond Massey in *Things to Come*, in which also appeared radio-Holmes and -Watson Cedric Hardwicke and Ralph Richardson.

In 1937, Rendel played the role of the Admiral (one of his many naval officer roles) in *The Spy in Black* with former-Watson Athole Stewart. In '39, Rendel was in the original *Goodbye Mr. Chips* with Lyn Harding and TV-Watson Nigel Stock. In 1940, Rendel appeared with a virtual galaxy of fellow Holmeses from three media—Clive Brook (screen), Sir John Clements (phonograph), and Stewart Granger (television) in the film *Convoy*.

Although he was widely disparaged as Sherlock Holmes, Robert Rendel had one attribute that is essential for the character, but that has been possessed by few if any other screen actors in the part: his preternaturally high forehead, speaking of the heroic profusion of those Holmesian gray cells. Eille Norwood had to compensate for the deficiency of expanse in his own countenance by actually shaving his temples, while Wontner and Granger gave the illusion by playing the role rather late in life when they were fortuitously rather balding. Rendel alone displayed the Baker Street brow.

Rendel's Watson, Frederick W. Lloyd, was in fact the more eminent of the two performers, which is not inappropriate for this story, in which Watson is left for so long to hold down the fort by himself while Holmes is off-screen.

Lloyd was born on 15 January 1880 in London, and made his film debut in 1930's *Balaclava*. Two other '30's films were *The W Plan* and *Temporary Widow*. The following year saw him appearing in *The Battle of Gallipoli;* in '32 he was seen in the first full-length film adapted for the screen by George Bernard Shaw himself—*Arms and the Man*. Lloyd's other films during the latter year included a role as the Advocate General in *A Gentleman of Paris* with Arthur Wontner, *Sleepless Nights,* and *Up for the Derby;* '33 saw him following his Watson stint with *The Crime at Blossoms, The Song You Gave Me,* and *Mixed Doubles*. In 1935, Lloyd made *Blossom Time,* and in 1936—*Everything is Thunder, Tell England, Radio Pirates,* and *The Beggar Student. April Romance, The Perfect Lady, The Great Gay Road, No Escape, Mademoiselle Docteur, Jubilee, Heidelburg, First and Last, Denham, Lt. Darling,* and *Weddings are Wonderful*—all kept Lloyd busy in 1937, one would suppose!

Lloyd was also a stage actor of some distinction, who appeared (like many others in this book) with the Old Vic company. The Duchess Theatre in London premiered Emlyn Williams' *The Corn Is Green* on 20 September 1938, and in the cast, besides author Williams and Dame Sybil Thorndike, was none other than Fred Lloyd, seemingly unexhausted by his previous year's grueling film schedule. It is curious to note that when *The Corn is Green* was filmed in Hollywood, Lloyd's stage role was filled for the cameras by another Dr. Watson—Nigel Bruce. There is still another odd Sherlockian link with this play, for Ethel Barrymore played the Thorndike part when the show crossed to New York, and after her brother John died she would from time to time play her character using John's mannerisms, delivery, etc.—a unique way of keeping his memory, and one which was noticed by very few in the audience (although by some).

Lloyd's character makeup in the play was very Watsonish: long and curly old-fashioned moustache, monocle, and gray hair brushed slickly back in military style, with a cigar perched in his mouth. His costumes ranged from the familiar tweeds to formal evening dress, and even straw hat and white trousers.

In 1940, Lloyd's film career resumed with *Twenty-One Days Together (21 Days)*, which had actually been filmed several years earlier for Holmesian producer-director Basil Dean but had been waiting in the can. Fred Lloyd's last film was David Lean's classic *Oliver Twist*, which had been done on the stage by Lyn Harding and H. A. Saintsbury.

The next year, on 24 November 1949 in Hove, England, Fred Lloyd died. He seems to have ranked among the sturdier and more capable screen Watsons, such as Morell and Houston: the Doctor's military background (even if a bit Blimpish) has been all too often overlooked by many of his other interpreters, for Watson should contrast with Holmes not only by his lesser intelligence, but also by his somewhat greater capacity when an everyday and prosaic sort of task needs to be faced. In this respect Watson resembles Sancho Panza to the Quixote of Holmes, for his greater earthiness is not always to his humorous disadvantage when the two clash verbally.

Hound's producer, Sir Michael Balcon, was one of the greatest influences to the good in British films for nearly half a century. Like Sam Goldwyn, David Selznick, or Val Lewton—producers who are not only businessmen but also exercise a truly creative influence on the quality of their product—Sir Michael was seemingly involved in just about everything of outstanding merit in the British cinema—from *Man of Aran* to *The Thirty-Nine Steps; Dead of Night* to *Tom Jones; and Kind Hearts and Coronets* to *Dunkirk*. Head of nearly all the major English studios or companies at one time or another—Gainsborough, Gaumont-British, Bryanston, etc.—he is probably most closely identified with his classic succession of Ealing pictures, which were so instrumental in reestablishing British films on the world market (as his Hitchcock-directed efforts had done originally years before). The three films Balcon made while briefly in charge of MGM-British in '38–9 are all such gems that one wishes the connection could have been prolonged: *A Yank at Oxford, The Citadel* (with stage-Holmes Sir Felix Aylmer and radio-Watson Sir Ralph Richardson), and *Goodbye Mr. Chips,* in which Balcon cast his old *Baskervilles* star Rendel.

Edgar Wallace, coauthor of this version of *The Hound,* was one of the most prolific of mystery novelists, and despite the speed with which he wrote them many of his books like *Dark Eyes of London* are minor classics with finely convoluted plots and deeper characterizations than one might expect. An occasional star in the recent series of German films based on Wallace's works has been Fritz Rasp, who, of course, figured prominently in the two most recent German versions of *Der Hund von Baskerville.* Edgar Wallace is probably best known to film audiences, however, for his (very slight, actually) participation in *King Kong,* which was only released after the great mystery-concoctor's death. With the keen sense of plot construction so manifest in Wallace's books, it is hard to understand how the '32 *Hound* can be as suspenseless and hard to follow as it was accused of being.

The film's editor, Ian Dalrymple, also cut Arthur Wontner's *Storm in a Teacup* in '37, and went on to become a very prominent screenwriter, producer, and director: in '39's *Q Planes* he originated a memorable screen detective character who would have figured in a series had not his interpreter, Ralph Richardson, refused to ever play him again! The same year Dalrymple made *The Lion Has Wings* with former-Watson Ian Fleming; and Dalrymple directed Wontner and André Morell in *Three Cases of Murder* ('54), but the duo was not, alas, cast in it as the Baker Street partners.

In our next chapter we must now jump back in time to the last days of 1930, when the cameras at Twickenham began turning on a rather cheaply made film called *The Sleeping Cardinal;* for that was the film that inaugurated the Arthur Wontner series of Sherlock Holmes adventures. These were to be the first truly classic transferences of Holmes to the screen, for at last all the elements had come together: Wontner was not only a superb actor, but physically he seemed to have stepped right off the pages of the *Strand* magazine; and unlike his illustrious predecessor Norwood, Wontner was not denied the use of speech. We shall dwell on Arthur Wontner and his Holmes series at some length because together with the subsequent Rathbone films they mark undoubtedly the most flawless Sherlockian cinema that has ever been made or is ever likely to be made.

18

Arthur Wontner

Arthur Wontner was born in London on 21 January 1875. He began his stage career in Ryde, on the Isle of Wight, when he appeared as Sir Thomas Tenby in Marie Corelli's melodrama *Sorrows of Satan*, which was later filmed by both G. B. Samuelson and D. W. Griffith. Wontner's acting career lasted until 1955, and branched out to include films, radio, and television—in all three of which media he played Sherlock Holmes between 1931 and 1951.

From Wight he went to Margate and spent eight months with Sarah Thorne's company, during which he played nearly thirty leading parts and got a very firm grounding in his art; ironically, when many years later Wontner starred in the first British production of Bernard Shaw's *Village Wooing*, one of his speeches required him to vehemently deny that he had ever been to Margate! Wontner left Miss Thorne's troupe to join that of Louis Calvert, in which Eille Norwood at one time also served a spell. Wontner played Poins during Calvert's tour of *Henry IV, Part II*, and then debuted in London in 1898 as Comte de Rochefort in *The Three Musketeers*. In a revival of that play thirty-two years later, Arthur was promoted to the part of Richelieu himself—a role that he shared with Massey and Saintsbury; Christopher Lee has, of course, been in the recent film versions of the Dumas story.

Like those of Rathbone and Granger, Wontner's pre-Holmesian image was essentially that of the romantic swashbuckler. Curiously enough, Wontner and Rathbone shared the same profession before they went on the stage as well—both beginning their working lives in London insurance companies. Besides each having played Holmes, there are a number of other striking parallels in the lives of the two actors: each played Pontius Pilate and Louis XI, for example; and they actually appeared on the stage together in a play in September 1926, *The Captive*, which was put on in New York and not in London as one might expect. We will find many more such links as we proceed.

Like Eille Norwood and John Barrymore, Arthur Wontner also played the role of Raffles—Wontner on the stage 1906. Arthur played Captain Hook in 1916, like those two screen-Moriartys Torrence and Harding.

To resume Wontner's career where we digressed from it, in 1899 he appeared in *Change Alley, The Upper Hand*, and *The Ghetto*—all in London—and then began four years of touring as leading man under the management of such stars as Mrs. Lewis Waller, Mr. and Mrs. Charles Sugden, and Edward Compton (with whom Norwood was also associated). During this period Arthur added another fifty parts to his already extensive repertoire. Then in 1903 he was engaged by Beerbohm Tree to appear in Australia, and during Wontner's stay of over two years in that country he played Baron Bonelli in *The Eternal City* (he was often to be cast as Italian or Jewish characters) and added another fourteen new parts to his list.

Back in London in '06, Wontner was in such plays as *The Weavers, The Great Conspiracy, The Christian, Idols*, and *An Englishman's Home*, and had a great personal success in 1909 as Raymond Fleuriot in the much-filmed play *Madame X*. In April of 1910, Wontner joined Lyn Harding for the Shakespeare Festival at His Majesty's Theatre, where Wontner played Bassanio in *Merchant of Venice*, and Laertes in *Hamlet*.

Arthur Wontner, seen here in a character study from
Sign of Four, 1932, is still considered by many
aficionados to have been the perfect Sherlock
Holmes. (Courtesy National Film Archives of the
British Film Institute)

A very early portrait of Wontner, with a rare autograph.

Some of his other plays during this period were *The Great Mrs. Alloway, Society, A Bolt from The Blue*, and *Grace*. He joined Harley Granville-Barker at the Court in 1911 to appear as Martin in John Masefield's *The Witch*, and remained with that management to play the prophet Iokanaan in Wilde's *Salome* the following year. Later in '12 he was to rejoin Granville-Barker to play Orsino (also a Rathbone role) in *Twelfth Night*.

Also in the cast of that production of Shakespeare's comedy was Dennis Neilson-Terry, who was himself to play Sherlock Holmes on the stage; the future Hollywood actor Frank Conroy; another stage Holmes in Felix Aylmer; and Granville-Barker's wife Lillah McCarthy—a very great stage actress who must have been impressed with Wontner's work with her in this play, for she later presented an inscribed color portrait of him in his rather Moorish makeup to her niece. (Wontner strikingly resembles Rathbone and Wilmer in *their* various Arabic roles.) Granville-Barker's comments on the character of Orsino give us some idea of how he must have directed Wontner in the role, and also show how major a coup it was for Wontner to be cast in it by that director, since it demonstrates how much more control to the play Orsino was given by Granville-Barker than by most directors: he calls the character "that interesting romantic"; and of Orsino's lines—"Why should I not, had I the heart to do it, / Like the Egyptian thief at point of death, / Kill what I

love?/A savage jealousy that sometimes savours nobly"—Granville-Barker remarks that

on that fine fury of his . . . I believe the last part of the play was to have hung. It is too good a theme to have been meant to have been so wasted . . . one can discover, I believe, amid the chaos scraps of the play [Shakespeare] first meant to write . . . the revelation of Olivia's marriage to [Orsino's] page [as he supposes], his reconciliation with her, and the more vital discovery that his comradely love for Viola is worth more to him after all than any high-sounding passion is now all muddled up with the final rounding off of the comic relief. The character suffers severely. Orsino remains a finely interesting figure; he might have been a magnificent one.

The director goes on to say of Orsino that he is not only passionate but "conscious of the worth of . . . passion in terms of beauty" and compares him to a Spanish Grandee of the time of Drake. He speaks of the "Delicate still grace of the dialogue between Orsino and Cesario"; it is interesting that Granville-Barker is very firm on the point that Elizabethan dramatic verse must be spoken with great speed—interesting because

Another autographed portrait, with Wontner looking more like Sherlock Holmes than Holmes himself.

when Wontner came to play Holmes he spoke much more *slowly* in the part than most other interpreters of it have done!

Some of the other plays Arthur was appearing in during this period were *The King and the Countess* (as Edward III), *Lady Patricia, Pelleas and Melisande, The Marionettes,* and *The New Sin* (as Hilary Cutts, who was to be played the next year, 1913, by Eille Norwood). Before 1912 was out, Wontner was playing the title role in the spectacular Drury Lane production of *Ben Hur,* and he rounded out the year as Edward Voysey in *The Voysey Inheritance* (and, of course, in his above-mentioned *Twelfth Night*).

Over the next few years Wontner was in *Esther Castways,* Wilde's *Ideal Husband, Outcast,* and *Philip the King.* Macqueen-Pope praised him highly in Sir George DuMaurier's 1913 revival of *Diplomacy,* and said that the famous "three man scene" had never been better performed; then at the beginning of '15 Arthur was cast as the mythical King Richard VIII in *Kings and Queens,* with Sir George Alexander opposite him as the equally spurious Emperor Frederick IV: the production earned Wontner a Haselden caricature in *Punch.* In this play Wontner sported the small moustache he often wore in his non-Sherlockian roles, and played a rather petulant young man who is depicted in the cartoon as threatening to kill his mother, Queen Elizabeth—it was a comedy. He rounded out the year with *On Trial* and his performance as Captain Hook in the annual Christmas production of *Peter Pan* (being cast in that highly popular role was in itself quite an accolade).

Also in 1915, Arthur Wontner began his film career, and he was seldom to be off the screen over the next four decades. His first film was *The Bigamist,* and in '16 he made *Frailty,* costarring with none other than his fellow Holmes-to-be Eille Norwood; that same year our old Holmesian friend Fred Paul presaged Lubitsch by attempting a silent version of Oscar Wilde's highly verbal *Lady Windermere's Fan,* and Wontner was in the cast.

Wontner was still active on the stage in '16 as well, playing in *The Iron Hand* and impersonating royalty again as Prince Charles of Galania in *The Happy Day.* The next year he created the part of Baldassarre in the enormously popular musical *Maid of the Mountains.* Wontner costarred in three musicals with (Miss) Jose Collins, and in '23 they made a series of films together. Arthur was not, however, primarily known as a musical performer so much as a "romantic lead," and for a time in the teens and twenties he was one of the most sought-after stars on the London stage.

Another of his 1917 parts was that of Julian Rolfe in *The Yellow Ticket*—when the play was filmed, Laurence Olivier got the role. Some of Wontner's next plays were *By Pigeon Post, Our Mr. Hepplewhite, A Voice from the Minaret, Sakuntala,* and *One Night in Rome;* but when in 1920 he attempted to go into management he was not altogether successful, despite the partnership for a time of Lady Wyndam. He seems to have begun at the

Globe Theatre before moving to the Comedy, and although his production of *Romantic Age* was successful enough to warrant a transfer to the Playhouse, another play by Basil Rathbone's kinsman A. A. Milne seems to have failed, and *A Lady Calls on Peter* did not last a month. In '21, Wontner was back acting for others in *Fulfilling of the Law,* and at the St. James' in January of the next year he was starring in Mary Roberts Rhinehart's classic mystery play *The Bat;* his role of Detective Anderson might seem at first to precurse Sherlock Holmes, but of course Anderson turns out to be the malevolent title character himself! Before '22 was out, Arthur played yet another Prince in *The Beating on the Door,* and in '23 he did *Love in Pawn* as Samuel Levi, *Eye of Siva,* and (replacing Bertram Willis) played Czar Peter in *Catherine.* He was also back on the screen that year, making (besides his Jose Collins series) *Bonnie Prince Charlie;* the next year Wontner was playing that Prince's great-uncle, Charles II, in a stage musical by the film's costar, Ivor Novello, entitled *Our Nell* (it ran for 140 performances). "The Merry Monarch" has also been played by radio-Holmes Hardwicke, and his brother James II was played by Rathbone on TV. Wontner and Rathbone have each been cast repeatedly as haughty aristocrats, though the haughtiness of Holmes is entirely of a different variety, being based not on superiority of birth, but on superiority of intellect. Holmes is rude, but no snob.

In '24, Wontner also played (in a benefit for the King's Pension Fund for Actors) in *The Ware Case*—Clive Brook was to star in the film version, although not in Wontner's role. Wontner then went on to replace Robert Lorraine in *Tiger Cats* opposite Edith Evans, and also found time for two more films: Henry Irving's old hit *Eugene Aram* and *The Diamond Man.* In 1925, he was seen in *You and I,* as Wangel in Ibsen's *Lady from the Sea,* in *The Lavender Garden, The Desire for a Change* and *Henry VIII* (as the Duke of Buckingham, in Sir Lewis Casson's production). Wontner played in Shelley's *Cenci, Martinique* and *The Debit Account* in '26 before crossing the Atlantic to make his New York debut at the Empire on the 29th of September as D'arguines in *The Captive* with Rathbone. Arthur stayed in New York to do *Mariners* in March, then returned to London briefly for *The Unknown Woman.* Over the next few years, however, Wontner was to spend a large proportion of his time in the United States, which perhaps partly explains the great and unexpected success his first rather cheaply made Holmes film was to meet in this country. (There are, of course, other salient factors, as we shall see, such as the character of Holmes himself!)

Wontner toured the United States as Sir John Marley in *Interference,* then repeated it for New York audiences before taking the play out on tour again; in the meantime he had been back to London again for a brief run in *The Man They Buried* at the Ambassadors (which has been for the last umpteen years the home of Agatha Christie's seemingly eternal mystery *Mouse-*

Arthur Wontner as the title character in Mary Roberts Rinehart's famous play "The Bat," with Eva Moore as Miss van Gorder.

trap). With '29's *Because Of Irene,* Wontner was back in London for good, although there was later talk of his going to Hollywood. He finished the year in *Time And The Hour.*

In 1930 he filmed *The Message,* was in *This Way To Paradise,* and then returned to the play in which he had made his London debut in the previous century, *The Three Musketeers*—following which, destiny caught up with him as he was cast to play the imitation Holmes character Sexton Blake in the play of that name. Wontner's uncanny resemblance to the original Sidney Paget illustrations of Sherlock himself inescapably struck many observers of the play, and he was immediately signed to play the Baker Street sleuth in the film *The Sleeping Cardinal.* (Previously he had discussed the possibility of a Holmes play with Doyle, but nothing came of it.)

For British audiences Arthur Wontner is as indelibly associated with the character of Sherlock Holmes as is Basil Rathbone for Americans, although the almost birdlike quickness and dynamic energy of the latter's interpretation (in contrast to the deliberate and rather tiresomely ponderous delivery of Wontner) is certainly far closer to Doyle's intentions.

One is perhaps more persuaded when watching Wontner that one is looking at the off-handed Holmes himself and not just a superlatively brilliant actor. Certainly his calmly authoritative manner is one of the reasons why the Wontner series is the favorite of most devout Holmesians (We shall, of course, examine both series later in depth, and contrast their rival merits.)

The Sleeping Cardinal (under the new title of *Sherlock Holmes' Fatal Hour* for American consumption) was highly successful in New York, and ran for over a nearly unprecedented (for a British film) month, much to the shame of Warner Brothers, who had foolishly given it to one of their small subsidiary companies for distribution in the United States. One can sympathize with Warners slightly, though, for a British writer of the time ('31) in *Picturegoer Weekly* frankly labeled the film a "quota quickie"—under British law, distributors and exhibitors must book a certain minimum percentage of British-made product, and the shoestring-budgeted films that often resulted in compliance were the dregs of the industry (but often gave needed employment to great talents on the way up or down).

Mr. William K. Everson has, however, assured the present writers that the film was in fact several cuts above the average "quota" item; certainly the sometimes imaginative sound and lighting effects betray some care lavished on the production, and the small scenic budget is made into a virtue by the great verisimilitude of 221B, which is portrayed as the somewhat tacky and grundgy place it must surely have been within the original financial grasp of a pensioned soldier and the unknown practioner of the unheard of profession of "consulting detective." However, as we shall see, the film sorely misses exteriors.

The *Picturegoer* writer announced that the American success of the film had led to a Hollywood contract for Wontner, and foresaw a George Arliss-type success for him; but the offer apparently came to nothing, for Wontner did not go to Hollywood. His British film career was at its height though, and 1932's *A Gentleman of Paris* cast him as Judge Lefevre, with Vanda Greville as his leading lady and Sybil Thorndike, Peter Lawford (as a child), and former-Dr. Watson Frederick Lloyd all in the cast. That same year Wontner played a Jekyll-Hyde type of character in *Condemned to Death*, with Jane Welsh (from *Sleeping Cardinal*), Edmund Gwenn, and Gillian Lind in support of him (Regrettably this was retitled from the more evocative *Jack O'Lantern*.) The plot strikingly resembled Fritz Lang's famed Dr. Mabuse entry, with an executed murderer exerting an influence on the personality and actions of the Wontner character through hypnosis.

Wontner continued his stage career at the same time, and during '32 he was also in *Napoleon* at the New Theatre in the role of Joseph Fouche, which, as it happened, was to gain Arthur a knighthood—not, however, from the King of England, for it was the insignia of Knight of the Order of the Crown of Italy with which he was decorated! During this same very busy year Wontner returned to his old Granville-Barker success of *Twelfth Night* to attempt the new part of Malvolio, and even managed to squeeze in a run of *Philomel* in November!

And as if this were not enough, two further pictures in Wontner's Holmes series were also released in '32: (*The Strange Case of*) *The Missing Rembrandt* and *The Sign of Four*. In 1933, he was at the Strand Theatre (a good place for Holmesian actors: not only was it the name of the Magazine, but Eille Norwood had played there in 1901) in *Sally Who?*, featuring Wontner as Hugh Perryn. He subsequently played in *The Joker* and *What*

Happened to George, then in '34 took on the role of Pontius Pilate in *Good Friday*, beating Rathbone's film by a year. Wontner replaced Nicholas Hannen in *Without Witness* in May, and in June costarred once again with Sybil Thorndike—this time in the British debut of Bernard Shaw's *Village Wooing*. Wontner was wickedly made up with an enormous beard to look like Lytton Strachey, and with his dark glasses and (naturally) bald head he made a fine subject for the caricaturing pen of Haselden in *Punch* once again. In December, Wontner once again presaged Rathbone (and followed in the footsteps of Saintsbury) when he incarnated Louis XI in *If I Were King*.

The Triumph of Sherlock Holmes and *Line Engaged* were filmed with Wontner in 1935, and on the stage he was in John Barrymore's old vehicle *Justice*, *The Skin Game*, and *Duet by Accident*. His 1936 films were *Dishonor Bright* (with the young George Sanders, whose brother Tom Conway was to be Holmes on radio) and *Second Bureau*, and his sole play *The Great Experiment*. The next year featured Wontner in his last Holmes film, *Siver Blaze*, and also in *Thunder in the City*, *Storm in a Teacup* (scripted by Rendel's *Hound* editor Dalrymple, with Rex Harrison and Vivien Leigh) and *The Live Wire* (remade from the George Pearson picture). On the stage he was charmingly named Major Warminside in *The Day Is Gone*. Wontner devoted himself entirely to the screen in '38, but it is no wonder he forsook the stage when we consider that he appeared in *Just Like a Woman*, *Kate Plus Ten*, *The Terror*, *Thirteen Men and a Gun*, and *Old Iron*. In '39, Arthur was back on the boards as Isaac Goldberg in *Sons Of Adam*, but his theatrical work was now beginning to wind down, though he toured in a play by Agatha Christie during the Second World War and appeared in four more plays in London following it. His film career continued strong, however, and he introduced his characterization of Sherlock Holmes to a new medium in 1943 when he played in the BBC's *Boscombe Valley Mystery* on the radio. His Dr. Watson in that one, Carleton Hobbs, was himself to go on to become *the* voice of the Baker Street Sleuth for the next three decades.

Tragedy struck Arthur Wontner in 1943 also, however, when his first wife died. Born Rosecleer Alice Kingwell, she had been an actress under the name of Rose Pendennis. Wontner later married again, to Florence Eileen Lainchbury. He had two sons and a daughter. In 1943, Arthur was also in *The Life and Death of Colonel Blimp*, but that film is so long that his part is often entirely eliminated when it is scheduled for television. Notable for the remarkable achievement of sympathetically portraying a German in World War II Britain, *Blimp* also features Deborah Kerr (and James Knight, who had last been seen in a *Sexton Blake* picture).

Blanche Fury in '47 paired Wontner with another Sherlock in Stewart Granger; in 1950, Arthur was in *The Elusive Pimpernel*, which had first been made by Maurice Elvey thirty years before, and this time around featured Jack Hawkins and David Niven.

Then in 1951, Wontner conquered yet another medium with his Holmes, when he played the character on TV at the age of seventy-six in conjunction with the Festival of Britain. His most memorable television performance, however, was probably in the male lead of Pinero's *Private Room* with Mary Jerrold. A '52 film was *Brandy for the Parson*, and the next year Wontner was in *Sea Devils* for Raoul Walsh, and had a highly effective role in *Genevieve*, in which he manages to create a very deep impression even though only appearing briefly at the end.

In 1955, Arthur Wontner made his last film. Appropriately enough it was *Three Cases of Murder*, and he was paired with future-Watson Andre Morell; before the end of the year Wontner retired—but only from acting, for he became a used-book dealer, having been a private collector for years, particularly of books on angling (he also collected stamps, played golf, and angled himself). He was sometimes, naturally enough, to be found in a theatrical memorabilia and book shop in London's Barter Street.

His career considered as a whole was, of course, a vast one, for he played more than 250 roles on the stage alone, not to mention the three other media in which he performed; but it is for his Sage of Baker Street that he is best remembered. He made such a devastating effect on British audiences with his interpretation of Sherlock Holmes, which he did not begin to play until he was fifty-six and looking, alas, even a bit older, that when Basil Rathbone made his debut in the part at the age of forty-seven, Graham Greene's review considered that the South African was too "young" for the part—although actually, he was considerably closer to the age of Holmes in the original stories, where it is implied that he was about forty in 1895 (the period of his heydey).

To Americans accustomed to the vivid, electric, brusk, and brisk performances of Rathbone in the role, Wontner must seem more like a slow-moving, elderly retired gentleman than Holmes, for even his diction is rather slurred in an upper-class manner as contrasted with the clipped tones of Basil; but Wontner was idolized in the part by fans, critics, and Holmesians alike, as some of the notes to our accounts of his films will help show. To complete the parallels between the two actors, it is positively frightening to come across the old turn-of-the-century *Strand* illustrations to the stories and find some that could pass for literal portraits of Wontner and others that are dead likenesses of Rathbone. (*see illustrations*)

Wontner was a founding member of British Actors' Equity and its first treasurer. Besides the great actors we have mentioned, he also performed with Sir Henry Irving, Mrs. Patrick Campbell, Sir Herbert Tree, and Sir John Martin-Harvey. For twenty-five years Wontner was a member of the Committee of the Actors' Orphanage, and his portrait hangs in the Garrick Club in London. He also belonged to the Stage Club.

In the thirties Wontner had been living first near Regent's Park, and was later reachable care of The

The Honorable Ronald Adair (Leslie Perrins) is granted an interview with the painted title character of *The Sleeping Cardinal*. The portrait is executed on solid steel, and behind it lurks the voice of Moriarty.

Spotlight (Club) in Cranbourn Street, but when he died in December of 1960, it was at his home in Burnham, Buckinghamshire. He was survived by his second wife, his daughter, and his son, Hugh Wontner, M.V.O., director of the D'oyly Carte Opera Company. Another son, Hilary, became a noted actor and spiritualist (as was Sir Arthur Conan Doyle).

THE SLEEPING CARDINAL; in the United States: **SHERLOCK HOLMES' FATAL HOUR** on screen, but copyrighted as **SHERLOCK HOLMES'S FATAL HOUR**

Date of Release: March or 20 July 1931; copyrighted in the United States, 10 July 1931

Running Time: 7,648 feet; 84 minutes; 75 minutes; 8 reels

Production Company: Twickenham Film Studios Ltd; distributed in Britain by Warner Brothers; distributed in the United States by First Division Pictures Inc. (Harry H. Thomas, President) and AmerAnglo Corp. (Arthur A. Lee, President).

Producer: Julius Hagen

Director: Leslie S. Hiscott

Screenplay: Cyril Twyford, H. Fowler Mear, Leslie S. Hiscott, and Arthur Wontner (some of his own dialogue)

Based on: *The Final Problem*, *The Empty House* and (uncredited) Gillette's play.

Director of Photography: Sidney Boythe (or Blythe)

Assistant: William Luff

Editor and Assistant Director: Jack Harris

Art Director: James Carter

Sound: Baynham Honri; recorded at Twickenham Studios on RCA Photophone system.

Lab Work: George Humphries Co. Ltd.

Wontner accentuated Holmes' pensiveness and gentlemanliness, perhaps at the expense of the sleuth's more manic moods. This outstanding study is also from *The Sleeping Cardinal*.

CAST

Sherlock Holmes	Arthur Wontner
Dr. Watson	Ian Fleming
Mrs. Hudson	Minnie Rayner
Ronald Adair	Leslie Perrins
Kathleen Adair	Jane Welsh
Professor Robert Moriarty	
(Col. Henslowe)	Norman McKinnel
Thomas Fisher	William Frazer
	(or Fazan)
Tony Rutherford	Sidney King
Inspector Lestrade	Philip Hewland
Marstan	Gordon Begg
Col. Sebastian Moran	Louis Goodrich
No. 16	Harry Terry
J. J. Godfrey	Charles Paton

SYNOPSIS: This is another of those hard-to-find films that we were able to screen, so we will treat it in some depth and also print a number of illustrations in order to help give the reader a better notion of the Wontner series as a whole.

The opening robbery-murder sequence is achieved more by the use of sound effects than by sight, for very little is actually visible; but, paradoxically, the sound effects are in themselves rather pedestrian and uninteresting, and the striking impression created by the scene is achieved by the starkly simple lighting effects: most of the screen is pitch dark, with only a slash of light diagonally across the floor of the bank, and another appearing as a door is opened. When the guard is killed, he sprawls dying in the patch of brightness on the floor, as if trying to find in the light safety from the darkness into which he feels himself falling. This eloquent sequence is so good that it is rather disappointing that no other visual or sound

effect in the entire film that follows even comes close to this quality, the film's merits lying more in the acting than the cinematic techniques.

There is indeed some moving camera work in the succeeding card game (and elsewhere in the picture), together with some dissolves; and whenever an excuse can be found for the lights being switched off, some of the dramatic composition of the first scene is echoed; but as a rule the lighting is flat and insipid, and many opportunities for exciting visual exposition are abandoned in favor of boring verbal recapitulation of off-screen action (such as the discovery of Adair's body and the attempts on Holmes' life). Credit must be given for this imaginative use of sound in the first sequence, though—something that was quite remarkable for 1930 when the film was begun.

The card game in the apartments of Ronald Adair (of the Foreign Office) and his sister Kathleen provides a good example of the film's low budget, since a large housefly is clearly visible creeping over the table, rather more out of place in such elegant surroundings than it would be in Mrs. Hudson's (in this film) distinctly lower-class establishment.

Ronald has the disturbing habit of always winning at cards, and when an extra ace is discovered on the floor, the burly Thomas Fisher leaves in a huff, followed shortly by one of the other players. Col. Henslowe, an old friend of the Adairs' father from India, who has only one arm and a rich Scots accent, remains to dispense kindly advice, and another family friend has earlier dropped by for a brief visit—Dr. Watson. As played by Ian Fleming, Watson is rather dapper and in fact behaves with somewhat excessive friendliness to Kathleen, taking her arm in very gallant fashion—this is not, however, a slick charmer, but only a very gentle gentleman. Kathleen wants Watson's advice on Ronald's gambling, and the good Doctor offers to ask Holmes to give the young man a few stern words, but Kathleen is at first afraid that Holmes might "arrest" her brother, though she subsequently agrees. Watson also tries his hand at a little deductive reasoning, and makes out a very good case for identifying the owner of a hat that he picks up from the Adair's table, but though he pronounces the feat "elementary," he turns out (of course) to be quite wrong!

After all the guests have left, there is a pleasant visual effect when Kathleen enters the darkened room where her brother is playing the piano; first she is seen as a dark silhouette against the light of the opened door, and then as she enters and is struck by the single light source she becomes a bright figure against a black background. The glasses that stand on the table are filled with light, acting like lenses in the dark room. Ronald is called out by a sudden message, allegedly to the Foreign Office, and after he leaves the butler creeps into the room to examine the extra card as the sequence ends.

We are now transported to Baker Street, but before we get an actual glimpse of Holmes' and Watson's rooms, the screen is filled by the newspaper which is

Ian Fleming's very dapper and chivalrous Dr. Watson seems to be getting a bit overchummy with the troubled Kathleen Adair (Jane Welsh) in *The Sleeping Cardinal*.

being perused by the latter, describing the murder in the bank strongroom, and the fact that no money appears to be missing. Watson himself is enjoying an after-breakfast smoke with his paper (he indulges in cigarettes à la Roland Young, as well as his pipe), while Mrs. Hudson clears the table.

Minnie Rayner, in this role, presents a very different image from Mary Gordon of the Rathbone series: Rayner is fatter, a bit more slovenly, and somewhat more tacky in appearance with her pendulous earrings; and far from being a restrained Scotswoman, she is very much a boisterous Cockney. But she is quite warm as a motherly image, and seems to be on a very much more equal footing with her lodgers; positively chummy, in fact, and far from formal. It is a delightful characterization, and Mrs. Hudson is far more central to the action of this film than she is in any of the Rathbone films; indeed, she is the leading lady.

Our first epic-making glimpse of Wontner as Holmes is considerably delayed for heightened interest, and we hear his disembodied voice before we see him: at last, fifteen minutes after the beginning of the film, Holmes peers his undeniable head around the corner of his old easy chair, puffing on his curved

and drooping pipe and surrounded by books, and delivers the wonderful line, "My dear Mrs. Hudson, you've always been a temptation to me," assuring her that he is serious by truthfully adding that "jokes are not my strong point." His dressing gown is refreshingly shabby-looking, contrasting markedly with Rathbone's elegantly tailored and immaculate number.

Holmes' obligatory opening deduction is brought up to 1930's date by a reference to the batteries being run down on Watson's car, and the Doctor of course pronounces Sherlock's feat "rather wonderful," prompting the rejoinder (what else?): "Elementary, my dear Watson!" Holmes at first seems ready, in his usual thoughtless fashion, to let the poor Mrs. Hudson struggle with no aid whatsoever out the door with the tea tray, but then, uncharacteristically, he actually holds the door open for her—surely a first!

"Have you ever heard of Robert Moriarty?" the detective asks his colleague (using the Gillettian first name for the Professor); Watson astonishingly seems to entirely disbelieve even in the existence of the said Professor. Holmes goes on to give the audience a clue as to the archcriminal's identity in the film by suggesting that Moriarty may even be disguised as someone with whom Watson is acquainted. Inspector Lestrade (pronounced here with a long *a*) now enters

Peeping out from behind his chair is Arthur Wontner, affording us the very-first-ever glimpse on screen of himself in the role of the Great Detective, in *The Sleeping Cardinal*.

Holmes (Arthur Wontner) explains to Watson (Ian Fleming) how to calculate the amount of pound notes that can be wrapped up in a particular sheet of brown wrapping paper found at the scene of a crime.

and agrees with Watson in ranking Holmes' faith in Moriarty as the monarch of crime with a belief in the Easter Bunny; but Holmes notes to the inspector: "You and I so often disagree," thus clueing in new members of the audience that Lestrade's opinion is not to be given too much credence. The police detective and the private discuss the bank murder, and Holmes makes a great deal of a seemingly useless clue—a piece of brown paper found in the safe, eventually evolving the hypothesis that the paper was used to wrap up counterfeit bank notes, which were taken into the vault and substituted for those that were stolen, thus accounting for the fact that no shortage was discovered. He advises the Inspector to have all the ports watched so that the stolen notes cannot be smuggled abroad, and even calculates how many notes could have fit in the brown parcel (by folding it at the creases, etc.)

The scene now switches again to Ronald Adair, who is not in the Foreign Office but is being brought blindfolded through a sliding door for an interview with "The Sleeping Cardinal". After Adair is left seated alone in the room, the lights go down everywhere except on a painting of that tired prelate (where they intensify), and the hollow voice of Professor Moriarty booms out from nowhere discernible. The Cardinal blackmails Adair into using his diplomatic passport to smuggle out the booty, and so incenses the poor fellow that he takes a punch at the painting—but, alas, the Professor has taken the precaution (as he tells us) of having the picture executed on steel, and poor Ronald does himself an injury. The alternative he is offered for compliance is a gun in a box on the desk, thoughtfully furnished by the spurious Sacred Prince.

We return now to 221B, which is an excellent set indeed—just the sort of digs one would expect to be tenanted by two old single men; one feels that perhaps

if the cushions were removed from one of the easy chairs, one might find last week's dirty laundry ferreted away. The famous "VR" of bullet holes is not to be detected on the walls, but there are the pair of crossed assegais, and under them an animal skin is hanging. One feels that perhaps Dr. Watson was at sea like Dr. Conan Doyle (since they both went to Edinburgh University), as there are tiny sailing-ship replicas in use as bookends; the books themselves are very numerous. There is a small alligator on the table, and a soda syphon for whiskey.

Kathleen Adair is paying a call to the premises continuing to be concerned about her brother. Holmes assures her that he can persuade the young man to cease cheating at cards, and delivers himself of

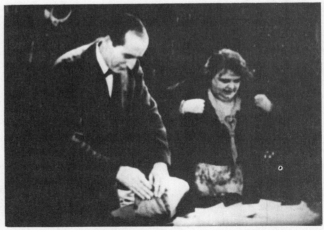

Holmes (Wontner) completes his brown-paper experiment as Mrs. Hudson (Minnie Rayner) prepares to bustle out of the house on a fool's errand to which she has been unsuspectingly sent by a messenger of Moriarty.

some classic lines like "Ha! I thought so." Mrs. Hudson is so ready at the door to show Miss Adair out that the conclusion is inescapable that the old landlady has been listening; Mrs. Hudson has apparently just come from the kitchen or else has been too slovenly to change out of her grimy apron.

Dr. Watson now receives a mysterious phone call from someone he does not know, requesting his medical services in an emergency and giving their name as Smith: "I seem to know that name," says Holmes, tipping alert members of the audience to the deception that is to follow. Watson asks Holmes to take down the address for him and the detective scrawls on a piece of paper which he gives to the doctor and then complacently speeds him on his way. In the meantime, a rather shabby looking Cockney street urchin, a small girl, has called at Mrs. Hudson's stuccoed kitchen doorway, which has a delightful back-alley ambiance, and so aggravates the stout lady with some involved story that the latter fastens on her enormous hat with an enormous pin and explains to Holmes that she, too, must temporarily go out for a moment. When he is left alone in the house, Holmes becomes all action, peering out the window, arming himself with a pistol, clapping his hands and rubbing the palms together with delighted excitement, and finally hastening to sit down with his pipe so that he will be ready to receive his expected guest—for Moriarty has, of course, lured everyone else away so that he might have a private interview with the Great Detective.

When the professor at last makes his entrance, he is so bundled up that he is almost totally unrecognizable. With his enormous scarf, dark glasses, and cane he rather strongly resembles the character of mole in the comic strip *Pogo*. The succeeding action between the two great nemeses is drawn very closely from William Gillette's play, although it is not so credited (in the American titles at least)—of course this scene originally derives from Doyle's story *Final Problem*.

Although Moriarty produces a small pistol, the exchange between the two great intellects is carried on in a highly civilized and polite (if somewhat sarcastic) fashion, with Holmes courteously inviting the Professor to sit down. As in the play, the Professor displays a surprisingly bad memory, being forced to consult his pocket notebook in order to recall the exact dates on which he was incommoded by the detective—these are, of course, updated to such recent vintages as '29. Holmes explains to Moriarty that before Watson had left he had given him a note which contained, instead

Arthur Wontner as Holmes interviews the Emperor of Crime (Norman McKinnel, foreground) in a scene lifted without credit from William Gillette's play.

146

Seen from the opposite angle is Professor Moriarty, clad in his Gillettian scarf.

of the Smith address, a request to return to the Baker Street chambers in five minutes; so the Professor is necessarily brief in his threats. Before he leaves, he is warned by Holmes that he should "never give way to sudden impulses," and after Watson returns, the sleuth explains to him that Moriarty has erred in visiting him, for the Professor has enabled both his dental work and his boots to be noted (although Holmes was so transparently obvious when he eyed the boots that it is difficult to believe that Moriarty did not notice his interest). Holmes further reveals that the brown paper found in the vault bears the remains of a label identifying it as having come from the Professor's bootmakers (who, as it happens, also supply footwear to the Doctor). Upon first catching sight of the fantastically garbed Moriarty, Watson is given the priceless line: "What's the matter with him?"—one of the questions, of course, with which entire books have perplexed themselves in vain.

The scene naturally switches at this point to the boot-shop basement, where a notably tame-looking edition of Col. Sebastian Moran is holding forth in person, and the voice of Moriarty is heard over a speaker in the ceiling, slyly abusing "that great detective, Dr. Watson," and his illustrious friend. Pending the imminent arrival of that duo, a door is made to appear unused by spraying cobwebs over it (a clever use of a commonplace studio device to create an unusual screen effect). Holmes arrives clad in exactly the same sort of modern hat worn by Rathbone and Brook in their updated adventures, and wearing a dark overcoat. It is worth noting that even without the traditional Sherlockian costume of deerstalker and inverness, Wontner is unmistakably the great detective himself, his incarnation being almost more spiritual and psychological rather than physical. Watson cannot credit the notion that his very own bootmaker might be up to anything un-English, and says, "I say Holmes, this does seem rather absurd"; but Holmes silently inspects the room in what Doyle has

referred to as his "Red Indian" character, leaving Lestrade and his men (who have accompanied him) to occupy themselves with the more obvious business; Sherlock, of course, turns up the concealed press used to print the counterfeit notes, and after he and Lestrade break down the cobwebbed door they also find the inoffensive Watson bound and gagged in a chair in the "Cardinal's" secret room, whither he had been spirited from a cabinet he was helpfully inspecting.

The action now returns to Baker Street, where we see Holmes taking his pipe tobacco not from his immortal Persian slipper, but from an ordinary cylinder, although this lapse in Sherlockiana is mitigated by his lighting his pipe with a coal drawn from the fire with a pair of tongs—a charming sequence. The striking parallels that exist between Holmes and Moriarty are pointed up in a bit of dialogue here, as Watson asks how Moriarty could have known about a certain point at issue, and Holmes rejoins, "How do I know?"—rather harking back to the 1908 Holmes film where he solved the ape murder more by intuition than cold reason.

Switching back to Ronald Adair's study, we return to the imaginative use of sound of the beginning sequence for a moment, when on-screen we see only the motionless form of Adair slumped over his table, and off-screen we hear the sound of a door breaking in. It must be emphasized that this disassociation of image from sound, though commonplace today, was highly original in the "Mickey Mousing" days of 1931, and undoubtedly Baynham Honri is to be given the credit for these innovative techniques, since the soundman was a rather more creative figure than director Hiscott. A touching moment follows when we glimpse Adair's weeping old serving woman, whose hair is tied up in rags to be set—yet another glimpse of lower-class London we are afforded in this film (and seldom in most other Holmes films).

In the investigation that follows, Holmes provokingly tells Lestrade, "You carry on, I'll just amuse myself," and proceeds to amuse himself with his magnifying glass—seated, of course, while everyone else in the room is standing! In the interview with Col. Henslowe, Holmes displays his wide-ranging grasp of obscure learning when he demonstrates himself knowledgeable enough about tiger-hunting to trip up the old India hand.

"I say, Lestrade, this is grotesque," says Watson when Kathleen is accused of her brother's murder; but Holmes, far from offering to help the poor girl, merely remains sitting complacently like a grinning Buddha, before bestirring himself to demonstrate that Ronald was shot through the window—thus ushering in the sequence of the film that is drawn from *The Empty House*. Moriarty has once again succeeded in clearing the area for his nefarious doings by luring away the police with fights in pubs and other such seamy diversions. Having disposed of Adair, he proceeds to close in on Holmes, and after a number of

147

(off-screen) attempts on the detective's life the scene is set for the climax.

As Holmes reclines in his easy chair in Baker Street, clasping his hands in feverish thought, Dr. Watson attempts to take the detective's temperature, having earlier wondered with Lestrade if Sherlock was "all there." Holmes has indeed been comporting himself in a rather abstracted way, preoccupied as he is with the case. Wontner's Holmes, far from being the mere "action-adventure" figure of so many other portrayers of the role, is very much the man of thought, and spends a good bit more of his time in deduction than derring-do. Now, while he is speaking, we suddenly see the pieces fall together in his mind as his voice trails off in the middle of a sentence and his face is suffused with a beatific calm. He shortly gives a clue to those dense members of the audience who need one by referring obliquely to the Scots.

There is a nice silhouette of Moriarty ascending the stairs of the empty house across the way from 221B, and then we see the Professor level his gun at what seems to be the silhouette of Holmes behind his window shade. But as a gunshot disposes of Sherlock's shadow, the lights come up in the empty house and Moriarty is apprehended. We are then treated to a delightful shot of the portly Mrs. Hudson stretched on the floor covered with bits of plaster from the bust of Holmes which that lady has been pluckily holding up to the window shade (unlike in the original story, it is a bust of Holmes himself, and not of Caesar).

"Really, Mr. Holmes, this is a bit too much," says the long-suffering landlady, who is rewarded by Holmes be being told she is "far above ordinary women."

When the police show Holmes Moriarty's specially made rifle, Holmes, the connoisseur, cannot resist admiring the workmanship of what was nearly the instrument of his own death. With a disdain for vulgar publicity, Holmes tells Lestrade that he will not appear in the case himself but resign all credit to Scotland Yard: "It's not easy to throw dust in your eyes, Lestrade," he says, and goes on to explain that he deduced the true identity of Moriarty by the first molar on the upper left, which was "badly filled with gold." And who is Moriarty? Why, none other than Col. Henslowe, who is exposed as having faked both his missing arm and his Scotch burr. The alert viewer may perhaps already have noted the similarity in Norman McKinnel's resonant intonation for both characters, but actually the disguise is quite a good one. The chameleonlike ability of complete disguise is, of course, yet another of the Holmes-Moriarty common traits.

When he is unmasked, Moriarty lapses from suave intellectual gentleman to savage beast, and tries to throttle Holmes in sheer desperate pique, having to be restrained by almost everyone in the room for the film's only burst of really physical action. "We shall meet again, Mr. Holmes," is his parting prophecy; though when they do so two episodes later, Norman McKinnel will have metamorphasized into the some-

Moriarty unmasked by Holmes, with his "missing" arm revealed. Again we see a beast at bay looking out from the eyes of the evil mathematician. From left: Phillip Hewland as Inspector Lestrade, McKinnel, Wontner.

what bulkier shape of Lyn Harding. Holmes, for his part, is comforted after his near-scrape with a motherly pat on the back by Mrs. Hudson—something one could not visualize transpiring between Rathbone and Mary Gordon, whose relationship was far more formal.

Holmes, Watson, and Lestrade now settle themselves down to some stiff drinks—these are highly "clubbable" fellows; but Holmes betrays his incorrigi-

Minnie Rayner clears the breakfast table for her two star boarders. Arthur Wontner at left; note the cigarette in Ian Fleming's mouth. *The Sleeping Cardinal*, 1931.

148

bly Bohemian untidiness by taking off his shoes and putting them up on Mrs. Hudson's clean table in order to don his slippers. The landlady is of course outraged by this all-too-typical mistreatment of her furniture, and in order to placate her, the Sage puts a handkerchief on his shoulder and takes up his violin, charming Mrs. Hudson out of her fury with his melodious strains.

For a film made on a tightly limited budget in a "tin hut" film studio, *Sleeping Cardinal* is a very good film indeed, owing mainly to the quietly authoritative performance of Wontner and the humorously understated one of Fleming, but also because the very paucity of the budget has contributed to a gritty flavor of lower-class realism in a few incidental scenes—a quality that almost convinces more than the lushly "period" effects of some of the bigger-budgeted Holmesian epics.

Wontner's Holmes contrasts with most other interpretations of the role by his accentuation of Holmes' humorously detached view of most human activities, coupled with a sort of indulgently kind treatment of his mental inferiors—the incorrigible eccentricity is not at all missing, but only handled more subtly and, hence, believably.

REVIEW (*Picturegoer Weekly*, 25 July 1931, by Lionel Collier):

> One of Conan Doyle's stories, which proves that he still has no peer as a creator of crime fiction.
> The intricate plot is very well worked out and Arthur Wontner's rendering of Sherlock Holmes wholly convincing, even to the smallest mannerisms.
> Naturally the picture depends rather more on its dialogue than its action, but there is not a moment when your interest is allowed to flag. Looking realistically sinister, Norman McKinnel makes a very convincing Prof. Moriarty. [Here Collier gives the whole plot away, of course!]
> I found, however, that Ian Fleming was a little stagey as our friend Watson, but after all, it is a very difficult part, since even in fiction the character is somewhat difficult to believe in. I take my hat off to Leslie Hiscott for getting so much out of a difficult screen subject.

The distinguished Sherlockian Vincent Starret wrote: "No better Sherlock Holmes than Arthur Wontner is likely to be seen and heard in pictures in our time . . . his detective is the veritable fathomer of Baker Street in person."

Ian Fleming was Wontner's Watson in four of the five movies in the series—it should hardly be necessary to add that he was *not* the same person as the author of the "James Bond" stories! (In the American release-print of *Sleeping Cardinal*, our Ian's first name is mistakenly given as "Jan.")

Ian Fleming, who was the perfect English gentleman on screen, was, like many another classic "English" type, born outside the confines of the British Isles—in Melbourne, Australia, to be precise,

on 10 September 1888. He made his film debut in *The Ware Case* in 1928—a subject that was later to be filmed with Clive Brook and that was played on the stage by Arthur Wontner. Other than his series of Watson portrayals, in which he was properly ineffectual without seeming to be a complete dolt, Fleming's other films included *The Crouching Beast*, '35 (directed by former Stoll staffer W. Victor Hanbury); *When Thief Meets Thief*, '37; *The Lion Has Wings*, '39 (with fellow-Watson Ralph Richardson); *The Briggs Family*, '40; *Hatter's Castle*, '41 (a tiny but important role as Sir John); *Appointment with Crime, George in Civvy Street* (both '46); *Captain Boycott*, '47 (with future-Holmes Stewart Granger); *Quartet*, with André Morell, his fellow Dr. Watson, '48; *Woman in Question*, '50 (known in the United States as *5 Angles on Murder*); *Norman Conquest*, '53 (an episode of the detective series with radio-Holmes Tom Conway); *Murder Will Out* the same year (the title had earlier been used by Rathbone series director Roy William Neill); *High Flight*, '57; *Bluebeard's Ten Honeymoons*, '59; *Too Hot to Handle*, '60 (with Christopher Lee, who was to play Holmes two years later; released in the United States as *Playgirl After Dark*); *Trials of Oscar Wilde*, '60 (the real-life Marquis of Queensbury in this is thought to have inspired *The Sign of Four*—also known as *The Man With the Green Carnation* and *The Green Carnation*); *No, My Darling Daughter*, '61; and a final detective story with 1965's *Return of Mr. Moto*.

The only one of the Wontner series in which Fleming did not play Dr. Watson was *The Sign of Four*, in which he was replaced by Ian Hunter for the same reason that had caused Hubert Willis to be dropped for Arthur Cullin: a younger man was wanted to romance Mary Morstan. Actually, Fleming would have been quite capable of this chore himself, judging by the mildly romantic byplay he has with Jane Welsh in *Sleeping Cardinal*; but he was perhaps judged to have too mild a presence for a heartthrob.

If not as noticeable a Watson as Bruce or Willis, or as

Moriarty disguised as the one-armed India Campaign veteran Col. Henslowe (Norman McKinnel).

vigorous a one as Morell or Houston, Fleming struck exactly the right balance with the character. He does not miss the comedy inherent in the part, but stops well short of making him ridiculous; one feels that his sedate company was just the unobtrusive sort Sherlock Holmes would have wanted in a roommate, whereas the Watson of Reginald Owen was so strident and bumptious that he surely would have driven poor Holmes up the walls!

Ian Fleming died in London on the first day of 1969.

Norman McKinnel makes a splendid Moriarty in this film, though he perhaps enjoyed playing the Col. Henslow sequences more, since he was able to make richly theatrical use of his native Scots accent; for, like his fellow Napoleon of Crime, Ernest Torrence, Mrs. Hudson Mary Gordon, and Conan Doyle himself, McKinnel was born in Caledonia—in Dumfries, specifically. McKinnel was a major figure on the British stage, and the author of the highly successful play *The Bishop's Candlesticks*. In 1911, McKinnel was in *Money* with Lyn Harding, who years later was to replace him as Moriarty in the Wontner series. He starred in *The Truth About Gladys* by Rathbone's kinsman A. A. Milne for 124 performances in 1921, and three years later he was personally praised for his performance in the George Arliss part in Galsworthy's *Old English*, though the production itself was not a success.

That immortal portrayer of Sherlock Holmes H. A. Saintsbury was also a shrewd critic, and in his book, *Letters Of An Unsuccessful Actor*, he makes the following prophetic comments on McKinnel (in the play, *The Lost Leader*):

> I could not accept Norman McKinnel as the embodiment of Parnell. I have always thought of Parnell as a sympathetic person and McKinnel in any part that is not, at least, sinister is—well, in my opinion, unsuited.
>
> McKinnel's case is similar to that of that very brilliant actor Charles Cartwright, who never failed, until, under his own management, he insisted on playing the hero.

Norman McKinnel made his film debut in 1915 with *The Shulamite* for Harold Shaw at London Films (who made several Conan Doyle subjects and many Hubert Willis pictures). Some of McKinnel's other early films were *Dombey and Son*, 1917, *Hindle Wakes*, '18, and its remake nine years later; all three of which were directed by Norwood series originator Maurice Elvey. McKinnel was in *Pillars of Society* for G. B. Samuelson (who had also produced the *Hindle*) in 1920, and made the World War I propaganda film *Eat Less Bread*. Six feet tall, Norman McKinnel made an ideal Professor Moriarty, encompassing the Emperor of Crime's animal ferocity as well as his subtle cunning. Throughout *The Sleeping Cardinal*, he plays his role with the same brand of humor that Arthur Wontner brought to Holmes—neither actor was guying his character; rather, both were playing characters who stood somewhat outside the mainstream of human

Norman McKinnel, Professor Moriarty in *The Sleeping Cardinal*, seen here without makeup.

endeavor and smiled indulgently on mere mankind (yet another of the Holmes-Moriarty parallels, of course).

Sleeping Cardinal's director, Leslie S. Hiscott, was to direct two more episodes of this series—*The Missing Rembrandt* in '32 and *Triumph of Sherlock Holmes* in '35. Of the remaining two in the series, some continuity was offered in '32's *Sign of Four* as well, since it was produced by the director of one of the Clive Brook series, Basil Dean. The final (1937) Wontner episode, *Silver Blaze*, was directed by a newcomer in Thomas Bentley but had a script coauthored by H. Fowler Mear, who had worked on three of the previous entries.

Leslie Hiscott may have done rather pedestrian work, but he surely deserves some credit for getting this series off to such a good start and for encouraging the creative work of Honri, Boythe, and Wontner. Born in London in 1894, Hiscott began his film career in Italy (like his fellow Twickenham staffer, George A. Cooper) in 1919, later becoming an assistant director for the British branch of Famous Players-Lasky. Although he was also a novelist, most of his prolific directorial output was frankly "quota quickie" in nature, though frequently (as with *Sleeping Cardinal*) he was able to transcend this classification to a degree. Hiscott began his career as a director with the *Mrs. May* series in 1925, and made several other silents, but he did not really hit his full stride until he made his first sound picture in 1930—*At the Villa Rose*, a remake of the old Maurice Elvey picture. During the next six years, Leslie Hiscott would direct nearly four dozen feature films! A few of the more notable of these, mostly made at Twickenham (like his Holmes films) or for British Lion at Beaconsfield, were the following: *The House of the Arrow*, '30; *Alibi* and *Black Coffee*, '31; *Murder at Covent Garden, The Crooked Lady* (with "Mrs. Watson" Isobel Elsom), *Double Dealing,* and *When London Sleeps*—all in '32. Also that year Hiscott directed former-Holmes Raymond Massey in the remake of the old C. Aubrey Smith detective picture *Face at The Window.*

Picturegoer Weekly devoted some space to the production, which also featured "Mrs. Watson" Isla Bevan and a Watson-type specimen of "Boobus Britanicus." "Twickenham is giving us another of its murder-mystery-horror-thrill specialties," said the magazine, suggesting that the studio was in some ways a forerunner of Hammer. Miss Bevan, the writer noted, "is very well suited to this melodramatic type of film . . . I am glad Twickenham has got under way again; they generally have an interesting cast there, and an interesting story, even if it is apt to be bloodcurdling."

Later that year the magazine compared the Twickenham staffers to the Bab Ballad character Simple James: " 'A deed of blood, and fire and flames/Was meat and drink to Simple James' . . . [Twickenham] particularly enjoy a good obscure murder." It is interesting to recall that the two major talkie Sherlock Holmes series (Wontner and Rathbone) were each made by studios that were heavily identified with horror films—Twickenham and Universal. This may demonstrate that the appeal of the Holmes stories does not lie entirely in their brilliant character studies, but that, for the average moviegoer at least, the melodrama of the plots is also a key factor; *The Hound,* of course, is by far the most popular story for screen purposes.

Face in the Window was subsequently filmed once again, in '39 with stage Holmes, Tod Slaughter.

To resume the career of Leslie Hiscott, in 1933 he made (among many other films) *The Stolen Necklace, Stickpin* (with Francis L. Sullivan from *Missing Rembrandt*), and *Marooned*; '34 saw *Flat No. 3, Passing Shadows, Crazy People,* and *The Big Splash; Annie Leave the Room, Death on the Set, Three Witnesses, Inside the Room,* and *A Fire Has Been Arranged* were all made in '35. After this date Hiscott's career began to wind down a little, to the extent that during the next year he directed only three films, as compared to the eight or twelve features he had been accustomed to knocking off in that span of time. Hiscott remade another Maurice Elvey feature with 1937's *Fine Feathers;* Hiscott's 1940 version of *Tilly of Bloomsbury* was the third of that subject: G. B. Samuelson (in another Holmesian link) having produced it in '21, and Sydney Howard having appeared in the '31 edition as well as in

Hiscott's. Some of Hiscott's other films were *The Seventh Survivor*, '41, *The Butler's Dilemma*, '43, *The Time of His Life*, '55, and *Tons of Trouble*, '56. As Hiscott's directorial chores gradually became fewer, he turned to production management. In his long career he was associated with comedy quite as much as with mystery, but like so many of the once-prominent figures in our book, if he is remembered at all today it is for his connection with Sherlock Holmes.

In 1931 *Picturegoer* described Leslie Hiscott as "a typical Englishman, tall and clean limbed," and said "his *House of the Arrow* and *Sleeping Cardinal* have made British talkie history." He died in 1968, never having had his prolific career reevaluated like those of so many American directors of "Bs" have been; the merits of *Sleeping Cardinal* and his other Wontners suggest that some of his other "quickies" might bear a second look.

THE MISSING REMBRANDT; THE STRANGE CASE OF THE MISSING REMBRANDT

Date of Release: February or 20 August 1932; United States copyright 18 May 1932

Fleming looks more like the expected image of Watson in this double-pipes shot with Wontner from *The Missing Rembrandt*, **second in their series. The detail on the walls of 221B is splendidly done. (Courtesy National Film Archives of the British Film Institute)**

Running Time: 7588 feet; 8 reels; 84 minutes
Production Company: Twickenham Film Studios,
  Ltd; PDC; copyrighted in United States by First
  Anglo Corporation
Producer: Julius Hagen Productions
Director: Leslie S. Hiscott
Screenplay: Cyril Twyford, H. Fowler Mear and
  Arthur Wontner
Based on: *Charles Augustus Milverton*
(British "A" or "U" Certificate)

CAST

Sherlock Holmes	Arthur Wontner
Lady Violet Lumsden	Jane Welsh
Claude (or Claud) Holford	Miles Mander
Baron von Guntermann	Francis L. Sullivan
Dr. Watson	Ian Fleming
Carlo Ravelli	Dino Galvani
Pinkerton Man	Ben Welden
Inspector Lestrade	Philip Hewland
Mrs. Hudson	Minnie Rayner
Marquess de Chaminade	Anthony Holles
Manning	Herbert Lomas
Chang Wu	Takase

SYNOPSIS: The second of the Wontner series, this
one began filming before the end of December 1931,
and was completed early the next year. The plot
expanded Doyle's story considerably, and transformed the blackmailer Milverton into an unscrupu-
lous American millionaire art dealer, who forces an
opium-addicted artist to steal a Rembrandt from the
Louvre and also (in an echo of *Scandal in Bohemia* and
the Gillette play) some compromising letters from
Lady Violet.

The sets included an elaborate opium den in
London's Chinatown (Limehouse), and cast carry-
overs from the last episode included not only Wontner,
Fleming, and Hiscott, but Jane Welsh and scripters
Mear and Twyford. Philip Hewland repeated as
Lestrade, but the character did not appear in the next
episode, and when Lestrade returned for the last two
of the series he was played by two different actors.
Minnie Rayner remained on as Mrs. Hudson in all but
the next picture (which was for a different studio).

Miles Mander was later to reappear in several
episodes of the Rathbone series across the Atlantic.

REVIEW (*Picturegoer Weekly*, 20 August 1932, by
Lionel Collier):

c** (Good; also suitable for children)
  Arthur Wontner is "Sherlock Holmes", and in this
picture he is excellent, giving a characterization
which makes Conan Doyle's famous detective "live"
on the screen.
  The tracking down of a master criminal who hides
his activities under the cloak of a respectable art
dealer is intriguing and Holmes's deductions are
well pointed.
  Hiscott has, perhaps, failed to get much movement into his story, but this deficiency is amply made

up for by the excellent way in which he has directed
Arthur Wontner, on whom the main interest is
continually focused.
  The atmosphere of Baker Street and Limehouse
are realistic, and all through respect has been paid to
the tradition with which this famous character is
inseparable.

THE SIGN OF FOUR

Date of Release: May or September 1932; United
  States copyright 14 August 1932, and released there
  that same month.
Running Time: 6,897 feet; 7 reels; 75 minutes; 76
  minutes
Production Company: A.R.P. Studios; Associated
  Talking Pictures Ltd. (later known as Ealing
  Studios) in conjunction with the American com-
  pany Radio; released in the United States by World
  Wide.
Executive Producer: Basil Dean
Producer: Rowland V. Lee
Director: Graham Cutts (although some sources have
  credited both producers with a hand in the direc-
  tion).
Director of Photography: Robert de Grasse
(British "U" Certificate)

CAST

Sherlock Holmes	Arthur Wontner
Mary Morstan	Isla Bevan
Dr. Watson	Ian Hunter
Jonathan Small	Ben Soutten
Thaddeus Sholto	Miles Malleson
Major Sholto	Herbert Lomas
Inspector Athelney Jones	Gilbert Davis
Bailey	Roy Emerton

**Sherlock Holmes (Arthur Wontner) pours on the
insincere charm in search of useful clues to the
mystery of *The Sign of Four*, disguised effectively as
an old tar. (Courtesy National Film Archives of the
British Film Institute)**

Another scene from *The Missing Rembrandt* with even more Sherlockian detail. Pictured are Wontner, Rayner, and Fleming in their usual roles.

Holmes (Wontner) at his perennial violin in *The Sign of Four*. (Courtesy National Film Archives of the British Film Institute)

Bartholomew Sholto	Kynaston Reeves
Captain Morstan	Edgar Norfolk
Mrs. Hudson	Clare Greet
Tonga	Togo
Tattoo Artist	Mr. Burchett

SYNOPSIS: The film was fairly faithful to the Doyle novel, although surely Miles Malleson and Kynaston Reeves must have been totally unbelievable as twins! Also, the character of Holmes himself was made rather more vigorous and athletic than Wontner was accustomed to play him, apparently because producer Lee wanted to make the Great Detective into a somewhat more virile and conventionally romantic character. Wontner wore the same modern hat he had worn in *Sleeping Cardinal* in lieu of deerstalker, and was also burdened with an ankle-length overcoat.

Ian Hunter at the age of only thirty-two was perhaps the most youthful of all screen Watsons, and could have passed for Holmes' son—Wontner was fifty-seven at the time, and Fleming had been forty-four when the previous picture was made. A youthful Watson is, of course, required in this story, however, to woo Mary Morstan—though some reviewers apparently thought the romance had been added by the filmmakers!

Since this film was made for one of Twickenham's rivals, Minnie Rayner and Philip Hewland were absent, but Herbert Lomas oddly enough was carried over from *The Missing Rembrandt*, though not in the same role.

REVIEWS: The film was criticized for poor lighting and photography, and Lionel Collier had this to say about it in the 24 September 1932 *Picturegoer Weekly:*

> Conan Doyle's story loses most of its grip in this picturisation. This is because a prologue at the beginning practically gives the whole plot away and leaves the matter of detection too obvious to be interesting to any great extent.
>
> The story concerns a treasure revealed to a certain Major Sholto, commandant of a convict settlement, by a convict.
>
> Sholto finds it, murders his companion, and returns to England. Terrified on learning that the convict has escaped, Sholto makes his two sons send a valuable string of pearls, anonymously, to his murdered companion's daughter.
>
> The girl is worried by the threatening letters she receives and calls in Sherlock Holmes, who clears up the mystery.
>
> Arthur Wontner is, as usual, a perfect Holmes and Isla Bevan quite a good heroine.

Two *Picturegoer* interviews that were made on the set of this film during shooting are worth quoting from. The 13 February issue contains this one:

> At Ealing this week I received a sharp rebuke from a corpse. I was standing on the *Sign of Four* set, critically inspecting a dummy head of a murdered

man which just showed over the back of a chair, and which, they told me, had been there for four days.

"It's hair looks a bit stringy," I remarked; "What's the idea of that?" "There is an old and honoured motto," the dummy reminded me, turning round and fixing me with a stern eye: "*De Mortuis nil nisi bonum.*"

Then I realised it was Kynaston Reeves, a clever actor whom I've known for about eight years.

"I've been dead four days. . . . The others simply act round me; I know all their parts by this time, word for word. I listen as from another world, and musn't even prompt them."

The interviewer went on to praise the atmospheric sets that were built for the film, and particularly singled out the 221B sitting room as looking so realistic that it seems to have been lifted bodily out of a real house and set down on the sound stage. In addition, his testimony that Basil Dean directed at least some of the film, despite the directorial credit to Graham Cutts alone, was especially valuable as coming from an eyewitness.

Kynaston Reeves was a descendant of the seventeenth-century Shakespearean actor Ned Kynaston. Born in 1893, his film career stretched from 1919 to 1970, the year before his death, when he appeared in *Anne of the Thousand Days*. Reeves appeared with Christopher Lee in *Captain Horatio Hornblower, R.N.* in '51; with Lee's Watson, Thorley Walters, in *Carlton-Browne of the F.O.* in '59, and is credited by two sources with appearing in *Sherlock Holmes*: we have not been able to find him in the credits of any of the films that have bourne that title, but it seems likely that Reeves could have played one of his innumerable bits in one of the London-filmed sequences of the Barrymore version. Reeves' part may even have been cut from the final print, as was his role in the Twickenham *Frail Women*, directed by Maurice Elvey in '32.

The next interview appeared on 5 March, and was with the actress who played Dr. Watson's future wife in *Sign of Four*, Isla Bevan. The interviewer would seem to have been rather taken with Miss Bevan, describing her as "Slim . . . young . . . green-eyed . . . blonde," with "scarlet finger nails" and "vivid red lips." He seems to find it hard to comprehend that the actress had only left a Belgian convent three or four years previously.

Speaking in her dressing room waiting to be made up while a scene was in process of being filmed, Isla rambled over an assortment of topics: "My grandfather was Frank Danby, the comedian. . . . I've got to confess that I adore bull fights. Oughtn't I to? Perhaps not." She had been picked out of the chorus by Noel Coward for *Bitter Sweet*, and subsequently was on the stage in the United States: "Looking back upon it it seems to me that I scarcely ever slept; there were so many parties." Miss Bevan seems to have overlooked the presence in the film of Mrs. Hudson, unless the landlady was added to the cast later, for she says that "I am playing the only feminine role in *The Sign of Four*." With Isobel Elsom, she is the only one ever to have actually played Mrs. John H. Watson on the screen,

154

In another characteristic scene from *Sign of Four*, Wontner seems to have sprung directly from the pen of Sidney Paget. (Courtesy National Film Archives of the British Film Institute)

although that patient lady (Watson was so often over at Holmes'!) has often been mentioned as an off-screen character.

Although this film was just a one-shot venture for Ealing, there are a number of links with other Holmes series beside the presence of Wontner and Lomas: World Wide, who distributed *Sign of Four* in the United States, was to perform the same function the following year for Reginald Owen's *Study in Scarlet*; Miles Malleson (Reeve's brother this time out) would go on to appear in the '59 version of *The Hound*; producer Rowland V. Lee had worked on the Brook-Holmes *Paramount on Parade* and made several non-Sherlockian films with Basil Rathbone (with whom Watson Ian Hunter appeared in several films); and, of course, executive producer Basil Dean had directed the '29 Clive Brook *Return of Sherlock Holmes*.

Ian Hunter was, like Basil Rathbone, a native of

South Africa, having been born in Cape Town in 1900. As Ian Fleming was an Australian, neither of Wontner's Watsons was a "native" Englishman (nor, as it happens, was Rathbone's, as Nigel Bruce was born in Latin America!).

Hunter made his stage debut in 1919, and entered films in 1922 with *Mr. Oddy*; some of his subsequent British films were *A Girl of London*, '25, three films for Alfred Hitchcock—*Downhill, Easy Virtue*, and *The Ring*—all in '27, *The Physician*, '28 (with Miles Mander), and *Valley of the Ghosts* the same year for G. B. Samuelson. Hunter's first sound film was *Escape*, made in 1930 for Basil Dean, and this was followed by *Sally in Our Alley*, '31, for Dean and Elvey, *The Water Gipsies* the next year for the same team, *Orders is Orders* with radio-Holmes Sir Cedric Hardwicke, in '33, *Something Always Happens, The Church Mouse*, and a detective role in *Death at Broadcasting House* with Robert Rendel (all of '34), *The Phantom Light* and *Morals of Marcus* (written and directed by Mander in '35), and many others before Ian left for Hollywood, where he played

Theseus in *A Midsummer Night's Dream* in '35—former-Holmes Maurice Costello had been in the 1909 version. Some of Hunter's many other Hollywood films were to be *The White Angel*, '36; *That Certain Woman*, '37; *The Adventures of Robin Hood*, '38 (as King Richard I, with Rathbone; Cushing and Douglas Wilmer are two other screen Sherlocks who have made versions of the legend); *Tower of London*, '39 (again with Rathbone and Mander); *Ziegfeld Girl*, *Strange Cargo*, '40; and *Dr. Jekyll and Mr. Hyde*, '41 (as Lanyon; the subject has been associated with Benham, Norwood, Barrymore, Cushing, and Lee).

After his World War II service was completed, Ian Hunter returned to British films, making the mystery *Bedelia* in '46. Some of his later films in that country were *The White Unicorn*, '47; *Edward my Son*, '48 (by Mycroft Robert Morley); *Appointment in London*, '52; *The Battle of the River Plate* with Douglas Wilmer and Christopher Lee in '56, and *Fortune is a Woman* the same year (again with Lee); *Dr. Blood's Coffin* and *The Queen's Guards* (with Raymond Massey)—both in '61; and '62's *Guns of Darkness*.

Although Ian Hunter never in his long career quite reached the heights, his youth and leading-man status made him, like Donald Houston, an unusual Watson. Both actors were able to emphasize the qualities of steadiness and reliability that made Watson so valuable to Sherlock Holmes—qualities that were sometimes neglected in the characterizations of such better-known Watsons as Willis, Fleming, and Bruce, brilliant though they all were. Andre Morell, of course, also shared this image of capability and resourcefulness, but played the good Doctor at a rather late age.

Sign of Four's director, Graham Cutts (1885–1958), was in his day the mentor of Hitchcock and Clive Brook, having come into film production from the exhibition end of the business and going on to make such films as *While London Sleeps*, '22; *The Rat*, '25, and its sequels *Triumph of the Rat* in '26 and *Return of the Rat* in '29, *She Couldn't Say No*, '39, and some documentaries and shorts in the forties as his career declined.

Rowland V. Lee, the producer, was an American and had begun his film career as an actor with Thomas Ince in 1918; he directed *The Mysterious Dr. Fu Manchu*, with its imitation Holmes and Watson characters (and stage-Holmes O. P. Heggie in the cast), in '29, then crossed over to Britain in 1932 to take up an executive position at Ealing for Basil Dean, although he was soon back in Hollywood. He directed such other Sherlockian actors as von Seyffertitz, Brook, and Rathbone, though not in Holmes pictures.

THE TRIUMPH OF SHERLOCK HOLMES

Date of Release: 26 August 1935, although previewed on 25 May 1935 and reviewed in February.
Running Time: 7,544 feet; 84 minutes; 83 min.; 82 min.
Production Company: Real Art Productions, Ltd. (Twickenham); Gaumont; distributed by Great Britain Distributors.
Producer: Julius Hagen
Director: Leslie S. Hiscott
Screenplay: H. Fowler Mear, Cyril Twyford, and Arthur Wontner
Based on: *Valley of Fear, Final Problem*, and (uncredited) Gillette's play.
(British "A" Certificate)

CAST

Sherlock Holmes	Arthur Wontner
Professor Moriarty	Lyn Harding
Ettie Douglas	Jane Carr
John Douglas	Leslie Perrins
Dr. Watson	Ian Fleming
Cecil Barker	Michael Shepley
Ted Balding	Ben Welden
Boss McGinty	Roy Emerton
Col. Sebastian Moran	Wilfred Caithness
Inspector Lestrade	Charles Mortimer
Mrs. Hudson	Minnie Rayner
Ames	Conway Dixon
Captain Marvin	Edmund D'Alby
Jacob Shafter	Ernest Lynds

SYNOPSIS: The film followed Conan Doyle's novel very closely, but introduced a number of new sequences. As the story opens, Holmes is preparing to retire from Baker Street to his bee farm, although very regretful that Moriarty is still at large. Before the sleuth has finished his moving, however, he is visited by the wily Professor, who threatens him in a scene that virtually duplicates the Holmes-Moriarty interview of *The Sleeping Cardinal*. This development prompts Holmes to come out of retirement, of course.

Holmes suspects that Moriarty is behind the mysterious apparent murder of John Douglas, a former Pinkerton detective who resided at a lonely country

Dr. Watson (Ian Fleming) comprehends his studious companion as little in *The Triumph of Sherlock Holmes* as he ever did.

house known as Birlstone Manor, where Holmes travels to investigate. Douglas' wife Ettie tells Holmes the story of her husband's early life in America, and this prolonged flashback sequence (which is very faithful to Doyle) takes up the bulk of the film's running time.

Ettie's account leads Holmes through a series of deductions to the solution: that the body found was not that of Douglas but of his enemy Balding, an underling of Moriarty; and that Douglas is still alive. At this point Moriarty himself arrives at Birlstone, not realizing that his agent is dead, and after a confrontation with Holmes, Watson, and Lestrade, the Professor falls from the top of a ruined tower when he is shot by Holmes. The apparent death of his nemesis leads Holmes to believe that his own career is finally closed, and he returns to his retirement.

In the next film of the series, *Silver Blaze*, Sherlock is still retired until Moriarty once again rears his indestructible head (cloaked in its usual voluminous scarf, of course). This notion of "retiring" Holmes was no doubt incumbent on the filmmakers owing to Wontner's very apparent age—he was sixty when this film was made, and sixty-two in the next.

This film marked the return of the Wontner series to Twickenham (although the studio was temporarily operating under a different name), and many of the old standbys from the previous episodes were back: Fleming, Rayner, Leslie Perrins, Ben Welden, Mear, Twyford, Hagen, and Hiscott. There was, however, a new Inspector Lestrade in Charles Mortimer, who replaced Philip Hewland and would himself be replaced in the next episode by John Turnbull. And, of course, that outrageously melodramatic star of the '31 *Speckled Band*, Lyn Harding, took over the role of the Napoleon of Crime from Norman McKinnel. Although Harding's somewhat broad style of acting did not gel exactly right with the naturalistic underplaying of Arthur Wontner, he would continue in the role for *Silver Blaze*, as well.

REVIEWS: *The Kinematograph Weekly* for 7 February '35 had extremely high praise for Wontner's performance as Holmes, calling him "excellent" twice, "exceedingly fascinating" and "great," although they had only faint praise at best for the rest of the film, finding the story treatment, though faithful to Doyle's "ingenious" original, rather unimaginatively transferred to the screen. They felt, however, that the appeal of Wontner and the title were quite strong enough for the film to be easily exploitable and to appeal powerfully as family and juvenile fare "to the masses."

The review also considered that

story treatment is a trifle haphazard, but the drama is ... interspersed with thrills and illuminated by the bright deductions of Holmes and his cross-talk with the well-meaning Watson. . . . Ian Fleming is a trifle too stupid as Dr. Watson, but he nevertheless makes a good foil; and Lyn Harding, Leslie Perrins and Jane Carr acquit themselves adequately. . . . The film is quite good Sherlock

The Triumph of Sherlock Holmes. **Arthur Wontner ponders a find in this screen adaptation of "The Valley of Fear." Rather balding already in his first Holmes film, Wontner was so noticeably aging in his last two films that it was felt necessary to indicate that Holmes was retired! (Courtesy National Film Archives of the British Film Institute)**

Holmes, but it would have been better had a more even feeling of balance been preserved. Too much footage is devoted to the American flashback ... and not enough to the solving of the crime. Holmes is the character in whom all interest is centered, and much entertainment is lost during the period the fascinating character is absent. . . . The country house interiors admirably fit the major action, while the flashaback is convincingly American in atmosphere. Lighting and photography are satisfactory.

H.D.T. in The British Film Institute's *Monthly Film Bulletin* of 20 February–20 March 1935 had this to say of *The Triumph of Sherlock Holmes:*

The film . . . follows the plot of the novel fluently and with considerable ingenuity, except for the now indispensable appearance of Professor Moriarty. Arthur Wontner is the only Sherlock Holmes. His playing throughout is in perfect character and he seems to have walked straight out of the Sidney Paget illustrations. . . . It is, therefore, disappointing that Dr. Watson should have been transformed from the bushy-mustached Victorian practitioner into a dapper contemporary. It is true Ian Fleming is successful in getting his laughs, but many would prefer him to have carried on the classical tradition. Lyn Harding, in an impossible part, came very near to presenting a credible "Napoleon of Crime." Roy Emerton's Boss McGinty is a perfect piece of character acting. For the rest, the film moves—the brisk American sequence is particularly effective— the photography is good, but the triumph is Arthur Wontner's. Suitability: Adults, Young People, Family.

Picturegoer Weekly's reviewer L. C. (presumably Lionel Collier) wrote in its 24 August 1935 issue:

> Arthur Wontner is a perfect Sherlock Holmes, and it is good to see him again as the world's most famous fictional detective. Unfortunately, the story is not too well told; there are very few really convincing scenes of crime detection and much too much footage is expended in showing the early life in America of the supposed victim of a murder mystery.
>
> Sherlock Holmes is prompted to withdraw from retirement by a threat made by his old enemy, Prof. Moriarty. He has reason to believe that the archfiend is behind the mysterious murder of John Douglas, and he goes to the victim's lonely country home.
>
> In the end he crosses swords with Moriarty, whose death re-closes his career.
>
> Ian Fleming rather overdoes the traditional obtuseness of Dr. Watson, but good support comes from Lyn Harding as Moriarty, and Leslie Perrins and Jane Carr are both good.

SILVER BLAZE; in the United States: MURDER AT THE BASKERVILLES

Date of Release: 15 July 1937 or 25 October '37; released 1941 in the United States.
Running Time: 6,358 feet; 6,258 feet; 71 minutes; 70 min.
Production Company: Twickenham Film Productions Ltd; Associated British P.C.; released in the United States by Astor Pictures Corp.
Producer: Julius Hagen
Director: Thomas Bentley
Screenplay: Arthur Macrae, H. Fowler Mear and Arthur Wontner
Based on: *Silver Blaze* and *The Hound of the Baskervilles* (British "U" Certificate)

CAST

Sherlock Holmes	Arthur Wontner
Professor Moriarty	Lyn Harding
Diana Baskerville	Judy Gunn
Dr. Watson	Ian Fleming
Sir Henry Baskerville	Lawrence Grossmith
Jack Trevor	Arthur Macrae
Mrs. Straker	Eve Gray
John Straker	Martin Walker
Inspector Lestrade	John Turnbull
Colonel Ross	Robert Horton
Colonel Sebastian Moran	Arthur Goullet
Mrs. Hudson	Minnie Rayner
Miles Stamford	Gilbert Davies (or Davis)
Silas Brown	D. J. Williams
Bert Prince	Ralph Truman
Stableboy	Ronald Shiner

SYNOPSIS: The film is quite faithful to Conan Doyle's original short story, which with its numerous characters lends itself well to expansion into a feature, and is obviously movie potential with its climactic horserace. This version does, however, drag in Professor Moriarty and even Sir Henry Baskerville from other stories—additions that can only be considered padding but which add to the drama and atmosphere nonetheless.

Holmes and Watson are in Devon to visit their friend Sir Henry Baskerville, when Holmes' aid is invoked by the neighboring Colonel Ross in the case of the disappearance of the Colonel's horse, Silver Blaze. Not only is the horse discovered to be missing on the very day it is to participate (as the favorite) in a big racing event, but its groom, Hunter, is found dead from opium poisoning. Later, the trainer, Straker, is also discovered apparently murdered on Dartmoor. The chief suspect is Jack Trevor, who is in love with Sir Henry's daughter Diana, since Trevor has bet on the horse favored after Silver Blaze to win him five thousand pounds; Trevor was also seen near Silver Blaze's stable on the night of the crime.

Holmes proves, however, that none other than Professor Moriarty has a hand in the business. For a huge bribe by a bookmaker named Miles Stamford (who has overlaid the favorite), the Napoleon of Crime has stooped to this (for him) rather petty affair and has undertaken to see that the favorite does not go to the post. Moriarty exerts his influence on Straker to nobble Silver Blaze, but at this point, the synopses of the film diverge—one saying that the horse kills Straker, and the other that Silver Blaze is guiltless of both deaths. In any event, Holmes finds the stolen horse and enables it to enter the race by blacking over its white "blaze" mark and thus disguising it.

Just as the favorite is nearing the winning post, though, its jockey is shot by Col. Sebastian Moran, under orders from Moriarty. The Colonel is disguised as a newsreel cameraman, with his silent air-gun concealed in a movie camera positioned at the finish line.

Dr. Watson, however, at last has his moment of glory in the Wontner series, since it is he who trails one of the criminals to the lair of Moriarty. The Professor, alas, succeeds in capturing the intrepid physician, and is just about to throw the poor fellow down an empty elevator shaft when Holmes and Lestrade make an opportune entrance and save the day (and the Doctor).

This was Arthur Wontner's swan song as the Great Detective on film, though as we have noted he was to continue to play him on radio and TV for some years. Of the old regulars, Fleming, Harding, Hagen, and Mear were all back for *Silver Blaze*, but there was a new Lestrade in John Turnbull, a new director in Thomas Bentley, and a new coscripter in Arthur Macrae (who also played the juvenile lead in the picture). Ronald Shiner, billed last as the Stableboy, would later become a popular star in Britain.

REVIEWS: One of the audiences for this film's first

Wontner's last appearance as Holmes on the screen: *Silver Blaze*. **Ian Fleming is Watson at left, and the Great Detective, arms folded, is unmistakeable in the center, unregenerately supercilious to the last. (Courtesy National Film Archives of the British Film Institute)**

London run laughed so boisterously in the wrong places that *Silver Blaze* was withdrawn from the program for two days; but after the London press vigorously excoriated this "sacrilege" to "the great man" the film was revived for a successful run with no further incidents (although this experience, together with Wontner's increasing age, perhaps was one of the reasons for the demise of this classic series).

Kinematograph Weekly reviewed *Silver Blaze* in its 8 July 1937 issue:

Arthur Wontner, as the detective, an unforgettable figure. Certain popular hit.... Good for all types and ages.... Production ... is packed with excitement and surprises.... Arthur Wontner's performance as Sherlock Holmes is easily the best

histrionic contribution ... he succeeds triumphantly in convincing us that he would really have deduced the main elements and perpetrator of the crime.... Lyn Harding is unctuously ferocious: Ian Fleming is a prize rabbit as the docile Watson; John Turnbull ... appropriately blustering and wooden-headed.... [The acting of Gilbert Davis, Judy Gunn and Eve Gray also came in for praise.]

Scenes on the moors, in the racing stables and in Sir Henry's country mansion have been devised with an expert eye for visual effect. The racehorse sequences are suitably sensational (though there seems to be a technical error in the actual running of the race), and Holmes' lodgings in Baker Street, present us with the looked-for surrounding and appurtenances of the detective's domestic menage ... rattling good ... novel kinema effects.... Superb performance ... by Arthur Wontner.

Director Thomas Bentley, though new to the Wontner series, was by no means a newcomer to films, having entered the profession in 1912 with *Leaves from the Book of Charles Dickens*. He was the foremost

159

An off-screen portrait of Wontner in 1937, the same year as *Silver Blaze*.

and Conan Doyle; the eccentric London characters created by these two Victorian scribes would not have batted an eyelid had any of them chanced to meet one another coming out of a fogbank, and those two old bachelors, Pickwick and Holmes, might have passed more than one agreeable evening in conversation before a blazing hearth, drinks in hands. Dickensian characters have been created for the stage and screen by such major Sherlockian interpreters as H. A. Saintsbury, Lyn Harding, Harry Benham, Maurice Costello, Basil Rathbone, Roland Young, Reginald Owen, Christopher Lee, Cedric Hardwicke, Fred Lloyd, and Ralph Richardson, and one can only wish that some enterprising producer will give Sherlock Holmes a chance at cracking Charles Dickens' unfinished and unsolved mystery classic *Edwin Drood*, especially now that he has disposed of Jack the Ripper. (*See our chapter on Study in Terror.*)

Thomas Bentley and Arthur Wontner had worked together on screen projects before *Silver Blaze*, for Bentley was the director of the 1923 series in which Wontner had costarred with Jose Collins. Some of Bentley's many other films were *A Master of Craft*, '22; *Old Bill Through the Ages* and *After Dark*, '24; two versions of *Young Woodley* ('29 and '30); *Hobson's Choice*, '31; *The Scotland Yard Mystery*, '33; *A Night Alone*, '38; *Dead Man's Shoes*, '39, and (what must have been something of an indignity) an episode of the rather atrocious comedy series starring Arthur Lucan in comic drag, *Old Mother Riley's Circus*—Thomas Bentley's last film as a director, in 1941.

We must now say goodbye to the Wontner series, but before we proceed to the next truly great Holmes series, that of Basil Rathbone (and director Roy William Neill), we must pause to take note of the Holmesian films that were being made during this period in Germany and Eastern Europe. Perhaps the best of them, *Der Mann, Der Sherlock Holmes War*, is not properly a true Holmes film at all, and must wait for our final section devoted to satires to be treated properly.

interpreter of Dickens of his time, having begun impersonating that writer's characters for the music-hall circuit in 1901. His other Dickens films were *Oliver Twist*, 1912; *David Copperfield*, '13; *The Old Curiosity Shop* and *The Chimes*, '14; *Barnaby Rudge* and *Hard Times* the following year; and *The Adventures of Mr. Pickwick* and a second version of *Old Curiosity Shop* in '21. When sound came in, Bentley made still a third *Old Curiosity Shop*—this one in '34. He was a natural choice to direct Sherlock Holmes, since there is, of course, a great affinity between the worlds of Dickens

19
German and Czech Films

LELICEK VE SLUZBACH SHERLOCKA HOL-MESE (Lelicek in the Service of Sherlock Holmes) Czechoslovakia

Released: 1932
Running Time: 2,044 m=6,704ft.=74½ min.
Production Company: Elektafilm AS
Producer: Jan Reiter
Director: Karel (Karl, Carl) Lamac
Screenplay: Vaclav Wasserman
Adaptation: Hugo Vavrise
Photography: Otto Heller and Jan Stallich

CAST

Frantisek Lelicek	
Fernando XXIII, King of	
Portorico	Vlasta Burian
Sherlock Holmes	Martin Fric
Jeho Sluha James (footman)	Fred Bulin
Queen Kralovna	Lida Baarova
Conchita	Eva Jansenova
Prime Minister	Theodor Pistek
Court Marshal	Cenek Slegl
Royal Officer	Zvonimir Regez
Photographer	Eman Fiala

Dr. Watson does not appear in this one, and Holmes himself seems to be only making a "guest appearance."

Director Karel Lamac later went to Germany where (after a name change) he made another Holmes picture in '36. *(see our next entry.) Lelicek* cameraman Otto Heller, however, left Czechoslovakia for Britain, where he proceeded to shoot over three hundred features, including *Mr. Emanuel*, '44, with stage-Holmes Felix Aylmer; the classic *Queen of Spades*, '48; *The Winslow Boy*, '48, with radio-Holmes Cedric Hardwicke; *Ipcress File*, '65; *Alfie*, '66; and *Duffy*, '68.

After *Lelicek* there were to be no more Czech films about Holmes until 1971. However, it seems most appropriate to leap forward here to examine that film—*Touha Sherlocka Holmese*—before we return to the career of *Lelicek* director Lamac and his version of *Der Hund von Baskerville*, which he made after migrating to Germany.

TOUHA SHERLOCKA HOLMESE (Sherlock Holmes' Desire) Czechoslovakia

Released: 1971
Running Time: 1,090m=3,576 ft.=40 minutes
Production Company: Czechoslovak Film
Director: Stepan Skalsky
Screenplay: Ilja Hurnik and Stepan Skalsky

CAST

Sherlock Holmes	Radovan Lukavsky
Dr. Watson	Vaclav Voska
Lady Abraham	Vlasta Fialova
Lady Oberon	Marie Rosulkova
Maestro	Bohus Zahorsky
Conductor	Eduard Kohout
Lord Biddleton	Miroslav Machacek
Mr. Wrubelski	Vlastimil Brodsky
Sir Arthur Conan Doyle	Josef Patocka

We have no further information on this film, but judging by the excellent *Death of Tarzan*, which was made in their country only a few years before, the Czechs seem well able to treat a capitalist hero with sincere understanding.

Here, though, we will rejoin Lamac in Germany with his second Holmes film.

DER HUND VON BASKERVILLE (Germany)

Date of Release: 1936; or 12 January 1937
Running Time: 2,255m=7,398 ft.=82 minutes
Production Company: Ondra-Lamac-Film G.m.b.H.
Director: Karel Lamac
Screenplay: Carla von Stackelberg
Photography: Willy Winterstein
Music: Paul Huhn

CAST

Lord Henry Baskerville	Peter Voss
Lord Charles Baskerville	Friedrich Kayssler
Beryl Vendeleure	Alice Brandt
Barrymore	Fritz Rasp
Sherlock Holmes	Bruno Guttner
Dr. Watson	Fritz Odemar
Frau Barrymore	Lilly Shonborn
Stapleton	Erich Ponto
Dr. Mortimer	Ernst (or Ernest) Rotmund
Mrs. Hudson	Gertrude Wolle (or Walle)

(perhaps listed only as "Holmes' Landlady")

Lady Baskerville	Hanna Waag
Lord Hugo Baskerville	Arthur Malkowski
Selden (Convict)	Paul Rehkopf
?	Klaus Pohl
	Horst Birr
	Ernst A. Shaah
	Ika Thimm
	Kurt Lauermann

This was the second Holmes outing for both director Lamac (*Lelicek*) and costar Fritz Rasp, who was essaying a different role than he had in the previous German version of *Der Hund*, and being billed absurdly high for the red-herring role of the butler Barrymore—an indication of Herr Rasp's popularity.

This version was apparently rather more faithful to Doyle than the long *Hund* series of the teens and twenties had been, though it retained the notion of the Baskervilles having a castle rather than a humble manor house. Holmes was portrayed as rather more Germanic than he had been in the hands of Carlyle Blackwell, too, and costumed in a continental-looking cap and a leather overcoat over a polo-necked jersey.

Der Hund von Baskerville of '36 also has the melancholy distinction of having been a favorite with Adolf Hitler, who had a print of it in his private collection—it was found in Berchtesgaden in 1945.

SHERLOCK HOLMES, ODER GRAUE DAME; SHERLOCK HOLMES: DIE GRAUE DAME

Date of Release: 26 February 1937
Running Time: 2,517m (8,258 feet)=92 min.
Production Company: Neue Film KG
Director: Erich Engel (or Engels)
Screenplay: Erich Engel and Hans Heuer
Based on: *The Deed of the Unknown* by Muller-Puzicka

CAST

Sherlock Holmes	Hermann Speelmans
Lola	Elizabeth Wendt
Maria Iretzkaja	Trude Marlen
Baranoff	Edwin Jurgensen
Harry Morrel	Theo Shall
Inspector Brown	Ernest Karchow
John, Holmes' servant	Werner Finck
Jack Clark	Werner Scharf
James Hewitt	Hans Halden
Archibald Pepperkorn	Henry Lorenzen
Wilson	Reinhold Bernt
Frau Miller	Eva Tinschmann

This film was not based directly on any Doyle story, but rather on a play by Muller-Puzika called *The Deed of the Unknown*, which did not have anything at all to do with Sherlock Holmes! However, the presence in the title of our old friend "The Gray Lady" suggests that this movie must have been inspired at least in part by the 1909 Nordisk film of that title, and since that old Danish picture was itself based on the Germans' favorite story of *The Hound of the Baskervilles*, it seems possible that some echoes of Doyle other than just Holmes himself must have filtered down into the '37 *Graue Dame* after all, however far removed from their source!

The director and coscripter, Erich Engel, must have felt rather ill at ease with the aristocratic setting of this film, since he was most at home with comedies about lower-middle-class life. But the Germans seem to love seeing Holmes among the upper classes, as witness their constant elevation of the status of the Baskerville family. The names of the characters are mostly of an obviously English cast like "Brown," "Wilson," and "Jack Clark," but one hopes that "Archibald Pepperkorn" was intended as a humorous character. It is a pity that "Inspector Brown" appears in place of any of the Doylesque policemen, but the real shocker is that Sherlock Holmes turns out to be working hand in hand with the Geheimpolizei (!), despite the film's English setting, thus completing his transformation into the "shrewd secret policeman" the Germans envisioned in '29. The saddest thing of all about this film, though, must be the absence of Dr. Watson, replaced by a character named John, who is presented as Holmes' *servant*. One would hope that this German Holmes behaved in as egalitarian a manner to his "servant" as the original Holmes behaved toward Mrs. Hudson and Billy, with whom there was never any question of inferior social status.

It is possible that "John" many have been only another Geheimpolozei agent, however, who was merely masquerading as a servant, because for most of the film Holmes himself is disguised as a criminal named "Jimmy Ward," and "John" may perhaps have been intended as the supposed servant of this illusory character rather than of Holmes himself.

Hermann Speelmans, as Sherlock, was somewhat plump, once again harking back more to the old Nordisk image than to the original conception of the character.

Now, however, we transfer our attention from this distorted image of the Baker Street Sleuth to an image that, for most people around the world, is that of the veritable one-and-only Sherlock Holmes himself—we speak, of course, of Basil Rathbone, who has surely formed the public conception of this character more than anyone else except Conan Doyle himself, and whose Watson made so indelible an impression that, even after twenty-nine years and numerous other fine actors in the role, when a TV comedian today does an impression of Dr. Watson, it is always really an impression of the unique personality of Nigel Bruce.

20

The Basil Rathbone Series

To the millions of current-day Sherlock Holmes fans, especially in the United States, just the thought of the Great Detective conjures up the image of Basil Rathbone. Rathbone, while not as prolific a screen Holmes as Norwood, nevertheless achieved a popularity never before realized by any screen Holmes, and his films are still playing to their fifth decade of film (and television) audiences. Never before has an actor—any actor—become so identified in the minds of so many with the character he has portrayed on the screen.

Rathbone's fourteen films as Holmes (fifteen if you count the parody musical *Crazy House,* in which he has little more than a cameo role as Holmes) have played and are playing to millions of people in many countries, in theaters, on television, in colleges, in film festivals, and anywhere someone might find a projector and a blank wall to use as a screen.

At the time of this writing, the first film of the series, Twentieth-Century Fox's *The Hound of the Baskervilles,* made in 1939, has just finished a record-breaking four-month run of continuous showings at a New York City film-revival theater, playing with Buster Keaton's *Sherlock, Jr.* and a filmed interview with Sir Arthur Conan Doyle—playing to audiences ranging in age from infant to octagenarian who lined up for tickets down the block and around the corner.

Also within the last month, the second film of the series, Fox's 1939 *The Adventures of Sherlock Holmes,* was shown on New York television as a late movie.

Needless to say, we saw them both, along with countless other Holmes fans (or is "addicts" a more appropriate term?).

BASIL RATHBONE

Rathbone's Holmes made him one of the most popular figures in American cinema, but at the same time nearly destroyed his career as an actor because his own superb portrayal of the world's favorite detective obscured so many other brilliant performances by this versatile, all-around character actor.

The curse of "type-casting" had already restricted Rathbone's activities long before he played Holmes, ever since his interpretation of the wicked Murdstone in *David Copperfield.* "Murdstone has haunted me . . .," Rathbone told the Los Angeles *Times* in 1936, "it's closed instead of opening doors to me."

His portrayal of Murdstone did get him a series of jobs, but seldom as anything but a villain. Playing these "heavies" only served to reinforce the image of Rathbone as a villain, which led to another film role as a rogue, which impressed producers even more with his talents as a rogue, which got him a role as a scoundrel, etc. The rut he was stuck in kept getting deeper and deeper. When he played Holmes from 1939 through 1946 on the screen, and in addition on stage, television, and over two hundred radio performances, producers forgot about everything he had done before Holmes, and he couldn't get the work he deserved.

He never again reached the plateau of good roles that he had enjoyed before Holmes, and eventually wound up working on such ignoble films as *Ghost in the Invisible Bikini* and *Hillbillies in a Haunted House.* It was a tragic end to a brilliant career; a career that displayed

Rathbone actually wore the deerstalker in the first two of his fifteen screen appearances as Sherlock Holmes. All of the subsequent episodes in his series were laid in contemporary settings, though the cap did figure as an unworn prop in the third film.

Basil Rathbone's talents in such roles as Richard III in *Tower of London*, Sir Guy in *The Adventures of Robin Hood*, the Marquis St. Evremonde in *A Tale of Two Cities*, Capt. Pasquale in *The Mark of Zorro*, Major Brand in *The Dawn Patrol*, and Pontius Pilate in *The Last Days of Pompeii*.

Even the part of Holmes eventually frustrated and bored Rathbone, and it is painfully obvious to the viewers of the Fox and Universal Holmes series. The series of fourteen films start out very good, even underrated, and decrease in quality and content as the series progresses. This is partially due to the deteriorating storylines and dialogue, but it is also due to a tiredness or lack of interest on the part of Rathbone himself. The ultimate insult to this fine actor was what was beginning to happen off-screen—that people he met or that saw him on the street confused or ignored his true identity and called him "Mr. Holmes," even asking him to sign autographs as "Sherlock Holmes."

He returned to his true love, the stage, after the Holmes series, and kept busy with dramatic readings, summer stock, and radio, in addition to an occasional

Of all the performers of the role, Basil Rathbone was probably the most successful in projecting the nervous intensity of Holmes. An actor of electric presence, his Baker Street Sleuth seemed to be a coiled spring always on the alert to jump into action.

movie or television role, but he never again played a major role in a major film.

Philip St. John Basil Rathbone was born on 13 June 1892 in Johannesburg, South Africa, son of mining engineer Edgar Philip Rathbone and musician Anna Barbara George Rathbone. He was also related to that noted actor Sir Frank Benson and writer A.A. Milne, who incidentally wrote a Sherlock Holmes parody.

After a difficult cross-country train journey during the Boer War, the Rathbone family, now numbering four with the birth of Beatrice in 1894, sailed for England and settled in London. The year was 1896. The retreat from war-torn South Africa was complicated by the fact that Edgar was suspected of being a spy, and that in Durban, while waiting for a ship sailing for England, Anna, Basil, and Beatrice spent several weeks in the hospital with typhoid fever.

Young Basil attended Repton School, and there expressed his first interest in the theater by writing a play entitled *King Arthur*. Basil had every intention of pursuing an acting career upon graduation in 1910, but his father persuaded him to at least try the business world, and secured Basil a position with the Liverpool, London and Globe Insurance Company for a year.

It was a long and dull year indeed for young Basil, and as soon as it was over, he auditioned with a scene from *The Merchant of Venice* for the Stratford-Upon-Avon Shakespeare Festival, which had been founded by Rathbone's cousin, Frank Benson (soon to become Sir Frank Benson). Benson saw Basil's potential talent and gave Basil a job with the number two company.

Basil's stage debut was in the part of Hortensio in *The Taming of the Shrew* on 22 April 1911 at the Theatre Royal in Ipswich. Basil toured England, Scotland, and Ireland with the company, earning thirty shillings a week ($4.50 U.S.), and playing with the main company at Stratford in such roles as Orsino in *Twelfth Night*, Laertes in *Hamlet*, and the Duke of Aumerle in *Richard II*.

In 1913 the company toured the United States, and Basil was there, as Paris in *Romeo and Juliet*, Lorenzo in *The Merchant of Venice*, Fenton in *The Merry Wives of Windsor*, and Silvius in *As You Like It*. In 1914 he married Ethel Marion Foreman, also in the Benson Company. Their son Rodion was born in July 1915.

Rathbone's London stage debut was at the Savoy Theater in 1914 in *The Sin of David* by Stephen Phillips, in the role of Finch.

Rathbone enlisted in the British Army and served in France, being awarded the Military Cross in September 1918. Rathbone's younger brother, John, born shortly after the family's arrival in London, died in the war. Shortly after returning to civilian life, he separated from his wife Marion.

In August 1919, he went back to work for Sir Frank Benson's successor, W. H. Savery, and the New Shakespeare Company at Stratford-Upon-Avon, for five pounds a week. He worked on four productions during that season, and had good parts to play: Ferdinand in *The Tempest*, Cassius in *Julius Caesar*,

Florizel in *The Winter's Tale*, and, his personal favorite, Romeo in *Romeo and Juliet*.

When the London production of *Peter Ibbetson* was casting in 1920, Rathbone competed with Henry Daniell (later to play Moriarty in 1945's *The Woman in Green*, and parts in two other Rathbone Holmes films) and George Ralph for the title role, but since Rathbone asked for the smallest salary, he got the part.

The play opened in February 1920 to disappointing reviews, but Rathbone's performance was generally praised. Despite the short run of the play, enough important theater people saw and liked his work that he began to get calls for some important roles.

Peter Ibbetson's leading lady, Constance Collier, also did the same play with John Barrymore about this time.

Rathbone played opposite Mrs. Patrick Campbell in *Madame Sand*, based on the romance of George Sand and Alfred de Musset, at the Duke of York Theatre. The play was not generally liked, but, again, Rathbone got encouraging reviews.

Basil starred as Major Wharton in W. Somerset Maugham's *The Unknown*, another short run. Two other plays took Rathbone through the end of 1920.

Maurice Elvey, producer-director, had noticed the young Rathbone, and hired Rathbone for two films for the Stoll Company, famous for so many Norwood Holmes films shooting at nearly the same time. *The Fruitful Vine*, a love story costarring Valya and Robert English, was shot and released in September 1921. *The Innocent*, although filmed later, was released earlier, in March 1921, and starred Madge Stuart. The story was adapted for the screen by William J. Elliott, who also adapted many of the series of Norwood Holmes films. While working for Stoll studios, Rathbone came into contact with several other people who were also involved in the Norwood Holmes series: cinematographer W. Germain Burger, art director Walter Murton, editor H. Leslie Britain, and Madame d'Esterre, who played Mrs. Hudson for Norwood's Holmes.

Rathbone then returned to the Royal Court Theatre to star as Prince Hal in *King Henry IV, Part 2,* and as Iago in *Othello*.

Rathbone's Broadway debut came the following January (1922), as Count Alexei in the comedy *The Czarina*.

Back in London, Rathbone played George Conway in Maugham's *East of Suez* in His Majesty's Theater for nearly a year. The director was Basil Dean, who in 1929 was to direct Clive Brook in *The Return of Sherlock Holmes*.

The School for Scandal, Basil Rathbone's third film, was released in August 1923—a costume comedy directed by Bertram Phillips. Rathbone then returned to Broadway for his first really big success—the role of Dr. Nicholas Agi in *The Swan*, with Eva Le Gallienne and Philip Merivale. The production opened on 23 October 1923 to excellent reviews for both Rathbone and the play in general. The play ran for 255

performances and made Rathbone a star. Soon after *The Swan* opened, Rathbone met Ouida Bergere at a party, but it was three long years before Basil could obtain a divorce from Marion and marry Ouida.

During this period, Rathbone made his American screen debut, 1924's *Trouping with Ellen*, an Eastern Production, with Helene Chadwick, Mary Thurman, Gaston Glass, and a young Tyrone Power.

Rathbone toured major United States cities with *The Swan* until the spring of 1925, when MGM hired him for *The Masked Bride*, which starred Mae Murray and Francis X. Bushman. The picture started filming with Josef von Sternberg directing, but he was replaced by Christy Cabanne after only two weeks. The film was released in November 1925, and the New York *Times* called Rathbone's performance "most commendable."

October 1925 saw Rathbone costarring on Broadway with Elsie Ferguson in *The Grand Duchess and the Waiter*—a comedy staged by Frank Reicher, which included in the cast Alison Skipworth and Frederic Worlock, who was later to enjoy roles in five of Rathbone's Holmes films. The show ran less than a month.

Rathbone married Ouida Bergere in April 1926. Ouida not only made a good wife for Basil, but also a good business advisor. His salary increased steadily as a direct result of Ouida's influence.

Rathbone played a German agent in 1926's *The Great Deception*, with Ben Lyon and Aileen Pringle.

Several Broadway productions occupied Rathbone's time before his next film, including the very successful *The Command to Love*, which also had a national tour after a long Broadway run, and *Judas*, which was written by Rathbone and Walter Ferris and starred Rathbone in the title role, but was received poorly and closed soon after opening.

MGM's 1929 talkie *The Last of Mrs. Cheyney* gave Rathbone second billing to Norma Shearer and his first chance to speak on screen. The film, released in July, was directed by Sidney Franklin and photographed by William Daniels. Rathbone's role of Lord Arthur Dilling was played on stage by Roland Young. One of 1929's major successes, *The Last of Mrs. Cheyney*, made Rathbone a very sought-after actor in Hollywood. He did well turning down the Broadway production of *Death Takes a Holiday* to take the film job.

1930 was a busy year for Basil Rathbone, who starred in no less than seven films: *The Bishop Murder Case* (as detective Philo Vance), *A Notorious Affair* (as a violinist), *The Lady of Scandal, This Mad World, A Lady Surrenders, The Flirting Widow*, and *Sin Takes a Holiday*, with Constance Bennett and Kenneth MacKenna.

In December 1930, he returned to the stage for *A Kiss Of Importance*, which Lionel Atwill directed. Atwill was later to play Moriarty to Rathbone's Holmes in *Sherlock Holmes and the Secret Weapon*, and also Dr. Mortimer in *The Hound of the Baskervilles*. February 1931 found Rathbone starring with his old friend Henry Daniell in fifteen performances of "Heat Wave" at the same theater.

Laurence Olivier's illness forced RKO to replace him for *A Woman Commands*, which also starred Pola Negri. Olivier's replacement—Basil Rathbone, playing Capt. Alex Pasitsch.

The cast also included Roland Young, H. B. Warner, and Anthony Bushell. Roland Young got the best reviews, but more important to Basil Rathbone, the film convinced a number of producers that Basil Rathbone was *not* a good choice to play a romantic lead.

After ninety-six performances of *The Devil Passes* with Diana Wynyard on Broadway, Rathbone returned to England. He worked on two plays and three films while in England, notably the film *Loyalties*, with Miles Mander and Alan Napier, and directed by Basil Dean. The film was reviewed as the finest in Basil's career up to that time. This 1933 film also featured Athole Stewart, who had played Watson to Raymond Massey's Holmes in 1931's *The Speckled Band*.

Rathbone toured the United States for seven months with a three-play repertory company. The tour began in October 1933 and covered eighty-six cities. Rathbone played Robert Browning in *The Barretts of Wimpole Street*, Morrell in Shaw's *Candida*, and Romeo in *Romeo and Juliet*, which later opened up on Broadway. The company also included Orson Welles, Brenda Forbes, George Macready, and Helen Walpole.

In May 1934, Rathbone was contracted by David O. Selznick to play Mr. Murdstone in MGM's *David Copperfield*, the cast of which included W. C. Fields, Lionel Barrymore, Freddie Bartholomew, Maureen O'Sullivan, Roland Young, and Lewis Stone. George Cukor directed, and the picture was released in January 1935; Rathbone was an overnight sensation and became Hollywood's supreme screen villain.

Almost immediately, Selznick cast him in *Anna Karenina* as the insensitive husband, with Greta Garbo and Frederic March, and directed by Clarence Brown. Rathbone's performance was given excellent reviews, and this role was regarded as his best screen role to date. His character, Karenin, is similar to Holmes in that he projects a cold unemotional exterior—inwardly, though, Karenin is full of emotion, as Rathbone subtly indicates by wringing his hands in the great confrontation scene with Garbo as Anna, who is blind to his deep feelings and sees only the outside persona.

Basil and Ouida finally and permanently moved to Los Angeles during this period.

Rathbone's next screen role was as Pontius Pilate in *The Last Days of Pompeii*, starring Preston Foster as Marcus. Reviewers were nearly unanimous in hailing Rathbone's performance as the best thing about the film. RKO released this Merian C. Cooper Production in October 1935.

Columbia's *A Feather in Her Hat* followed, with Pauline Lord, Louis Hayward, Billie Burke, and Wendie Barrie.

MGM's *A Tale of Two Cities*, released in November 1935, saw Rathbone cast as Marquis St. Evremonde in a cast that also included Ronald Colman, Elizabeth Allen, Reginald Owen (who also played both Holmes and Watson in films), and Henry B. Walthall. Costing a million dollars to make, this lavish spectacular motion picture has become a classic, and Rathbone's reviews were excellent.

Next followed his first swashbuckler, *Captain Blood*, starring Errol Flynn, Olivia de Havilland, and Lionel Atwill, directed by Michael Curtiz, and released by First National (Warner Bros.) in December 1935. Rathbone played pirate captain Levasseur, and despite the brevity of the part, his duel on the beach with Errol Flynn was the most memorable scene in the film.

Two insignificant feature films followed—MGM's *Kind Lady* and twentieth-Century Fox's *Private Number*—both with Rathbone as the "heavy."

Rathbone was nominated for the Best Performance by a Supporting Actor Academy Award for his portrayal of Tybalt in MGM's *Romeo and Juliet*, which starred Leslie Howard as Romeo, Norma Shearer as Juliet, John Barrymore as Mercutio, and C. Aubrey Smith, Edna May Oliver, Reginald Denny, and Andy Devine. The 1936 film was directed by George Cukor and produced by Irving Thalberg. William Daniels' beautiful photography and the exquisite costumes and sets added to the lavish production.

The New York *Times* raved: ". . . and Basil Rathbone, a perfect devil of a Tybalt, fiery and quick to draw and an insolent flinger of challenges. No possible fault there." The film was released in July 1936. Rathbone lost the Oscar to Walter Brennan for his performance in *Come and Get It*.

Rathbone's first film in color was the Technicolor *The Garden of Allah*, starring Marlene Deitrich and Charles Boyer, and directed by Richard Boleslawski for Selznick (released by United Artists in November 1936). Rathbone's part was small, but his reviews were excellent.

Rathbone signed a two-picture contract with Warner Bros., which produced *Confession* and *Tovarich*, which starred Claudette Colbert and Charles Boyer. Both were released in 1937. Also in 1937, United Artists released *Love From a Stranger*, in which Rathbone played opposite Ann Harding.

RKO's *Make a Wish*, released in August 1937, was one of Rathbone's few nonvillain roles. The film featured child star Bobby Breen, and Rathbone's reviews were good; as a whole, audiences and reviewers seemed surprised that Rathbone could play a good guy at all!

Rathbone turned down a major role in *The Hurricane* to do *The Adventures of Marco Polo* with Gary Cooper. (NOTE: Raymond Massey, a screen Holmes in his own right, got the part in *The Hurricane*.) *Marco Polo* was a weak film, directed by Archie Mayo for Samuel Goldwyn, and was released in February 1938.

One of Rathbone's most remembered villainous roles was that of Sir Guy of Gisbourne in Warner Brothers' Technicolor epic *The Adventures of Robin*

Hood, which starred Errol Flynn, Olivia de Havilland, Claude Rains, Ian Hunter (screen Watson in Arthur Wontner's 1932 *The Sign of Four*), Eugene Pallette, and Alan Hale. The direction, by Michael Curtiz and William Keighley, was excellent, and production values very high. Rathbone once again duels Flynn and loses, in a most memorable finale. The film won three Oscars: for Original Music Score, Editing, and Set Decoration. The budget was two million dollars, a record for 1938.

If I Were King followed in September 1938 from Paramount. Rathbone stole the show from star Ronald Colman with his portrayal of hunchback King Louis XI, and was nominated for the second time for Best Performance by an Actor in a Supporting Role, but once again Rathbone lost out to Walter Brennan for *Kentucky*.

Errol Flynn and Basil Rathbone appeared together for the third and final time in *Dawn Patrol*, released by Warner Bros. in December 1938, directed by Edmund Goulding, and also starring David Niven and Donald Crisp.

Universal, having successfully revived the Frankenstein monster for *Bride of Frankenstein*, filmed a second sequel to the box-office smash *Frankenstein*, calling it *Son of Frankenstein*, and featuring Basil Rathbone in the title role. Boris Karloff returns as the Monster, and Bela Lugosi appears as Ygor, the mad shepherd who befriends and controls the Monster. Lionel Atwill, later to play Moriarty, plays the good Inspector Krogh, and Gustav von Seyffertitz, John Barrymore's Moriarty, is also in the cast. Rowland V. Lee, who produced Arthur Wontner's *Sign of the Four* in 1932, directed *Son of Frankenstein*.

Darryl Zanuck of Twentieth-Century Fox signed Basil Rathbone to play Sherlock Holmes and Nigel Bruce to play Dr. Watson in *The Hound of the Baskervilles*. Rathbone, noting more than just a passing resemblance between himself and the classic Sherlock Holmes portraits by Frederic Dorr Steele, felt that he was a logical choice for the role, although he probably regretted that resemblance later, after he had become bogged down playing the part of the Great Detective.

The first film in the series (although Zanuck did not plan on creating a series at the time) was *The Hound of the Baskervilles*.

This Holmes story was Zanuck's (and Rathbone's) favorite, and the resulting film is excellent. Richard Greene, as Sir Henry Baskerville, received top billing over Rathbone, but was left far behind Rathbone's superb interpretation of Doyle's character. Information about this and the other Rathbone Holmes films follows in the next section, but we will cover Rathbone's non-Holmes films here.

After *The Hound*, Rathbone costarred in *The Sun Never Sets*, with Douglas Fairbanks, Jr. Rowland V. Lee produced and directed this June 1939 release, which also featured Lionel Atwill and C. Aubrey Smith, but which failed because of a ludicrous storyline.

The Hound of the Baskervilles had done well enough at the box office that Fox decided to make a sequel, *The Adventures of Sherlock Holmes*, based on Gillette's play. The resulting film was released in August 1939, and was even better than its predecessor. Fox thought two Holmes films were enough, and did not attempt a third.

NBC Radio began the *Sherlock Holmes* radio show about this time, and hired Rathbone and Nigel Bruce to repeat their by then famous movie roles. The first show was broadcast on 2 October 1939, and the series continued at NBC until 1943, when it moved to the Mutual network, though retaining the talents of Rathbone and Bruce for a total of 275 episodes in seven years.

Universal contracted Rathbone for two films released in September and November 1939, respectively. First was *Rio*, directed by John Brahm, which saw Rathbone as an imprisoned financier escaping from a French penal colony. The cast included Victor McLaglen, Sigrid Gurie, Robert Cummings, and Leo Carillo. The second Universal picture of 1939 was *Tower of London*, again teaming director Rowland V. Lee with Rathbone and Boris Karloff. Also in the cast were Barbara O'Neil, screen-Watson Ian Hunter, and Vincent Price. Rathbone brilliantly played the evil hunchback Richard III.

Paramount's *Rhythm on the River* was next, released in August 1940. A musical featuring Bing Crosby and Mary Martin, the film provided a welcome vacation for hard-working Rathbone, giving him a small but important part as a composer.

Too old (forty-seven) to fight when the Second World War began, Basil and Ouida did what they could to support the British War effort—organizing benefits, raising money, hosting visiting dignitaries, etc.

Rathbone's nastiest screen villain came in Fox's 1940 *The Mark of Zorro*, in the person of Capt. Esteban Pasquale, playing opposite Tyrone Power and Linda Darnell. Once again displaying his dueling skill, Rathbone nevertheless could not avoid two superficial cuts inflicted by a less-than-expert Tyrone Power. The film was directed by Rouben Mamoulian, and also included in the cast Gale Sondergaard (who later played the Spider Woman in the Holmes film of that name), Eugene Pallette, and Montague Love. *Variety* called Rathbone "particularly effective."

A varied assortment of rogues, scoundrels, murderers, spies, and one role as an FBI agent saw Rathbone through 1941 and 1942. The films were Paramount's *The Mad Doctor*, Universal's *The Black Cat* (no relation to the Poe story), United Artists' *International Lady*, Universal's *Paris Calling*, MGM's *Fingers at the Window*, and *Crossroads*, also from MGM.

In April 1942, MGM, having contracted Rathbone for five years beginning 29 December 1941, agreed to loan him to Universal for a series of low-budget thrillers based loosely (sometimes too loosely) on Sir Arthur Conan Doyle's Sherlock Holmes stories. Universal had bought the rights to use the stories and characters from the Doyle estate for the sum of 300,000 dollars.

Hired with Rathbone were Nigel Bruce as Watson, Mary Gordon as Mrs. Hudson, and Dennis Hoey as Inspector Lestrade (although Hoey was not to play the part in all of the films). Mary Gordon's other filmatic endeavors before playing Mrs. Hudson throughout the Rathbone series included *Little Minister*, 1934; *The Irish in Us* and *The Bride of Frankenstein*—both 1935; *The Invisible Woman*, 1941 (with former-Sherlock John Barrymore); *The Mummy's Tomb* (with former-Moriarty George Zucco) and *The Strange Case of Dr. RX* (with still another Moriarty, Lionel Atwill)—both in 1942. Also, Dennis Hoey—Rathbone's Inspector Lestrade—not only reprised his bumbling Scotland Yarder in *Frankenstein Meets the Wolfman*, 1943, but also did so in *She-Wolf of London*, 1946.

The twelve Holmes films that followed over the next five years were modernized to the extent of having them take place during the then current Second World War. This, of course, gave Holmes the opportunity to combat Nazi spies and saboteurs, to indulge in airplane flights and car chases, and to make eloquent patriotic speeches about the inevitable triumph of the Allied forces over the Teutonic menace.

Rathbone did take breaks in his Holmes schedules to do other films, playing a Gestapo officer in MGM's *Above Suspicion* in 1943 with Joan Crawford and Fred MacMurray.

Rathbone and Bruce also parodied themselves as Holmes and Watson in Universal's Olsen and Johnson slapstick vehicle *Crazy House,* also in 1943.

In 1944, Rathbone again played hookey from Baker

Basil Rathbone and Nigel Bruce, without doubt the best remembered and best loved of all filmic Holmeses and Watsons. They are seen here in the second film of their series, *Adventures of Sherlock Holmes*, 1939. (Courtesy National Film Archives of the British Film Institute)

Street to support Red Skelton and Esther Williams in MGM's *Bathing Beauty,* and in another swashbuckler for Paramount (also with Nigel Bruce), called *Frenchman's Creek.* This beautifully Technicolor-photographed film starred Joan Fontaine and Arturo deCordova and was directed by Mitchell Leisen.

In between the last two Holmes films, *Terror by Night* and *Dressed to Kill,* Rathbone took time out to make *Heartbreak* for RKO, costarring with Ginger Rogers, Jean Pierre Aumont, and Adolphe Menjou.

Of course, all through the period of the Holmes films, Rathbone was actively working in radio, not only as Holmes, but for productions of *The Christmas Carol* (as Scrooge), and *The Phantom of the Opera* (in the title role). He also narrated the second half of Walt Disney's animated feature *Ichabod and Mr. Toad,* based on *The Legend of Sleepy Hollow* and *The Wind in the Willows.*

After the last of the Holmes films, Rathbone, bored with playing the same character for so long, moved back to New York, hoping to return to his first love—the stage. Several moderately successful plays and a lot of radio work kept Rathbone busy until the spring of 1947, when he began work on *The Heiress,* a play based on Henry James' *Washington Square.* The play opened in September to excellent notices, played for over a year on Broadway, then went on tour. In March 1948, Rathbone received the Antoinette Perry Award for his performance.

Plays, radio, and live television roles kept coming in for the next five years, and Rathbone was not to appear in another film until 1954's Paramount production of *Cassanova's Big Night,* which starred Bob Hope and Joan Fontaine.

We're No Angels followed in 1955, starring Humphrey Bogart, Aldo Ray, Peter Ustinov, Joan Bennett, and Leo G. Carroll. This pleasant comedy about three convicts escaping from a penal colony and befriending a shopkeeper's family on Christmas Eve was directed by Michael Curtiz and released by Paramount in June.

The Court Jester, released by Paramount in January 1956, once again put a sword in Rathbone's hand when he played the wicked Sir Ravenhurst with Danny Kaye, Glynis Johns, and Angela Lansbury.

The Black Sleep cast Rathbone with Akim Tamiroff, Lon Chaney Jr., John Carradine, and Bela Lugosi in a mild horror film from United Artists in 1956.

Columbia's massive political epic *The Last Hurrah* starred Spencer Tracy, Jeffrey Hunter, Diane Foster, Pat O'Brien, Donald Crisp, and James Gleason; it features Rathbone as Tracy's political nemesis. Produced and directed by John Ford, this two-hour film was released in November 1958.

Basil Rathbone played an evil sorcerer in United Artists' 1962 *The Magic Sword,* a childrens' film with Estelle Winwood and Gary Lockwood.

Rathbone made five cheap thrillers for American International Pictures between 1962 and 1967, the first being *Tales of Terror,* directed by Roger Corman, a collection of short Poe stories in which Rathbone plays an evil hypnotist in the final segment. Next came *A*

Comedy of Terrors, which boasted the collective horrific talents of Rathbone, Karloff, Lorre, and Price. The *Queen of Blood* was an alien vampire whose spaceship had crashed on Mars and who was rescued by Rathbone, John Saxon, and company. Rathbone and Karloff appeared together for the last time in *Ghost in the Invisible Bikini,* a combination beach-blanket-horror quickie. The last AIP film was *Voyage to a Prehistoric Planet,* which utilized Rathbone's talents in only one day's filming.

Rathbone's last two films were both with John Carradine—*Autopsy of a Ghost,* shot in Mexico and never released in English; and something called *Hillbillies in a Haunted House,* about which the less said the better.

Basil Rathbone died a month later, on 21 July 1967, of a heart attack at age seventy-five.

The last ten years of the actor's life were not marked so much by his infrequent movie roles, but by his other activities: summer stock, radio, live television, stage, narrations, poetry readings, dramatic readings and recordings, and his one-man show, *An Evening With Basil Rathbone,* and the many recordings of Sherlock Holmes stories, Poe Stories, and horror and ghost stories.

Also worth mentioning is the unsuccessful play written by his wife Ouida about Sherlock Holmes. The play, though "blessed" by Doyle's son Adrian, closed after three performances. Jack Raine played Watson, and Thomas Gomez, who had played a German spy in *Sherlock Holmes and the Voice of Terror,* played Moriarty. The play was described by reviewers as "untidy, cumbersome, and uneven," and Rathbone's performance as "too emotional."

Howlett, quoted by Baring-Gould, had this to say: "The physical resemblance of Rathbone to the Sidney Paget illustrations was quite striking and, next to Arthur Wontner, probably no one has been so happily cast."

Basil Rathbone on Sherlock Holmes (from Rathbone's autobiography, *In and Out of Character*):

> Had I but one Holmes picture, my first, *The Hound* . . . , I should probably not be as well known as I am today. But within myself, as an artist, I should have been well content. Of all the "adventures," "The Hound" is my favorite story, and it was in this picture that I had the stimulating experience of creating, within my own limited framework, a character that has intrigued me as much as any I have ever played. But the continuous repetition of story after story after story left me virtually repeating myself each time in a character I had already conceived and developed.

NIGEL BRUCE

Nigel Bruce played Dr. Watson to Basil Rathbone's Holmes in fifteen films and throughout Rathbone's two hundred-plus Sherlock Holmes radio programs (except for one where they switched roles).

Bruce's interpretation of Dr. Watson has become the "definitive" Watson, despite the fact that his interpretation is quite a different character than Doyle created. Nevertheless, Bruce made such an indelible impression as Watson that since 1939 almost all impressionists who have done Watson have really been doing Bruce.

Bruce was born in Ensenada, Mexico on 4 February 1895, which makes him three years younger than Rathbone, which is hard to believe watching their films together. Bruce was the son of a Scottish baronet and his wife who were travelling in Mexico when Nigel was born. Nigel was educated in England and fought in World War I, sustaining a leg injury that confined him to a wheelchair for three years.

Nigel Bruce made his stage debut in 1920 in *The Creaking Chair,* which starred C. Aubrey Smith. In 1922 he married Violet Shelton and they had two children, Jennifer and Pauline. He played in *Two White Arms* in London, which ran for 149 performances, in 1928, and shortly thereafter made his debut in silent films. His film career began just as sound films began, and he did quite well in this new territory.

Some of his films were *Red Aces* (1929); *The Squeaker* (1931); *Escape* (1931); *The Calendar* (1931); *Lord Camber's Ladies* (1932); *Channel Crossing* (1933); *Stand Up and Cheer* (1934); *The Lady Is Willing* (1934); *Treasure Island* (1934); *The Scarlet Pimpernel* (1935); *Becky Sharp* (1935); *She* (1935); *The Trail of the Lonesome Pine* (1936); *Under Two Flags* (1936); *The Charge of the Light Brigade* (1936); *The Last of Mrs. Cheyney* (with Basil Rathbone, 1937); *Kidnapped* (1938); *Suez* (1938); *A Dispatch from Reuters* (1940); *Hudson's Bay* (1940); *Suspicion* (1941); *This Above All* (1942); *Eagle Squadron* (1942); *Frenchman's Creek* (with Rathbone and Reginald Owen, 1944); and *Hong Kong* (1951).

He died of a heart attack on 8 October 1953.

Nigel Bruce did not just ride along on Rathbone's coattails; he contributed a great deal to the success of the Fox and Universal Holmes series. He is just as well known to the millions of fans and viewers of these films as Rathbone is, and, in fact, towards the end of the series, when Rathbone was tiring of the role and losing interest in the character, Nigel Bruce did not, and even impressed audiences and reviewers more than Rathbone with his performances.

Bruce's gift of subtle comedy, his apparent clumsiness, his under-the-breath mutterings, his proper British air, and above all his wonderful sense of dedication and loyalty to Holmes—all serve to make his "Watson" a very real, very human, and very lovable character.

Rathbone on Nigel Bruce (from *In and Out of Character*): "there is no question in my mind that (he) was the ideal Dr. Watson, not only of his time, but possibly of and for all time. There was an endearing quality to his performance that . . . humanized the relationship between Holmes and Watson."

A character study of Nigel Bruce as Dr. Watson in *Terror by Night.* **Bruce made such an indelible impression in the part that for the vast majority of people there is no other Watson. Those who have complained that he overaccentuated the comic aspects of the good doctor have forgotten what an outstanding *serious* actor he was. His comedy was never burlesque but always arose from genuinely human characterization. (Courtesy National Film Archives of the British Film Institute)**

ROY WILLIAM NEILL

Roy William Neill produced and directed eleven of the twelve Sherlock Holmes films made by Universal from 1942 through 1946, and contributed quite a bit to several of the screenplays. He was born Roland de Gostrie in Dublin 4 September 1892—the same year as Rathbone.

Neill began his career as an actor, making his stage debut in *Wildfire* with Lillian Russell. He became quite well liked as an actor, and starred in *Baby Mine* in London and in *O'Reggie* in the United States. He had also written two successful plays: *Prince O' My Dreams* and *Heart's Desire.* His first film was *Love Letters* in 1917 for Ince Productions.

He started directing films in 1922, including *The Iron Trail, What's Wrong with the Women, Toilers of the Sea, Broken Laws, The Kiss Barrier, Marriage in Transit, Black Paradise, The Cowboy and the Countess, Madame Spy* (1942), *Hoot Mon* (1939), *Murder Will Out* (1939), *His Brother's Keeper* (1939), *As the Devil Commands* (1933),

The Hound of the Baskervilles: **Nigel Bruce and Richard Greene (right) standing in Hollywood's notion of Dartmoor. (Courtesy National Film Archives of the British Film Institute)**

Although the train window is black in this still, in the finished film it is filled in by process-screen footage of the actual Dartmoor. Rathbone and Bruce in *The Hound of the Baskervilles*. (Courtesy National Film Archives of the British Film Institute)

Frankenstein Meets the Wolfman (1944), *Gypsy Wildcat,* and after the last of the Sherlock Holmes films, *The Black Angel* (1946). He died soon after completing this last film.

THE HOUND OF THE BASKERVILLES

Date of Release: 31 March 1939 in United States; September 1939 in Great Britain
Running Time: 7142 or 7169 feet (80 min.)
Production Company: Twentieth-Century Fox
Associate Producer: Gene Markey
Director: Sidney Lanfield
Screenplay: Ernest Pascal

Director of Photography: Peverell Marley, ASC
In Charge of Production: Darryl F. Zanuck
Art Directors: Richard Day and Hans Peters
Editor: Robert Simpson
Musical Direction: Cyril J. Mockridge
Costumes: Gwen Wakeling
Sound: W. P. Flick and Roger Herman
Set Decorator: Thomas Little
Publicity Drawings: Frederic Dorr Steele
British "A" Certificate

CAST

Sir Henry Baskerville	Richard Greene
Sherlock Holmes	Basil Rathbone
Beryl Stapleton	Wendy Barrie
Dr. James Watson	Nigel Bruce
Dr. Mortimer	Lionel Atwill
Barryman	John Carradine
Frankland	Barlowe Borland
Mrs. Jennifer Mortimer	Beryl Mercer
John Stapleton	Morton Lowry
Sir Hugo Baskerville	Ralph Forbes
Cabby (John Clayton)	E. E. Clive
Mrs. Barryman	Eily Malyon
Convict (Selden)	Nigel De Brulier
(possibly replacing *Harry Cording*)	
Mrs. Hudson	Mary Gordon
Roderick	Peter Willes
Shepherd	Ivan Simpson
Sir Charles Baskerville	Ian Maclaren
Bruce	John Burton
Jon	Dennis Green
Edwin	Evan Thomas
Coroner	Lionel Pape

SYNOPSIS: This film follows the novel quite closely.

The Baskerville legend originated in 1650 with the mysterious death of Sir Hugo Baskerville. Since then all male members of the Baskerville family have died violently. The most recent was Sir Charles Baskerville, who seems to have been killed by a ghost hound. His death leaves the mansion and estate to Sir Henry Baskerville. Dr. Mortimer, a family friend, is worried about Sir Henry and hires Sherlock Holmes and Dr. Watson to keep him alive. Watson and Sir Henry travel together to Baskerville Hall. Holmes also goes to the moor, but remains hidden. The housekeeper's brother is an escaped convict hiding on the moor, and the housekeeper and her husband have been leaving food and clothing out for him. Putting on Sir Henry's clothes, the convict is killed by the Hound, who has been trained to attack by the scent of the next victim's clothes by Stapleton—an heir to the Baskerville estate, anxious to kill Sir Henry. The next attempt to kill Sir Henry is foiled by Holmes and Watson, who kills the Hound, but not before Holmes is trapped in an abandoned mine shaft by Stapleton. Holmes escapes and returns to the scene in time to rescue Sir Henry and see Stapleton captured by the police.

A seance scene was written in that was not in the novel, and it served well to introduce other suspects in Dr. Mortimer and his strange wife.

There are sequences similar to the Norwood *Hound*, such as Watson leaping out of bed with a revolver. Some romance was also added in the person of Beryl Stapleton, who falls for Sir Henry (and vice versa).

The closing line, surprising for 1939, is Holmes' line: "Quick, Watson—the needle," referring to Holmes cocaine habit.

REVIEWS (From the *Spectator,* 14 July 1939; by Graham Greene):

The cinema has never yet done justice to Sherlock Holmes . . . atmosphere of unmechanised Edwardian flurry is well caught; the villain bowls recklessly along Baker Street in a hansom and our hero discusses plans of action in a four-wheeler. The genuine Holmes London, too, is neatly touched in through the cab windows. . . . Dartmoor is a rather gothic landscape. . . . What is wrong, surely, is Mr. Rathbone's reading of the Great Character: the good humor . . . and the general air of brisk good health . . . the deductions are reduced to a bare minimum and the plot is swollen . . . what we really need in a Holmes picture is far more dialogue and far less action. Let us be presented in a series of close-ups, as poor Dr. Watson was, with all the materials for deduction, and let the toothmarks on a walking stick, the mud on a pair of boots, the stained fingernail be the chief characters in a Holmes film.

Other reviewers said that Rathbone was the perfect Holmes, but maybe a trifle young; that Nigel Bruce was an excellent, if not quite Conanical, Watson; and that they worked very well together. Rathbone was forty-seven years old when this film was made. It is hard to understand the comments about his youth, except that Norwood and Wontner were considerably older when their films were made, and that reviewers must have been making mental comparisons between Rathbone and the older Holmeses.

Supporting players Carradine, Atwill, and Lowry also received good notices. Richard Greene received top billing because he was Fox's newest romantic lead, but delivered an unremarkable performance.

Criticisms leveled at the film included (but were not limited to) slow pace, sparse music, and unsatisfactory exterior sets on sound stages; but the film was popular, and inspired Fox to make a sequel that same year.

THE ADVENTURES OF SHERLOCK HOLMES

Date of Release: 1 September 1939 in the United States. March 1940 in Great Britain as *Sherlock Holmes*
Running Time: (various reported times) 85 min., 82 min., 81 min.
Production Company: Twentieth-Century Fox release of a Gene Markey Production.
Associate Producer: Gene Markey

Dr. Watson (Nigel Bruce) is extricated by the Tower of London guards from the overturned carriage where he has been summarily abandoned by his thoughtless colleague Mr. Holmes, who is in a great hurry to thwart Moriarty's scheme to steal the Crown Jewels. *Adventures of Sherlock Holmes*, **1939. (Courtesy National Film Archives of the British Film Institute)**

Executive Producer: Darryl F. Zanuck
Director: Alfred Werker
Screenplay: Edwin Blum & William Drake
Director of Photography: Leon Shamroy
Art Director: Richard Day & Hans Peters
Editor: Robert Bischoff
Musical Director: Cyril J. Mockridge
Set Decorator: Thomas Little

CAST

Sherlock Holmes	Basil Rathbone
Dr. Watson	Nigel Bruce
Ann Brandon	Ida Lupino
Jerrold Hunter	Alan Marshal
Billy	Terry Kilburn
Professor Moriarty	George Zucco
Sir Ronald Ramsgate	Henry Stephenson
Inspector Bristol	E. E. Clive
Bassick	Arthur Hohl
Mrs. Jameson	May Beatty
Lloyd Brandon	Peter Willes
Mrs. Hudson	Mary Gordon
Justice	Holmes Herbert
Mateo	George Regas
Lady Conyngham	Mary Forbes
Dawes (Butler)	Frank Dawson
Stranger	William Austin
?	Anthony Kemble Cooper

SYNOPSIS: The film opens with Moriarty being acquitted of murder. An instant too late, Holmes bursts in with new evidence. Leaving the courthouse in the same cab, Holmes remarks to Moriarty that he

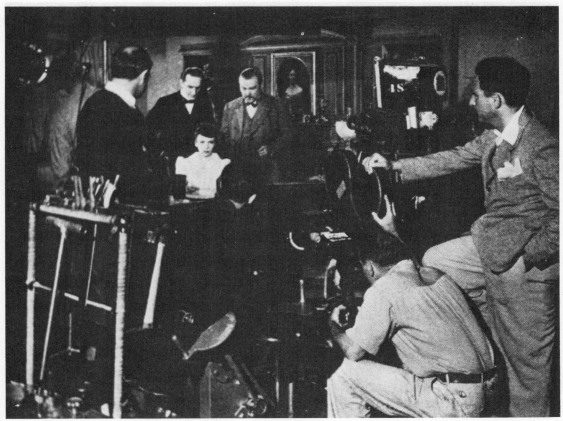

A production still from *Adventures of Sherlock Holmes*, showing Holmes (Rathbone) and Watson (Nigel Bruce) conferring with their client Ann Brandon (Ida Lupino). Director of Photography Leon Shamroy is visible, extreme right.

would like to present the Professor's brain pickled to a scientific society. "It would make an interesting exhibit," agrees Moriarty. Moriarty drops Holmes off at Baker Street and proceeds to his own abode, complete with greenhouse full of flowers, to formulate a scheme to humiliate and defeat Holmes. His plan calls for diverting Holmes' attention by presenting him with two cases; and knowing that Holmes will choose the more interesting of the two, concocts a complicated murder threat involving Ann Brandon and her family to mask the real crime—the theft of the Crown Jewels. Ann's brother Lloyd is mysteriously murdered, and Holmes, deeply involved in this investigation, sends Watson to guard the Crown Jewels. Unknown to Watson, the police escort with him is in reality Moriarty (having shaved off his beard) and his gang in disguise. Holmes manages to save Ann from the murderer, capture the murderer (who, by the way, is a South American Indian who kills with a bolo, limps on a clubfoot, carries a chinchilla foot for good luck, and plays very strange flute music throughout the earlier scenes), and get to the Tower of London in time to shoot it out with Moriarty, who falls off the Tower, presumably to his death (at least temporarily).

This film is probably the best of all the Rathbone Holmes films; it has everything working for it: a large enough budget, a fine cast, elegant sets and costumes, an exciting screenplay, a first-rate director, and beautiful photography.

REVIEWS (From *Variety*): "The Holmes character seems tailored for Rathbone . . . "

(From the *Sherlock Holmes Journal*, Winter 1970, review by Howlett): "Nigel Bruce gave a brilliantly acted portrayal of Dr. Watson (even if his interpretation seemed wrong) and George Zucco was villainous as Moriarty. . . . This was indeed a tremendous film."

SHERLOCK HOLMES AND THE VOICE OF TERROR

Date of Release: 18 September 1942 in the United States; 22 November 1942 in Great Britain
Production Company: Universal
Running Time: (various reported) 69 min., 65 min., 56 min.
Associate Producer: Howard Benedict
Director: John Rawlins
Screenplay: Lynn Riggs
Adaptation: Robert D. Andrews & John Bright
Based on: Doyle's "His Last Bow"
Director of Photography: Woody Bredell
Art Director: Jack Otterson

George Zucco, who made a suave and egocentric aesthete of Professor Moriarty in *Adventures of Sherlock Holmes.*

Editor: Russell Schoengarth (or Schoengart)
Musical Director: Charles Previn

CAST

Sherlock Holmes	Basil Rathbone
Dr. Watson	Nigel Bruce
Kitty	Evelyn Ankers
Sir Evan Barham	Reginald Denny
Sir Alfred Lloyd	Henry Daniell
General Jerome Lawford	Montague Love
Meade	Thomas Gomez
Admiral Fabian Prentiss	Olaf Hytten
Captain Ronald Shore	Leyland Hodgson
Jill Grandis	Hillary Brooke
Mrs. Hudson	Mary Gordon
Crosbie	Arthur Blake
Taxi Driver	Harry Stubbs

Working Title: *Sherlock Holmes Saves London* (we're glad they changed it!)

SYNOPSIS: Doyle's story "His Last Bow" about a German spy living quite respectably in England was modernized to World War Two London; which of course gave the scriptwriters (and therefore Holmes) the opportunity to make some rather stirring patriotic speeches, but the most famous of these was lifted right out of the Doyle original story, the closing passage about an "East wind coming . . ."

Holmes is hired by the British Inner Council to find the German agent in their midst who has been passing information to "The Voice of Terror"—a Nazi propaganda radio broadcaster who announces various acts of sabotage as they are happening: train wrecks, ships' sinkings, generator stations demolished, etc. Holmes in turn hires Kitty to spy on Meade, a known Nazi agent. Holmes deduces that a "Voice" prediction of an invasion on the Northern English coast is a diversion to cover the real invasion on the South coast, and persuades the Prime Minister to reinforce the area. Holmes unmasks the spy in the Council's midst, Sir Evan Barham, and rushes to the South coast in time to capture Meade and his other spies, but not in time to save Kitty, who is killed by Meade.

REVIEWS (From *Variety*): "Rathbone carries the Sherlock Holmes role in great style, getting able assistance from the flustery Bruce as Dr. Watson."

This first of the Universal low-budget modern thrillers is typical of the rest of the series, except that John Rawlins directed this one, and Roy William Neill all the others. The plot is a trifle silly, and the dialogue stilted, and the general production value "cheap." Logic, reason, and deduction are replaced by action, action, and more action.

Reginald Denny was a veteran of Barrymore's 1922 film; Henry Daniell was to appear several times in the series; and Thomas Gomez played Moriarty in Rathbone's stage play "Sherlock Holmes," written by his wife Ouida.

The villainous Nazi spy Sir Evan Barham (Reginald Denny) arranges an attempt on his own life to throw suspicion away from himself in *Sherlock Holmes and the Voice of Terror.* Here Watson (Nigel Bruce) inspects Barham's wounded hand as Olaf Hytten, Leyland Hodgson, Henry Daniell, Basil Rathbone, and Montague Love look on.

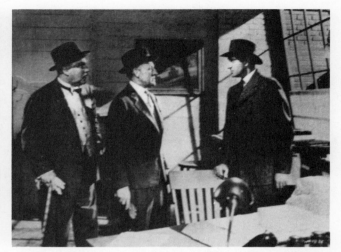

The opening sequence of *Sherlock Holmes and the Secret Weapon*. Disguised as an itinerant bookseller, Holmes (Basil Rathbone) demonstrates to Dr. Hans Tobel (William Post, Jr.) how the latter's valuable bombsight model can be concealed in a specially prepared volume.

Basil Rathbone and Nigel Bruce flank Holmes Herbert in the set for *Sherlock Holmes and the Secret Weapon*. Director Roy William Neill was a master at turning a routine set into a striking one by the use of simply achieved but sumptuous lighting effects. Note Rathbone's extravagantly Gordon Craigish hat.

SHERLOCK HOLMES AND THE SECRET WEAPON

Date of Release: December 1942 in the United States; 2 January 1943 in Great Britain
Running Time: 68 min.
Production Company: Universal
Associate Producer: Howard Benedict
Director: Roy William Neill
Screenplay: Edward T. Lowe, W. Scott Darling, Edmund L. Hartmann
Based on: Doyle's *The Dancing Men*
Adaptation: W. Scott Darling, Edmund L. Hartmann
Photography: Lester White
Art Director: Jack Otterson
Editor: Otto Ludwig
Musical Director: Charles Previn
Music Score: Frank Skinner

CAST

Sherlock Holmes	Basil Rathbone
Dr. Watson	Nigel Bruce
Charlotte Eberli	Kaaren Verne
Professor Moriarty	Lionel Atwill
Inspector Lestrade	Dennis Hoey
Dr. Franz Tobel	William Post, Jr.
Peg Leg	Harold deBecker
Mrs. Hudson	Mary Gordon
Meuller	Paul Fix
Braun	Robert O. Davis
Sir Reginald	Holmes Herbert
Brady	Harry Cording
Kurt	Phillip Van Zandt (or Harry Woods)
Gottfried	George Burr MacAnnan
Hoffner	Henry Victor

SYNOPSIS: Dr. Franz Tobel has invented a new and better bombsight, and with the help of Sherlock Holmes, manages to escape Nazi agents in Switzerland and travel to England. There he divides the prototype in four parts, entrusting each to a different scientist, and encodes the list of scientists into a code comprised of stick figures ("Dancing Men"). Moriarty, hired by the Nazis to get the bombsight, kidnaps Tobel. Holmes is left with the coded message, which he decodes and tries to get to the scientists before Moriarty does, but arrives too late in the first three cases. He masquerades as the fourth scientist, and when Moriarty shows up for the fourth part of the bombsight, Holmes tells him that the item is at Scotland Yard. Moriarty attempts to kill Holmes by draining his blood, but this takes much too long, and Watson and the police intervene. Moriarty dies (again) falling through a trap door into the river.

REVIEWS: This film gave Sherlock a better chance to do some real detecting and brain work, and did not have the emphasis on action like its predecessor in the Universal series. This episode was Roy William Neill's first Holmesian effort and shows a marked improvement in style, pace, and atmosphere. Universal was also apparently pleased, since Neill went on to direct ten more Universal entries.

SHERLOCK HOLMES IN WASHINGTON

Date of Release: 30 April 1943 in the United States; 8

February 1944 in Great Britain
Running Time: 6430 ft. (71½ min.)
Production Company: Universal
Associate Producer: Howard Benedict
Director: Roy William Neill
Based on Characters Created by Sir Arthur Conan Doyle
Original Story: Bertram Millhauser
Screenplay: Bertram Millhauser & Lynn Riggs
Director of Photography: Lester White
Editor: Otto Ludwig
Art Director: Jack Otterson
Musical Director: Charles Previn
Music Score: Frank Skinner

CAST

Sherlock Holmes	Basil Rathbone
Dr. Watson	Nigel Bruce
Nancy Partridge	Marjorie Lord
William Easter	Henry Daniell
Stanley	George Zucco
Lt. Peter Merriam	John Archer
Bart Lang	Gavin Muir
Detective Lt. Grogan	Edmund MacDonald
Howe	Don Terry
Cady	Bradley Page
Mr. Ahrens	Holmes Herbert
Senator Henry Babcock	Thurston Hall
Sir Henry Marchmont	Gilbert Emery
Clerk	Ian Wolfe

Two views of the Holmes-Moriarty conflict from *Sherlock Holmes and the Secret Weapon*. That splendid actor Lionel Atwill seemed to be just going through the motions as his umpteenth villain. Notice Rathbone's curious hairstyle, a bizarre echo of the decadent nineties, which was abandoned after the first few episodes in the "modern" Universal series.

SYNOPSIS: This was the first Rathbone Holmes film not based at least in part on a Doyle story. Holmes is trying to recover a document microfilmed and hidden in a matchbook by a British agent in the United States. The agent is killed, and the matchbook has been passed to another passenger on the train without her knowing what she is now carrying. Holmes is competing with Nazi agents also eager to recover the document. The Nazis kidnap the girl with the matches, and Holmes traces the spies and their captive to their antique-shop headquarters. Holmes is captured by the villains, but is rescued by Watson and the police just in time. The ringleader escapes, but Holmes captures him later with the elusive matchbook in his pocket, not realizing that he had the document with him all the time.

The Washington setting lent very well to Holmes' pro-Allies, anti-Axis, "hands-across-the-sea" patriotism propaganda messages, but the poor script made this film second-rate.

REVIEWS (From the *Hollywood Reporter*): "Basil Rathbone is just what he should be in the title role, and Nigel Bruce is supplied with much bright comedy of which he is quick to make the most."

SHERLOCK HOLMES FACES DEATH

Date of Release: 17 September 1943
Running Time: 68 min.

Sherlock Holmes in Washington was undoubtedly the weakest episode of the series, but it gave Rathbone a chance to speak some Winston Churchill lines. The young lady in the photo that Holmes is studying is Marjorie Lord, and Thurston Hall had a splendid cameo as a glad-handing United States senator. Note the un-Sherlockian cigarette. (Courtesy National Film Archives of the British Film Institute)

Production Company: Universal
Producer: Roy William Neill
Director: Roy William Neill
Screenplay: Bertram Millhauser
Based on: Doyle's *Musgrave Ritual*
Director of Photography: Charles Van Enger
Art Director: John Goodman & Harold MacArthur
Editor: Fred Feitchans
Musical Director: H. J. Satter

CAST

Sherlock Holmes	Basil Rathbone
Dr. Watson	Nigel Bruce
Sally Musgrave	Hillary Brooke
Captain Vickery	Milburn Stone
Dr. Sexton	Arthur Margetson
Brunton	Halliwell Hobbes
Inspector Lestrade	Dennis Hoey
Phillip Musgrave	Gavin Muir
Geoffrey Musgrave	Frederic Worlock
Captain MacIntosh	Olaf Hytten
Lanford	Gerald Hamer
Clavering	Vernon Downing
Mrs. Howells	Minna Phillips
Mrs. Hudson	Mary Gordon
Jenny	Heather Wilde
2nd Sailor	Peter Lawford
Pub Proprietor	Harold de Becker

Nigel Bruce and Basil Rathbone in *Sherlock Holmes Faces Death*. Director Neill got some of his best lighting effects with an artificial light source behind bushes at a window.

SYNOPSIS: Watson has returned to his medical practice and is in charge of an army officers' convalescent home in Musgrave Manor. Holmes arrives after Watson's assistant, Dr. Sexton, is assaulted. Soon after Holmes' arrival, Phillip and Geoffrey Musgrave are both murdered, shortly after the tower clock strikes thirteen. The sole heir to the Musgrave estate, Sally, by custom in the family, has to read out the ceremonial "Musgrave Ritual," which Holmes believes to contain the motive for the crimes. As usual, Holmes' hunches are right, and using the Manor's main-hall floor as a giant chessboard and people as chess pieces, the "Ritual" leads them to a hidden cellar and a long-forgotten land grant, which proves to be the motive for the triple murder. The guilty party is tricked by Holmes with a blank-loaded revolver into confessing in front of Holmes, Watson, and Lestrade.

REVIEWS: This film is considered by many to be one of the best of the Universal series. The script is pretty good, the plot not only believable but interesting, the supporting cast more than adequate, and the atmosphere of mystery convincing.
(From the *Sherlock Holmes Journal,* Vol. 9, #1):
"The story was set during World War II and had many distinctive echoes of 'The Musgrave Ritual.' The 'reading' of the ritual in terms of chessmen upon a chess board was ingenius, and one would like to see the film again, so as to follow the clues with the benefit of knowing the solution."
NOTE: This film was released with *Pearl of Death* in Germany as *Sherlock Holmes Jagt Den Teufel von Soho* (Sherlock Holmes Hunts the Soho Devil).

THE SPIDER WOMAN (SHERLOCK HOLMES AND THE SPIDER WOMAN)

Date of Release: 21 January 1944 in the United States; 8 May 1944 in Great Britain
Production Company: Universal
Producer: Roy William Neill
Director: Roy William Neill
Running Time: 5606 ft. (62 min.)
Screenplay: Bertram Millhauser
Based on: Elements of *The Sign of Four*
Director of Photography: Charles Van Enger
Art Director: John B. Goodman
Editor: James Gibbon

CAST

Sherlock Holmes	Basil Rathbone
Dr. Watson	Nigel Bruce
Adrea Spedding	Gale Sondergaard
Inspector Lestrade	Dennis Hoey
Norman Locke	Vernon Downing
Radlik	Alec Craig
Adam Gilflower	Arthur Hohl
Colonel	Stanley Logan
Artie	Donald Stuart
Croupier	John Roche
Mrs. Hudson	Mary Gordon
Announcer	John Barton
Colonel's Wife	Lydia Bilbrook
Fortune Teller	Belle Mitchell
Fred Garvin	Harry Cording
Clerk	John Rogers
Boy	Teddy Infuhr
Charwoman	Marie de Becker

SYNOPSIS: A rash of "Pajama Suicides" plague London, and Holmes fakes his own death in order to work "underground" on the investigation. Disguised as a Hindu, he meets Adrea Spedding (played by Academy Award winner Gale Sondergaard), who turns out to be a veritable female Moriarty. Spedding has worked out an elaborate scheme, lending money in exchange for signatures on insurance-policy endorsements, making Spedding's accomplices the beneficiaries of the policies, and then murdering the insured to collect the money. The murders are also ingenius, committed by a spider whose venom drives the victim to suicide because of the intense pain it causes. The spiders are delivered to the victims' hotel rooms by a pygmy through an air shaft. The attempt to kill Holmes with the spider fails, as does a poison-gas attack on Holmes and Watson. The most exciting scene comes near the end, when a captured Holmes is tied behind a target in a shooting gallery at an amusement park and is shot at unknowingly by Watson. Holmes escapes in time to capture the gang, needless to say.

The character Spider Woman appealed to a large enough audience that a spinoff film was made without Holmes soon after, starring Gale Sondergaard and Rondo Hatton ("The Creeper" from *Pearl of Death*).

Combined with *The Scarlet Claw,* this film was released in Germany as *Sherlock Holmes Sieht Demtod Ins Gesicht* (Sherlock Holmes Faces Death), though it contained no footage from that film, which was also released in Germany under still another title.

REVIEW: (From the New York *Times*): "Basil Rathbone plays the versatile detective with his usual serene elegance."

THE SCARLET CLAW (SHERLOCK HOLMES AND THE SCARLET CLAW)

Date of Release: 26 May 1944 in the United States; 18 September 1944 in Great Britain
Running Time: 6657 ft. (74 min.)
Production Company: Universal
Producer: Roy William Neill
Director: Roy William Neill
Screenplay: Edmund L. Hartmann & Roy William Neill
Original Story: Paul Gangelin and Brenda Weisberg
Director of Photography: George Robinson
Musical Director: Paul Sawtell

Disguised as a Sikh soldier addicted to gambling, Holmes (Basil Rathbone) appears to be more interested in *The Spider Woman*'s eyes than her palm. Gale Sondergaard made a magnificent foil for the sleuth and their subtle battles of wits were perfectly balanced. (Courtesy National Film Archives of the British Film Institute)

Art Directors: John B. Goodman & Ralph M. DeLacy
Editor: Paul Landres
Special Photography: John P. Fulton

CAST

Sherlock Holmes	Basil Rathbone
Dr. Watson	Nigel Bruce
Potts	
Tanner	
Alistar Ramson	Gerald Hamer
Lord Penrose	Paul Cavanagh
Emile Journet	Arthur Hohl
Judge Brisson	Miles Mander
Marie Journet	Kay Harding
Sergeant Thompson	David Clyde
Drake	Ian Wolfe

Nigel Bruce, Arthur Hohl, and Basil Rathbone on the set of 221B Baker Street in *The Spider Woman*.

181

Nora	Victoria Horne
Father Pierre	George Kirby
Cab Driver	Frank O'Connor
Storekeeper	Harry Allen

SYNOPSIS: Holmes and Watson travel to the village of La Morte Rouge in Canada (an appropriate name—"The Red Death"), which has seen several ghastly and ghostly murders supposedly committed by a legendary phantom. Holmes soon deduces that there is nothing supernatural about the murders; that they are being committed by Alistair Ramson, an actor imprisoned nearby but now at large. He is killing the people he holds responsible for his imprisonment: the judge that sentenced him, the prison guard, etc. Ramson has adopted several disguises to aid him in his revenge, and Holmes adopts one himself to catch Ramson. The fight between Holmes and Ramson on the fog-bound swamp, and the Ramson fight and death at the hands of one of his victim's fathers, are highly effective and memorable.

REVIEWS: (From Michael Druxman's fine work *Basil Rathbone: His Life and His Films*):

The Scarlet Claw was, unquestionably, the best picture in the Sherlock Holmes series. The suspenseful screenplay by Roy William Neill and Edward L. Hartmann was almost a horror story and Neill's imaginative direction, aided by the superb special effects of John P. Fulton, turned the film into a minor masterpiece of that genre. . . . The production had many unforgettable moments: a dead woman's hand clutching a bellrope; the luminous "monster" stalking Holmes in the marsh; the murder of the judge, with the killer being disguised as a woman. Each scene helped to create a film that kept audiences guessing until the conclusion. . . . Rathbone and Bruce were at their best . . . and they received fine support from Gerald Hamer and Miles Mander.

THE PEARL OF DEATH

Date of Release: 22 September 1944 in the United States; 19 February 1945 in Great Britain
Running Time:(various reported) 6184 ft. (69 min.), 67 min.
Production Company: Universal
Executive Producer: Howard S. Benedict
Producer: Roy William Neill
Director: Roy William Neill
Screenplay: Bertram Millhauser
Based on: Doyle's *The Six Napoleons*
Director of Photography: Virgil Miller
Art Directors: John B. Goodman & Martin Obzina
Editor: Ray Snyder
Musical Director: Paul Sawtell

CAST

Sherlock Holmes	Basil Rathbone
Dr. Watson	Nigel Bruce

Sherlock Holmes (Basil Rathbone) struggles with Alistair Ramson (Gerald Hamer) in the final scenes of *The Scarlet Claw*, 1944.

Inspector Lestrade	Dennis Hoey
Naomi Drake	Evelyn Ankers
Amos Hodder	Ian Wolfe
Digby	Charles Francis
James Goodram	Holmes Herbert
Bates	Richard Nugent
Mrs. Hudson	Mary Gordon
The Creeper	Rondo Hatton
Teacher	Audrey Manners
Boss	Harold de Becker
Customs Officer	Leland Hodgson
Giles Conover	Miles Mander

SYNOPSIS: The Borgia Pearls are stolen from a museum by master jewel thief Giles Conover, but in his

A crew member is caught in the mirror in this *Pearl of Death* production still. Holmes (Basil Rathbone), in surgical garb, tries to explain the significance of a clue to Dr. Watson (Nigel Bruce) who is dumbstruck as usual. (Courtesy National Film Archives of the British Film Institute)

escape after the crime, he is nearly caught, and he hides the pearls inside the wet plaster of one of six busts of Napoleon. When he comes back later for the bust with the pearls, he discovers that the six busts have been sold. He and his homicidal sidekick, "The Creeper," track down the six owners of the busts and kill them. Holmes reaches the sixth and last bust owner first and impersonates him to wait for Conover's arrival. After a struggle, the "Creeper" kills Conover, and Holmes kills the "Creeper" (but only temporarily, because Universal revived him for several sequels without Holmes).

REVIEWS: Critics and fans liked this Holmes entry very much. It had all the things going for it that *The Scarlet Claw* had: good script, fine cast, imaginative direction, and superb photography—all combined to make a delightful film.

THE HOUSE OF FEAR

Date of Release: 16 March 1945 in the United States; 9 July 1945 in Great Britain
Running Time: (Various reported) 5986 ft. (66½ min.); 69 min.
Production Company: Universal
Producer: Roy William Neill
Director: Roy William Neill
Screenplay: Roy Chanslor
Based on: Doyle's *The Adventure of the Five Orange Pips*
Director of Photography: Virgil Miller
Art Directors: John B. Goodman, Eugene Lowrie
Editor: Saul Goodkind
Musical Director: Paul Sawtell

It turns out that *everyone* is guilty in *House of Fear*. Harry Cording, Paul Cavanagh, Holmes Herbert, Dick Alexander, and Cyril Delevanti (left to right) are advised to keep their hands up by Holmes (Basil Rathbone) and Inspector Lestrade (Dennis Hoey). Hoey's characterization of the Scotland Yard man was more broadly comic than Doyle envisioned, but remained thoroughly human. Pig-headed and invincibly stupid though he was, Lestrade was still capable of quick action and sincere feeling. Hoey's comic interludes with Nigel Bruce were marvelous.

Sherlock Holmes (Basil Rathbone, with pipe) questions Leonard Mudie in *House of Fear*. The hat Holmes is wearing is nearly identical to those sported by his earlier screen impersonators Brook and Wontner. (Courtesy National Film Archives of the British Film Institute)

CAST

Sherlock Holmes	Basil Rathbone
Dr. Watson	Nigel Bruce
Alastair	Aubrey Mather
Inspector Lestrade	Dennis Hoey
Simon Merrivale	Paul Cavanagh
Alan Cosgrove	Holmes Herbert
John Simpson	Harry Cording
Mrs. Monteith	Sally Shepherd
Chalmers	Gavin Muir
Alison MacGregor	Florette Hillier
Alex MacGregor	David Clyde
Guy Davis	Wilson Benge
Sergeant Bleeker	Leslie Denison
Angus	Alec Craig
King	Dick Alexander

SYNOPSIS: Rathbone began to run down in this film; his attitude is wrong, and it is obvious that he is beginning to tire of the role of Holmes. His performance is even called "pedestrian" by more than one reviewer. And anyway, Watson is the one that discovers the final clue to the mystery, although he does not realize it at the time, and gets himself kidnapped because of that discovery.

"The Good Comrades"—a club of men living together in a Scottish castle, and having set up a group insurance policy among themselves, declaring any surviving members as joint beneficiaries to the total insured amount—is slowly being decimated by a series of mysterious murders. The victims are first warned by receiving envelopes containing dried orange pips, in decreasing numbers—one for each surviving member. When the number gets to five, Holmes, Watson, and Lestrade arrive on the scene but are unable to prevent the reduction of the number of survivors to one—Alastair. All the others have disappeared, leaving only mutilated bodies. Watson notices that the late sea captain's favorite shag tobacco is missing, and is kidnapped for his observation. Holmes and Lestrade are not far behind, and discover the secret smugglers' cave below the mansion. All the "Good Comrades" are hiding there, having faked their deaths and substituted recently dead bodies from the local churchyard in order to collect the insurance.

Reviewers called this film "disappointing, lacking in interest, slow-moving, and dull."

THE WOMAN IN GREEN

Date of Release: 27 July 1945 in the United States; 20 August 1945 in Great Britain
Running Time: 6094 ft. (68 min.)
Production Company: Universal
Producer: Roy William Neill
Director: Roy William Neill
Screenplay: Bertram Millhauser
Based on Characters Created by Sir Arthur Conan Doyle
Director of Photography: Virgil Miller
Art Directors: John B. Goodman & Martin Obzina
Editor: Edward Curtiss
Musical Director: Mark Levant
Special Effects: John P. Fulton

CAST

Sherlock Holmes	Basil Rathbone
Dr. Watson	Nigel Bruce
Lydia Marlowe	Hillary Brooke
Professor Moriarty	Henry Daniell
Sir George Fenwick	Paul Cavanagh
Inspector Gregson	Matthew Boulton
Maude	Eve Amber
Onslow	Frederick Worlock
Williams	Tom Bryon
Crandon	Sally Shepherd
Mrs. Hudson	Mary Gordon
Dr. Simnell	Percival Vivian
Norris	Olaf Hytten
Shabby Man	Harold de Becker
Newsman	Tommy Hughes

SYNOPSIS: Several beautiful women in London have been murdered and have had their right forefinger amputated after their deaths. Scotland Yard is stumped (no pun intended), and Holmes is asked to help. Moriarty has arisen from the grave to become the prime suspect and indeed the culprit behind this complicated blackmail plot against Sir George Fenwick. The "Woman in Green" is an attractive hypnotist involved with Moriarty in the scheme, having hypnotized Fenwick into believing he committed the "Finger Murders" and planting the latest finger in his pocket. Fenwick is murdered by Moriarty when the blackmail attempt falls flat by Fenwick's plan to confess to the crimes. Holmes allows himself to be hypnotized and almost killed, but he is faking the trance, and Watson and Gregson arrive as usual in the nick of time. Moriarty once again perishes in a fall from a rooftop, and the rest of the gang is captured.

Henry Daniell was thought by many to be the "ideal" Moriarty, including executive producer Howard S. Benedict and Basil Rathbone himself. Clearly his superb performance in this film earns him a place in the Holmesian Hall of Fame, next to those other dastardly Moriartys Gustav von Seyffertitz, Lyn Harding, and Ernest Torrence. His performance was the most redeeming feature about this otherwise dreary film.

Universal had become a virtual stock-company of Holmes film character actors, much as had Stoll for the Norwood films. In addition to regulars Rathbone, Bruce, Mary Gordon, and Dennis Hoey (although replaced in this film by Matthew Boulton), this film featured such veterans of prior Rathbone Holmes films as Hillary Brooke, Henry Daniell, Paul Cavanagh, Frederic Worlock, Olaf Hytten, Harold de Becker, and Sally Shepherd.

Reviewers complained of a weak script, poor production values, disappointing direction, and a bored Rathbone.

PURSUIT TO ALGIERS

Date of Release: 26 October 1945 in the United States; 4 February 1946 in Great Britain
Running Time: 65 min.
Production Company: Universal
Executive Producer: Howard S. Benedict
Producer: Roy William Neill
Director: Roy William Neill
Screenplay: Leonard Lee
Director of Photography: Paul Ivano
Art Directors: John B. Goodman & Martin Obzina
Editor: Saul A. Goodkind
Musical Director: Edgar Fairchild

CAST

Sherlock Holmes	Basil Rathbone
Dr. Watson	Nigel Bruce
Sheila	Marjorie Riordan
Agatha Dunham	Rosalind Ivan
Mirko	Martin Kosleck
Jodri	John Abbott
Prime Minister	Frederic Worlock
Sanford	Morton Lowry
Nikolas	Leslie Vincent
Kingston	Gerald Hamer

Hillary Brook is *The Woman in Green*, and with her friend Moriarty (Henry Daniell) she waits for the supposedly hypnotized Holmes (Basil Rathbone) to take one step too many. Rathbone's favorite Moriarty, and probably the cinema's most restrained interpreters of the role, Daniell would also have made a fine Holmes himself, given the opportunity. Certainly in *The Sea Hawk*, Daniell successfully stepped into another role that seemed to have been tailored for Rathbone. (Courtesy National Film Archives of the British Film Institute)

Gregor	Rex Evans
Restaurant Proprietor	Tom Dillon
Johansson	Sven Hugo Borg
Gubec	Wee Willie Davis
Clergyman	Wilson Benge
Ravez	Gregory Gay
Woman	Dorothy Kellogg

Mary Gordon is depicted here as a rather more stern and forbidding character than her grandmotherly Mrs. Hudson for the Rathbone Holmes series.

185

Pursuit to Algiers: **(left to right) Marjorie Riordan, Nigel Bruce, Basil Rathbone, Leslie Vincent. (Courtesy National Film Archives of the British Film Institute)**

SYNOPSIS: The bulk of the film takes place on an ocean liner, on which Holmes and Watson are escorting King Nikolas to Algiers to be delivered into the hands of a representative of his government. Unfortunately, there are assassins on board who have other ideas. The king and Holmes are kidnapped, but the criminals are captured and the king is revealed to be a decoy while the real king was travelling as a ship's steward.

This is probably the worst of the Rathbone Holmes films, marred by a second-rate script, lackadaisical direction, extreme low-budget production values, and poor acting (except for Nigel Bruce, who has some wonderfully comic moments, and even sings "Loch Lomond").

TERROR BY NIGHT

Date of Release: 1 February 1946 in the United States; 8 June 1946 in Great Britain.
Running Time: 60 min.
Production Company: Universal
Executive Producer: Howard S. Benedict
Producer: Roy William Neill
Director: Roy William Neill
Screenplay: Frank Gruber
Based on Characters Created by Sir Arthur Conan Doyle
Director of Photography: Maury Gertsman
Art Director: John B. Goodman
Editor: Saul A. Goodkind
Musical Director: Mark Levant

CAST

Sherlock Holmes	Basil Rathbone
Dr. Watson	Nigel Bruce
Major Duncan Bleek	

(Col. Sebastian Moran)	Alan Mowbray
Inspector Lestrade	Dennis Hoey
Vivian Vedder	Renee Godfrey
Lady Margaret Carstairs	Mary Forbes
Train Attendant	Billy Bevan
Professor Kilbane	Frederic Worlock
Conductor	Leyland Hodgson
Hon. Ronald Carstairs	Geoffrey Steele
Inspector McDonald	Boyd Davis
Mrs. Shallcross	Janet Murdoch
Sands	Skelton Knaggs
Mr. Shallcross	Gerald Hamer
Mock	Harry Cording
Guard	Charles Knight

SYNOPSIS: Short but fast-moving, this film corrected many of the things that were wrong with previous films: Neill and Rathbone have greatly improved their performances; the script was very good; and the whole production was considerably more of what all Holmes films should be, but which all too few are.

Hired to safeguard the "Star of Rhodesia" diamond while en route from London to Edinburgh by fast train, Holmes and Watson discover the owner dead and the gem stolen. Interrogating the passengers in their inimitable fashion, they suspect the crime is the handiwork of Col. Sebastian Moran, Moriarty's right arm. Moran's air-gun proves to be a very effective weapon, indeed, as two more people are murdered. Watson and Lestrade help Holmes expose Moran's disguise as Duncan Bleek; and unfooled by phony policemen, Holmes does some fantastic sleight-of-hand in a darkened railway car and manages to set up the rest of the gang for Lestrade to capture. The gem is returned to the rightful owner, and all is well in the world.

Dennis Hoey returned to the series as Lestrade, and delivered his usual competent and sometimes comic performance. Alan Mowbray, veteran of Clive Brook and Reginald Owen Holmes films as well, makes a fine "heavy."

DRESSED TO KILL (SHERLOCK HOLMES AND THE SECRET CODE in G.B.)

Date of Release: 7 June 1946 in the United States; 26 August 1946 in Great Britain
Running Time: 6477 ft. (72 min.)
Production Company: Universal
Executive Producer: Howard S. Benedict
Producer: Roy William Neill
Director: Roy William Neill
Screenplay: Leonard Lee
Adaptation: Frank Gruber
Director of Photography: Maury Gertsman
Art Directors: Jack Otterson & Martin Obzina
Editor: Saul A. Goodkind
Musical Director: Milton Rosen
Based on a Story by Sir Arthur Conan Doyle

Alan Mowbray returns to the world of Baker Street after a hiatus of thirteen years. In this scene Dr. Watson (Nigel Bruce, right) seems to suspect that his old friend Major Duncan Bleek (Mowbray, left) may not be all he seems. Holmes (Rathbone) looks on with interest.

CAST

Sherlock Holmes	Basil Rathbone
Dr. Watson	Nigel Bruce
Hilda Courtney	Patricia Morrison
Gilbert Emery	Edmond Breon
Colonel Cavanagh	Frederic Worlock
Inspector Hopkins	Carl Harbord
Evelyn Clifford	Patricia Cameron
Detective Thompson	Tom P. Dillon
Hamid	Harry Cording
Kilgour Child	Topsy Glyn
Mrs. Hudson	Mary Gordon

SYNOPSIS: One wishes that such a long series of Holmes films would never end, or at least if it must end, let it end with a bang. Alas, this is not the case. *Dressed to Kill* is the final episode of Rathbone as Holmes (except for his all-too-brief attempt at staging his wife's play on Broadway and several one-shot TV appearances) and it is indeed an unfortunate movie. An inept script, uninspired direction, and mediocre acting by Rathbone close the series with a whimper instead of the desired bang.

The script follows the same formula used in *Pearl of Death* and *Secret Weapon*; Holmes and the criminals are in a race with each other for the prize—in this case, stolen Bank of England engraving plates. Holmes and the criminals, led in this case by a beautiful but deadly woman, have the same clues, and are searching for, in this case, music boxes made in prison by an inmate who has coded the tunes played by the boxes. Needless to say, Holmes gets there first and sets a trap for the gang, which, needless to say, is successful.

Everything seemed to go wrong with this entry: the supporting cast was barely adequate; Rathbone seemed fed up with the character of Holmes; and one of the most redeeming features of the film was Watson's impression of a duck.

There is also a very lyrical use of the moving camera in the sequence where Holmes and Watson descend the stairs at the meeting place of the "buskers" (London street musicians), while an old music-hall cockney song is being sung in the background. And the film makes haunting use of the tune played on the music boxes themselves, for it is repeated with subtle variations on each of the boxes in turn, whistled by Holmes, and finally played on the piano by Holmes' busker friend.

This repetition of a single theme on a number of

Dressed to Kill, **1946: By the end of the series, Rathbone's Holmes had become very melancholy and world weary. Patricia Morrison, pictured here with Rathbone, made the detective's cleverest feminine foil since Irene Adler.**

lone instruments was also used to telling effect in Rathbone's second Fox film, and was quite a sound-track innovation in those pre-*Third Man* days of overorchestrated film scores.

CRAZY HOUSE

Released: October 1943
Production Company: Universal
Running Time: 80 min.
Associate Producer: Erle C. Kenton
Director: Edward F. Cline
Screenplay: Robert Lees & Frederic I. Rinaldo
Director of Photography: Charles Van Enger
Art Directors: John B. Goodman & Harold H.
    MacArthur
Editor: Arthur Hilton
Musical Director: Charles Previn

Rathbone and Bruce played Holmes and Watson in a brief unbilled appearance in this Olsen & Johnson vehicle.

This was the end of the last of the great Sherlock Holmes film series. There have not been any attempts to date to revive Sherlock Holmes as a series character. After this last Rathbone film in 1946, there was not even another single Holmes film for thirteen years—the longest hiatus Sherlock Holmes has ever taken from the screen.

We're sure that at least a partial explanation for this long pause in the filmic history of Sherlock Holmes was that the role of Holmes was so inseparable from Basil Rathbone that for a long time producers were afraid that the public would not accept any Holmes but Rathbone, and any Watson but Bruce.

The three greatest Sherlock Holmes series—Norwood, Wontner, and Rathbone—had an advantage impossible to enjoy for a single film. After the first entry in a series, the characters are firmly identified in the minds of the audience. They need not be constantly reestablished in each subsequent entry. This eases the screenwriters' burden considerably, and was a saving economically as well; it is not necessary to spend the first twenty minutes of a film introducing the regular characters, but you can get right into the meat of the story. This won't help if the stories are weak, as was the case in some of the Rathbone Holmes films, but it is generally true for a series of this type.

In 1959, Hammer Films in England and director Terence Fisher apparently felt that the time was right to revive *The Hound,* the spectre of Rathbone's Holmes having diminished somewhat. We Holmesophiles know that that image will never die; Sherlock Holmes will always be at least partly Basil Rathbone.

21
Peter Cushing

THE HOUND OF THE BASKERVILLES (British)

Date of Release: March or June, 1959 (although there was some sort of press showing as early as 15 November 1958).

Running Time: 7,772 feet; 87 minutes; 84 min.

Production Company: Hammer Film Productions Ltd.; released in the United States by United Artists

Director: Terence Fisher

Executive Producer: Michael Carreras

Producer: Anthony Hinds

Associate Producer: Anthony Nelson Keys

Director of Photography: Jack Asher

Screenplay: Peter Bryan

Editor: James Needs

Art Director: Bernard Robinson

Musical Director: John Hollingsworth

Music Composed By: James Bernard

Holmes's Costumes: Peter Cushing

Production Manager: Don Weeks

Color: Technicolor

(Wide Screen)

(British "A" Certificate; United States, "R")

CAST

Sherlock Holmes	Peter Cushing
Dr. Watson	Andre Morell
Sir Henry Baskerville	Christopher Lee
Cecile Stapleton	Marla Landi
Sir Hugo Baskerville	David Oxley
Dr. Mortimer	Francis de Wolfe
Bishop Frankland of the Isles	Miles Malleson
Barrymore	John Le Mesurier
Stapleton	Ewen Solon
Perkins	Sam Kydd
Mrs. Barrymore	Helen Goss
Servant Girl	Judi Moyens
Servant	Dave Birks
Lord Caphill	Michael Hawkins
Lord Kingsblood	Ian Hewitson
Mrs. Goodlippe	Elizabeth Dott
Selden	Michael Mulcaster

Holmes (Peter Cushing, right) and Watson (Andre Morell) spring into action in *The Hound of the Baskervilles*. (Courtesy National Film Archives of the British Film Institute)

SYNOPSIS: The film begins with a prologue set in 1740, portraying the origin of the legendary Hell-Hound which haunts the Baskerville family. Sir Hugo Baskerville and his depraved companions, Lords Caphill and Kingsblood, roast one of Baskerville's manservants alive by holding him over an open hearth, and then torment the dead man's rebellious daughter, who is chased by Baskerville and his pack of huntinghounds to the ruins of an ancient abbey on Dartmoor. As an unearthly howling seems to pursue Sir Hugo, and crazed by fear of the sound, he stabs the girl to death. But even as she dies the supernatural baying is heard again, and, as Sir Hugo turns to face it in horror, the Hound of Hell appears from among his own pack and tears out the nobleman's throat.

The curse of Sir Hugo, the legend recounts, is upon the Baskerville family and its descendants in the shape of a "Hound from Hell," bringing to each succeeding generation calamity, violence, and untimely death, which, though it is sometimes peaceful, always comes early to the family.

The scene now switches to the "present" (turn of the century) in Sherlock Holmes' Baker Street study where Dr. Mortimer of Devon has been narrating the legend to Holmes and Watson. Holmes discounts the tale and asks to hear the details about the mysterious death of Sir Charles Baskerville, who has recently been found dead in the same abbey ruins on the moor. Mortimer tells Holmes that "never in all my medical career have I seen such a look of horror on a dead man's face." He adds that the howl of the hound was heard at the same time. Holmes eventually deduces that the dead man was running in panic across the moor. Mortimer retains Holmes and Watson to safeguard the interests of the heir to the baronetcy, Sir Henry Baskerville, who is due to arrive in London from South Africa, and when Sir Henry reaches his hotel room the Baker Street Duo are summoned by the doctor.

Sir Henry is barely able to escape with his life when a deadly tarantula spider appears and crawls onto his shoulder. "If you fear for your life, don't move," cries Holmes walking slowly toward him until he is near enough to brush off the creature with his cane and beat it to death. Holmes warns Baskerville that his life continues to be in grave danger. The sleuth arranges for Dr. Watson to accompany Baskerville to his family estate in Devonshire, and insists that Sir Henry must not go out on the moor alone at night.

After arriving at Baskerville Hall, Dr. Watson and Sir Henry learn that a convict named Selden has escaped from the nearby prison and is believed to be hiding somewhere on the moors. The following day while out exploring, Dr. Watson makes a wrong turn and begins to sink in the treacherous mire, but is rescued by a neighboring farmer named Stapleton and the latter's daughter, Cecile. The Stapletons accompany Watson back to the Hall in order to keep him from further mischief, and when Sir Henry meets Cecile, he becomes very attracted to her.

Sir Hugo Baskerville (David Oxley) attempts to roast his ungrateful servant (David Birks).

A well-realized 221B Baker Street set in *The Hound of The Baskervilles*, as Holmes (Peter Cushing, right) explains a clue to his colleague (Andre Morell).

During the night, Watson and Sir Henry see a strange light out on the moor, which is evidently signaling to someone in the Hall, and they go out in search of its source. In the vicinity of the old abbey, they come across the escaped Selden, and the shock of the encounter causes Baskerville to exhibit symptoms that reveal to Dr. Watson that the young man suffers from a heart condition similar to that of his late uncle, Sir Charles. After returning the baronet to his manor house, the Doctor returns alone to the ruins for a further investigation, and unexpectedly comes upon Sherlock Holmes.

It turns out that Holmes has been secretly present in Devon for some time, and has questioned Selden. Holmes also traces the tarantula to the eccentric Bishop Frankland who lives nearby and reveals that one is missing from his collection; the sleuth gradually gathers together the relevant clues, eventually being

As Sir Henry Baskerville in *The Hound of the Baskervilles*, Christopher Lee is on the receiving end of a good scare (for a change).

Holmes (Cushing) explains to Dr. Watson (Morell) the significance of the painting of Sir Hugo Baskerville's hand.

led by them to investigate an old unused mine shaft, which he suspects may be the hiding-place of the Hound itself. Mortimer and Stapleton accompany him to this site, but then they separate themselves from him, and engineer the collapse of a tunnel, hoping to trap Holmes inside. The durable detective, however, manages to escape and, later, reappears safe and sound on Dartmoor. The convict Selden is less fortunate, and is found dead.

That same evening, Sir Henry is planning to meet clandestinely with Cecile, with whom he has fallen in love. Meanwhile, Holmes has learned that the dagger with which Sir Hugo had stabbed the servant girl (and which had been preserved all these years) has been stolen from the drawer in which it was kept, and he realizes that this means Sir Henry must be slated to die that very night.

A portrait of Sir Hugo has previously been stolen, and Holmes explains to Dr. Watson that this painting held the key to the entire mystery, for it revealed that the fingers on Sir Hugo's left hand were webbed—and the farmer Stapleton has this very condition on his own hand, revealing him to be an illegitimate descendant of the demonic baronet and, therefore, next in line of succession to the estate after Sir Henry.

During this time, Cecile Stapleton is continuing to lure Baskerville towards the abbey ruins, intending to make his death appear to be in revenge for the murder of the servant girl. She suddenly reveals her true feelings to Sir Henry: her bitter hatred because she believes her father to be the rightful heir to the estate and fortune. She tells Sir Henry how she lured his uncle out to the abbey just as she did him, and how she witnessed the murder by fright of the old man. "He died screaming," she says proudly and disdainfully. As she is speaking, the baying of the Hound is heard in the distance, rapidly drawing nearer.

Finally, the dreaded Hound of the Baskervilles makes its long-awaited appearance in the film, and it

Sir Henry (Lee) is clearly the worse for wear after his encounter with the Demonic Dog. Cushing sports the correct Holmesian headgear for hunting hounds on the moor—a homburg.

Left to right are Holmes (Cushing), Dr. Mortimer (Francis de Wolfe), Watson (Morell), and Sir Henry Baskerville (Christopher Lee).

must be admitted that Hammer's special-effects men have not exactly covered themselves with glory, for the beast looks none too horrendous, nor supernatural. It seems rather smallish and even friendly. Be that as it may, the Hound certainly glows a bit in the dark, and with fangs bared it bounds from the ruins and attacks Sir Henry. Just as the creature goes for Baskerville's throat, Sherlock Holmes shoots it (Holmes has been concealed nearby for some time, and perhaps has not been overhasty in taking action, though, of course, he obviously had to wait for the Hound to appear before he could do much). As the Hound is shot, Stapleton appears and attacks Dr. Watson, but meets his own death in the struggle with Andre Morell's very efficient and ex-military Baker Street Doctor. Cecile Stapleton breaks away and races madly into the mire, but she makes a wrong turn and sinks down too quickly for anyone to rescue her.

REVIEWS (*Daily Telegraph,* 15 November 1958, reviewed by Campbell Dixon):

It is characteristic of the screen that, though some of the best character touches seem to have vanished in Hammer Films' adaptation, pains have been taken to supply Peter Cushing's Holmes with all the familiar props, including a deerstalker and an assortment of pipes. They include the Tanganyika Meerschaum, for problems at their most baffling; the briar (filled from an old slipper in which he keeps his shag-tobacco) for furious activity; the long-stemmed rosewood [another source says cherry-wood] for meditative moments; and the cherry-wood smoked during moods of irritation or bad temper.

A later review in the same paper by the same critic:

"Really," an eleven year old girl observed sagely, when I mentioned the liberties taken with Doyle's text . . . "you wonder what the world's coming to!" And indeed you do. Nothing's sacred. This . . . is

not necessarily wrong . . . the adapter is free to make any changes he likes—on one condition. If his work is unfaithful, it had better be good.

The dialogue is indifferent. The producer (Anthony Hinds), having reasonably selected Peter Cushing to play Holmes, need not have cast two of the tallest men on the English screen, Francis de Wolff and Christopher Lee, to dwarf him.

Mr. Cushing makes Holmes a light-weight—light in voice, physique and personality.

Andre Morell, who cannot act badly, plays Watson very well.

Some people liked Nigel Bruce's bumbling burlesque of the doctor. Not I. But then I was never any brighter than Watson, whereas the people who mock him are all Holmeses.

(*Daily Express,* 26 March 1959):

. . . a merry little romp introducing Peter Cushing as the one and only Sherlock Holmes, complete with Dr. Watson, carefully reconstructed rooms in Baker-street "at the turn of the century", pipes of tobacco and all.

This novel by Conan Doyle is one always treated with exaggerated respect by people over the age of 40. Various films have been made out of it: they are usually successful.

Andre Morell (whom I last saw on the telly as Quatermass) is far too intelligent as Dr. Watson. Peter Cushing is excellent as Sherlock Holmes.

The ex-model Marla Scarafia, now renamed Marla Landi, makes a startling appearance as a lady murderess who lures the Baskervilles to their doom, what time her awful old dad lets loose the hound on them.

Peter Cushing does his best with all this soggy material and very nearly pulls off a triumph. Of the rest, however . . .

(*Evening Standard,* 26 March 1959):

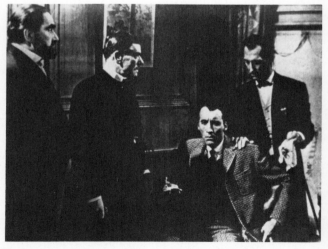

Holmes comforts a distraught Baskerville, as Mortimer and Watson look on.

Conan Doyle played effectively for a maximum of blood and thunder (the blood comes in several shades) with Peter Cushing the most prissily pedantic Holmes on record.

Miles Malleson contributes a wholly extraneous but delightful sketch of a bishop who collects tarantulas.

(*News Chronicle,* 26 March 1959): Reviewer Paul Dehn considered that Cushing's interpretation of Holmes "leaves all earlier impersonators except the late Arthur Wontner standing at the Baker Street post"—praise that must have inspired mixed feelings in Wontner, if he saw it, since, of course, he was still very much alive in 1959.

Of Cushing, Dehn continued:

the portrait's total impact is piercingly accurate.

Though we never see so much as a sniff, this Holmes' addiction to cocaine is implicit in the taut exaltation of his manner.

The blue eyes glitter with cool excitement; every tendon seems as tightly tuned as a string from the immortal violin; and the questing hawk's-head so swivels in the throes of observation that one can almost hear the brain brought to a fine fizz inside.

The voice, too, has a high tension which only once exceeds its permitted voltage and short-circuits in a positively Gielgudian flash of anger.

When Mr. Cushing's Holmes thunders: "I never relinquish a case!" he does so with the white-hot wrath of Hamlet crying "By heaven, I'll make a ghost of him that lets me!"

Dehn also notes that Morell is "earnest but never risible" as Watson, and has high praise for de Wolfe, Lee, and Malleson among the performers, scripter Peter Bryan, director Terence Fisher, and especially the film's music composer, James Bernard: "High, divided strings trace the advance of a tarantula-spider . . . screaming with great orchestral brilliance for us," Dehn says of one of the musical effects.

(*Star,* March 3, 1959): "Peter Cushing portrays Sherlock Holmes as something of a pompous dilettante and Andre Morell makes Dr. Watson someone far above the elementary."

(*Daily Herald,* 28 March 1959, reviewed by Anthony Carfew): "The Hound itself is a bit of a disappointment, but Peter Cushing is accurately irritable, precise and prissy as Holmes, and Andre Morell is the perfect Dr. Watson. The story of nastiness on Dartmoor is done with humour rather than horror. I hope there will be more Holmes films like this."

(*Daily Mail,* 28 March 1959):

Sherlock Holmes . . . is so insufferably self-satisfied, so aware of his "brilliance," so fond of showing off.

He is a clever little bumptious upstart, and I can't

even imagine how Dr. Watson stood him, except that Dr. Watson is so nice that he would put up with anybody.

Peter Cushing plays the indomitable Sherlock as an undersized prig with blazing blue eyes and an oversized opinion of himself.

Andrew (sic) Morell as Dr. Watson is the perfect gentleman at all times, even when sinking in a bog.

How I squirmed at the righteous indignation of Sherlock Holmes when a client offered to "pay him well." "My fees are on a fixed scale," he snaps.

But when the cheque comes at the end of the picture and it's a big one, does Shylock Sherlock send some of it back? Oh no. "He has been generous," he lisps.

Miles Malleson . . . is worth seeing.

(*Daily Mirror,* 28 March 1959, reviewed by Dick Richards): " . . . the old tale of crime and treachery on Dartmoor stands up very well.

Peter Cushing is a splendid Holmes. The film, while being 'Very elementary, Watson' has atmosphere and thrills."

(*Daily Worker,* 28 March 1959):

After a crude and brutal prologue *The Hound of the Baskervilles* . . . turns out to be a dull, badly produced melodrama.

Quite without atmosphere, despite a background of Dartmoor mist, ruined abbeys and baying dogs. The dialogue is hammy and the acting wooden.

But for sheer horror, nothing can beat this film's use of Technicolor—sick reds and blues and green all . . . round the edges.

(*Evening News,* 28 March 1959)

Hammer Films . . . do not seem to have done badly until you read the book again: then you wonder why they did not just stick to Conan Doyle's ready-made script.

New red herrings have been cooked up in a rather underdone way to meet the current appetite for sensation. . . . Holmes would have hated their untidiness.

And I very much doubt if Holmes would have taken the 1958 Ordnance Survey maps to Devonshire in 1888. Did you notice, Watson, that the ink used on the covers was red—a post 1939–46 innovation, I believe?

Peter Cushing makes a good enough Holmes, in one of his more irritable moods. . . . Andre Morell refuses to make the good doctor as fatuous as some of his predecessors did in this much-filmed subject.

Christopher Lee, Maria (sic) Landi, David Oxley, Miles Malleson, Francis De Wolff (sic) and the spreader of Technicolor blood all work valiantly.

(*News of the World,* 29 March 1959):

There's a comfortable air of Victorian cosiness . . . about *The Hound of the Baskervilles* . . . with Sherlock Holmes and Dr. Watson once more unravelling the mystery of the diabolical curse threatening the gallant Sir Henry Baskerville.

Those two accomplished practitioners in the Dracula-Frankenstein business, Peter Cushing and Christopher Lee, appear in the piece.

(*Observer*, 29 March 1959, reviewed by C. A. Lejeune; Miss Lejeune herself dramatized several Holmes stories for television):

By adroit manipulation of the Conan Doyle material, by cunning changes in the relationship of character, by the invention of new scenes of no relevance whatsoever, by resolutely avoiding any arrangement of the book which led, ineluctably, to a dramatic climax, they (Hammer) have managed to evolve a script which misses almost all the salient points of the original.

Peter Cushing is the new Sherlock Holmes. Curiously, for he has shown authority in other parts, he seems fussy, finicky and indeterminate in this one. Andre Morell . . . works hard to avoid buffoonery in a part in which a buffoon might have been more comfortable. The Hound is a nice hound: a large, friendly mongrel, he gave me the impression of a dog that would be good with children.

(*Sunday Dispatch*, 29 March 1959):

. . . with Peter Cushing and Andre Morell as an impeccably poised Sherlock Holmes and Dr. Watson, it generates real excitement without the taint of the old-style (Hammer) horror.

Peter Bryan's screenplay amiably catches the gaslight and hansom-cab essence of the Baker Street myth. And a polished cast (particularly Peter Cushing's gimlet-eyed Holmes) walk the razor-edge between period and parody without tripping over their deer-stalkers.

(*Sunday Express*, 29 March 1959, reviewed by Derek Monsey):

. . . a melodramatic horror-treatment . . . loses some of its eerie power . . . still makes its grisly impact.

But for good measure the film gives Sir Henry Baskerville a romantic interest in a Spanish girl who flaunts her petticoats around the Baskerville estates and lures him out onto the moor at night.

As the seductress Miss Marla Landi only proves again the old adage that good model girls . . . seldom turn into even tolerable actresses.

Peter Cushing, wearing deerstalker and pipe, and Andre Morell, trying hard to look stupid, give fine performances as Holmes and the block-headed Dr. Watson.

But they seem to be playing the whole grim story for heavy laughs. This—plus some very thin-blooded horror and a remarkably undersized hound—takes the sting out of a classic tale.

(*Sunday Times*, 29 March 1959 reviewed by Dilys Powell): "the rewritten, re-shuffled version . . . is a very mild shocker; a few nocturnal howls, hints of

nameless sacrificial rites, and the rest is whodunit and poor hungry doggie. Peter Cushing rather over-sprightly. . . . Andre Morell reliable."

The following day the daily version of the *Times* (London) reviewed the film again:

Holmes did not mean to be unkind—"If you had killed Watson you would not have got out of this room alive" is . . . more indicative of his real feelings than his almost automatic sarcasms—but still Holmes always knew what was going on, was always at the centre of things, while Watson hovered about in a fog.

In *The Hound of the Baskervilles*, Watson is on the spot and Holmes, in appearance at least, is on the receiving end. . . . (This film) can be forgiven for not following this particular aspect of the book . . . some other omissions, distortions, and additions are harder to understand . . . a melodrama of atmosphere, and that Mr. Fisher understands. . . . Holmes is a difficult part. . . . Peter Cushing makes an interesting attempt at it—the trouble here is that the affectations are, so to speak, too affected. . . . Andre Morell is a manly Watson who avoids being too much of a fool.

Finally, the next month, the *Times* treated the film to a final review, this time by David Robinson:

. . . relying more on mystery and suspense than on plain physical nastiness. Again one senses a rather more sophisticated approach than is usual with this class of film; when the spine-chilling gets really absurd, you have the reassuring feeling that the film-makers, too, know that it is comic.

I fear Holmesians will not approve, and it is no use pretending that it is anywhere near the level of the old James Whale horrors. Even so one can admire the film's pronounced period sense. The settings, Peter Cushing's deliberately mannered Holmes, above all the late-Victorian Gothic—ruins and mists and vaults, and stylishly sinister villains—are very well conceived.

(*S.P.C.*, 29 March 1959):

. . . good, stout Sherlock Holmes thriller in which Peter Cushing darts about the mists of Dartmoor to confound evil, and finally puts a number of well-placed bullets into the hound.

Dog-lovers won't mind this much since the hound has a weakness for eating people.

(*New Statesman*, 4 April 1959, reviewed by William Whitebait):

Peter Cushing, after a long line of hawks, makes a very bold descent on Dartmoor in the Master's most Gothic adventure. I can't say I managed to raise a shudder—except at the revelation that Holmes and Watson shared one very small room, with shelves of chemical bottles round and coats hanging behind the door."

(*Time and Tide*, 11 April 1959, reviewed by Charles Mac Laren):

Conan Doyle wrote nothing grimmer in the whole of the Sherlock Holmes saga and a re-reading of the book chills one to the marrow. The amazing thing is that Hammer, horror specialists, haven't got into their work a particle of the sense of doom and shock that is bound up in the pages of the original story. All the changes they have made are for the worse. Their horror isn't a patch on Conan Doyle's. They had a beauty in their hands and let it go. Andre Morell is a credible Watson and no buffoon. Given the chances the book afforded him, he might have proved very good indeed. Peter Cushing plays Sherlock Holmes with a curiously light touch. He isn't my Holmes, not by any means, but I'll allow him fair pass marks for an educated fancy.

And, finally, *Newsweek* of 8 June 1959 called Cushing "a living, breathing Holmes . . . the best . . . yet."

It may perhaps seem at first glance that we are treating this film in greater depth than it deserves, but although not part of an official series, it did spawn a number of other Holmes projects. The film's director, Terence Fisher, made a second Holmes film three years later (*Sherlock Holmes and the Deadly Necklace*) in which he promoted Christopher Lee from the role of Baskerville to that of Sherlock himself, and Lee later went on to play Sherlock's brother, Mycroft Holmes, in still a third film (*Private Life of Sherlock Holmes*). It seems that Fisher and Lee also made one more Holmes picture together, but that it has not yet seen the light of day; we will of course deal with all of these projects more fully in our succeeding chapters.

Cushing himself went on to play Holmes again in a BBC-TV series, and has more recently written the preface to a Sherlockian book, and we will be looking at both of these items again in his biography.

Hammer Films had, in fact, intended to make their version of *The Hound* the starting point for a whole series of Holmesian films, but the Doyle estate was apparently not overpleased with this initial effort and did not grant permission, although one would have thought that enough of the stories were in the public domain that Hammer might have proceeded anyway.

The film was the first Holmes adventure to be filmed in color, although it was not in fact the first time Holmes had appeared in a film with color sequences. That distinction belongs to 1930's *Paramount on Parade*, in which the Holmes segment, however, was filmed in black and white, hence our distinction.

Cushing was first announced for the part as early as July '58, and the shooting began at Bray Studios a month later. Christopher Lee was cast as Baskerville at the same time and Fisher was slated to direct, but the role of Watson had not yet been filled, and seems to have presented some difficulties that, however, the final acquisition of Andre Morell made more than worthwhile.

In October the film crew did some location shooting in the wild heathland near Frensham Ponds, Surrey, which for some reason was used as a standin for the real Dartmoor. Cushing was interviewed by Felix

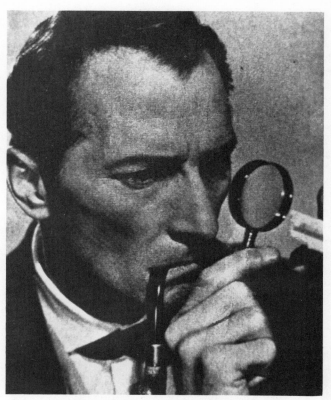

Peter Cushing studied his Conan Doyle with great care and emerged with the same kind of manic Holmes as had Basil Rathbone.

Barker for the *Evening News* at a pub called The Mariners after a morning of shooting on the moors. The article recounts how, despite the setting, Cushing was drinking only the W. C. Fields favorite: pineapple juice. Cushing was in a state of ecstasy, having just been presented by Albert Porter, the landlord, with a first edition of *The Hound*, illustrated by Sidney Paget. Cushing had studied the part with his usual scrupulous care, and is perhaps the only screen Holmes who truly made any attempt to play Holmes with the appropriate symptoms of a drug addict. He took the part very seriously, consulting the works of Doyle and Paget and even supplying his own costumes to be sure they would accurately match the Paget illustrations in the *Strand* magazine: "Fortunately my father left me a whole set," he told Barker. "Everything is accurate right down to the famous 'mouse-colored' dressing-gown which I charred with cigarettes to get the burns Holmes made during his experiments.

The producer had some absurd idea that I should not wear a deerstalker. I told them you might as well play Nelson without a patch over his eye!

But still I am avoiding the more obvious props—the things like the huge curved pipe and magnifying glass that make Holmes a music-hall joke.

Quite a bit of time I wear a homburg on the moors—which is absolutely right, I find."

Cushing described Holmes as "not the pleasantest of characters," which must have been something of a heresy to those who had grown up with the highly gentlemanly interpretation of Arthur Wontner, but which an objective observer must admit to be not far short of the mark. "Holmes didn't suffer fools, and he must have been insufferable to live with. He was always so right!" A case in point is that Cushing lit his pipe with a coal from the fire with tongs, as dictated by Doyle. Some other Cushing-introduced accuracies were the detective's habit of keeping his tobacco in a Persian slipper, and the pipes, themselves, of which there were a large variety to suit the various Holmesian moods (*see above for descriptions*); however, for some reason, Holmes is minus his violin in the film. Later, in a 1976 American movie called *The Great Houdinis,* Peter Cushing graduated up to the part of Holmes's creator, Sir Arthur Conan Doyle. Maureen O'Sullivan was Lady Doyle, and Cushing was given the chance to voice onscreen some of his own (and Doyle's) genuine belief in the immortality of the soul.

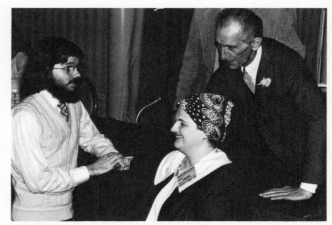

Coauthor Pohle with Peter Cushing. (Photo by Douglas C. Hart)

Modelling his costumes on the original Sidney Paget illustrations, Peter Cushing was very sparing in his use of the deerstalker.

A large pack of hounds was in attendance on the ridge above Frensham Ponds, being used in the seventeenth-century prologue sequence, but the casting of the title-*Hound,* of course, presented a bit more difficulty, since the beast was described in the original novel as a "foul, fearsome thing, a great black beast, shaped like a hound, yet larger than any hound that ever mortal eye rested upon." All of the versions we have seen of this story have failed lamentably in making the hound appear to be anything other than an ordinary specimen of the everyday variety of hound, and it is a great pity that no producer has ever realized that, although the "modern" hound is of course a fake disguised by Stapleton, the *legendary* Hound of the prologue should really fit the Doyle description; *King Kong* type animation would seem to be the obvious way to handle the original appearance of the beast, and surely the cost of the brief glimpse required would not be prohibitive.

Despite the location shooting, however, there were indeed some studio interiors used for Dartmoor in some scenes, with puffs of mist that were rather painfully obviously mechanical in origin, and artificial leaves, according to one source. The film's general attention to historical authenticity, though, is demonstrated again in the echoes of the real Sir Francis Dashwood and Hell Fire Club in the prologue.

Peter Wilton Cushing was born on 26 May 1913 at "Normandy," Godstone Road, Kenley, near the London suburb of Purley in Surrey, England. His father, George Edward Cushing, a quantity surveyor, must have encouraged Peter's interest in Sherlock Holmes, since he owned a set of original "Strands." But the boy's earliest childhood ambition—to be an actor—must have derived more from his grandfather, who was an actor with Sir Henry Irving's company. Edward Cushing had not only toured the United States theaters with Irving, but on 5 January 1892 appeared in Irving's production of *Henry VIII* with Lionel

Belmore, an actor-director who appeared with Irving in Conan Doyle's *Waterloo* many times between 1895 and 1904, and who years later went to Hollywood, where he worked in films with future-Moriarty Harry T. Morey and Basil Rathbone. However, the young grandson of his old colleague did not encounter him when Peter himself arrived in Hollywood in the late thirties, Mr. Cushing informed the present writers in an interview he was kind enough to grant us.

Edward Cushing, however, was really only a part-time actor, for he had already begun to work as a quantity surveyor before joining Irving. His son George, of course, went into the same profession, and later it was expected that Peter would follow in both their footsteps. The theater bug seems to have bitten Edward's children more permanently, however, for George's half-brother Wilton Herriott (for whom Peter was named) was a professional actor, and his sister Maude Aston also had a notable stage career. Peter's mother, the former Nellie Maria King, does not seem to have had any acting connections.

One might have expected that Peter's childhood hero would have been one of the great figures who were then treading the English boards, but in fact he idolized Tom Mix! He named his bicycle after Mix's horse, and at age 5 was already drawing his own comic strips featuring the movie cowboy. Years later Peter noted that he had "always found it easier to draw, paint or mime something than to describe it in words," and, besides his acting career, he has continued to work as an artist, having recently illustrated a book of children's stories written by fellow-actor Joseph O'Conor. His water-color paintings were exhibited in the West End of London in 1958.

Peter made his first appearance on the stage as a child, when he played an elf in a pantomime, and at eleven he was a puppeteer but received no encouragement from his parents to become a professional. When he was nine he was sent as a boarder to Shoreham Grammar School but was so homesick he was soon transferred to Purley Grammar School, remaining there until he was eighteen. Baffled by arithmetic, he excelled in drawing, theatricals, and rugger.

At Purley, Peter was active in the school plays, being especially successful in comic parts, for which he modelled his style on those of Chaplin and Keaton. During this time he was also pursuing his art studies at the then Croyden School of Art, under Percy Rendell.

After leaving school Peter tried to adhere to his father's wishes by taking a job as a "surveyor's assistant" (actually a glorified office boy) with the Coulsdon and Purley Urban District Council. Though he remained with them for four years, he spent as much of his time as possible continuing to act at his old school: "I couldn't stand monkeying around with a slide-rule," he said, and the architectural plans he drew up were so far from successful that "it was said . . . that any resemblance to a real building was purely

coincidental," says Cushing. Hoping to further his theatrical ambitions, he applied to the Guildhall School in London for an acting scholarship, but at his interview his indistinct and careless regional accent led the interviewer to say: "This isn't an audition. Speak in your normal voice."

"This *is* me normal voice," responded Peter. "I wanna go on the stage!" He was tutored by the school's James Cairns-James, but eventually was thrown out because of his seemingly incorrigible accent.

It must be hard for the many who are familiar with Cushing's faultless film diction to realize it is entirely the production hard self-discipline, mainly acquired by shouting his lines at the top of his lungs as he tramped over the downland (he still finds it easiest to learn his parts in the open air). At last, at the age of twenty-two, Cushing was hired for a walkon role as a "gum-chewing, teddy-bear coated creditor" in *Cornelius* with the Worthington Repertory Company at the Connaught Theatre in Sussex, playing his first important role for them as Captain Randall in *The Middle Watch* in 1935.

He had gotten this engagement by writing a total of twenty-one letters over a period of months to the head of the Company, who at last called him in out of sheer desperation to beg him to stop writing—and, instead, gave him a job when Cushing told him he had given up his surveying position. He was paid fifteen shillings a week, and required to double as assistant stage manager. As his salary just managed to cover his bed and breakfasts for the week, he was fortunate that many of the plays done at the theater featured eating scenes with real food supplied for the free publicity by local merchants. Otherwise, he subsisted mainly on tea.

After some months at the Connaught Theatre, Peter moved to the Grand Theatre in Southampton for nine months. Reading in his script that the character he was to play in *Lean Harvest* was "slightly merry" he "staggered onto the stage with balloons tied to the ends of my tie." In the Christmas pantomime *Dick Whittington*, Cushing was cast as the King Rat, but he eventually worked his way up to juvenile leads, and then moved to the William Brookfield Players at the Theatre Royal in Rochdale, and afterwards to Harry Hanson's Court Players in Nottingham, where he gratified a childhood dream by meeting not only Tom Mix, but the latter's equally famous horse Tony. At this theater, Cushing began to display his abilities as a character actor, and he was soon making the rounds of many more regional theaters.

Having by this time saved fifty pounds, he decided to try his luck in Hollywood, and (helped out with more money from his father) Cushing bought a one-way ticket to New York. Arriving there in September '38 he bought a one-way train ticket to Los Angeles and, after taking a room at the Y.M.C.A., sat down and wrote letters to all the major New York film company offices, informing them that he was on his way west. On the actual train trip, he passed the hat for a trio of college boys who were singing to earn back the money for their tickets.

At the Y.M.C.A. in Hollywood, Cushing told the clerk that he was staying for just ten days, as he would be in movies by the end of that time. He had, in fact, only enough cash left for two days, but before the ten had expired, he was indeed hired by James Whale for *The Man in the Iron Mask.* Cushing got the part by alleging that he was an expert fencer, although "I had never handled a foil in my life." Fortunately, when Peter threw himself on the mercy of the picture's fencing-master, the latter responded by teaching him all he knew about swordplay. The job paid seventy-five dollars and lasted four months, but in the finished film Cushing has hardly more than a cameo as a Rathbone-type swashbuckling villain who fences D'Artagnan (played by Warren William, in yet another link between Sherlock Holmes and The Three Musketeers). Cushing also served as Louis Hayward's standin during the split-screen sequences when the latter was playing twins.

Cushing's second Hollywood part was much more notable, as he was cast as Anne Shirley's husband in *Vigil in the Night,* in which Carole Lombard and Miss Shirley were the stars. Though billed only sixth, Cushing is very notable in the film, and it is ironic after all the trouble he took to lose his regional accent and acquire "The King's English" that his first film success should have been in a Lancashire dialect part! Several critics compared Cushing to Spencer Tracy, whom the English actor had always admired. At this point, though, when the war broke between Britain and Germany, Cushing was given the medical grading of 4C due to his old rugger injuries, and told to remain in Hollywood until further notice. But after a promising start, his film career was not really going anywhere, although he continued to be busy in small parts (apparently because his main studio, RKO, feared that he might be called up at any time and leave them with a half-finished role to reshoot).

He played a moustachioed don in Laurel and Hardy's *A Chump at Oxford,* and was cast as Clive of India in an MGM Passing Parade short, *The Hidden Master.* During the filming of the scene in which the young Clive attempts suicide only to discover that his loaded gun will not fire, Cushing first had the inner conviction that he himself would eventually know great success as an actor—a conviction that must have been sorely tried during the tribulations his career was to know for so long. Some of his other films during this period were *Women at War, They Dare Not Love,* '40, *Laddie,* and *The Captain of the Guard.* He was apparently also in a serial, but we have been unable to locate its title.

Cushing spent so much time at the home of his married friends Ida Lupino and Louis Hayward that a Hollywood gossip columnist printed the muddled item: "Ida Lupino is always speaking about her adopted son. He lives with them. People are always surprised when they meet him because he is 6 feet 2 inch Peter Cushing, the RKO actor" (Miss Lupino was the same age as Cushing at the time—and the RKO publicity department would seem to have added two inches to the actor's height, as well). "It was marvelous," Peter said of Hollywood. "It measured up to all my expectations."

As the news of the bombing of London reached him, Cushing was overwhelmed with homesickness and decided to return to New York in hopes of finding transportation back to Britain, but once on the east coast an emergency operation that barely saved his leg (it had become septic as a result of a burst blister) used up most of his savings, and he was stranded. Not even able to afford the Y.M.C.A., the actor had to stay at a Times Square flophouse. Finding no work in the Manhattan theater, Peter was forced to accept a job as a car-lot attendant at Coney Island. He was found to be overcareful with the cars and consequently too slow, and was fired after only one day. After this he became a soda jerk in a hash house, and then had enough saved to attempt the Broadway theatrical agents again with as little luck. Wandering forlornly about the empty theaters whenever he could sneak in, Cushing had a strong sense of deja-vu, which he attributed to the fact that his grandfather had appeared in some of those same theaters so long ago.

Finally reduced to $1.35, Peter had a strange impulse to rent one of the rowboats on Central Park, which he could hardly afford, and found on the floor of the boat a ten-dollar bill, on which he lived for the next three weeks, subsisting mainly on coffee and doughnuts. Eventually trying to find work as an artist in Greenwich Village, Cushing ran into his Hollywood friend John Ireland, who told the Englishman that rather than starve he should be collecting the eighteen-dollar a week unemployment benefits he had earned while in Hollywood. Cushing had not even known he was eligible! And the very next morning Peter was offered a five-month acting engagement in a summer camp in New York State—no salary, but food, lodging, and fresh air. Among other parts, he did the Leslie Howard role in *The Petrified Forest* (which seems a natural piece of casting since Howard's lookalike son Ronald was later, like Cushing, to play Sherlock Holmes).

Still anxious to return to England, Cushing wrote to Canadian Air Marshal Bishop, who advised him to cross the border in order to have more luck finding a berth on a home-bound ship, though the Marshal also pointed out that Cushing was not fit medically for the service. Just at this point, Peter got a job in a Broadway play which earned him the money he needed to get to Canada. *The Seventh Trumpet* played for a few weeks at the end of '41, and Cushing managed to save one hundred dollars. He headed first for Montreal, where he worked in the art department of a film studio on the sets of *49th Parallel,* which starred fellow-Holmes Raymond Massey and—Leslie Howard! Also holding down a job as a night clerk at the "Y," Cushing earned enough for his sea passage and left for Halifax to find a ship, but had a long wait before a berth would become available. The once-and-future movie star was forced to fill the time as a lowly usher in a movie theater—where he saw *Captains of the Clouds* a grand total of forty-eight times. He finally gained a temporary berth as a merchant seaman on a former banana boat, and set sail for home in January '42. The voyage was eventless save for the ship's pursuit by a German battleship and the fact that Cushing's feet were frozen solid in several inches of ice while he was on watch in the crow's nest. In February they reached Liverpool, which was crowded with ships sunk by the war. Cushing immediately went to his elder brother David's poultry farm where his parents were staying. His mother, who had not been expecting him, fainted when he walked in.

Turned down once again for the Services, he applied to stage-Sherlock Henry Oscar for an acting job with the E.N.S.A. (the British equivalent of U.S.O.) and was hired with alacrity. Touring the English countryside again was a great joy to Cushing despite the war, and he has always maintained his love of nature in Britain.

During the tour, a Leningrad-born, blonde and blue-eyed actress named Helen Beck joined the cast of the play, and she and Peter were married on 10 April 1943 in London. Her father was of Lancashire extraction but his family (like that of radio-Holmes Tom Conway) had been settled in Russia for generations, and had cotton mills there before the revolution. Helen, a former musical comedy actress-dancer, had appeared in *What Price Glory* in '26. She was to be by far the most important influence in the life and career of Peter Cushing, who has always been very firm in attributing all his success to her.

Lung congestion picked up in the drafty rooms with which they were furnished on the tour forced Peter to leave E.N.S.A.; and with Helen also becoming ill, the couple decided to settle in Kensington with her parents and only fifty pounds between them.

Peter's first London stage appearance came in August '43 when he doubled the roles of Czar Alexander I and Captain Ramballe in *War And Peace* at the Phoenix (after first playing it in Blackpool and Manchester). Parts followed in such plays as *Dark Potential, The Crime of Margaret Foley, Happy Few* and *While The Sun Shines*—when this play was revived in '47, Cushing's performance as the French Lieutenant so impressed Laurence Olivier's partner, Anthony Bushell, that he cast Cushing as Osric in his film version of *Hamlet*, which was released in 1949. Also in the cast of that one was an actor with whom Cushing was to appear in over twenty enormously successful films, and who was himself to play Sherlock Holmes—Christopher Lee, cast as Hamlet's heir, Fortinbras.

But this film, and the Cushing-Lee partnership, lie in the future; we must first return to September '45 when Peter appeared in *The Rivals* with Edith Evans.

Following that revival's five-month run, Peter and Helen entered a very lean period, and he was out of work for a year and a half with the exception of a total of a single week's work at the "Q" Theatre in the title role of *The Curious Dr. Robson*.

They were soon heavily in debt, and when Peter wanted to give his wife a Christmas present in '46 he had no money at all, but found an old piece of silk and painted Dickensian characters on it. This proved to be a Godsend, for he soon managed to get a contract as a silk-scarf designer!

Not long after this came *Hamlet*, and then Cushing and his wife were engaged by Olivier for his 1948 Old Vic Tour of Australia and New Zealand, during which Cushing played Clarence in *Richard III* (filmed later with Douglas Wilmer), and (among other parts) Joseph Surface, a part that has also been played by fellow-Holmes Wilmer and whose brother Charles Surface was played by H. A. Saintsbury. Peter remained with the company when it returned to London the next year, and two years later rejoined Olivier and Vivian Leigh for their double productions of *Caesar and Cleopatra* and *Anthony and Cleopatra*. There are more Sherlockian links here, for Stewart Granger was in the film version of the former and Wilmer in that of the latter.

Cushing had had one of his most outstanding personal successes during the first season in London with Olivier, when Peter was so overcome after his fourth curtain call (for Chekhov's *Proposal*) that Olivier had to push him back on stage where he received another four calls! After this though, ill health again struck Cushing and he was forced to retire for over six months. Olivier put him under contract anyway, and after a brief run in *The Gay Invalid* Peter rejoined Sir Laurence for the final season referred to above.

By this time, Helen had retired from her own career to help Peter with his, and when yet another thin period arrived she sat down and wrote to every name listed in the *Radio Times*, informing them that Mr. Peter Cushing was now available to TV work! She had always insisted he carry on when he was on the point of giving up acting. "She had such faith in me," he said. The biggest triumphs of his career were in fact just about to begin, for he was cast in *Eden End* on television in December '51, and he was soon one of the hottest TV stars in Britain.

In the next few years Cushing was to win four major television awards: Outstanding Actor from the *Daily Mail* for '53–54; Silver Screen Award in '54; the Guild of TV Producers and Directors Award for Best Performance in '54–55 (for *1984*); and the *News Chronicle* Award for Best Actor in '56. It was his horrific performance in *1984*, together with his role in *The Creature* (filmed with him in '56 as *The Abominable Snowman of the Himalayas*) that led to his becoming a horror star in Hammer Films.

Some of Cushing's other television appearances were in *Asmodee, Gaslight, Home at 7, Tovarich* (filmed with Rathbone), *Beau Brummel* (filmed with Stewart

199

Granger), *Pride and Prejudice, When We Are Married, Portrait by Peko, Moment of Truth, Uncle Harry, Rookery Nook, The Browning Version, The Noble Spaniard, The Moment of Truth, Epitaph for a Spy, The Road, Anastasia, The Winslow Boy* (played on the stage by Rathbone), *Peace with Terror, Julius Caesar* (filmed with Christopher Lee), *Monica, The Plan, Caves of Steel, Richard of Bordeaux, Great Mysteries* with Orson Welles, the United States TV-movie *Some May Live*, in 1967 and, of course, his Sherlock Holmes series.

One of the few actors at that time with a BBC contract, he played twenty leads for them in twenty months—though the contract was later eased up to require only three shows per year from the actor.

When Cushing came to replace Douglas Wilmer as Holmes on the BBC series in '68, he had of course already done the role before in *The Hound of the Baskervilles*, but he threw himself into restudying it with his customary intensity, and subjected himself to a vigorous regimen of swimming, diving, and running just to get into the physical shape he thought the Great Detective required. Peter gave up two movie offers that would have garnered him a considerably higher salary, in order to return to Baker Street. After rising at seven each morning and walking four miles down the Kentish coast (where he and his wife then lived), he would bash away at a tennis ball, letting it be retrieved by his dog Thumper, until both he and the dog were exhausted. Cushing would then sequester himself on the third floor of his shore house among his many books and consult both his fifteen TV scripts and his trusty bound *Strands*, frequently telephoning the BBC and asking them to correct too-modern lines. One script took Holmes to 1881 Paris and set a scene by the Eiffel Tower. Cushing informed the BBC that the said structure was not built until seven years later. "I mean, I don't want to be a pest, dear boy," he told an interviewer at the time, "but we do want the series to be right. I am having all my clothes specially made up to match the illustrations to the original magazine stories.

The pipes I will smoke in the series are being made up by Charatan's, the top people for pipes.

I have been studying the scripts since February (four months). In ten days we go to Dartmoor for locations in *The Hound* (which was redone for the new series). Then we will be at it until December in the studios." In Dartmoor, Cushing and his TV-Watson Nigel Stock filmed near Cleft Rock, not far from the Chase Hotel where Conan Doyle probably stayed in 1899 during his "local color" expeditions, which led to the writing of the original novel of *Baskervilles*.

Despite the fact that some episodes were written by the eminent Sherlockians Michael and Mollie Hardwicke (who later wrote the screenplay for *Private Life of Sherlock Holmes*, in which Chris Lee played Mycroft), the series was not overly well received by devout Holmesians. In the London *Sherlock Holmes Journal*, Anthony Howlett wrote that Cushing's

performances were, as acting craftsmanship, greatly

to be preferred to those of his predecessor in the earlier BBC series, but they were, alas, ineffective. . . . Holmes had authority . . . there was, behind all the eccentricity, an inner fire and strength of personality in him that could not be ignored. . . . But Peter Cushing gave us none of these things: his rather fey and twittery Holmes lacked any resemblance of power or real authority: without this, all Cushing's subtlety and excellent touches of Holmesian detail were lost . . . a surprising disappointment in so accomplished an actor whose work I usually greatly admire.

Despite such cavils from the True Believers, however, the Cushing series was extremely successful with the majority of the viewing public, and was sold to several other countries as well. The series was by far the most costly ever devoted to Holmes on television, though even so there were a few minor technical slipups, such as the presence in one segment of the camera crew!

In Cushing's early TV-star days, he attended a local church fete and made the acquaintance of Faith Tallack, a teenager who, though a great fan of his, was painfully shy as a result of her semiparalysis and spasticity. Cushing, who had known his own share of suffering, realized that the girl could use some friendship, and he and his wife began to send Faith postcards whenever he was on location, and to telephone her every week. Once when Faith was about to cancel her appearance as a mermaid in a charity carnival due to stage fright, she was heartened by a telegram from Cushing and went on to win a prize. Cushing even persuaded her to go to a dance, just to sit, telling her, "Of course people will stare. They stare at me. They'll stare at you—because you're beautiful." The general encouragement and personal involvement of Peter and Helen were of great benefit to Faith in helping her to get out of her shell, and Cushing has continued to be active in helping the handicapped— more recently spending much time recording books for the blind.

While his voluminous television appearances were taking up most of his time in the early '50's, Cushing still managed to continue his film career, and in 1953 he was in his second film with Christopher Lee, *Moulin Rouge*. He went to Spain for *The Black Knight* in 1954, another Rathbone-like swashbuckling villain, and an Arabic role such as has been played by so many Holmesian actors. In 1955, Cushing appeared in *The End of the Affair*, and in the following year he made *Time Without Pity, Magic Fire*, and yet another period role as Memn in *Alexander the Great*. It was *Curse of Frankenstein* with Lee in '57, however, that established the direction in which Cushing's career would go from now on, and that finally led him to the status of a truly international star.

Undoubtedly his best-known characterization, Cushing followed Rathbone in the role of Baron Frankenstein, and repeated it in *Revenge of Frankenstein*, 1958, *Evil of Frankenstein*, 1964, *Frankenstein*

Created Woman, 1967, *Frankenstein Must be Destroyed*, 1969, and *Frankenstein and the Monster from Hell*, 1972 (he also played the role in a cameo in *One More Time*).

In 1958, Cushing began another series with *Dracula* (*Horror of Dracula* in the United States), again with Lee. Cushing played the vampire's nemesis, Professor Van Helsing, in this one and its sequel, *Brides of Dracula*, '60, in which Lee did not appear. Lee, however, starred in the series without Cushing until '71, when Cushing returned as a modern-day descendent of Van Helsing in *Dracula A.D. 1972*—a role he has continued in *Dracula is Dead*, '72, and *Satanic Rites of Dracula*, '73; more recently, Cushing himself has assumed the role of Count Dracula in a film made in France—*The Big Funk*.

Although he is so closely identified with horror films, Cushing has actually seldom played a monster, but is usually (as with Van Helsing and Holmes) the hero who combats the monsters. A rare exception is his award-winning characterization of Grimsdyke in '71's *Tales from the Crypt*, for which he helped devise his own makeup.

Besides those that we have mentioned above, Cushing's films include the following (readers may determine his numerous costarring films with Christopher Lee by tallying these with the Lee filmography in our next chapter): *Violent Playground*, '57; *John Paul Jones*, '58; *Mummy* and *Hellfire Club*, '59; *Cone of Silence*, *Flesh and the Fiends*, *Sword of Sherwood Forrest* (as an enemy of Robin Hood in a role similar to those of Rathbone and Wilmer in other versions), and *Suspect* (known as *The Risk* in the United States), '60; *Fury at Smuggler's Bay*, *The Naked Edge*, *Cone of Silence*, and *Cash on Demand* (the latter two with his Watson, Andre Morell), '61; *Captain Clegg* (*Night Creatures* in the United States—Athole Stewart was in the earlier version, *Dr. Syn*), *The Man Who Finally Died*, and *The Devil's Agent*, '62; *The Gorgon* and *Dr. Terror's House of Horrors*, '64; *She* (again with Morell), *Dr. Who and the Daleks*, *The Skull*, and *Island of Terror* (*The Frightened Island*), '65; *Daleks Invasion Earth A.D. 2150*, '66; *Night of the Big Heat*, and *Torture Garden* (*The Garden*), '67; *Blood Beast Terror*, *Death's Head Moth*, and *Corruption* (by Donald and Derek Ford, scripters of the Holmes film *Study in Terror*) '68; *Incense for the Damned* and *Scream and Scream Again*, '69; *Vampire Lovers* (with Douglas Wilmer), *House That Dripped Blood*, and *I, Monster*, '70; *Tales From The Crypt*, *Fear in the Night*, *Doctors Wear Scarlet*, *Devil's Agent*, *Blood From the Mummy's Tomb*, *Twins of Evil*, '71; *Asylum*, *Nothing But the Night*, *Creeping Flesh*, *Bride of Fengriffen* (*And Then the Screaming Starts*), *Dr. Phibes Rises Again*, '72; *Horror Express*, '74; *The Legend of the Seven Golden Vampires*, '75; and at this writing (late '75) Cushing has just completed a role as "Scar," a reanimated Nazi in *Death Corps*, filmed in Florida with John Carradine, and is back in Britain making *The Satanist*.

He has still found time to occasionally appear on the stage as well, in such shows as *The Silver Whistle*, '56; *Sound of Murder*, '59; and *Thark*, '65.

A recent candid by coauthor Hart of Peter Cushing displaying the great warmth which he has too often hidden in his film roles.

With his "star" earnings, Peter and Helen had bought a house in Whitstable, Kent, on the estuary, and the two of them used to spend hours watching the wild seabirds circle the mud flats there. Completely devoted to his wife, Cushing has repeatedly told reporters over the years: "Without her encouragement and faith in me I would have been a failure." When Helen died in 1971, Peter was completely shattered.

After his initial solitude following her death, he involved himself with work, work, work, and more work—"the only therapy," he says.

Luckily, I have kept working constantly ever since and I like to be occupied. Time is the worst thing. It doesn't mean that I think less of her. Only the knowledge that we will meet again keeps me going. You have to believe in the next life or you could never reconcile the injustices in this one. I used to love spare time—since we did so much together, but I find now there are many things I can't enjoy doing, Helen was everything to me.

201

After his wife's death, Cushing received a great volume of letters from his many fans, and the actor answered every one of them personally. If not for his belief that he would be reunited with Helen, he said, "I could not face up to anything . . . in the meantime . . . I shall endeavor to give of my best in work and divers activities," which indeed he has. He has never felt that he was "slumming" by doing horror films:

I've never felt I'm wasting myself. You have to have a great ego to want to play Hamlet all the time, and I just haven't got that ego. . . . I don't believe there's much difference between the horrors of Shakespeare and the horrors of Bram Stoker (author of *Dracula* and an acquaintance of Cushing's grandfather). . . . If I were offered two plays at the same time and one was *Macbeth* and the other *Rookery Nook* I'd do *Rookery Nook* because I believe it has more attraction for the general public.

He felt that Hammer, especially,
make better and better films of the macabre kind, understanding what makes a good horror picture, getting to the heart of the matter.
. . . Hammer horrors have an authenticity of their own. . . . Horror films, I believe, are an escape valve in a world surrounded by the menace of catastrophe. They are a vacarious form of outlet amid pressures which tend to squeeze us into tight corners. They are, I think, necessary.

As for himself, Cushing was never part of the London social world: "He does go to Caprice sometimes," his wife had told an interviewer, "but it's only to sit at a corner table and have eggs and bacon, 15 shillings." His happiness was to share his beloved English countryside with her, and on winter mornings to make up the early morning fires for her in their quiet house on the silent, deserted beach. He is an expert on such games as "L'Attaque," and like Conan Doyle he is interested in collecting model soldiers. His old architectural training survives in his interest in building model structures, such as the miniature theater in which he puts on shows.

Since his wife's death, however, Cushing has spent much time away from his Whitstable home due to his self-imposed heavy work schedule. "He looked tired but immaculate," wrote a *Radio Times* correspondent in '72, and Cushing told him that nothing in his life could ever be the same again:

Since Helen passed on I can't find anything; the heart, quite simply, has gone out of everything. Time is interminable, the loneliness is almost unbearable and the only thing that keeps me going is the knowledge that my dear Helen and I will be united again some day. To join Helen is my only ambition. You have my permission to publish that . . . really, you know dear boy, it's all just killing time. Please say that.

Peter Cushing continues to be active in film. He has just made a 1976 yet-to-be-released film entitled *At the Earth's Core*, which is to be distributed by American International Pictures. Directed by Kevin Connor, the film is based on the novel by Edgar Rice Burroughs, and besides Cushing (who has the lead role), the film also stars Doug McClure and Caroline Munro.

Andre Morell, the '59 *Hound of the Baskerville's* Dr. Watson, was called by a reviewer in the *Sherlock Holmes Journal* (notoriously hard to please, as witness the above Cushing review) one of the few "really acceptable Dr. Watsons on the screen"; and the reviews we have quoted above of course bear out this judgment with their high praise for the exmilitary capability of Morell's interpretation as opposed to the blockheadedness of so many other performers in the role.

Born Andre Mesritz on 20 August 1909 in London, Morell was educated at Bath and at Belmont College, London. He joined the amateur Saint Pancras People's Theatre in 1930 and four years later made his professional bow in *Good Morning Bill* in Somerset. Then, after two years of repertory experience in New Brighton and Margate, Morell debuted in London with *Call It A Day* in 1936, subsequently appearing in such West End shows as *Sweet Aloes, They Came By Night,* and *The Last Straw* before 1938, in which year Andre joined the Old Vic Company. With the Vic he played in such shows as *Trelawny Of The 'Wells'* (which future-Holmes Robert Stephens was to do at that theater years later), *Romeo and Juliet* (with Stewart Granger), *The Rivals, Hamlet, The Devil's Discipline, Saint Joan,* and *The Tempest*; and he toured Europe and Egypt for them in *Henry V, Viceroy Sarah* and *Libel*.

Following the outbreak of war, however, Morell joined the Royal Welsh Fusiliers. Before the war, he said, he "did nothing else but theatre work"—now he was to spend six years commanding a company of infantry in the Far East, no doubt gaining the valuable experience that made him so superb as that old

Andre Morell's Dr. Watson was by far the most intelligent on the screen. Cushing is in the background of this outstanding 221B set.

Eastern campaigner John H. Watson. After the war was over, Morell came back to Britain and after only a month was in *Happy As Kings*, but after *Boys In Brown* he concentrated mainly on film work, with the exception of a brief return to the Vic in '52 and a few short seasons at the smaller "avant-garde" theaters. The reason he deserted the boards for the screen, said Morell, was that "I must do film work to pay my tax. Income Tax drives me into films. I would like to go back to theatre work."

Andre Morell's films include his debut, *Thirteen and a Gun*, with Arthur Wontner in 1938; *Ten Days in Paris*, '39; *Unpublished Story*, '42; *Quartet* (with Ian Fleming), '48; *So Long at the Fair* (for *Hound* director Fisher), and *No Place for Jennifer*, '49; *Madeleine, Seven Days to Noon* (as Folland; the film won an Academy Award for its original story), Hitchcock's *Stage Fright* (in which Sherlock Holmes is mentioned), *Trio*, (in which Morell played a doctor, and in which Sherlock Holmes is mentioned), *The Clouded Yellow*, and *Flesh and Blood*— all of them '50; *High Treason*, '51; *The Tall Headlines* and *Stolen Face* ("I do very little in it indeed"), '52; *His Majesty O'Keefe* (as Tetins), '54; *Three Cases of Murder* (as the psychiatrist Dr. Audlin, and again with Wontner) and *Summer Madness*, '55; *Bridge on the River Kwai*, '57; *Behemoth the Sea Monster* (*The Giant Behemoth* in the United States), '58; *Ben Hur* (as Sextus), '59; *Cone of Silence*, '60; Ray Harryhausen's *Mysterious Island* and *Cash on Demand* (in which "Watson" turns the tables as a charming bank robber by dominating Cushing), '61; *Shadow of the Cat* (a splendid villain), '62; *She* (with Cushing and Lee) and *Plague of the Zombies*, '65; *Mummy's Shroud*, '67; *Dark of the Sun* (a very moving role as Bussier), '68; and *10 Rillington Place* (as the Judge, with phonograph-Holmes Robert Hardy), '71.

He has also been very much evident on TV, being especially well remembered for his 1956 role as the Inquisitor in *1984*, in which Watson had his revenge by treating Peter Cushing very badly indeed. Morell played a similar role in *The Condemned*, but on being offered a third such outing refused, saying "I would like to play a comedy part—from my point of view it seems very desirable to get away from these gloomy existentialist roles." In short, he told an interviewer, he would like to play "any zonking good role." Some of his other TV work (he has also been much on British radio) was in *Trouble in the Sun*, *The Gay Lord Quex*, and *It's Midnight, Dr. Schweitzer*; undoubtedly his best-known role on the tube was the part of Quatermass in the famous science-fiction series, though he was not in any of the movies inspired by it.

Like Peter Cushing, Morell is interested in building model theaters, and made a minutely accurate edition of the Elizabethan Fortune Theatre. He also collects Staffordshire theatrical figures and Sunderland lustre jugs. It is astonishingly in view of his success as Dr. Watson that he has never repeated the part, but perhaps his own aversion to being "typed" has played a part in this situation.

Hound director Terence Fisher, of course, went on to direct the next Holmes film in our book as well, and David Pirie's book *A Heritage Of Horror* suggests that the character of the Baker Street Sleuth has great affinities for the distinctively personal world of Fisher's films, calling Sherlock, "the perfect Fisher hero, the Renaissance scholar with strong mystical overtones," and noting his lines in *Hound* that echo the vampire-fighter Van Helsing, such as, "I am fighting evil, fighting it as surely as you do." It seems, indeed, very probable that this Galahadism is an aspect of Holmes that accounts in part for his great revival of popularity in our own despairing age: his ability to make order out of chaos, and to put things "back in joint" when they seem hopelessly tangled and in-explicable. It is perhaps significant that modern audiences are particularly fascinated with Holmes' Quixotic struggle against that personification of evil—Moriarty.

Born in London in 1904, Fisher began in films as assistant editor to Ian Dalrymple, who is discussed earlier in our book. Some of his significant and characteristic films as a director include *So Long at the Fair*, '50 and *Stolen Face*, '52 (both with Morell); *Curse of Frankenstein*, '57 (and most of the sequels with Cushing); *Dracula*, '58; *The Man Who Could Cheat Death*, '59; *The Mummy, Stranglers of Bombay, Two Faces of Dr. Jekyll* (United States: *House of Fright*), and *Brides of Dracula*, '60; *Curse of the Werewolf*, '61; *The Gorgon*, '64; *Dracula Prince of Darkness* and *Island of Terror*, '65; *Night of the Big Heat*, '67; and *The Devil Rides Out* (*Devil's Bride* in America), '69. For television, he directed Boris Karloff in the detective series *Colonel March of Scotland Yard* and did the Richard Greene *Robin Hood* series for Hammer, subsequently directing Greene and Cushing in the feature version *Sword of Sherwood Forrest*. He has, of course, done many, many films with both Cushing and Lee.

In a 1967 interview Fisher noted that cinematographer "Jack Asher likes to go for strong color effects. And then you really have to stylize and discipline the colour." This makes it all the more remarkable that in *Hound* Fisher managed to induce Asher to achieve a very subtle muted effect with his pallet. Of Miles Malleson, highly praised as his Bishop Frankland in this film, Fisher commented, "I like working with Miles. . . . Give him two lines and he'll work through-out the scene"—and certainly Malleson makes his utterly extraneous role in *Hound* far more memorable than it deserves to be.

"Cushing . . . is a very deep thinker," noted the director; and speaking of his next Holmes, Fisher said, "Lee is a mime expert; he studied ballet at one time, and he can express emotion eloquently in the simplest physical movements, just in his walk."

Pirie believes that in Fisher's films, "The Universe . . . is strictly dualistic, divided rigidly between ultimate Evil," and goes on to say that in *The Hound of the Baskervilles*, Fisher "uses Conan Doyle's plot to estab-lish a stylish dialectic between Holmes' nominally rational Victorian milieu and the dark fabulous cruelty

Snapped at an off-camera party is director Terence Fisher, flanked by his Holmes from *Hound of the Baskervilles* (Cushing, left) and his Watson from *Sherlock Holmes and the Deadly Necklace* (Thorley Walters).

behind the Baskerville legend."

This interpretation, if true, would help to explain the point that baffled so many of the film's contemporary critics, namely, why had so much of the original plot been jettisoned to be replaced by far less-mysterious incidents? The reason would seem to be that Fisher saw the story as taking place on a different plane than the merely intellectual one, and felt that the interest in it lay not in the deductive process by which Holmes solves the case, but more on the sub- (or super-) conscious level where Holmes saves the *soul* of Baskerville from the vengeful and fatally fascinating Cecile, who acts as the physical instrument of punishment for the misdeeds of his ancestor.

22
Christopher Lee

SHERLOCK HOLMES UND DAS HALSBAND DES TODES; SHERLOCK HOLMES (LA VALLE DEL TERRORE); SHERLOCK HOLMES ET LE COLLIER DE LA MORT; SHERLOCK HOLMES AND THE DEADLY NECKLACE; SHERLOCK HOLMES AND THE NECKLACE OF DEATH; SHERLOCK HOLMES AND THE DEATHLY NECKLACE; THE VALLEY OF FEAR (West German, Italian, French)

Released: 1962; United States: '64; Great Britain: '68 (although originally set for release there in '65).

Running Time: 7,710 feet; 86 minutes

Production Company: CC/Criterion/INCEI; released in Britain by Golden Era

Producer: Arthur Brauner

Director: Terence Fisher and Frank Witherstein

Screenplay: Curt Siodmak

Based on: *The Valley of Fear*

Director of Photography: Richard Angst

Filmed in: West Berlin

CAST

Sherlock Holmes	Christopher Lee
Ellen Blackburn	Senta Berger
Dr. Watson	Thorley Walters
Professor Moriarty	Hans Söhnker
Inspector Cooper	Hans Neilsen
?	Ivan Desny
?	Wolfgang Lukschy

SYNOPSIS: The film followed the plot of Doyle's novel to some extent, though updated to a period that seemed to be somewhere in the first third of this century. At the end, though Holmes retrieves the necklace of the title, Moriarty gets away scot-free: apparently because a sequel had been shot back-to-back with the same cast and crew, in which the Professor would have gotten his comeuppance. The sequel, however, has not yet been released; it seems to have been based on the same premise as the next film in our book, *Study in Terror,* and each of them was known as *Fog* (from the Adrian Conan Doyle story) at one time or another—the Lee film was also known as *Sherlock Holmes Meets Jack the Ripper* (with Lee apparently in both roles), and *this* title was subsequently used for the novelization of *Terror* in Britain, to complete the confusion!

Christopher Lee had the following comments on *Deadly Necklace* in a 1968 interview (before the film's English release):

We should never have made it in Germany with German actors, although we had a British art director and a British director. . . . It was not taken from any specific story. Although it was called *The Valley of Fear,* it was not taken from that story. It was a hodge-podge of stories put together by the German producers, which ruined it. My portrayal of Holmes is, I think, one of the best things I've ever done because I tried to play him really as he was written—as a very intolerant, argumentative, difficult man—and I looked extraordinarily like him with the make-up. The picture, which, thank heavens, has never been shown here, really wasn't well done. It was a badly edited deplorable hodge-podge of nonsense. Everyone who's seen it said I was

One cannot think that Lee's aloof Holmes is averting his eyes from the corpse because he is in any way disturbed by it, so he must be eyeing something of more interest off-camera. (Courtesy National Film Archives of the British Film Institute)

as like Holmes as any actor they've ever seen—both in appearance and interpretation.

REVIEWS (*Sherlock Holmes Journal,* Vol. 7, 1964, reviewed by Anthony Howlett): "*Sherlock Holmes and the Necklace of Death. . . .* The title alone is sufficient comment on this new film. This is the Teutonic Holmes, perpetrated in Berlin in '62. . . . Dubbed into American. . . . I have read the synopsis—ouch!"

(*Sherlock Holmes Journal,* Winter '71, reviewed by C.G.P.): "Some of us will want to see this film, with its sinister secret coffin and stolen treasure, again."

(*Heritage of Horror,* 1973, by David Pirie): ". . . contains some fine sequences, but it was finally impossible to judge the version shown here because both Christopher Lee (Holmes) and Thorley Walters (Watson) were dubbed by mediocre American actors."

Having graduated from Sir Henry Baskerville to Holmes himself, Chris Lee went on a few years later to play Mycroft Holmes, which he did beautifully in *Private Life of Sherlock Holmes*—although he is entirely the wrong physical type for the portly and slow-moving (not to say sluggish) elder brother of Sherlock.

He has had still another link with Sherlock Holmes through his long association with the *Fu Manchu* series, which parallels the Holmes films at many points because of its imitation Holmes and Watson characters, Nayland Smith and Dr. Petrie; we will discuss these links in greater detail in our chapter on Douglas Wilmer, who has played both Holmes and Smith more than once.

Christopher Frank Carandini Lee was born in London on 27 May 1922. His godfather was a Battenberg—the family that is today the Royal one of Mountbatten. His father was a Colonel in the 60th King's Royal Rifle Corps and on his mother's side (the Carandinis, who date back to Charlemagne) Lee claims descent from the Borgias. He first appeared on the stage between the ages of nine and twelve when he

Perhaps the best-cluttered Sherlockian apartment in movies. Christopher Lee is the dreamy Holmes, and Thorley Walters warms his hands at the fire as Dr. Watson. (Courtesy National Film Archives of the British Film Institute)

performed in the annual Shakespeare plays at his prep school—Summerfields in Oxford; appearing with him in all of these ventures was his schoolmate Patric Macnee, with whom years later Lee was to appear on television in an episode of Macnee's series *The Avengers.* Lee went on to major in classics at Wellington College (although as a King's Scholar he could have gone to Eton), and was holding down an office job in the City (London's financial district) when the war began. He served in the South African Air Force during 1940–45 (joining at 17½), first as a fighter pilot and subsequently in Military Intelligence, where he was transferred as a result of his multilingual gifts (he speaks seven languages), which have since served him so well in international films.

"When I was demobilized after the war, I didn't really know what I wanted to do," said Lee. He was none too keen on returning to his ill-paying office job,

but did not really consider becoming an actor until the idea was suggested to him by his cousin Count Niccolo, who was the Italian ambassador in London at the time. The cousin arranged an interview with Filipo Del Guidice, the London-based Italian producer who ran Two Cities Films for J. Arthur Rank—and Lee was given a seven year contract!—even though some had considered him, at 6'4", too tall for films. He made his film debut in 1947 in *Corridor of Mirrors,* and has since then appeared in considerably more than one hundred feature films. Since his role as the Monster in 1957's *Curse of Frankenstein,* Lee has been primarily (and enormously successful—eighteen thousand fan letters per year) associated with horror films, but within the past few years he has begun to emerge in major "mainstream" films like *Hannie Caulder, Julius Caesar, The Three* (and *Four*) *Musketeers,* and *The Man with the Golden Gun*; and his career seems to promise even greater things for the future.

He has tended to be most at home with villainous roles, though: "All classic villains are the epitome of dignity," he says. "I have always tried to invest even the lowliest of 'creatures' with nobility and they are yet too

Christopher Lee as Sherlock Holmes. The moustache must be part of some disguise.

of the TV film *In Search of Dracula*, Lee journeys to Transylvania and appears not only as himself and the fictional count, but also plays the historic Vlad Dracula, a Wallachian prince known as the Impaler.

Although he played a similar role in *Terror of the Tongs*, '60, Lee's actual *Fu Manchu* series consisted of *The Face of Fu Manchu*, '65 (with TV-Watson and radio-Holmes H. Marion-Crawford as Dr. Petrie, a role he continued in most of the rest of the films); *Brides of Fu Manchu*, '66 (with screen-Holmes Wilmer taking over the role of Smith); *Vengeance of Fu Manchu*, '67; *Blood of Fu Manchu* (*Der Todekuss Des Doctor Fu Manchu*) and *Castle of Fu Manchu* (*Das Schloss Des Fu Manchu*)—both of '68. Besides his appearances with Wilmer in some of the episodes of this series, Lee previously acted with him in '56's *Battle of the River Plate*.

Although best known for his menaces, more recently Lee has been playing detectives, monster-slayers, and other "good" (if still characteristically supercilious and ill-tempered) characters in such films as *The Gorgon*, '64 (as Professor Meister); *The Night of the Big Heat* and *The Devil Rides Out* (*The Devil's Bride*, as the Duc de Richelieu), '67; *Scream and Scream Again*, '69; *Nothing But the Night* (his own coproduction and 111th film), '72; and *Horror Express*, '74. He has displayed his versatility as both Faust *and* Mephistopheles in *Katarsis*, '63, and gave one of his best performances as Jekyll and Hyde in 1970's *I, Monster*, which was far more faithful to Stevenson's book than most previous versions, except for its renaming of the principal characters to Marlowe and Blake. (Lee had played a supporting role in the earlier *Two Faces of Dr. Jekyll*, known in the United States as *House of Fright*, '59.) In '72's mistitled *Night of the Blood Monster*, he was especially fine as the real-life Judge Jeffreys, who is mentioned in one version of *The Hound of the Baskervilles*.

His career is indelibly associated in most peoples' minds with that of Peter Cushing, and they have made over twenty pictures together at last count—including, besides many of those mentioned above, *Hamlet* (Lee as Fortinbras), *Moulin Rouge*, '53; *The Mummy*, '59; *Dr. Terror's House of Horrors*, '64; *She* and *The Skull*, '65; *House That Dripped Blood*, '70; *Creeping Flesh*, '72; and *Island of the Burning Damned*. Recently they have each completed an episode of the TV series *Space: 1999*.

"I don't believe in double acts or teams," Lee told an interviewer in '72, speaking of his long association with Cushing, "but we have a good working relationship together. We anticipate each other and know how the other will react."

"After all that time," echoed Cushing, "you know a person very well!" Susan d'Arcy wrote in *Photoplay* that "they are a contrary pair and yet their very differences are probably one reason for their success: where Christopher Lee is assertive, slightly remote, majestically assured, Peter Cushing is gentle and perhaps more reserved." Lee has recently said of his old friend that Cushing was "the closest thing to a saint I've ever met."

deeply pathetic. . . . I stress the human element. I stress the sadness, the loneliness of evil."

Like such other screen Sherlocks as Rathbone and Granger, Lee has played in a large number of swashbucklers. He does some superb fencing in *Captain Horatio Hornblower*, '50 and *Pirates of Blood River* (as Captain La Roche, with Marla Landi from *Hound*), '63. He even doubled Rathbone's old nemesis Erroll Flynn in one film, and inherited Basil's role of the villainous Marquis St. Evremond in the '58 remake of *Tale of Two Cities*. Besides being a swordsman, he is a boxer and all-around athlete, as one would expect of an exstuntman.

The role with which Christopher Lee is most closely associated is, of course, Count Dracula. He first played the thirsty Voivode in '58's *Dracula*; and in the subsequent Hammer series he has starred in *Dracula, Prince of Darkness*, '64; *Dracula Has Risen from the Grave*, '68; *Taste the Blood of Dracula*, '69; *The Scars of Dracula*, '70; *Dracula A.D. 1972* (actually '71); *Dracula is Dead*, '72; and *Satanic Rites of Dracula*, '73. In addition, Lee made *Count Dracula* (*Nachts Wenn Dracula Erwacht*), a version more close to the original novel, in '70 (it contains one of his best performances). He has played the character in the satirical *Tempi Duri Per I Vampiri* (*Uncle was a Vampire*, for English-speaking audiences), and even contributed vampirish cameos to *The Magic Christian* and *One More Time*. In '75's theatrical release

Speaking of his own acting technique, Lee has said,

I underplay rather because I think so hard, and it shows in the eyes and in every little movement of the face and figure . . . which I attempt only when it means something. I believe in thinking, listening and standing still unless one really has to do anything. When the action comes, it should be quick, decisive—violent, if necessary—but always absolutely full of meaning. One should never do anything unless its absolutely essential; when you do need it, it's that much greater . . . it is again a question of the screen actor thinking and showing it in his eyes as opposed to the stage actor who actually does more physically.

Of the value of most of his work, he notes: Everybody likes to laugh, everybody likes to cry, everybody likes to be frightened, sometimes. I enjoy my job. . . . When the audience leaves the cinema they may realise the falseness of what they've seen, but while the film's still running I try to keep them totally convinced. . . . I have said it before, and I will say it again, there is not as much violence in all my so-called "horror" films as there is in one current film.

An avid reader of biography, and recently a judge of the London *Times* Ghost Story Competition, Lee is a perfectionist where his films are concerned, constantly insisting on script changes to preserve accuracy and often taking a hand even in the camera department. His Danish wife Brigitte is a painter, and they have a daughter named Christina.

Deadly Necklace director Fisher has said of Christopher Lee, "he knows how to project mood and inner feeling" due to his "very real understanding of mime," and it is to be hoped that this ability (too rare in modern cinema) will now begin to be more appreciated by "mainstream" audiences.

Among Lee's legion of films, other than those we have already mentioned, are *One Night with You, Song For Tomorrow, Saraband for Dead Lovers* (with Stewart Granger), *Trottie True, My Brother's Keeper, Penny and the Pownall Case*, and *Scott of The Antarctic*, '48; *Prelude to Fame* and *They Were Not Divided*, '49; *Valley of Eagles*, '51; *Paul Temple Returns* (based on the H. Marion Crawford radio series) and *The Crimson Pirate*, '52; *Innocents in Paris* and *The Triangle*, '53; *Dark Avenger, Destination Milan, The Death of Michael Turbin*, and *Final Column*, '54; *That Lady, Storm Over the Nile* (a beautifully played cameo as an old prisoner), *Alias John Preston, Cockleshell Heroes, Private's Progress*, and *Crossroads*, '55; *Moby Dick* (for John Huston; also in a production directed by Orson Welles), *Port Afrique, Beyond Mombasa*, and *Ill Met By Moonlight*, '56; *Fortune is a Woman, Bitter Victory*, and *The Truth About Women*, '57; *The Accursed, Battle of the V.I.*, and *The Doctor from Seven Dials (Corridors of Blood)*, '58; *The Man Who Could Cheat Death, The Treasure of San Teresa, Beat Girl*, and *Long Distance*, '59; *Too Hot to Handle, City of the Dead (Horror Hotel), The Hands of Orlac*, and *The Taste of Fear (Scream of Fear)*, '60; *Vampires Versus Hercules (Ercole Al Centro Della Terra), Das Geheimnis Der Gelben Narzissen*, and *Das Ratsel Der Roten Orchidee* (with Fritz Rasp, of the German *Hunds*), '61; *Im Namen Des Teufels*, '62; *Der Dämon Und Die Jungfrau*, and *Das Schlors Des Grauens*, '63; *Castle of the Dead (Il Castello Del Morti Vivi), La Crypty E L'Incubo* and *Horror Castle (The Virgin of Nuremberg)*, '64; *Rasputin—The Mad Monk* and *The Theatre of Death* (one of his finest parts), '65; *Circus of Fear* and *Das Rätsel Des Selbernen Dreiecks*, '66; *Die Pagode Zum Fünften Schrecken, Die Schlangengrube und Das Pendel, Diana Tocht er der Wildnis*, and *Five Golden Dragons*, '67; *Curse of the Crimson Altar (The Crimson Cult)* and *The Face of Eve*, '68; *The Oblong Box, Torture Chamber of Dr. Sadism*, and *Der Hexentoter von Blackmoor*, '69; and *Dark Places* and *Death Line*, '72; and *The Wicker Man*, '73.

At this writing, Lee is set to film the controversial Biblical tale *Passover Plot*, in Israel, and for his own production company Charlemagne (in cooperation with Hammer) he is planning *To the Devil a Daughter*.

Thorley Walters, who plays Dr. Watson in *Sherlock Holmes and The Deadly Necklace*, makes a distinct contrast to Terence Fisher's last Watson, Andre Morell, since Walters returns rather to the mold of Nigel Bruce and gives us a somewhat older and slower-witted edition of the good doctor, though no "Boobus Britanicus" by any means. Walters has been around for quite awhile, but it seems to have been only in the last few years that this splendid actor has begun to get anything like his just recognition. In 1968, Walters played Dr. Watson in a cameo in the British film *The Best House in London*. At this writing he is on very prominent display as King Edward VII in the television series *Jennie*, based on the life of Lady Randolph Churchill.

Like his fellow-Watson H. Marion Crawford, Walters has taken a turn as Sax Rohmer's Dr. Petrie—in Chris Lee's *Fu Manchu* series. Another film with Christopher Lee was 1964's *Dracula, Prince of Darkness* (as Ludwig); with Peter Cushing, Walters was in *Suspect*, '60; *Frankenstein Created Woman* (a very Watsonish part), '66; and *Frankenstein Must be Destroyed*, '69. In '61, Walters made *Invasion Quartet* with stage-Holmes John Wood, and the same year with TV-Sherlock Ronald Howard he did *Murder She Said*. Among the other films of Thorley Walters are *Carlton-Browne of the F.O. (Man in a Cocked Hat*, '59); *The Earth Dies Screaming*, '64; *The Wrong Box*, '66; and *Vampire Circus*, '71. In May '72 he had a notable role in *The Lotus Eaters* on BBC-TV, as an elderly man breaking up under the strain of being away from England.

Thorley Walters later reprised his Dr. Watson opposite the Sherlock of Douglas Wilmer in 1975's *Adventure of Sherlock Holmes' Smarter Brother*.

23
John Neville

A STUDY IN TERROR; FOG (British)

Date of Release: 4 November 1965
Running Time: 95 minutes; 94 min.
Production Company: Compton-Cameo Films (Michael Klinger, Chairman, and Tony Tenser)/ Tekli/Sir Nigel Film Corp.; released in Britain by Rank and in the United States by Columbia Pictures.
Executive Producer: Herman Cohen
Producer: Henry E. Lester
Director: James Hill
Screenplay: Donald and Derek Ford
Based on: *Fog* by Adrian Conan Doyle, and "Characters Created by Sir Arthur Conan Doyle."
Director of Photography: Desmond Dickinson
Editor: Henry Richardson
Art Director: Alex Vetchinsky
Music: John Scott
Special Effects: Wally Veevers
Costumes: Motley
Assistant Director: Barry Langley
Sound: H. L. Bird and John Cox
Color: Eastmancolour
Locations: London
(British "X" Certificate)

CAST

Sherlock Holmes	John Neville
Dr. Watson	Donald Houston
Edward Osborne, Lord Carfax	John Fraser
Dr. Murray	Anthony Quayle
Annie Chapman	Barbara Windsor
Mycroft Holmes	Robert Morley
Angela Osborne	Adrienne Corri
Inspector Lestrade	Frank Finlay
Sally	Judi Dench
Prime Minister	Cecil Parker
Duke of Shires	Barry Jones
Singer	Georgia Brown
Joseph Beck	Charles Regnier
Home Secretary	Dudley Foster
Max Steiner	Peter Carsten
Chunky	Terry Downes
Polly Nichols	Christiane Maybach
Cathy Eddowes	Kay Walsh
Simpleton	John Cairney
Mary Kelly	Edina Ronay
Landlady	Avis Bunnage
Mrs. Hudson	Barbara Leake
P. C. Benson	Patrick Newell
Liz Stride	Norma Foster
First Streetwalker	Donna White

SYNOPSIS: In 1888, Jack the Ripper is terrorizing London's East End slum, Whitechapel. Holmes becomes intrigued in the case after the murders of Polly Nichols (who had just lifted a "Swell's" purse, and is left floating in a horse trough), and Annie Chapman—like the Ripper's first (killed before the opening titles) and all of his subsequent victims, the pair are streetwalkers.

Someone mysteriously sends Holmes a case of surgical instruments through the mail, complete except for a missing postmortem scalpel (the largest), which subsequently proves to have been the one used by the killer. Holmes' notes the crest on the case: "Ha!,

Sherlock Holmes (John Neville) saws placidly away as his brother Mycroft (Robert Morley, center) prepares to have apoplexy. *Study in Terror*'s version of the Great Sleuth's elder brother Mycroft was not exactly as easygoing as the Doyle original, but Donald Houston (right) was perhaps the best-balanced Watson ever, neither too bright nor too buffoonish. (Courtesy National Film Archives of the British Film Institute)

John Neville in an untenable position in *Study in Terror*. (Courtesy National Film Archives of the British Film Institute)

the coat of arms of the elder son of a Duke! Quick, Watson, pass me my 'Burke's Peerage,'" says the sleuth, who discovers that a scion of the house of the Duke of Shires was the owner, and further deduces that the case had been sent to 221B by a woman. "Come Watson," says Holmes, "there will be another murder tonight. Let us scour the streets of Whitechapel for the missing clue."

Holmes is too late to save Liz Stride, who has failed to "move along" fast enough after being requested to do so by the "peelers" (police). Holmes does, however, trace the surgical case to a pawnbroker's shop ("in a narrow street facing South and business is bad," he has deduced), run by one Joseph Beck who tells him that it was pawned by a girl named Angela Osborne.

Holmes visits Osterly Park where he finds out that the Duke's second son, Lord Carfax, has been disowned by his father and his present whereabouts are unknown.

Holmes' search for Angela Osborne leads him to the Whitechapel charity organization run by bearded, radical missionary and surgeon, Dr. Murray, who, it develops, also works as a coroner and in the morgue on the Ripper's victims.

In his mercy work, he is assisted not only by his niece, Sally, and a gentle simpleton with a harmless necrophiliac foot fetish, but also by Sally's fiance, Lord Carfax. Carfax explains to Holmes that his brother Michael was married to Angela, a prostitute, and that since his brother's disappearance he has been paying blackmail money to a pubkeeper named Max Steiner to hush up this affair. Steiner's sleazy premises are one of the chief targets of Dr. Murray's reforming zeal, and Holmes not only pays the pub a visit—"I wish to see the owner of this doubtful establishment"—but also returns to Dr. Murray's soup kitchen disguised as a Cockney derelict.

In the meantime the British Government is under the gun because the Ripper murders continue unsolved, and the Prime Minister and Home Secretary request their associate Mycroft Holmes to ask his brother's official assistance in the case. ("Mycroft," says the Premier, "I've sent for you because you have the tidiest and most orderly brain in her Majesty's Civil Service"; "Mr. Prime Minister, I cannot deny it.") As Mycroft enters 221B, Sherlock is holding forth on the violin, and the elder brother comments, "It was a sad day when mother gave you that thing."

Inspector Lestrade is, as usual, disconcerted by the opinion of Holmes regarding the man they are looking for. "This is a madman with certain medical skills," believes the Baker Street Sage, "considerable intelligence and education."

Holmes is not far from the scene when the Ripper claims his next victim, Mary Kelly: Miss Kelly has just invited the camera, which is taking the Ripper's point of view, up to her room for a little fun. Holmes pursues the killer, but loses him in Dr. Murray's surgery; however, in a showdown with the doctor, the sleuth demands all essential information about the missing Michael; Murray reluctantly reveals that Michael is none other than the pathetic idiot who assists him in his medical work.

The young man's sanity snapped, the doctor explains, when he got into a fight with his wife and Steiner over the plot to blackmail the Duke. In the struggle, Steiner had thrown an uncorked bottle of acid at Michael, but it had hit Angela instead, scarring her horribly and forcing her to lead a life of complete withdrawal. Holmes takes Michael home to the Duke, and then returns to the scent.

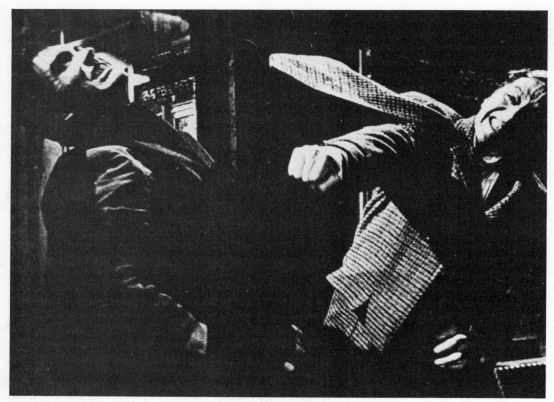

Jack the Ripper (John Fraser) is handily dealt with by Sherlock Holmes, the "baritsu" student of Baker Street (John Neville).

Holmes and Watson have had an encounter with some footpads outside Steiner's pub, but defended themselves adequately with their sword canes, which they had with them since they were formally dressed in their "out-on-the-town" togs at the time: "Nothing like a piece of cold steel, eh, Holmes?" asks the good doctor; "Brisk work, Watson!" agrees his companion.

Undeterred by this encounter, however, the sleuth now returns to the establishment. Too late to save Cathy Eddowes, he hopes to be in time to prevent the murder of Angela.

He confronts her in her concealed bedroom, and she gives him her own version of her career as a prostitute and her married life with Michael, and explains that she had sent the surgical instruments to Holmes in hopes of arousing his interest in the mystery.

Finally the Ripper appears by her darkened bedside, but Holmes is waiting in readiness, and confirms the fact that all of the murders have been committed in the attempt to find Angela by her vengeful brother-in-law. "Good evening, Lord Carfax!" cries the Great Detective, whereupon Holmes and the Ripper grapple in a fierce fight, during which a lamp is overturned and the room catches on fire, and Carfax, Angela, and the faithful Steiner all perish. Holmes escapes as the building is consumed in flames.

"Lestrade has his three buckets of ash," he tells Watson. "We will keep the name."

But how, Watson wants to know, did Holmes escape from the burning pub?

"You know my methods. Hmph, my dear Watson— it's well known that I am indestructible!"

REVIEWS (*Daily Mail,* 3 November 1965, reviewed by Cecil Wilson):

. . . its idea of London's East End in the 1880s— toytown backstreets, fog swirling over the cobbles, quaint *My Fair Lady* cockneys, louder as well as larger than life—smacks of Hollywood.

John Neville . . . aquiline, arrogant, deer-stalker hatted, violin-scraping and elegantly cab-drawn, has the true Baker Street air.

Donald Houston . . . at once dog-like and bovine, trotting meekly at the master's heels and perpetually gasping at his deductive powers.

. . . . the obvious temptation was to humanize the sleuth with a little sex.

But he remains wedded to his work and in love with himself.

You may well ask what business tarts have with the respectable world of Sherlock Holmes and no doubt the ghost of Conan Doyle is asking the same question.

James Hill's bustling direction.

. . . next time how about starring "The New Sherlock Holmes," as they call him, in a genuine old Sherlock Holmes story?

212

(*Sun*, 3 November 1965, reviewed by Ann Pacey):

At first gory glance it looks as if Compton's *Study* . . . is going to play up the horror horribly.

But a mere glance at the cast list is reassuring.

Directed by James Hill, with plenty of boozy, bawdy, beautiful period atmosphere, *Study* emerges as a vastly entertaining juggling act between truth and fantasy.

Tensely and thoroughly deserving of its 'X' cert at times, the film is still discreet with its shocks and generous with its wit.

. . . the unsolved mystery . . . smoothly unravelled by the imperturbable Holmes, with the mystified aid of the bluff and comfortable Dr. Watson.

Neville, with his long, serious face and faintly tongue-in-cheek approach is a superb Holmes.

Houston does a beautifully-timed job as Watson . . . the rest of the exceptional cast are excellent.

Study will almost certainly prove to be only the first of a series.

Why? It's elementary. It bears all the marks of success.

(*Daily Express*, 4 November 1965, reviewed by Leonard Mosley):

The idea of involving the famous fictional detective with the sordid series of real murders in the East End has paid off.

For that most of the credit is due to director James Hill, who has recreated the atmosphere of Edwardian London with uncanny success, so that not only does every Whitechapel scene look like the noisome slum it undoubtedly was, but also seems to smell of gin and cheap perfume.

Of gaiety too. Most of the doomed girls (particularly that super-trooper Barbara Windsor) go to their deaths with a flaunt of their hips and a laugh on their lips.

Garter-snappers, all of them.

John Neville plays the supercilious and self-confident Sherlock Holmes with just the right touch of hauteur. Donald Houston is his naive side-kick, Doctor Watson. . . . there are some fruity interventions from Robert Morley and Cecil Parker as a couple of pompous pillars of Government.

(*Evening News*, 4 November 1965, reviewed by Felix Barber):

Sherlock Holmes, whom John Neville provides with just the right profile, discards all the long-cherished theories.

After going into a brown study over his violin, and without troubling Watson for the hypodermic, he comes up with quite a different solution.

But a bit slow off the mark, you may think.

Donald and Derek Ford . . . show him as a bit laggardly, but then they want us to enjoy a full blood ration.

Holmes's disguise is so impenetrable that the audience spots him immediately, and so presumably does the Ripper.

One suspect is an East End doctor (very suspi-

cious, as he is played by an expensive star, Anthony Quayle).

No actor, I begin to think, will ever be the perfect Sherlock Holmes. Basil Rathbone was probably the best.

Mr. Neville looks right, and has the necessary strength, but the script denies him that touch of mystic authority and towering intellectualism which the character demands.

(*Times*, 4 November 1965): John Neville, the unidentified reviewer found, was

Not perhaps everyone's idea of Holmes, any more than Donald Houston is everyone's idea of Watson (surely the ideals were Basil Rathbone and Nigel Bruce?), but the casting will serve, especially in the present case where period feeling in the dialogue is almost non-existent and there is a decided tendency to caricature the whole thing and even, horror of horrors, play the great Holmes himself for laughs.

. . . the film is quite viewable. It finds some unhackneyed surprisingly genuine-looking London locations, and visually it is all very attractive. The supporting cast . . . is distinguished, and the only major complaint against it, once one adjusts to the convention in which it is made, is that Mr. James Hill's direction seems to rely more on freezing our blood intermittently with a series of Jack-the-Ripper murders given in gruesome detail than on keeping the narrative moving smoothly forward between whiles.

(*Daily Telegraph*, 5 November 1965, reviewed by Patrick Gibbs): Holmes in this film, according to the critic,

"is merely a caricature, for all the care and skill of John Neville's performance.

Obviously the authors have not been after pastiche but horror (as in horror-comic), in the style of Grand Guignol of Victorian melodrama.

Holmes receives through the post (one authentic touch, at least) a box of surgical instruments. . . . So starts the trail through a very dense maze with its centre a Whitechapel pub with Georgia Brown singing away as if this were "Stars and Garters."

Inquiries involve a number of engaging actors rather than satisfying characters. . . . Cecil Parker glimpsed momentarily as a bearded Prime Minister, presumably Salisbury; Barry Jones as a Duke of Shires who lives perversely in the Home Counties. . . . But all tend to sink in the thick plot, and of all Watson's exclamations it is his "incredible, my dear Holmes" which is most apt, though some will find a stronger adjective.

(*The Guardian*, 5 November 1965, reviewed by Richard Roud):

The best thing about *Study* is . . . its production values. A nice sense of period and sensitive art direction are the most distinguished elements of this story of the battle between Jack the Ripper and

Sherlock Holmes. Or rather, begging the billing's pardon, "the new Sherlock Holmes." Well, played by John Neville or not, I think I liked the old Sherlock Holmes better. With all the murders, all the stars and guest stars . . . the purest bit of pleasure comes from Georgia Brown, who knocks out "Ta-Ra-Ra-Boom-De-Ay" and "These Hard Times."

(*Financial Times*, 5 November 1965, reviewed by David Robinson):

. . . this is distinctly the least dignified and the most entertaining film so far directed by James Hill—a good deal more successful and satisfying on its own terms than his respectable pictures, such as *The Kitchen* and *The Dock Brief*.

Much of the film's success must be credited to its neat, light script by Donald and Derek Ford (for whom a period thriller seems an up-grading; the last film of theirs I recall was *The Yellow Teddy Bears*). They quite wittily send up the Holmes persona and the long-shot logic of his deductions; but at the same time are admirably conscientious in constructing the narrative and winding up the suspense of their preposterous story.

John Neville . . . has the right looks and presence. Of the rest of the impressive cast . . . Barbara Windsor and Kay Walsh as Whitechapel tarts are quite the most positively endearing.

(*Spectator*, 5 November 1965, reviewed by Isabel Quigley):

John Neville looks remarkably right for Sherlock Holmes; too handsome, perhaps, but that's allowable film-maker's license. In *Study* Holmes' (till now sacred) person is attached to a non-Holmesian nonsense of a story about Jack the Ripper . . . . A cross between James Bond and Professor Higgins (sexily cool in all the colourful provocation), with sword-stick, flowing cape, apparent powers of levitation, an asbestos body, and the faithful Watson, of course puffing along behind, he moves in on his man. An embarrassingly distinguished cast wastes its energies on nothing.

(*Daily Worker*, Britain, 6 November 1965, reviewed by Nina Hibbin):

The gruesome ripping up of bodies isn't exactly Holmes' cup of blood. But the two approaches to crime are entertainingly married in *Study* which is more in fun than in deadly earnest.

John Neville makes the best screen Sherlock to date—as stern, fastidious and elegant a gentleman as ever sported a deerstalker, with exactly the right blend of poker-faced spoofer for this sort of film. Donald Houston is an engaging, pompous, teddy-bear of a Watson, and the two go together like ham and eggs.

In the sleazy Whitechapel pub . . . the only ray of light comes from Georgia Brown, belting out Ta-Ra-Ra-Boom-De-Ay by the quart.

. . . dialogue is lively, amusing and genuinely earthy, but the story itself is weak. It leans too heavily on sleuthings down back alleys, knifing brawls and easily gained confessions.

. . . some dazzling deductions—but only in the background.

(*Sunday Telegraph*, 7 November 1965, reviewed by Robert Robinson):

. . . some remarkably good fake dialogue. "Though not in yourself luminous, Watson, you are an excellent conductor of light" advances the idiom splendidly, and the Holmesian syntax for instant deduction is caught to perfection.

. . . very little violence has been done to the myth. . . . There are more disembowelings than Moriarty could either provoke or approve, but the emphasis is still on the suspense or adventure of the thing . . . the atmospherics (a thought too rich in J. Arthur Rank oystermongers with that special clean dirt on their faces) are seldom merely theatrical, operating for the most part like a tide that helps the story along.

As for the magus himself, in the person of John Neville he is faintly camp, faintly Restoration, altogether too young (PH—though he was 40, 6 years older than Holmes would have been at the time of the story!). . . . Donald Houston is a serviceable Watson, but the hit of the picture is Mycroft . . . I knew that he had been Robert Morley from the beginning of time.

(*Sunday Times*, 7 November 1965, reviewed by Dilys Powell):

High jinks in an English pub on screen are apt to lower my spirits, and I felt distinctly the worse for the tararaboomdeay in the bar-room scene which opens *Study* . . . perhaps I was expecting too much . . . the writers, Donald and Derek Ford, have turned out some creditably Holmesian scenes. And the patter is there all right. . . . But the playing . . . isn't whole-hearted enough to make this Jack the Ripper story either chilling or hilarious. One or two happy moments, though; for instance the doctor's mate at the morgue fondling corpses's feet. Robert Morley as Mycroft supplies a welcome touch of absurdity, and as Watson Donald Houston, despatched by the great detective on the usual enigmatic mission, produces the proper mutton-headed bewilderment. The standard of appearance among busy Jack's street-walker victims is high.

(*Time*, 25 November 1965):

. . . stylish send-up of costume chillers as well of that silly ass with the deerstalker and the magnifying glass. . . . Hill hoses the screen with such a preposterous torrent of catchup that gross horror becomes Grand Guignol.

John Neville and Donald Houston play Holmes and Watson with a quaint and slightly stilted charm that defines them as exactly what they are: impressive pieces of Victorian bric-a-brac. Houston gustily presents the doctor as a tintype of the ruddy regimental; Neville drily displays the detective as a standard Victorian eccentric, an intellectual who beneath a mask of pedantry conceals a sad little secret: he is really just a middle-class boy who never quite made Eton and never quite got over it.

. . . dialogue . . . can be seen to issue from their lips on little cross-stitched samplers, which just sort of hang there on the screen and give off a faint scent of sachet.

(*Monthly Film Bulletin*, British Film Institute, December 1965):

The problem with Sherlock Holmes these days is what to do with all those absurd passages of high-speed deduction which end with the inevitable moo of admiration from Dr. Watson and the bland "Elementary, my dear Watson." James Hill and his script-writers have reverentially chosen to play it straight, with the result that *Study* marks time lamely in the intervals between its conventionally shock-cut murders, while John Neville and Donald Houston uncomfortably mouth their lines as if suspecting that nobody will listen. The plot is agreeably tangled, and there are two good marginal performances (Peter Carsten and Adrienne Corri): but the film's only real saving graces are Alex Vetchinsky's charmingly period sets . . . and the pleasantly muted colour.

(*Films in Review*, August–September 1966):

. . . well acted, directed and produced British programmer from a story of their own in which they combined the prowesses of Sherlock Holmes and Jack the Ripper. John Neville is a credible Holmes, and the direction of James Hill, the production design of Vetchinsky, and the costumes of Motley, lift this inexpensive black-&-whiter above the level of routine entertainment.

(*Daily News*, 3 November 1966, reviewed by Kathleen Carroll):

". . . snappy, handsomely mounted production . . . with John Neville a crisp, shockproof Holmes and Donald Houston a worshipful Watson."

(*New York Times*, 3 November 1966, reviewed by A.H. Welles):

". . . The entire cast, director and writers, play their roles well enough to make wholesale slaughter a pleasant diversion."

(*Monster Mania*, April 1967):

Neville fits into the proceedings perfectly. And he can rattle off the most convoluted, stilted Holmesian dialogue with the best of them.

Neville is a bit too slight of build and stature to project with any effectiveness the dynamic side of Sherlock Holmes' personality.

Watson, too, has had life breathed anew into his stuffy, rotund figure. Donald Houston . . . adds yet another aspect to Watson's character—a shy continental charm. Not as bumbling and moronic as Nigel Bruce . . . not as "straight" and cultured as Andre Morell—Mr. Houston strikes a perfect medium . . . he has spiced the role with a blushing bashfulness. He and Mr. Neville blend perfectly in the . . . screen chemistry which worked so well for the Rathbone/Bruce team . . . *and not so well for Peter Cushing and Andre Morell*.

When not wrestling with the rhetoric given to him . . . Mr. Morley uses his bushy eyebrows and portly frame to the hilt.

Sir Arthur Conan Doyle's son Adrian not only had a hand in the script of this venture, but also contributed to its financing as trustee of his father's estate; in partnership with the American Henry E. Lester he had originally planned not only to film more combinations of Holmes-and-horror, but also to base a television series called *The Sir Arthur Conan Doyle Theatre* on his father's works and film versions of the elder Conan Doyle's *The White Company* (one of the books featuring Sir Nigel, from whom Doyle and Lester took the name of their film company) and his Brigadier Gerard stories—only the latter was made. Lester had represented him on Cushing's *Hound*.

Adrian Conan Doyle paid a visit to the set of *Fog* (as it was then known) after shooting began on 10 June 1963. He approved very strongly of Donald Houston's interpretation of Dr. Watson: "So completely, utterly right for the part," said Doyle, taking a step back from the burly actor to take in his overall appearance more fully. "At last Dr. Watson will appear as a character in his own right. I've always until now thought that the poor chap has been rather badly done by."

Houston agreed fully about the usually unsympathetic treatment that Watson was usually given by those who played him:

Sherlock Holmes's genius would dwarf any normal intelligence, but that's no reason for imagining that Watson should always be treated as a bumbling, doddering idiot; while he couldn't match Holmes's brilliance he was certainly no fool. Conan Doyle presented him as a man who already had a number of considerable achievements to his name before he even met Holmes: this conflicts with the picture of the man as an idiot, as he has often been portrayed before. After all, these two men shared a flat as well as their working lives. How could Holmes have born it if he had been living in close proximity with an idiot?

The above comments of Conan Doyle and Houston serve to point up how mistaken the many critics were who insisted that the film was tongue-in-cheek. Neville and Houston indeed played their parts with humor, but far from mocking Holmes and Watson, they were playing them as men of wit. The sense of aloof superiority displayed by Neville is that of Holmes towards the other characters and not of Neville toward Holmes; and Houston plays Watson as a warmly human character whose foibles spring from his very three-dimensional existence.

Like *The Sign of Four*, this story contains characters who are to some extent patterned after the real-life Douglas family (the Marquis of Queensbury and his son Lord Alfred), and this resemblance is pointed up by the presence in the cast of three of the actors who played the leads in the two film versions of the Wilde-Douglas trials five years previously: Neville, Morley, and Fraser.

Another touch of very sound Holmesiana comes when Holmes manages to disarm a thug who is several times his own size, merely with a flick of the wrist—surely he is practicing the Oriental art of "Baritsu," known only in the Doyle stories!

Coproducer Henry Lester, however, would have preferred to see other affinities in the Sherlockian prowess. "Everything James Bond knows he has learned from Sherlock Holmes," the American stated in a publicity release—though one would hardly think that it was quite *everything*, unless Holmes was up to rather more mischief than is reliably recorded.

A nameless Compton P. R. man underlined this notion by writing: "No longer is Holmes the old fuddy-duddy which the public tended to classify him as in the past, he's now way-out and with-it"—one can only hope that the perpetrator of that has seen the error of his ways.

Several years after playing the Sage of Baker Street, John Neville appeared on the British TV series, *The Rivals of Sherlock Holmes*, in the role of the immortal neo-Holmesian detective, Dr. John Thorndyke, who was distinguished by exactly the same sort of supercilious manner and scientific method as his better-known colleague. Though in a subsequent episode of the series he was replaced in the part by Barrie Ingham (with stage-Watson Peter Sallis as Thorndyke's right-hand man Dr. Jervis), Neville went on to re-create his interpretation of Holmes himself for the Broadway stage in 1975, when he stepped into John Wood's inverness in the Royal Shakespeare Company's revival of the Gillette play.

John Neville was born in 1925, and graduated from the Royal Academy of Dramatic Arts in London. As leading man for the Old Vic, he alternated the roles of Othello and Iago with Richard Burton, and played in that theater's cycle of nearly all of Shakespeare's plays. In a Vic tour of the United States, Neville played Hamlet, Richard II, and Romeo, returning to New York more recently to star in an abortive musical version of Nabokov's *Lolita*.

Some of his other London appearances were in *School for Scandal* (like Saintsbury, Rathbone, Cushing, and Wilmer), *Lady from the Sea, Irma La Douce, Once More With Feeling*, and the original production of *Alfie*, in which he created the title role. At the Chichester Festival, Neville played in *The Threepenny Opera* and *The Doctor's Dilemma;* then in the midsixties, he had a very successful spell as the director of the Nottingham

Playhouse. For the last few years Neville has been resident in Canada, where he is currently Artistic Director of the Edmonton Citadel Theatre.

His film career so far has not been extensive, although in addition to his well-received Holmes in *Study* he was also praised in 1963's *Unearthly Stranger*, one critic commenting that it was mainly his performance in that little-known thriller which made it at all memorable. With his *Study in Terror* co-star, Morley, he made the aforementioned *Oscar Wilde*, as "Bosie" Douglas and Wilde, respectively. Neville's role was taken by John Fraser in the rival Peter Finch version, which also featured Ian Fleming. The Mad Douglases of the Wilde case also partly inspired both *Study in Terror* and Doyle's original *Sign of Four*, by the way.

Neville's other pictures include *Billy Budd*, '62; Hitchcock's *Topaz*, '69; and *Waterloo*, '70 (with radio-Holmes *and* Moriarty Orson Welles). On television, apart from *The Rivals of Sherlock Holmes*, Neville is undoubtedly best remembered for his performances as the Duke of Marlborough on the *First Churchills* series. In 1965, he received the O.B.E. from the Queen for his services to the theater.

The remark of one critic that as Holmes he "mouthed his lines as if suspecting that nobody will listen" seems far from the mark when written of an actor who is as voice-conscious as Gielgud (himself a radio-Holmes); and other critics passed the equally baffling judgments that he did not have the right profile; was too young, too small; and played the part tongue-in-cheek. Even the verdict that he is "recognizable" as the disguised Holmes is unfair, since it should be mentioned that his Cockney-characterization at that point is one of the best cameos in a film that is full of outstanding ones.

The real "sin" of the film was undoubtedly that it fell just betwixt and between two dissimilar genres, and pleased neither the Holmes purists nor the horror fans. The individual achievements of Neville, and especially Houston, seem hard to fault.

Donald Houston followed the tradition of Andre Morell and, as we have seen, played Watson as an intelligent man capable of assessing evidence on his own—not in the Holmes class; but then who is? Houston also managed, however, to lose very little of the character-comedy touches brought to the role so memorably by Hubert Willis and Nigel Bruce. In addition, Houston is far less strident than were Reginald Owen or Colin Blakely, making him surely a far less nerve-wracking roommate, and perhaps the most fully rounded Watson so far on the screen.

Donald Houston was born in 1924 in Tonypandy, Wales. He shared Dr. Watson's Scots connections, however, for Houston's father was a native of Dundee who had come to Wales to play professional football for Swansea Town, where he met and married Donald's mother. It was *her* mother who brought the boy up, however, for the younger woman died when her son was only six. Houston's grandmother was known for miles around the Rhondda Valley as "Mrs. Jones the Milk," and encouraged the boy to become a football player like his father.

"But soon after I was fourteen my whole world changed," remembered Houston. "I had never been inside a theatre—yet suddenly had the urge to act." So he abruptly abandoned his sporting dreams, and eventually in '40 went to join the Pilgrim Players in Fowey, Cornwall. The Pilgrim Players asked him to lose his accent as quickly as he could, though "like all Welshmen, I was tremendously proud of it. The Pilgrim Players were not impressed."

Houston travelled all over the country with this troupe, appearing in such locales as church halls and air-raid shelters; and following this initial stint of two years he joined an Oxford Repertory group in '43 for a few months before he went into the R.A.F. in December.

Initially trained as a rear gunner and radio operator, in '44 he was found to be among those redundant crews that (lacking a skilled trade—acting didn't count, apparently) were offered a choice between going into the Army or the mines. Houston chose the latter and became a "Bevin boy," as they were called in honor of the Parliamentarian.

After the war he rejoined the Oxford Company, and made his London bow in '47 with *The Master Builder*. In 1948, Donald Houston became famous "overnight" as a beefcake star in *The Blue Lagoon*, although it was not until some years later that he broke this mold and gained the great respect as a serious craftsman, which he still holds. He found it very hard to live down the tag of "one-time miner." "I wanted so hard to be taken seriously," he said. "I was desperately anxious to be regarded as a worthwhile actor."

It was his performance in the original stage version of Dylan Thomas' play *Under Milk Wood* (written for the radio and since filmed) that Houston finally achieved real critical recognition. As the Narrator, with a total of 178 separate speeches in two and one-quarter hours, he was the hit of the Edinburgh Festival in '56 and in London; and although the New York critics were not overfond of the play itself, they too acknowledged the brilliance of Houston in it. He thought at first that he would never memorize the part, but "suddenly the magic rhythm of Thomas' prose took control," he said. "The words flowed on then."

As a result of this success, he received many lucrative offers but chose instead to join the Old Vic in 1960, which paid no extravagant salary but offered him the chance to extend his artistic powers in such plays as *As You Like It, The Double Dealer, St. Joan, Henry V* (in which Houston was directed by John Neville), and *What Every Woman Knows*.

In addition, Houston has appeared in over sixty television programs and about the same number of films. He has recently costarred in a comedy series with Sheila Hancock on the former medium, and appeared

(like his fellow-Watson H. Marion Crawford) on the *Danger Man* show (*Secret Agent* in the United States).

His film career actually began as long ago as 1941, and some of his other pictures are *A Girl Must Live* (his debut); *A Run For Your Money*, '49; *Dance Hall*, '50; *My Death is a Mockery* and *Crown Hollow*, '52; *The Red Beret, Small Town Story, The Large Rope*, and *Point of No Return*, '53; *Doctor in the House, The Devil's Pass*, and *The Happiness of Three Women*, '54; *The Flaw* and *Double Cross*, '55; *Find the Lady*, '56; *Yangtse Incident, The Surgeon's Knife*, and *Every Valley*, '57; *A Question of Adultery, The Man Upstairs, Danger Within*, and *Room at The Top* (one of his favorite parts), '58; *Jessy*, '59; *The Mark*, '61; *Twice Round the Daffodils, The Prince and the Pauper, Maniac* (for Hammer, a very un-Watsonish role), and *The Longest Day*, '62; *Doctor in Distress* and *Carry on Jack*, '63; *Carry on Sailor*, '64; *The Viking Queen*, '66; and *Don't You Cry*, '70.

Married to actress Brenda Hogan, whom he met in repertory, Houston has a grown daughter, Sian, and maintains a flat in London and a seventeenth-century house in Kent. Houston had long had the idea of playing Watson to Neville's Holmes, and their off-screen friendship and professional association greatly enhanced the believability of the on-screen fondness for each other of the Baker Street Duo—a quality that has sometimes been missed by screen Watsons and Holmeses who have become too preoccupied with Holmes' rudeness to his humble associate.

Robert Morley, who made such a perfect screen Mycroft, even if he did not perhaps succeed in suggesting the character's slovenly and lazy qualities, was an Old Bensonian-like Eille Norwood and Basil Rathbone. Perhaps the only actor who could have been better cast as Sherlock's brother would have been the late Francis L. Sullivan, who did indeed appear in the Wontner series in another part.

Study's director James Hill was to achieve great success the following year with his screen version of *Born Free*, the popularity of which in the United States seems to have prompted a belated release of the Holmes film there at last. Hill, born in 1919, had previously made such films as *The Stolen Plans*, '52; *The Clue of the Missing Ape*, '53; and the screen version of Arnold Wesker's *The Kitchen*, '61—and this range from thriller to social-consciousness served him in good stead with *Study in Terror*, in which the presence of both elements serves both to enhance the grimy period-flavor and make the horror more believable.

Screenwriters Donald and Derek Ford scripted *The Black Torment*, '64, and four years later wrote and coproduced *Corruption*, a very interesting attempt at true Grand Guignol, which furnished Peter Cushing with one of his few truly monstrous roles.

John Scott, the film's composer, was very highly praised for his subsequent score for the '72 *Antony and Cleopatra*, which featured Douglas Wilmer, another film that has been unjustly neglected.

With the presence in the cast of Kay Walsh, we see

yet another example of the conjunction of the worlds of Dickens and Sherlock Holmes; for the aging tart played by Miss Walsh in *Study* seems very much like the woman her Nancy in *Oliver Twist*, '48 (with Fred Lloyd), might have become had she not been murdered by Bill Sykes.

Frank Finlay, Inspector Lestrade in this one, had a pseudo-Holmesian role in *The Deadly Bees* that following year, but although Holmes appears in *A Taste for Honey*, the novel by H. F. Heard on which that film was based, he is for some reason absent in the movie itself!

This phenomenon of a Holmes film without Holmes is not, however, unique, for Vitagraph's 1907 *Caught* was a version of *The Red-Headed League*, which substituted the police force for Holmes; and in *The Hypnotic Detective* of 1912, we find a very faithful version of *The Norwood Builder*, wherein Holmes is replaced by a moustached and monocled gentleman named Professor Locksley! This sort of thing is all the more surprising when we consider how often the films in which Holmes *does* appear bear considerably less resemblance to Doyle's stories!

24

Robert Stephens

THE PRIVATE LIFE OF SHERLOCK HOLMES
(British-United States)

Date of Release: United States: 28 October 1970; Great Britain: 3 December 1970.
Running Time: 125 minutes
Production Company: Mirisch Prod. Co./United Artists
Producer and Director: Billy Wilder
Screenplay: Billy Wilder and I.A.L. Diamond
Set Design: Alexander Trauner
Color: De Luxe/Panavision
Filmed in: Pinewood Studios
Locations: Inverness, Scotland; Malta

CAST

Sherlock Holmes	Robert Stephens
Dr. Watson	Colin Blakely
Mrs. Hudson	Irene Handl
First Gravedigger	Stanley Holloway
Mycroft Holmes	Christopher Lee
Gabrielle Valladon (Delvaux)	Genevieve Page
Rogozhin	Clive Revill
Mme. Petrova	Tamara Toumanova
Bird Woman	Catherine Lacey
Queen Victoria	Mollie Maureen
Von Tirpitz	Peter Madden
?	Robert Cawdon
?	Michael Balfour
Inspector Lestrade	George Benson

SYNOPSIS: The film was originally intended to be much longer than the version eventually released, with four stories honed down to three and finally only two, and all of the episode about the room where everything was upside-down, together with the Malta and Lestrade material completely removed; a prologue showing a modern Watsonian grandson opening the famous battered tin dispatch-box of "stories for which the world is not yet prepared" was also drastically curtailed.

As it stands, the film begins with a spurious Bernard Shaw anecdote transferred to Holmes: A Russian

The very tempting Genevieve Page puts the Misogynist of Baker Street to a severe test. (Courtesy National Film Archives of the British Film Institute)

ballerina suggests that she and Holmes have a child together, so that the infant will inherit her looks and his brain. Holmes attempts to squirm out of the proposition by suggesting that their offspring may have the opposite set of attributes, but since this fails to extricate him he is forced to decline on the grounds that he is too emotionally attached to—Dr. Watson!

This notion caused much grief to devout Holmesians, but in fact it is quite clear in the context of the scene that Holmes is not at all serious about the suggestion. The story, however, in the film, reaches the ear of the Diaghlev-like ballet impressario Rogozhin, who helpfully tries to fix up poor Watson with some of the male members of the Corps de Ballet. When the good doctor learns of the falsehood Holmes has coined, he becomes totally distraught, and asks the detective if it would be impertinent to ask if the allegation was founded on fact.

"Yes," says Holmes, "—it would be impertinent." This ambiguous answer is not resolved until later in the film when Holmes recounts his famous Conanical speech about the most charming woman he had ever known having poisoned people for their insurance money, and indeed most of his circle of feminine acquaintances being criminals. His naturally ensuing

The Private Life of Sherlock Holmes was private indeed. The sleuth (Robert Stephens) looks very much like the cocaine and morphine user Doyle described prior to Holmes' visit to Tibet. (Courtesy National Film Archives of the British Film Institute)

Irene Handl was an ill-tempered Mrs. Hudson in *Private Life*. One wonders if she will welcome the assistance of Holmes (Stephens) in her game of solitaire. (Courtesy National Film Archives of the British Film Institute)

misogyny is overcome in this film by a romance with the beautiful Belgian Gabrielle Valladon, and the film succeeds extremely well as an old-fashioned love story, which is told with such restraint that there is hardly a kiss—a state of things that so surprised Billy Wilder's usual audience that it no doubt accounts in large part for the film's financial failure.

Besides his mistrust of women, Holmes' drug addiction is also emphasized in this film, although not in any "sensational" manner. Rather, Holmes' addiction deeply influences Stephens' whole interpretation of the character, just as some critics felt it did Cushing's, but in an entirely different direction. For, while Cushing emphasized Holmes in his hyperactive phase, Stephens presents him when the pendulum has swung to the other extreme and Holmes is lethargic and depressed. This Holmes is a study in the almost-failed genius; of the stripe of Coleridge or DeQuincey—a man of great natural powers that have been reduced to the point where they cannot function unless they are stimulated by the very drugs that have atrophied them in the first place. Stephens, consequently, gives us a very melancholy Holmes, more melancholy even than Norwood or the Rathbone of the last few films. In this film, when Sherlock behaves in his classically rude and peevish manner, we are given a bit more motivation behind his actions to help explain why. Some purists have complained that this naturalistic approach goes to make Holmes a lesser character, but it also makes him a more human one, which can only be a gain.

Irene Handl's Mrs. Hudson gives vent to the passions that must have been pent up within screen Mrs. Hudsons for the past half-century, and soundly harangues the great sleuth for his untidy and bohemian mistreatment of her premises.

The final blow for the poor landlady occurs when a Belgian lady named Gabrielle Valladon arrives in a state of dishevelled confusion at the door to ask the detective's help in finding her missing husband. Gabrielle is put up for the night, and even wanders naked into Holmes' room in what appears to be a fit of somnambulism, seeming to mistake him for her husband. Holmes, of course, does not take advantage

Robert Stephens does not look overgrateful to this helpful crew member in *Private Life of Sherlock Holmes*. (Courtesy National Film Archives of the British Film Institute)

of the distraught girl, despite the low suspicions of Dr. Watson and Mrs. Hudson the following morning.

Holmes decides to masquerade as Madame Valladon's husband, and their search involves them with a number of curious incidents: dead canaries mysteriously keep cropping up in odd places; the Loch Ness Monster is sighted by the trio (for Watson has, of course, accompanied the "honeymooners"); and Holmes' brother Mycroft appears to take an interest in the case on behalf of the British government.

It eventually develops that Gabrielle is in fact working as a spy for the Germans, as was her dead husband, trying to get information on the "Monster"—which turns out to be a charmingly Jules Vernesque submarine the government is testing as an experimental secret weapon. The poor canaries, tended so lovingly by Catherine Lacey's eccentric "Moms" in an empty storefront, are used in the experiment to detect gas in much the same way as they are in mines.

As she is being wheeled away in a carriage to her eventual execution, Gabrielle flashes a message to the watching Holmes via her "parasol-code" (opening and closing it à la Morse), and we see that, although she is yet another of the "dishonest" types who have come the sleuth's way, Gabrielle has reciprocated his unspoken love.

A very touching final scene shows us Dr. Watson sitting down unhappily to pen the adventure, while Holmes drifts off into a drug-induced euphoria. Even though Gabrielle is not Irene Adler, the purist can hardly complain, for she is quite as clever as *The Woman*, and equally successful in bamboozling Holmes.

Tribute must be paid, too, to Stephens and Genevieve Page (who appeared in *El Cid* with Wilmer) for making us believe this highly stylized and quintessentially "old-fashioned" romance—perhaps the only such on the screen for many, many years.

REVIEWS (*Sherlock Holmes Journal,* winter 1970, reviewed by Anthony Howlett):

> . . . extravagantly mounted, glossy, beautifully photographed, expertly directed, amusing and preposterous . . . dialogue is essentially modern in tone. . . . The vulgar feud between Holmes and Mrs. Hudson, albeit an affectionate one, would . . . have been alien to both their natures . . . never would Holmes have shouted at her . . . ["The landlady stood in deepest awe of him, and never dared to interfere. . . . She was fond of him, too, for he had a remarkable gentleness and courtesy in his dealings with women."—*The Dying Detective*] . . . a gentle, even melancholy charm pervades . . . the film.
>
> Robert Stephens's appearance is tolerably acceptable, but he affects a namby-pamby petulance of voice and manner that is wholly and irritatingly wrong.
>
> Colin Blakely's hysterical and somewhat vulgar Dr. Watson is amusing in a childishly obvious sort of way, but, in view of the good portrayals over the last

11 years . . . I had hoped it would be realised that we have grown out of the Boobus Britannicus image.

. . . beautifully suave portrait of Mycroft Holmes by Christopher Lee . . . although it is disconcerting to find the corpulent and untidy Mycroft transformed into such a lithe and elegant figure. . . . Genevieve Page . . . is enchanting.

(*The Times*, 4 December 1970, reviewed by John Russell Taylor): "*The Wilder Shores Of Love.* . . . If Wilder came to scoff at Sherlock Holmes, he remains to pray at the shrine."

A few echoes of the longer version of the film survived after its release, for George Benson was listed in the role of Lestrade in the Radio City Music Hall souvenir-program during the film's American premiere, and the same program also contained a photograph of Stephens as Holmes in which he is depicted in sideburns, whereas he lacks them throughout the film as it now stands. Likewise, on the film's London bow there were photographs outside the theater that depicted the Malta sequence.

The film itself made a few errors in dating, but such slips as these are, of course, quite in the Watsonian tradition: the date of the first publication of the *Strand Magazine* and of the first London performance of *Swan Lake* were both given incorrectly, and that of the original appearance of *The Hound of the Baskervilles* was pushed back a total of seventeen years.

The original version of the film gave larger parts both to Watson's grandson, who retrieved the manuscript which recounts the tales from the bank vault where it has lain forgotten, and also to Petrova and Rogozhin—the latter evidently having been troubled with some sort of peculiarly delicate personal problem of his own.

Robert Stephens went on to replace John Neville in the Broadway revival of Gillette's Holmes play in 1975, and also played Max Carrados, yet another of the *Rivals of Sherlock Holmes* in the British television series of that name.

For his Holmes film, Stephens had to learn to row stroke for a team of eight—the sequence was yet another of those fated never to actually appear in the film.

Born in Bristol, England in 1931, Stephens was originally associated on the stage with the "Angry Young Man" school of drama, which flourished at the Royal Court Theatre. Eventually, however, Stephens came to be known as a classical actor, and when he created the part of the Emperor Atahualpa in *Royal Hunt of the Sun* at the Old Vic, it was said of him that he was "an actor who could play a god." He played many other leading roles at the Vic where he was also associate director in such plays as *Trelawny of the "Wells"* and *Private Lives*.

On TV, Stephens made an exciting Marc Antony in Shakespeare's *Julius Caesar*, playing the famous orator as a rabble-rousing politician with an evangelical style. Former-Lestrade Frank Finlay was Brutus. More

recently, Stephens was in the multipart American TV-movie *QB VII*.

Stephens' first film was 1960's *Circle of Deception*, and since then he has appeared on the screen in *A Taste of Honey, The Queen's Guards*, and *Pirates of Tortuga* (as the notorious real-life buccaneer Sir Henry Morgan), '61; *Cleopatra* (with Douglas Wilmer), *The Inspector* (*Lisa* in the United States; with radio-Watson Finlay Currie), and *Lunch Hour*, '62; *The Small World of Sammy Lee*, '63; *Morgan a Suitable Case For Treatment*, '66; and *Romeo and Juliet* (as the Prince, rather than one of the roles played by Barrymore or Rathbone in the '36 version), and *The Prime of Miss Jean Brodie* (with his wife Maggie Smith), '68.

Robert Stephens' interpretation of Sherlock Holmes was radically different from that of virtually all his predecessors; but, although the Holmesian purists objected vigorously, it seems to us that the character of the Great Detective is large enough in scope to permit many different (but equally valid) readings. The gushing romantic Sherlock of Barrymore and the petulant and grumpy one of Brook may both have overstepped the bounds of poetic license; but as for Wontner's kindly gentleman, Rathbone's rapier-sharp adventurer in the early episodes and his brooding Holmes of the latter ones, which echoed Eille Norwood, Cushing's drug-sodden white-hot enthusiast and Stephens' near-ruined prodigy—all of them are plausible faces of Conan Doyle's great creation.

The really odd thing is that none of these splendid Holmeses of the screen has looked like Doyle's *physical* description of his character anymore than Sidney Paget's *Strand* illustrations did. For the original scarecrow of Baker Street, we must go back as far as 1914 and gaze on the homely but striking features of James Bragington in the first *Study in Scarlet*.

Colin Blakely played Watson with much the same sort of aggravating vigor that characterized the performance of Reginald Owen in the role. (Surely Holmes would have thrown them both out into the street after the first few days of trying to share digs with them and think at the same time!) It is very surprising to find that an actor of Blakely's genius and subtlety has given such a cheap and obvious slant to a part that is capable of much more (as Morell and Houston have both shown).

Even when played for comedy, as he was by Willis and Bruce, Watson still contains great reserves of humanity, but (at least in the much-cut version we now have) Blakely manages few touches of sincere feeling until the final sequence. We can only suppose that director Wilder is to blame for this narrowness in the conception of Watson, for we know too well of how much better Blakely is capable.

Born in Northern Ireland in 1930, Colin Blakely was, like Stephens, for some years a leading man with the National Theatre at the Old Vic. That company's director, Laurence, Lord Olivier, has compared Blakely's physical stage movement to that of "a young lion." On TV, Colin played Frank Finlay's stage role of Christ in the play *Son of Man,* and his film performances include the classic Smokey Pickles in *Charlie Bubbles,* '67, which is particularly memorable for the scene in which Blakely and Albert Finney playfully dump their lunch platters on one another's heads.

He is also notable in *This Sporting Life,* '62; *The Informers,* '63; *The Long Ships,* '64; *The Spy With a Cold Nose* and *The Day The Fish Came Out,* '67; *The Vengeance of She* (a sequel to the film whose numerous versions have starred Blackwell, Bruce, Cushing, Lee, and Morell), '68; *Decline and Fall (Decline and Fall of a Birdwatcher,* in the United States; with *Private Life of Sherlock Holmes* costar Genevieve Page), '68; and *Alfred The Great,* '69. With his costar in this last film, Vivien Merchant, Blakely recently had a great stage success in her husband Harold Pinter's play *Old Times.*

Billy Wilder does not, of course, immediately strike out as the obvious director for either a Holmes story or an old-fashioned romance, but with the exception of Watson, who gets the sort of farcical treatment one might have feared, the film succeeds stunningly well indeed on both levels.

Private Life was first announced for production in May 1963, and was at that time expected to star Peter O'Toole as the Great Man and, possibly, Peter Sellers in the role of Watson—later still Ringo Starr, of all people, was apparently considered for the Good Doctor. In an announcement of July '64, O'Toole and Sellers seemed to be firmly cast, and filming was slated to begin in the summer of '65 in Hollywood and Europe. It was not, however, until May '69 that the cameras finally began to turn on the subject, and most of the nineteen-week shooting schedule was spent at Pinewood Studios in Britain, with the exception of the Scottish and Maltese locations.

As he began shooting, Wilder commented: "The last thing I want to do is to guy the stories in any way. We hope to treat Holmes and Watson with respect but not with reverence, and to reveal a certain amount of the natural humor."

He underlined this ambivalent attitude to his subject in another interview, when he said that the film was "not a comedy and it's not serious! . . . You know the oil is there, if only you can tap it. On the other hand, if you're not sure there's any oil there in the first place, you may only strike piss. But it's like the thing we have in the picture about 'with your brains and my body we must make a beautiful baby.' It could turn out wrong."

Fundamentally, though, Wilder's feelings towards Holmes were very affectionate: "To me he is wildly romantic—elegant, all that Baker Street setting, great sharpness, precision, and imagination. One of the great minds of the twentieth century. This film isn't camp. It's a valentine to Sherlock."

His "screenplay" seems to have been largely in his head, for neither Stephens nor Blakely had any idea how the film would end until near the end of shooting. Wilder personally searched out many of the little objects that were used to decorate the shelves of 221B,

and he was highly delighted with the extremely detailed and lived-in-looking set, according to Genevieve Page, who called him "the best director any of us has ever worked with." Miss Page was especially struck by his kindness: "We lost our Loch Ness Monster, but he didn't seem to worry too much. . . . He was more concerned to go over and comfort the man who had made it who was upset about it disappearing."

The late Adrian Conan Doyle, who had figured so prominently in the making of our last film, also had a hand in this one, in his capacity of trustee of the Conan Doyle literary estate. The younger Doyle stipulated very firmly in his contract that Wilder's script could in no way "Parody or disfigure my father's original portrayal of Sherlock Holmes. I am very sure that I shall receive the moral support of those countless friends of Sherlock Holmes in my determination that the original conception shall be respected," wrote Doyle from his Swiss Chateau in February '69 to a British newspaper.

Some may suspect that Wilder honored his end of the agreement more in the breach than the observance—but in many respects he has done Holmes more good on the screen by his freshly seen interpretation than any number of films might have done that only repeated the same old formulas, tried and true though they are.

For we must bear in mind that there was a time when the views of Holmes displayed by such as William Gillette and Basil Rathbone were considered to be too radical departures from the Doyle original, and yet the image of Holmes that most people hold today derives almost as much from these two actors as it does even from the great author himself.

Clive Revill, whose part of Rogozhin was much curtailed in the final print, was later to replace Philip Locke in the role of Professor Moriarty after the above-mentioned Royal Shakespeare revival of Gillette's *Sherlock Holmes* had transferred to Broadway. Revill remained in the cast when its original star, John Wood, left, and consequently played opposite the new Holmses of Patrick Horgan (who filled in briefly, and had been in the Holmes musical *Baker Street* previously as well as recording some Sherlockian tales for the blind), John Neville, and Robert Stephens!

Revill's Moriarty was perhaps a shade reminiscent at times of his Fagin in *Oliver,* and he rather overdid the melodrama, whereas Locke never edged over into burlesque no matter how much of the "old" he gave the part. All in all, though, even with the enormous pompadour he was given to raise his forehead to Moriartian heights, Revill made a magnificent Napoleon of Crime, and we can only hope that his serpentine interpretation will eventually find its well-deserved way to the screen.

Although those distinguished and prolific Holmesians Michael and Mollie Hardwicke do not seem to have worked directly on *Private Life*'s screenplay, they did turn the script into a novel of the same title, which

223

many of the True Believers found to be more acceptable than Wilder's unbleached heresies. The Hardwickes have, of course, written on Holmes and Doyle in books and adapted the adventures of both detectives into virtually all the media—stage, radio, TV, and even phonograph records (they also directed these last ventures, which featured Robert Hardy as Sherlock, and Nigel Stock, from the Cushing and Wilmer TV shows, as Watson).

25
Douglas Wilmer

THE ADVENTURE OF SHERLOCK HOLMES' SMARTER BROTHER

Production Company: Twentieth-Century Fox
Director: Gene Wilder
Director of Photography: Gerry Fischer, BSC
Production Designer: Terence Marsh
Filmed at Shepperton Studios, England
Released: December 1975

CAST

Sigerson ("Sigi") Holmes	Gene Wilder
Bessie Bellwood	
(Music Hall Singer)	Madeline Kahn
Sgt. Orville Stanley Sacker	Marty Feldman
Professor Moriarty	Leo McKern
Sherlock Holmes	Douglas Wilmer
Doctor Watson	Thorley Walters
(Opera Singer)	Dom De Luise

This picture, obviously a comedy, represents the directorial debut of Gene Wilder, who has been so delightfully involved with zany Mel Brooks for so long (*The Producers, Blazing Saddles, Young Frankenstein*). With him are Kahn and Feldman, veterans of *Young Frankenstein* (Kahn was also in *Blazing Saddles*); Dom De Luise, well-known American comic and star of William Gillette's play *Too Much Johnson* on the stage; Douglas Wilmer and Thorley Walters, certainly no strangers to the roles of Holmes and Watson; and Leo McKern, Australian stage actor, whose occasional film roles are memorable, to say the least.

The film is full of marvelous sight gags and slapstick,

with a sprinkling of double-entendre and off-color puns. The storyline is vague and implausible, but it serves its function—to thread together the beads of Wilder's vaudevillelike vignettes of hilarity, such as a duel between Wilder and a mechanical fencing machine powered by Feldman's bicycling, and a coach-roof battle between Wilder and the bad guys, using giant boots and gloves as weapons, and an attempt on the lives of Wilder and Feldman that leaves their posteriors unclothed without their realizing it.

Leo McKern's Moriarty was the high point in the film, as Wilmer and Walters have only miniscule on-camera appearances. Marty Feldman serves as a surrogate Watson for Wilder; "Orville Sacker," Feldman's screen name, is very close to "Ormond Sacker," Conan Doyle's original choice for the name of Sherlock's sidekick, before he settled on "Watson."

Douglas Wilmer is no novice in Baker Street, for he first donned the deerstalker back on 18 May 1964, when the British television series *Detective* presented a one-hour adaptation of *The Speckled Band*, which featured Wilmer as Holmes and Nigel Stock as Dr. Watson.

Detective, as it happened, was hosted by Rupert Davies in the role of Inspector Maigret—a role that has also been played by Heinz Rhumann, who played Watson in the German film *Der Mann, Der Sherlock Holmes War*, which we will deal with in our next chapter.

This adaptation of *Speckled Band* was by the late playwright Giles Cooper, on one of whose plays Edward Albee based his *Everything in the Garden*, and whose TV play *Unman, Wittering and Zigo* was filmed in

Sherlock Holmes (Douglas Wilmer) is forced to take a back seat to his brother Sigerson in *The Adventure of Sherlock Holmes' Smarter Brother*, recently filmed in England. The existence of Sigerson Holmes was postulated in scholarly fashion by the late William S. Baring-Gould, but surely he could not have imagined Gene Wilder in the role. (Courtesy BBC Television)

1970 with Douglas Wilmer. The *Sherlock Holmes Journal* noted of *Speckled Band*:

> ... the details of Holmesiana were splendidly correct—no nonsense with curly pipes and "Elementary my dear Watson" ... in Douglas Wilmer we had a fine Holmes. In appearance reminiscent of the younger Basil Rathbone, he gave an original and very acceptable interpretation. With a bit more "bite" and authority in his portrayal, he could perhaps become *the* screen Holmes of today.

Produced by David Goddard and directed by Robin Midgley, the production was so successful with the general public that it was repeated in September and a series was announced, making its bow on 20 February 1965 with the same actors and producer. Its twelve episodes ran until May, and then a season of repeats lasted into November of the following year. The series

was credited with a steady average of ten to eleven million viewers, no mean feat for Britain.

Beverly Nichols interviewed Wilmer for *Woman's Own* the latter year under the title *I Meet the Living Spirit of Sherlock Holmes*, but in the *Sherlock Holmes Journal* opinion was a bit more divided this time out: when the series was revived in September '68, Percy Metcalfe wrote that "Douglas Wilmer, to my mind, gave a far more realistic Sherlockian representation than does Peter Cushing"; but Michael Hardwicke found Cushing's "performances ... greatly to be preferred to those of his predecessor." The Holmes Society's Michael Pointer in his book *The Public Life of Sherlock Holmes* records the opinion that Wilmer was not "sufficiently sympathetic" as the Great Detective.

Despite these varying verdicts, however, Wilmer is so utterly perfect for the part in physical appearance and such a fine acting craftsman that it was inevitable he would continue to be associated with Holmes. Before this present Holmes film, Douglas Wilmer took his turn on *The Rivals of Sherlock Holmes* television series, as had Neville, Stephens, and stage-Watson Peter Sallis. Cast as S.F.X. Van Dusen, *The Thinking Machine*, Wilmer delivered a flawlessly Sherlockian interpretation—much aided by the fact that the story, *Problem of Cell 13*, was transposed from an American setting to a British one.

Wilmer's TV-Watson Nigel Stock was highly praised as a Conanical doctor in the vein of Morell and Houston, and proved his durability by not only remaining in the series when Cushing took over, but, subsequently, also playing the part on a series of records opposite the Holmes of Robert Hardy.

Douglas Norman Francis Wilmer was born in London on 8 January 1920, the son of Harry Bradlaugh Wilmer and the former Kate Tavener. Educated at King's School in Canterbury, Douglas began as a student of architecture but later entered the Royal Academy of Dramatic Arts to train for a stage career. He made his professional bow in 1945 as Robert Browning in *The Barretts of Wimpole Street* at the Repertory Theatre in Rugby, and first appeared on the London boards the following year playing Rathbone and Granger's old role of Tybalt in *Romeo and Juliet*, the monstrous Gilles de Rais in *Saint Joan* (in a subsequent production he would graduate to the part of Warwick), and also appearing in *The Wise Have Spoken* and *In Time To Come*—all of these during Basil C. Langton's tenure of the King's Theatre, Hammersmith. At the Aldwych in '47, Wilmer was in *Macbeth*, and then he joined the Shakespeare Memorial Theatre (now the Royal Shakespeare Company) in Stratford. For the '49–'50 season, he moved to the Oxford Playhouse, and before the end of the year was at the Old Vic where he remained for two seasons before touring South Africa with them in '52.

Back in London he played Theobald Thin in *Blind Man's Buff* before making his film debut in '54's *Men of Sherwood Forrest*. Wilmer's resemblance to Rathbone has always verged on the uncanny, so it seems likely he was cast in this film as a sort of followup to Basil's Guy of Gisbourne in the Errol Flynn *Adventures of Robin Hood*; Peter Cushing, too, had a similar role in the subsequent *Sword of Sherwood Forrest*.

Some of Wilmer's other films are *The Right Person*, '55; Olivier's *Richard III* (Cushing had, of course, been in Olivier's stage version), *Passport to Treason*, and *The Battle of the River Plate* (with Christopher Lee and Ian Hunter), '56; *An Honourable Murder*, '60; *El Cid* (as a Moor), '61; *Cleopatra* (as the treacherous eunuch, with Robert Stephens), '62; *Fall of the Roman Empire* (with Finlay Currie), '64; *One Way Pendulum* (repeating his stage role as the Judge, one of his favorite parts, from the original Royal Court production), '65; *Khartoum* (as another North African, with Sir Ralph Richardson), '66; *Cromwell* (as Sir Thomas Fairfax, with Robert Morley), *Vampire Lovers* (as Baron Hartog, with Cushing, '70; and *Antony and Cleopatra* (as Agrippa), '72.

One of the few modern actors who looks at home in period costume, Wilmer played two splendid swashbuckling Rathbonesque villains in Ray Harryhausen's fantasies *Jason and the Argonauts*, '63; and *The Golden Voyage of Sin Bad*, '74.

During all this time, Wilmer was of course continuing to be active on stage and television. At the New Lindsey Theatre in '54 he directed *Grey Fedora*, and some of his subsequent stage appearances were in *The Way of the World* '56, *Madame De; Traveller Without Luggage; Marriage of Mr. Mississippi*; and *Ulysses In Nighttown*—all of the latter at the Arts Theatre in '59, and the last play transferring to both Paris and Amsterdam for additional performances. His first television appearance was as long ago as 1946, and besides those shows we have mentioned above he was, among many others, in *The Protectors*, as Commander Whiting—a bearded villain who looked distressingly like the "Schweppervescence" man of the TV commercial.

Married to Elizabeth Melville, Wilmer's hobbies are wine and riding. Because of his association with the *Fu Manchu* film series, this seems an appropriate place to discuss the many close links between those films and Sherlock Holmes.

The character of Fu Manchu was created in 1913 by Sax Rohmer (Arthur Sarsfield Wade), who was perhaps inspired to some extent by the 1895–1901 "Dr. Nikola" stories by Guy Boothby (who is represented in one of the *Rivals of Sherlock Holmes* volumes). Fu, however, has retained his popularity far more strikingly than Boothby's character.

Fu Manchu himself, with his Shakespearean brow, rather resembles Professor Moriarty, since both of them are scientists of genius who control great crime empires. Despite their titles, however, far more space in the Fu novels is devoted to Nayland Smith than to Fu Manchu. Sir Denis Nayland Smith of Scotland Yard is an exceedingly close pastiche of Mr. Sherlock Holmes, and his associate, Dr. Petrie, is quite transparently Watson. These two represent the forces of

good, and are usually the only things standing between the Insidious Doctor and world domination. As with Holmes and Moriarty, there is a good deal of ambiguity in the relationship between Smith and Fu.

In the novel *Drums of Fu Manchu*, the latter (for his own selfish reasons it must be admitted) is out to remove all the world's dictators from power, and in the last novels of the stories he has become an anti-Communist who works *with* Smith.

Besides the literary links, the film versions of the Smith-Manchu clashes also have many Holmes connections. Wilmer played Nayland Smith in both *Brides of Fu Manchu*, '66, and *Vengeance of Fu Manchu*, '67—both of them with Christopher Lee. TV-Watson H. Marion Crawford played Dr. Petrie in most of Lee's series, with Thorley Walters taking a hand in one episode. For the last two, Wilmer was replaced as Smith by Richard Greene, who had played Lee's own role of Sir Henry Baskerville in the Rathbone *Hound of the Baskervilles*. (Lee's first Smith was Nigel Green.)

In *Brides*, the apartment of Smith and Petrie is so much like 221B that it even has crossed assegais on the wall. Although the early episodes of the series were set in the proper early twentieth-century period, the later ones (more cheaply made) became contemporary in setting.

The first Fu Manchu films were made by Eille Norwood's studio, Stoll, in 1923, with H. Agar Lyons as the Evil Genius and, as Nayland Smith, Fred Paul. Paul was, of course, associated with the Holmes films of Bragington, Saintsbury, and Norwood, although he never actually played the part himself.

Apparently much taken with the role of Smith, he followed this initial series of fifteen—*The Mystery of Dr. Fu Manchu*—with *Further Mysteries of Dr. Fu Manchu* the next year in eight segments. This time Paul also scripted and directed in addition to playing Smith, and Lyons was back in the role of Fu, with Humberston Wright repeating his characterization of Dr. Petrie.

A few years later, in 1928, Paul directed a series called *Dr. Sin Fang Dramas*, which gives us Holmes two generations removed, since Paul's own character Lt. John Byrne is an imitation Nayland Smith, and Smith is an imitation Holmes. Agar took on the obviously derived title role, but when he repeated it in 1937 Fred Paul was no longer involved with the series.

Warner Oland played Fu Manchu on the screen four times between 1928 and 1932, clashing with Sherlock Holmes himself in Clive Brook's *Paramount on Parade*. Oland's "daughter" in his last episode, Anna May Wong, costarred with Reginald Owen in *Study in Scarlet*.

When Boris Karloff inherited the mantle of the Manchus in '32's *Mask of Fu Manchu*, Nayland Smith was played by Lewis Stone, who had previously starred in the first version of Conan Doyle's *Lost World*. In 1941's serial version of *The Drums* with Henry Brandon, William Royle played the misnamed "Sir Nayland Smith," and Olaf Hytten was Dr. Petrie.

At this point, of course, we have finished with the

legitimate films of Sherlock Holmes and entered into the shadowy realm of those films that contain only echoes of the Great Detective—pastiches, satires, incidental references, etc. These quasi-Holmes films, however, are in fact even more numerous than the genuine article, so we will have rather more to look at before we have finished with the denizens of Baker Street.

Some of the films in our next chapter, like *They Might be Giants,* are so close to the Real Thing as to be almost indistinguishable, while others like *The Falcon Strikes Back* seem so tenuously connected that it is astonishing to watch radio-Holmes Tom Conway fall into a Holmes-Watson dialogue with his crony Goldie Locks.

26

The Apocryphal Adventures of Sherlock Holmes
(Parodies, Pastiches, and Near-Misses)

MISS SHERLOCK HOLMES—(United States)

Released: December 1908
Production Company: Thomas A. Edison, Inc.

SYNOPSES and REVIEWS (*The Film Index,* 5 December 1908):

Jack Rose and Jim Dalton both in love with Nell, who favors Jack. Dalton, speculating, loses heavily, steals from safe. To divert suspicion, places securities in Jack's overcoat pocket. Observed by Nell. She removes securities from Jack and places them in Jim's pocket.

(*New York Dramatic Mirror,* 12 December 1908):

This is an inconsistent and complex story; none too easily followed, although it is admirably mounted and fairly acted. Two clerks in a brokers office love the broker's daughter. She returns the good clerk's love, but papa opposes. The bad clerk is a defaulter and seeks in some obscure way, to fasten his crime on his rival. The girl very badly disguises herself as the office boy, fooling papa and the whole office force, but not the spectators. Oh, my no! Her fat legs would give her away in any picture. In this guise she remains in the office at night, unknown to papa, who obligingly keeps slight watch on his darling child. The bad clerk enters and opens the safe to steal more money and the girl slams the door shut locking him up till morning, when she lets him out just in time to clear the good clerk, who is about to be arrested. Then she lets her hair down to show the rest of the actors that she is not a boy. They might not have known it otherwise.

It is curious to see that the plot, which seemed so utterly unmysterious to the first writer, was so hard to follow for the second, who is also perhaps overblunt in his comments on poor Miss Sherlock Holmes' physical charms.

This idea of a feminine edition of the Great Detective was revived in 1912 with Vitagraph *The Pipe,* featuring Sherlie Homes; next came Crystal's 1913 *Homlock Shermes,* which featured no one of that name in the plot, but rather a girl detective named Pearl.

The Edison company themselves returned to the subject with *The Sherlock Holmes Girl,* a one-reeler, copyrighted on 20 December 1913. Bliss Milford was the title character, and she also seems to have played some role behind the camera. The plot presented her as a hotel maid who spots a totally nondescript man, and decides to shadow him since he is suspiciously average-looking. He turns out, of course, to be a jewel thief.

It is interesting that both of these Edison efforts lived up to their titles to some extent—the first by giving the detective a disguise; the second by utilizing the Holmesian logic that gave us the celebrated Curious-Case-of-the-Dog-in-the-Nightime hypothesis (". . . the dog did nothing in the night time—that was the curious incident!").

Edison managed to eke out one more pseudo-

Sherlock in 1909, *A Sqeedunk Sherlock Holmes*, and it would be instructive to know if it, too, contained any quasi-genuine touches.

SHERLOCK HOLMES, JUNIOR (United States)

Date of Release: 20 July 1911
Production Company: Rex

Little Sherlock Holmes, Jr., reads of the doughty doings of his hero-god, and at once determines to become a detective himself. Providence favors him by at once giving him a mystery to solve. His father has noticed that in some weird, unaccountable fashion the whiskey in the decanter is ever vanishing, and father swears he doesn't drink it as fast as all that. So Sherlock Holmes, Jr., assigns himself the task of discovering who tampers with his father's soothing beverage. Concealed behind a table, he sees Bridget, the cook, come in and at once proceed to get on the outside of a man's size pull on the flask. At once the embryo detective makes his report to his father, with the astonishing solution of the mystery. The father decides to use Dr. Brown's Sure Cure for the Liquor Habit on the cook, and obtains a bottle of the fluid. This he puts in the room near the whiskey, intending to pour some in the bottle a little later. Sherlock Holmes, Jr., discovers the bottle, and follows the "Do It Now" maxim. There are friends visiting the house at the time, who are sitting on the lawn with his parents, awaiting tea which the maid is to bring them. Sherlock, Jr., pours a goodly quantity of the fluid into the tea. One of the results of taking the liquid is falling into a deep slumber, and in a few moments the host and hostess and guests are fast asleep. Then happens along Bridget's beau, the policeman, for whose particular benefit Bridget essays to go inside and procure a glass of "buttermilk." After inbibing, the policeman forgets all about everything except that he is awfully drowsy, and the next thing he, too, is asleep. It must have been contagious—or could Bridget not have forgotten herself?—but at any rate, she, too, wanders off into the Land of Nod. Then Sherlock dons the policeman's clothes and club, and marches through the house, monarch of all he surveys.

At this opportune moment, two burglars arrive on the scene, and seeing the sleepers, think they have been transferred to Burglar's Paradise. They sneak upstairs, fill their bags with silverware and then fall for the whiskey on the table, little Sherlock watching eagerly. At last they get themselves off, followed by the creator of all the mischief, but they have not gone far when they are overcome by the liquor cure and fall in their tracks to sleep. Little Sherlock now takes the manacles from the policeman's coat pocket, and ties both legs of the burglars together. In due time the household awakes, they seek the boy, and eventually find him covering the two burglars, prisoners of Sherlock, Jr.

The "father" in this film is, of course, *not* Sherlock Holmes, Sr., we assume. Child editions of the Great Detective were not uncommon on the silent screen.

This same year Gaumont in France was lensing *Bobby Turns Detective*, with their five-year-old star; it was released in Germany as *Fritzchen Als Sherlock Holmes*. Also in France, Eclair anticipated their Treville series with *Little Sherlock Holmes* that year. In 1912, Pathe gave us a small boy made up with a beard in *A Midget Sherlock Holmes*, and back in America, Powers made *Baby Sherlock*, with the diminutive detective recovering some stolen money.

Undoubtedly the most interesting of these juvenile-Holmeses was seven-year-old Matty Roubert, whose feature-length film, *The Waif*, was released in Britain by the Globe Film Company on 24 July 1916. The film contained several fantasy sequences in which the boy plays various heroes à la Walter Mitty, and judging by the stills in *Pictures and the Picturegoer* the Holmes sequence seems to have been a very elaborate and highly accurate parody with all of the true Holmesian trimmings—most likely inspired by the Gillette film *Sherlock Holmes* and Saintsbury's *Valley of Fear*, both of which had been released shortly before, and which naturally contained the best interpretations of Sherlock heretofore on the screen.

THE *TWO SLEUTHS* SERIES (UNITED STATES)

As might be expected, the major manifestation of Holmesian fooling on the early silent screen sprang from the freakish brain of the great Mack Sennett. Although Sennett appeared by himself in 1911's *A Desperate Lover*, planted under a deerstalker cap and bearing a magnifying glass, the actual *Two Sleuths* series was inaugurated at the same studio, Biograph, when Sennett was joined on screen by Fred Mace for the split-reel *$500.00 Reward*, released on 21 August '11.

The two Sleuths themselves—Fred Mace and Mack Sennett—at Keystone in 1913. The scowls apparently denote intense brain activity.

Although both comics with their beefy appearances seemed more suited to the role of Watson, each of them was in fact costumed as Holmes in the series, in which their attempts to emulate the deductive methods of the Great Sleuth invariably culminated in the usual Sennett apocalyptic mayhem. In this first film, they attempt to assist the police but predictably end at cross-purposes with them. They were more happy in their relations with film audiences, and a total of eleven more pictures were ground out over the next few years—at first in New York for Biograph, and then for Sennett's own California studio. A final film, with Mace by himself cast as either "Sureshock Holmes" or "Surelock Homes" was made at the rival company Majestic. With the exception of this last one, all of the series were directed by Sennett.

After *$500.00 Reward*, there followed in rapid succession *Trailing the Counterfeiters*, on 12 October 1911; *Their First Divorce Case*, 2 November; *Caught with the Goods*, 25 December; and *Their First Kidnapping Case*, 10 April 1912.

The latter, running 413 feet, introduced Eddie Dillon as the sleuths' half-witted assistant, no doubt patterned after Watson. Dillon would turn up twenty years later in Brook's *Sherlock Holmes*. In this film, the luckless trio is retained to find a kidnapped baby, but mistakenly assume that a baby with a contagious disease is the one they are looking for; at the end they are quarantined in a hospital by the Public Health Department. This plot is a good example of the cruel humor that characterizes much of Sennett's early work, though we assume that the real kidnapped child must have been safely accounted for somewhere in the film—Sennett did have a way of forgetting such petty details, though.

At this juncture Sennett left Biograph and headed West, being joined by Mace, who had departed previously, and the first Sleuths film under Mack's own aegis was *At It Again*: they were at it on 4 November 1912, and the subsequent episodes for Keystone were *A Bear Escape*, 25 November; *The Stolen Purse*, 10 February 1913; *The Sleuths' Last Stand*, 3 March; and *The Sleuths at the Floral Parade*, 6 March.

Floral Parade, as its title indicates, owed its genesis to the same sort of Sennettian economy that produced Charlie Chaplin's famous Little Tramp debut, *Kid Auto Races at Venice*. Whenever the thrifty producer got wind of any public festivity (or catastrophe) that lent itself to filmic purposes, he was in the habit of dispatching a cameraman and a few comics to improvise a short, using that background. This particular film was the outcome of a bit more premeditation, for Mace and Sennett were making official personal appearances in the Pasadena parade that January, costumed in their deerstalkers and long tweed overcoats, and smoking their pipes (an indication of how popular the Sleuths series was at this time). Mabel Normand was also scheduled to ride in the Sennett florally decorated car (which won second prize), but the whimsical pseudo-detectives locked

Miss Normand in her dressing room, and as a result she was so late in arriving at the parade grounds that she missed the car and kept frantically trying to catch up with it. This action, and the presence of Ford Sterling as a plant in the watching crowd, accounted for the film's slender plot.

After this episode, Fred Mace departed for Majestic, where he made the above-mentioned solo effort *The Tongue Mark* in his familiar sleuth regalia. Sennett made one more film in the series sans Mace, *Their First Execution*, 15 May 1913, although it is plain from the title that someone else had taken over Mace's character in this one; we are unable to supply his name.

THE *SHERLOCKO* AND *WATSO* SERIES (UNITED STATES)

Although proving less durable than *The Two Sleuths*, the protagonists of these films represented much closer parodies of Holmes and Watson. Imp released *The Flag of Distress* early in 1912, featuring a detective named Mr. Sherlocko, but this seems not to have been derived from the comic-strip characters on whom Champ Exclusive Pictures (Champion Film Co.) based their first Sherlocko and Watso film, *The Robbery at the Railroad Station*, 26 February 1912.

The strip, created about a year before, had found its way as far afield as Brazil, but the film versions (there was at least one further episode) do not seem to have caught on despite the fact that Champ timed the first one to coincide with the advance publicity that the Treville-Moyse Holmes series was receiving.

A glance at the stills we have included will reveal as close a similarity to Mutt and Jeff as to Holmes and Watson, but the resemblance to the second duo was still a good deal more than that of most other silent comedies that appropriated the Great Detective's name and little else.

Champ did their best to sell the initial entry to exhibitors: *The Robbery at the Railroad Station*, proclaims their trade advertisement,

"introduces these strange but popular characters at their ingenius trade, solving a mystery surrounding the theft of a railroad lantern—A dark deed! See the film and learn how they solve it.
Do you realize what it will mean for you to advertise *Sherlocko and Watso* for your theatre? Don't you see the profitable results? Of course you do, and you're not going to miss them!"

The exhortation seems to have been of little avail.
There were several other attempts at satirical Holmes series in this early period, but none of them met with the success of Sennett and Mace. Pathe turned out three *Charlie Colms* epics in France in 1912: *Charlie Colms and the Knave of Spades*; *Charlie Colms and the Dancer's Necklace*; and *The Dandies Club*.
Solax in the United States entered the fray in '13 with *Burstup Homes, Detective*, and *Burstup Homes's*

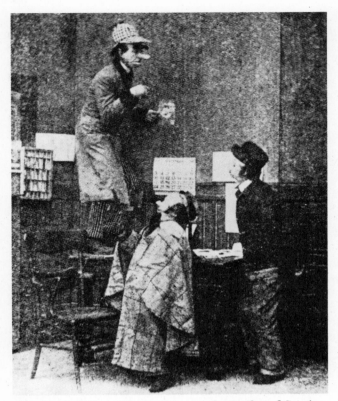

Two scenes from *The Robbery at the Railroad Station*, one of the short-lived Sherlocko and Watso series. The masked characters resemble Mutt and Jeff quite as closely as they do Holmes and Watson.

Murder Case; and Herlock Sholmes appeared in Gaumont's '13 *The Amateur Sleuth*—this name would crop up again in the Marionette film *Herlock Sholmes in Be-A-Live Crook*, but since that was not made until seventeen years later and based on the 1929 Clive Brook image, it seems to have been just a coincidence of the rather obvious name. It was made in Britain by Assoc. Sound Films.)

A large number of one-shot titles also proliferated. In France, Gaumont made *Detective Barock Holmes and His Hound* in 1909. Among the United States companies, Lubin created *Hemlock Hoax, The Detective* in '10. Thanhouser experimented with *Suelock Jones, Detective* in '12 before they made their Benham *Sign of Four*. The same year Comet rejoiced in *Mr. Whoops, The Detective*. Kalem inflicted *Sherlock Bonehead* on a world that can hardly have been prepared in 1914. In 1915, Bruce Mitchell wrote and produced *Sherlock Boob, Detective*, and the Mica Film Corp. released it on 9 January '15.

Vitagraph had the disagreeable notion of featuring Sherlock Ooomph in their 1916 *A Villainous Villain*. He was played by the rotund Hughie Mack, a former undertaker, and comic Larry Semon wrote and directed this tale of the Great Detective crossed in love.

Britain was less active in this field, but in December '15 Fred Evans played Sherlokz Homz in *A Study in Skarlit*, which was released by Comedy Combine-Sunny South (Pioneer) in approximately 2000 feet. Professor Moratorium was handled by Will Evans, and both Evanses collaborated on the writing and directing chores.

SHERLOCK BROWN

Date of Release: 26 June 1921
Running Time: 4,800 feet; 5 reels
Production Company: Metro Picture Corp.
Produced, Original Story, and Directed by: Bayard Veiller
Screenplay: Lenore J. Coffee
Photography: Arthur Martinelli
Art-Technical Director: A. F. Mantz

CAST

William Brown	Bert Lytell
Barbara Musgrave	Ora Carew
Hilda	Sylvia Breamer
J. J. Wallace	DeWitt Jennings
Frank Morton	Theodore von Eltz
Chief Bard	Wilton Taylor
General Bostwick	Hardee Kirkland
Henry Stark	George Barnum
Sato	George Kuwa

Besides the title, the presence in the list of characters of the name Musgrave is another Holmesian echo, just as we would expect to find, since Bayard Veiller later went on to work on the screenplay of Clive Brook's *Sherlock Holmes*. George Kuwa, incidentally, was a pre-Warner Oland screen Charlie Chan.

The hero of this one wants to become a detective, so he writes to an agency and receives a tin badge for five dollars. Brown is presented with his first case by Lt. Musgrave, who has been robbed of a secret government formula for explosives. Hospitalized in delirium, Musgrave babbles the name Wallace to his sister Barbara, who discovers that a man of that name has hidden the formula in a flower pot. Barbara and Brown follow Wallace to his apartment, and during the ensuing struggle Brown accidently discovers the formula. Barbara escapes with it but falls foul of more conspirators before she can deliver it to a government agent. After more complications and the obligatory climactic chase, Brown tracks down the formula, captures the conspirators, and wins Miss Musgrave.

A few years later Metro returned to the subject of Holmes, as we shall see from our next entry.

SHERLOCK, JR.

Date of Release: United States copyright, 22 April 1924
Running Time: 5 reels
Production Company: Metro Pictures Corp.
Producer: Joseph M. Schenk
Codirectors: Buster Keaton and Clyde Bruckman
Written and Adapted by: Clyde Bruckman, Jen Harvey, and Joe Mitchell

CAST

The Boy	Buster Keaton
The Girl	Kathryn Mc Guire
The Villain	Ward Crane
The Girl's Father	Joe Keaton
?	Horace Morgan
?	Jane Connelly
The Villain's Henchman	Erwin Connolly
?	Ford West
	George Ives
	John Patrick
	Ruth Holley

SYNOPSIS: Although it is one of the acknowledged giants of screen comedy, and by far the best-known of all Holmes parodies, *Sherlock, Jr.* actually has very little indeed to do with Sherlock, Sr. The prowess in disguise of Keaton and his assistant (who is far too competent to be Watson, even Andre Morell's) is the chief point of convergence.

There is also a supporting character called Gillette, and *Sherlock, Jr.* appears in a top-hatted image that echoes that of Barrymore in his *Sherlock Holmes* of a few years earlier, which would have been the best-known Holmes film to Keaton's American audiences. A few touches of ratiocination and a magnifying glass and we have enumerated the lot.

Fundamentally, this brilliant film is not concerned with Holmes at all as the focus of its comedy, but with Keaton's usual and highly individual subject preoccupations and screen techniques.

Buster Keaton as the luckless cinema projectionist in his immortal *Sherlock, Jr.* The Great Stone Face would not have been a bad choice for a serious Holmes adventure on the silent screen. (Courtesy National Film Archives of the British Film Institute)

The film's best-remembered sequence features Keaton as a cinema projectionist who falls asleep and dreams that he has walked onto the screen. As the backgrounds change behind him in the film that is being projected, the somnambulist remains in the same place, so that when he tries to sit on a doorstep the scene changes and he finds himself at the foot of a wall, then he just avoids being run over by a train; before he finishes taking a step, he is on a rock in the sea; he tries to dive and lands in the desert; finally he is kicked out of the screen by the villain—all of which was done entirely inside the camera, with Keaton positioning himself in the exact same relationship to the camera every time it was moved to a new location. No optical effects were used at all.

Blamed for a robbery of which he is innocent in the "real" portion of the film, in the "dream" section Keaton is transformed into the brilliant detective who solves the mystery. One of the best moments has Keaton placing what seems to be a large paper-covered hoop in a window, and then, when he is pursued by the villains, diving through the window and coming out on the other side disguised in a dress that he has placed in the hoop!

Even more startling is the effect when the great sleuth's ubicquitous assistant (who is always turning up in the nick of time outfitted in some unlikely disguise) opens up the lid of a box he is holding so that Keaton can dive not only through the lid, but clear through the assistant's body, and completely disappear.

As in many of his films, Buster has supplied his father Joe with a good supporting part—this time playing the heroine's father.

The great surrealist Luis Bunuel has had high praise for this film.

REVIEW (*New York Times*, 26 May 1924):

As one watches *Sherlock, Jr.* being unfurled on the . . . screen, one might observe with a sigh after 500 feet have passed, that it is about time the comical Buster Keaton skipped into action. Just about then you realize that something has happened—one of the best screen tricks ever incorporated in a comedy—then laughter starts, and for the balance of the picture you smile, snigger, chuckle, grin and guffaw.

This is an extremely good comedy which will give you plenty of amusement so long as you permit Keaton to slide into his work with his usual dedication.

Among the other great silent clowns (even if somewhat lesser lustre than Keaton) who tried their hands at a Holmes satire was the Sennett alumnus Mack Swain (1876–1935), whose *Sherlock Ambrose* probably echoed his mentor's *Two Sleuths* series: with his beefy build and thick moustache, Swain would seem to have been better suited to the role of Dr. Watson, though—unlike Keaton, the Great Stone Face.

Sherlock Ambrose was directed in two reels by W. S. Fredericks for the whimsically named L-Ko Motion Picture Kompany, and "kopyrighted" on 16 March 1918. Oliver Hardy gave us "Sherlock Pinkham."

Sennett's chief rival, Hal Roach, made a film called *Sherlock Sleuth* in 1925, released by Pathe Exchange, Inc. and copyrighted 4 May. The Three Stooges contributed *Shivering Sherlocks* and Lou Costello garbed himself in regulation deerstalker with pipe for both *Abbott and Costello Meet the Invisible Man*, '51, and *Abbott and Costello Meet Dr. Jekyll and Mr. Hyde*, '53—the latter being a full-dress turn-of-the-century costume picture with Bud Abbott also in inverness cape.

Not even Edgar Bergen's wooden protege was found lacking in qualifications to personate the great sleuth, and *Charlie McCarthy, Detective* was filmed in '39, with full Rathbonesque regalia.

Among other silent Holmesian travesties that we have not mentioned so far, were (in America) *The Kid and The Sleuth* and *The Right Clue*, both Imp, '12; *Cousins of Sherlock Holmes*, Solax, *A Would-Be Detective*, Gem; and *The Case of the Missing Girl*, Solax—all '13; *Shorty and Sherlock Holmes*, Broncho, '14; *A Society Sherlock*, Universal, and *The Great Detective*, Kalem, '16.

Britain, meanwhile, as we have noted, was less active in the pseudo-Sherlock sweepstakes. In 1911, Cricks and Martin presented *A Case for Sherlock Holmes*; the title, however, was meant to convey no more than such an expression as "one for the books," since nowhere in the film does Holmes himself put in an appearance. It was actually a "trick" film in the vein of Melies or *Sherlock Holmes Baffled*, with a thief repeatedly escaping capture by metamorphosing into different characters.

Urbanova, founded by the transplanted American

In both of these stills from *Der Mann, Der Sherlock Holmes War*, Hans Albers sports the soft cloth cap so beloved of German Holmeses. Heinz Ruhmann, on the right in both stills, was a very youthful Dr. Watson. One hopes that the Germanically neat set in the first still is not meant to pass for 221B.

Charles Urban, produced *A Canine Sherlock Holmes* in '13, the plot of which surely needs no elucidation. This film was shot on location in Brighton, and was distributed by Gaumont.

In France, Eclipse came up with *A Neat Trick* in 1911, and three years later Pathe subjected the sage to a further indignity with *Moritz Triumphs Over Sherlock Holmes*. The same year Eclair returned to the subject of their popular Treville-Moyse series with yet another film in which Holmes comes out the loser—only its German title, *Gontran als Sherlock Holmes*, has been preserved.

As if there were too few Holmes films in Germany with the concurrent series of Neuss, Larsen, Bonn, et al, in 1916 Eiko-Film eked out *Die Hand*.

There were fewer overt satires in the sound era.

Alfred Goulding directed a two-reeler for the Vitaphone Corporation called *Sherlock's Home,* which was written by Jack Henley and Glen Lambert and copyrighted on 29 September 1932; but most humorous references to Conan Doyle's character were more oblique.

A Van Bueren two-reeler of '33 or '34 called *The Strange Case of Henessy* was actually aimed at S. S. Van Dine's Philo Vance (its hero was called Silo Dance), but had a Holmesian echo in the detective's costume—by this time, however, deerstalker, pipe, inverness, magnifying glass, etc. had come to be associated more with detectives in general than specifically with Sherlock Holmes, so that it would be little instructive to enumerate more than we have of the many equally tenuous examples of this type.

More direct references are in such films as the '41 *Black Cat,* in which one of the characters asks of Basil Rathbone: "Who does he think he is—Sherlock Holmes?" Mycroft rates a mention in *The Ruling Class,* '72, and the '47 Johnny Mack Brown Western *Valley of Fear,* directed by Lambert Hillyer, owes a bit more to Doyle than just its title, for there are many touches of scientific deduction in this range mystery. Holmes is mentioned also in *Them,* '54, but, again, there would be little point in enumerating all such casual mentions.

Here, however, we arrive at the two greatest Holmes parodies made for the screen. They follow the originals so closely, in fact, that it is debatable whether they actually belong in this section at all.

DER MANN, DER SHERLOCK HOLMES WAR (The Man Who Was Sherlock Holmes) (Germany)

Date of Release: 15 July 1937
Running Time: 3,072m (10,079 feet)=112 min.
Production Company: UFA
Director: Karl Hartl
Screenplay: R. A. Stemmle and Karl Hartl

CAST

Sherlock Holmes	Hans Albers
Dr. Watson	Heinz Ruhmann
Mary Berry	Marieluise Claudius
Jane Berry	Hansi Knotek
Madama Ganymar	Hilde Weissner
Monsieur Lapin	Siegfried Schurenberg
Sir Conan Doyle (The Man Who Laughed)	Paul Bildt
Polizei-Director	Franz W. Schröder-Schrom

SYNOPSIS: Two down-and-out private detectives trying to boost their sagging business disguise themselves as Holmes and Watson and race to solve the first mystery they happen on before their real identities can be discovered. The pair succeeds in fooling all the passengers on a train into believing them, and eventually recover a stolen blue Mauritius stamp. The sequences involving the thieves were handled seriously, but most of the rest of the film was comic in treatment.

"Holmes and Watson" keep encountering a nameless Englishman who bursts into laughter every time he sees them. Finally, at the end of the film, after the two detectives have been arrested and brought to trial, the mysterious gentleman manages to clear them by testifying that there are in fact no such people as Sherlock Holmes and Dr. Watson!

His name, it turns out, is "Sir Conan" [sic] Doyle. His presence in the film (and indeed those of "Holmes" and "Watson") is a rare example of sympathetic portrayal of an Englishman in a Nazi film. The film was very popular before, during, and after the war, even as far afield as Prague, and has recently resurfaced on West German television.

Hans Albers (1892–1960) began in German films playing slick rascals and adulterers in such films as the original Sternberg-Dietrich *Blue Angel,* '30. Over the subsequent four years, however, he was cast as the romantic hero in a series of films (mainly for Erich Pommer at UFA), which visualized the typical fantasies of the bourgeois, according to Siegfried Kracauer, and Albers became the top favorite German movie star.

In *Monte Carlo Madness,* '31, Albers was cast as the crazy captain of an operetta cruiser, and the same year in the classic *Mädchen in Uniform* his photograph was worshipped by a group of aristocratic young girls. In '32 he was in the science-fiction film *F. P. 1 Does Not Answer* with Peter Lorre (the "F. P." stood for "Floating Platform"—floating not in space but on the sea); the same year he also played an amorous clown in *Quick* and a telegraph-operator who finds himself in high society in *The Victor.* Some of his other films were *Gold* (another sci-fier), '34; *Baron Munchausen* (a fantasy), '43; and *Der Letzte Mann,* '55.

Besides playing Sherlock Holmes, Albers shared another part with Stewart Granger, for the German created the character of *Old Shatterhand,* the Continental Cowboy whose durable series lasted long enough for him to be played on the screen not only by Granger, but also by former Tarzan Lex Barker.

Kracauer commented on Albers' screen personality:

He quivered with radiant vitality, was extremely agressive and like a born buccaneer seized any opportunity within his reach . . . whether attacking enemies or courting girls, it was all done in an unpremeditated way—as if he were driven by changing moods and circumstances rather than by the steadfast will to realise a project. . . . Fortuna on her part pursued him with the persistence of a loving woman and lent him a helping hand whenever he stumbled. . . . This human dynamo with the heart of gold embodied on the screen what everyone wished to be in life.

Heinz Ruhman, like Hans Albers, began his film career before the Nazi takeover, and like Albers, also, though he appeared in films during the Third Reich, he survived well into the postwar era with his popularity if anything greater.

Born approximately 1908, Ruhman made *Drei von Tankstelle* in '30. More recently he has rejoined the screen detective fraternity by incarnating Georges Simenon's classic *Inspector Maigret* on the screen (in France). In '65, Ruhmann was outstanding among an all-star cast as a Jewish salesman in *Ship of Fools*.

THEY MIGHT BE GIANTS (United States)

Released: 1971; Great Britain: March '72
Running Time: 88 minutes; in Great Britain: 86 min. (7,714 feet)
Production Company: Universal/Newman-Foreman; distributed in Britain by Rank.
Producer: John Foreman (and, uncredited, Paul Newman)
Associate Producer: Frank Caffey
Director: Anthony Harvey
Photography: Victor Kemper
Screenplay: James Goldman
Based on: Goldman's own play
Production Superviser: Jack Grossberg
Production Designer: John Lloyd
Editor: Barry Malkin
Music: John Barry
Sound: Nathan Boxer
Assistant Director: Louis A. Stroller
Set Decorator: Herbert Mulligan
Color: Technicolor
(British "U" Certificate)

CAST

Dr. Mildred Watson	Joanne Woodward
Sherlock Holmes (Justin Playfair)	George C. Scott
Wilbur Peabody	Jack Gilford
Blevins Playfair	Lester Rawlins
Daisy	Rue McClanahan
Dr. Strauss	Ron Weyand
Grace	Kitty Winn
Grace's Boyfriend	Peter Fredericks
Maud	Sudie Bond
Miss Finch	Jenny Egan
Peggy	Theresa Merritt
Messenger	Al Lewis
Mr. Small	Oliver Clark
Telephone Operators	Jane Hoffman
	Dorothy Greener
Sanitation Men	M. Emmet Walsh
	Louis Zorich
Telephone Guard	Michael McGuire
Policeman	Eugene Roche
Mr. Brown	James Tolkan
Brown's Driver	Jacques Sandulescu
Mr. Bagg	Worthington Miner
Mrs. Bagg	Frances Fuller
Teenage Boy	Matthew Cowles
Teenage Girl	Candy Azzara
Police Lt.	John McCurry
Chief	Tony Capodilupo
Usher	F. Murray Abraham
Winthrop	Staats Cotsworth
Chestnut Vendor	Paul Benedict
Store Manager	Ralph Clanton
Cab Driver	Ted Beniades

SYNOPSIS: Justin Playfair, a lawyer, has withdrawn into a fantasy world since his wife's death. He dresses, speaks, and behaves like Sherlock Holmes. Blevins Playfair, his brother, wants to get him certified insane and committed in order to take control of his estate, the incentive partly being that Blevins is being blackmailed for a large sum that he cannot afford.

At a clinic where he is taken, Justin intrigues psychoanalyst Dr. Mildred Watson by diagnosing one of her most baffling patients accurately with preternaturally Holmesian deductions: "Holmes" theorizes that the mute Mr. Small, though fat and ungainly, believes himself to be Rudolf Valentino, who was of course a silent star—hence Small cannot speak.

"My best to Vilma Banky," murmurs the sleuth in parting to the patient, who is grateful for being at last recognized.

Dr. Watson feels that Justin is a classic paranoid, but after calling on him in his 221B-esque den, she is persuaded to aid him in his "investigations" just as her namesake did, because the sleuth has successfully analysed Mildred's own frustrations and mental troubles.

Holmes is in hot pursuit of his ancient nemesis, Moriarty, and treats everything that crosses his path as a clue, including the amount of "twenty grand" mentioned in his brother's blackmail note—taking it to refer to a street address, Number 20 Grand Street!

Holmes and Watson wander all over New York City on the trail: through a telephone switchboard office; an old library whose equally ancient librarian has always secretly cherished a desire to be "The Scarlet Pimpernel"; the apartment of an old couple who have successfully locked out the world since 1939 and cultivated their indoor jungle of a garden for both a self-sufficiency of food and aesthetic satisfaction; and a crumbling 42nd Street movie theater where Holmes and the other balcony patrons are accustomed to resort seeking escape from the modern world in the simpler ethos of old Western films.

The deductive duo is trailed during all this odyssey by the blackmailer, who wants to help Blevins get Justin's money so that he can more readily be paid off. While Holmes is somewhat bashfully bringing flowers to his "dear Watson," who has rather ineptly cooked dinner for him in her apartment, he is shot at and barely escapes with his life.

Continuing to be pursued and to pursue the elusive Napoleon of Crime, at the film's end Holmes and Watson are joined by an army of all the lonely eccentrics whom they have met in the course of their circumambulations: Mr. Small the mute, the old couple, the nurse who helped Holmes escape from the clinic, the telephone operators, trashmen, cops, Justin's sister-in-law, and the moviegoers (whose sanctuary has been invaded by porno films). All of these people, it appears, have long cherished a "secret identity" like Justin and the elderly librarian.

At one point, hotly pursued, Holmes seizes the microphone at an enormous 1984-ish all night supermarket and creates chaos by announcing giveaway prices for various items, thus setting off a near riot in which his assailants are hopelessly entangled.

Finally, all alone together at night before a tunnel in Central Park, Holmes and Dr. Watson await the imminent approach of the great Moriarty himself, who is heard in the form of an approaching hansom cab with clip-clop of horse's hooves and jingling bridle—or perhaps it is an approaching train; we do not see, and the ending is left ambiguous with a fade to white, in keeping with the title that refers to Don Quixote's windmills which might of course really be giants after all.

REVIEWS (*Monthly Film Bulletin*, 17 May 1972, reviewed by Penelope Houston):

. . . Moriarty is elevated to the status of an all-purpose symbol for dreads and terrors . . . the great Holmes merges into the greater Quixote. . . . Part of the film's extraordinarily captivating quality perhaps comes from a realisation of how near the edge [of "neo-Capra . . . whimsy"] its straying . . . well-turned and exact elegance of the dialogue . . . powerful resonances of the Holmes legend linked to the script's specific and incongruous incidents . . . sure-footed, balanced direction of the players. . . . Dr. Watson . . . tries to approach [Holmes] as a patient, and ends up joining him on the trail—to admonitions of, "Watson, where's your pluck?" This whole long sequence is entirely theatrical; and never stagey . . . Scott's character modulates beautifully from the inhuman Holmesian responsibility of being always right (his defense against the Moriarty terrors) to the softening admission of a mistake . . . last scene . . . is bewitching . . . sense of something immense and invisible coming at them out of the night.

(*Films and Filming*, 18 May 1972, reviewed by Gordon Gow):

. . . neo-Holmes is confronted by a female psychoanalyst . . . they are gradually linked in a kind of fantasy that appears to hold more substance than the reality of New York, a city of sleazy streets and occasional graces, against which they operate in crazy quest of a symbolic Moriarty.

Their real enemy is the anti-individual systemised life, so different from the clean-cut justice of the Western films that are admired by our latterday Holmes. . . . Dr. Watson leaves her customary work . . . and lends herself to the idealism of Holmes, and to his fears as well, being transported into admiration after he has analysed her own bleak condition all too clearly.

. . . author James Goldman . . . has not quite sustained his diverting and mildly sentimental idea. . . . Anthony Harvey . . . gets in a few nice

touches when pools of light are isolated in surrounding darkness . . . cuteness and cumbersomeness intrude too often upon such interesting intentions.

George C. Scott played a Holmesian sort of detective in *The List of Adrian Messenger* with Clive Brook, and his famous *Patton* also featured Douglas Wilmer. *Giants* screenwriter Goldman and director Harvey had previously made *Lion in Winter* with TV- and phonograph-Watson Nigel Stock, also; but otherwise this film has few links to the "legitimate" Holmes works on the production side.

Goldman's original theatrical version of this story had premiered in London on 28 June 1961 with Harry H. Corbett as Holmes and Avis Bunnage as Dr. Watson, and the link with Cervantes was coincidentally underscored by the presence in the cast (as Blevins Playfair) of Roy Kinnear, who made a highly successful Sancho Panza at the Old Vic.

In this film the relationship of Holmes and Watson is somewhat reversed in order to bring it into closer harmony with that of Quixote and Sancho; whereas the Knight was the idealist to his squire's down-to-earth materialist, Holmes was the materialist in the Baker Street partnership and Watson the romantic—despite the superficial resemblance to the earlier duo resulting from one of its members being tall and thin and the other stocky (this qualification, after all, fits Laurel and Hardy equally well!).

It is true that beneath his self-proclaimed coldly scientific exterior, Holmes concealed a chivalrous, benevolent, and rather old-fashioned heart; nevertheless, his ideals were exactly the opposite of Don Quixote's, for the great sleuth was concerned to reduce mysteries to explicable facts, and not to *inject* mystery into too mundane reality.

Still, there are indeed correspondences of personality between the two sets of immortal creations, and it is interesting that Peter O'Toole, who was originally cast as Holmes in *Private Life,* later played Quixote in *Man of La Mancha.* Boris Karloff, too, who played the retired and bee-keeping Holmes (under the alias of "Mr. Mycroft") on the radio and TV, played an eccentric Spanish scientist who believed himself to be Quixote (on an episode of *I Spy.*)

All in all, *Giants* must rank as one of the sincerest attempts ever to transfer Sherlock Holmes to the screen, for the film treats this highly complex character with a good deal more respect (and deserved ambiguity) than very many of the so-called "straight" adaptations of the original Doyle stories. As with the Czech *Death of Tarzan,* it seems that the liberation from slavish convention permitted by an overtly "satirical" framework has allowed the filmmakers to come closer to the fundamental *spirit* of the original literary creation, and interpret it in more truly cinematic terms than would be possible with a more literal attempt at translation from one medium to the other.

Since *Giants,* there have been two more ventures into the realm of Sherlockian parody, but since both were hard core porno films—one *The Adventures of Shirley Holmes,* and the other one whose mere title can hardly be repeated in these pages—". . . the rest is silence."

Edgar Allan Poe's detective character C. Auguste Dupin, of course, actually preceded Conan Doyle (and every other writer on scientific deduction), so it is not exactly correct to speak of Dupin's screen adventures as having been inspired by those of Sherlock Holmes. Still, the original Dupin was very close to Holmes in character as well as methods, and some filmmakers have not been slow to notice this and make him appear even closer. Two examples are the British *Dupin and the Stolen Necklace* (Urbanova, '12) and the much later ('42) American *Mystery of Marie Roget*.

This second one was a poverty-row effort picked up for distribution by Universal, who were then engaged in the Rathbone-Holmes series. One might suspect that part of the film's appeal to Universal was the fact that it fielded the equivalent to a spare Holmes-and-Watson team in the event of emergencies, for Patrick Knowles (as Dupin) and Lloyd Corrigan were virtually carbon copies of Rathbone and Nigel Bruce.

Surprisingly enough, however, the many screen versions of *Murders in the Rue Morgue* seem to have gone out of their way to downgrade the very close Holmes-Dupin resemblance and turn the Chevalier into a conventional juvenile lead. In the '32 and '54 versions (the latter retitled *Phantom of the Rue Morgue*), Dupin was presented as a love-struck medical researcher. The 1914 version seems not to have played up Baker Street links, and that of '71 turned the original Poe tale into a play within the main film story. *Marie Roget* was filmed earlier by Universal in '31, and, of course, we have already seen how the *Rue Morgue* plot was appropriated for a "legitimate" Holmes vehicle in 1908.

A caricature of King Baggot wearing a deerstalker appeared in the American magazine *Motion Picture Stories* in July 1914, and three months later in the British *Pictures and the Picturegoer*. It did not, however, refer to any screen portrayals of Sherlock Holmes by the actor, but to his series of "King, the Detective," adventures that had commenced late the previous year with *The Jarvis Case*. This series, though, does indeed seem to have had some affinities with Holmes. *Moving Picture World* noted at the time:

> Mr. Baggot made extensive studies in . . . the latest discoveries of sciences that might be of use in detecting the criminal. . . . King, the detective, surrounds and fills his house with appliances of science. For instance, when a person calls at the front door he simply presses a button and immediately the figure waiting outside is shown in relief on a screen before him.

Baggot starred in, wrote and directed the series. Despite the caricature, he seems not to have worn a deerstalker in the series but rather the sort of soft-checked cap worn by Francis Ford in *A Study in Scarlet* and by so many of the German Holmeses and Holmes-imitators.

Here we have effectually ended our chronicles of Sherlock Holmes on the Screen, but we must glance at a few of the Great Detective's appearances on television, in documentaries, and other such nearly related endeavors before we bid farewell to Baker Street for the final time.

27

The Televised Adventures of Sherlock Holmes

(Together with his exploits on Madison Avenue and other related topics)

The story of Holmes on TV is actually a bit outside the province of our book, but there are a few aspects of this phase of his career that overlap the films sufficiently to deserve a look here.

First we should glance briefly at Holmes on the radio. Between 1930 and 1943 every one of the dramatizations was written by Edith Meisner and produced in the United States, and Miss Meisner did not finally sever her connection with the various series until '48. The first radio-Holmes, appropriately enough, was William Gillette, who played the detective again in '35, and whose old stage play was dramatized without him by Orson Welles three years later. Welles was Holmes that time out, but nineteen years later on the other side of the Atlantic, Welles went to bat for the opposite team by playing Moriarty in the Gielgud-Richardson series.

Between Gillette's two appearances, Richard Gordon monopolized the role of Holmes on the radio, except for one stint in '35 by Louis Hector—himself an erstwhile Napoleon of Crime. Gordon was back in the role in '36, then in '39 the first of the many Rathbone-Bruce series made its bow.

Rathbone, of course, dominated the United States airwaves with his classic interpretation of the part even as he did cinema screens, but by '46 he had grown very weary indeed of Baker Street, and though Bruce remained as Watson, Tom Conway took over the ratiocinative chores.

It is curious to realize that the *Falcon* picture we mentioned earlier, in which Conway spoke a few lines of Sherlockian dialogue, was actually made several years *before* he did the Holmes series with Bruce. It, thus, comes more under the heading of coincidence than "in" joke, unless he had indeed been mentioned for the radio series earlier.

It seems probable, too, that Universal must have contemplated bringing Conway into the filmic Holmes series as well, after the irrevocable departure of Rathbone from that additional sphere. Certainly Conway would have been physically perfect for the part, and Nigel Bruce was anxious to continue the series.

Meanwhile, Holmes had bowed on British airways in the familiar voice of Arthur Wontner. His Watson, Carleton Hobbs, was to go on to play Mycroft and, most importantly, Holmes himself in so many radio series over the next four decades that for most Britains he has become *the* voice of the Great Detective.

Wontner also introduced his deductive alterego to the television screen during the Festival of Britain in '51. (The Holmesian Exhibition of the Festival was also chronicled via a *Pathe Pictorial* newsreel that year, called *The Sage of Baker Street*.)

Other British radio Holmeses over the next few years were John Cheatle, Cedric Hardwicke (with Finlay Currie as his Watson), and Laidman Browne, whose Watson, Norman Shelley, was subsequently to join Hobbs' famous series in this role; many of their episodes were written by Michael and Mollie Hardwicke. After one series with John Stanley in America had run its course and another was in progress, the British returned to the fold with *The Adventure of the Speckled Band,* introduced by Adrian Conan Doyle. Finlay Currie was Dr. Watson, and with his Scots accent it was easy to accept him as an Edinburgh University Bachelor of Medicine (or a standin for the Scots Dr. Arthur Conan Doyle). He had a new Holmes in Howard Marion-Crawford, and Marion-Crawford was to be associated so closely with Holmesian projects in two other media over the next twenty years that his career deserves an extended look.

There had been an American television broadcast of *The Three Garridebs* with Louis Hector as early as 1937; Alan Napier and Melville Cooper had incarnated the Baker Street Duo in a 1949 *Speckled Band* in the United States; Alan Wheatley and Raymond Francis handled a brief BBC series in 1951; and Rathbone himself joined Martyn Green for a last bow in *The Black Baronet* in 1953 (based on an Adrian Conan Doyle original).

But by far the most important of the early TV appearances of the Great Detective was the series of thirty-nine twenty-seven-minute episodes made in Paris (of all places) by Guild Films and originally released in the United States by Motion Pictures for Television in 1954. Marion Crawford was demoted to the role of Watson, and Leslie Howard's lookalike son Ronald was cast as Sherlock Holmes.

Ronald Howard, thirty-six at the time, said that he saw Holmes as someone who was not without charm and a sense of humor, and appearances were made in the series by such other notable performers as Delphine Seyrig and Paulette Goddard; but the indelible impression was made by Marion-Crawford, for he survived the demise of this series to play the pseudo-Watson Dr. Petrie in most of the Christopher Lee Fu Manchu series in the late sixties, outlasting such transient (though excellent) Nayland Smiths as Nigel Green, Douglas Wilmer, and Richard Greene.

Howard Marion-Crawford was the grandson of the American writer of ghost stories F. Marion Crawford (without the hyphen), but his career was mostly in England. Educated at Clifton with Trevor Howard, Marion-Crawford then entered the Royal Academy of Dramatic Arts in London and won the Galsworthy Prize for playing Henry VIII in *The Rose Without a Thorn.*

Marion-Crawford made his radio debut in 1935, and his gift for imitating literally dozens of different accents earned him the title of "the man with a thousand voices."

When he was selected to portray New York City Mayor Fiorello LaGuardia on the radio, Marion-Crawford listened to only a few seconds of recordings of the mayor and then within five minutes had his voice down flawlessly. In one serial episode the actor was cast as four different characters: an RAF officer, a Cornish pubkeeper, a black American, and a Burmese girl!

When the war broke out, Marion-Crawford enlisted first in his father's old regiment the Irish Guards, but, as a friend later noted, "He got tired of foot-slogging so he transferred to the RAF as a navigator." Among the wartime figures Marion-Crawford impersonated on the radio were Mussolini, Goerring, and Rommel.

Baring-Gould felt that Marion-Crawford's TV series "portrayed Watson as the sturdy fellow he really was," and the actor's many other television appearances included roles in the *Secret Agent (Danger Man* in Britain) and *Saint* series.

He appeared in over one hundred films, and although a bit too beefy to re-create his radio Sherlock Holmes on the screen, he played Dr. Petrie in most of the episodes of the Christopher Lee *Fu Manchu* series: *Face of Fu Manchu* in 1965; *Brides of Fu Manchu* in 1966; *Blood of Fu Manchu*; and *Castle of Fu Manchu* in 1968.

Although some of the Nayland Smiths in this series (other than Wilmer) were not especially Holmesian, Marion-Crawford was rather more like Dr. Watson than a good many of the performers who have played the good doctor under his original name! The residence of Smith and Petrie was an excellent rendition of 221B Baker Street, though Mrs. Hudson was replaced by a stunning young Asian lady named Lotus.

On the stage he appeared in *The Kensington Squares, The Pied Piper* and *Chips With Everything,* and some of his other film roles were in *Forever England* (1932), *Freedom Radio* (1940), *The Rake's Progress* (1945), *The Hasty Heart* (1949), *The Man in the White Suit* (with future-Lestrade George Benson, 1951), *Where's Charley?* (1952), *The Silken Affair* and *Reach for the Sky* (1956), *Nowhere to Go* and *Virgin Island* (1958), *Lawrence of Arabia* (1962), and *The Charge of the Light Brigade* (as Sir George Brown, with his old friend Trevor Howard, and radio-Holmes John Gielgud; 1968).

Married three times, Marion-Crawford was survived by two sons. His widow, New Zealand actress Germaine Anderson, was returning from that country overland through India when Marion-Crawford, reading in his London home, succumbed to a heart attack at the age of fifty-five in November of 1969.

The Man with the Twisted Lip, 3214 feet long (thirty-six minutes), had been shot originally as a pilot for a television series, but wound up being released to British theaters by Vandyke Pictures in April 1951. It featured John Longden as Sherlock Holmes and Campbell Singer as Watson, and was directed by Richard M. Grey. Hector Ross played Neville St. Clair.

From the late forties to the present, Holmes has continued sporadically on the radio, played in the United States by Ben Wright in 1949 and 1950 with Eric Snowden as Watson; in Sweden by George Arlin in 1960 and 1971, by Stig Ericson in 1967, and by Jan Blomberg in 1974; and in Switzerland in 1967 by Marcel Imhoff.

In Britain all this time the voice of Holmes was that of Carlton Hobbs, and Dr. Watson sounded very much like Norman Shelley. There were a few exceptions to this hegemony, though, for on a 1960 broadcast Hobbs was joined briefly by a new medical colleague in

Leslie Perrins, reappearing from non-Watson roles in the old Wontner film series. In 1961, Hobbs' Holmes conversed with none other than Nigel Bruce, whose voice survived on recordings though his soul had departed this sphere eight years earlier; Alan Wheatley resurfaced as the sleuth in 1954 in a script written by the authoress of his old television series, critic C. A. Lejune, and Gielgud and Richardson took a crack at the Baker Street Duo, also; Hugh Manning and Leigh Crutchley had the roles in 1958, and Richard Hurdall and Bryan Coleman in 1959.

Despite all this competition, Hobbs and Shelley have proved by far the most durable, and in 1975, as we prepare this book for the press, some of their BBC episodes were being played regularly even in New York City.

On television, meanwhile, the 1954 series was succeeded by those of Wilmer and Peter Cushing. There were then several offerings that were distinctly off-trail: a comedy pilot with Paul Lynde, of all people, as the Great Detective; another satirical offering with John Cleese and William Rushton as the star residents of Mrs. Hudson's establishment; and a program called *Dr. Watson and the Darkwater Hall Mystery*, which gave us Edward Fox as the much abused junior partner given a chance to tackle a problem without the interference of Holmes. Italian TV has also joined the fray.

Television commercials featuring Holmes and Watson began to be made in 1966, and are continuing at this writing: the pair has been used to invoke the merits of Farmer's Wife Double Devon Cream; to persuade viewers to heat their homes with Esso Oil; to imbibe Carlsberg Lager; play "Clue," the detective board-game; and to chew Carefree Sugarless Gum!

An advertising film of 1970 released theatrically was *The Bizarre Adventures of Sherlock Holmes and Imperial Oil*. Even the trained ape "Zippy" donned a deerstalker for a "Sea Monkeys" commercial, and Charles Schulz's ever-popular character "Snoopy" wore a deerstalker and carried a magnifying glass for a children's television special.

The most recent televised escapade of Sherlock Holmes, though, was the 1972 color version of *The Hound of The Baskervilles*, an ABC-TV made-for-television movie first shown in June of that year.

THE HOUND OF THE BASKERVILLES (United States)

Running Time: 90 minutes (with commercials)
Production Company: Universal
Director: Barry Crane
Screenplay: Robert Williams
Director of Photography: Harry Wolf, A.S.C.

CAST

Sherlock Holmes	Stewart Granger
Dr. Watson	Bernard Fox
Stapleton	William Shatner
Dr. Mortimer	Anthony Zerbe
Miss Frankland	Sally Ann Howes
Beryl Stapleton	Jane Merrow
Frankland	John Williams

SYNOPSIS: The film opens with a London lamp-lighter causing the unmistakable shadow of Sherlock Holmes to fall over the screen. There is an excellent glass shot of a London exterior sunset, with sidewalk stalls, flower girls, etc. Holmes walks home to 221B Baker Street, where he proceeds to find the cane Dr. Mortimer has left behind. An effective touch has Holmes light his pipe from the hearth fire with a long splinter of wood.

Bernard Fox gives us a muttering Watson like that of Nigel Bruce, and also narrates the flashback of the Baskerville legend. Regrettably, the entire mystery is given away by the fact that William Shatner is very recognizably cast as both Sir Hugo Baskerville and his supposedly secret descendant Stapleton. Otherwise, though, the legendary sequence is quite well told visually without overheavy reliance on expository narration, and the Hound itself is refreshingly supernatural-looking—looking wolfish and glowing with blue light.

A few noticeably Far Western sets (such as Medicine Bow from Granger's *Shiloh* series) are used for London, and most of the "exteriors" are done in the studio, but despite this there is a fair amount of care taken with the period atmosphere, and the London Natural History Museum is accurately rendered.

Granger's Holmes is a bit heavy-set and snow-white-haired, but his forehead displays the proper Shakespearean loftiness and his reading of the part is excellent, with the same dynamic vigor that so distinguished Basil Rathbone. Both actors, of course, had reputations on the screens as cads and period swashbucklers before they migrated to Baker Street, and this sort of background helped them steer clear of making Holmes too considerate or too modern.

Granger's dark red dressing gown, though, is hardly "mouse-colored"—a concession to color photography, no doubt. His string tie, too, seems un-Conanical. For street dress the detective varies his familiar deerstalker and tweed Inverness cape with a black Inverness and hat exactly resembling those worn by Eille Norwood fifty years before. He also carries a walking stick.

Though he plays him with great good humor, Bernard Fox gives us the familiar Boobus Britannicus, and Granger's Holmes takes a wicked delight in proving the poor doctor's deductions about Mortimer's cane to be totally off the mark. His friendship for Watson is not neglected either, though, as he persuades the reluctant medico to avail himself of a second brandy.

This Holmes is no ascetic, and seems to be quite a connoisseur of his wine. The Baskerville family is generously furnished with a castle—shades of the German Schloss from the old *Hund* films! Some authentic-sounding dialogue has found its way into the script though, such as "The litmus paper, Watson!"

and "That moss only grows on rocks" (one knows that Holmes has surely composed a monograph on the subject).

On the moors Dr. Watson wears the same sort of hat that he did in the Morell *Hound*, and as he taps the wine kegs very gently with the barrel of his gun, Fox seems very much the old military man, quite capable of holding down the fort during the fifteen minutes in which Holmes seems to be absent from the screen. Actually, the sleuth has returned during the last five, naturally, but Granger's disguise is certainly one of the very best of a filmic Holmes to date. The slightness of the actual makeup only serves to accentuate the brilliance of the actor's character playing as the supposed old beggar.

We have a glimpse of Holmes the misogynist when he pats Dr. Mortimer sympathetically on the back after catching a glimpse of the latter's harridan of a wife. Surprising and unaccountably, when some hastily improvised false explanations are called for, Dr. Watson "wings" his a good deal more believably than does Holmes.

There is an interesting supernatural touch at the end of the film after Holmes has grappled with and beaten the faked Hound, for another Hound is heard baying in the distance, suggesting that Stapleton perhaps did not need to create his own version after all. The sound, Holmes suggests, "must be merely the wind," and Watson agrees with him, but the viewer is gratified to think that all of the ghostly trappings have not been merely the result of a hoax—an anticlimax that even the presence of Holmes had never quite managed to avoid in previous versions.

At the film's end Sherlock Holmes is back among his chemicals in Baker Street, looking very elegant (and a bit dilettantish) in a black dressing gown and white scarf. Dr. Watson, on the track, notes that his learned friend is a genius, but has a bothersome sense of humor—an aspect of the character that the witty Granger has effectively accentuated, although he has also given us some of the Eille Norwood melancholy, with the same lowered lids. Granger has his own tricks of speech in the role, speaking in staccato phrases and accenting the last syllables.

It is a pity that the series for which this film served as the pilot never materialized, for, besides the outstanding Granger-Fox performances, the technical effects are all thoughtfully achieved. The softly focused background in an early outdoor sequence serves to minimize the fact that it is a studio interior, but also bathes the background figures in a nostalgic Seurat-like haze that is very lovely in color. Good use is also made of subjective moving camera shots from the point of view of the characters.

At another point the camera takes the point of view of a *clue* as Holmes raises his magnifying-glass until he brings himself into focus for the viewers—a not uncommon but effective simile for the workings of the sleuth's mind as he perceives the significance of the evidence with sudden clarity.

Violin music makes a fine musical accompaniment, which, despite its seemingly painful obviousness for a Holmes film, seems to have been seldom used for this purpose, except in the Rathbone series (in which the "Londonderry Air" wafted us up to 221B in one of the episodes).

The litigious Mr. Frankland reverts to his proper self in this version, being appropriately unfrocked from the Bishoply Cloth of the (first) Cushing version; Lestrade, too, puts in an appearance, together with a seldom seen member of the original Baker Street Irregulars, a Mr. Cartwright.

We have already noted many of the links between Stewart Granger's career and those of his fellow-Holmeses in our earlier chapters, but a connection we have not touched on is his film of *Moonfleet* '55; for the J. Meade Faulkner novel on which it was based contains not only the name "Sherlock" but the more esoterically Doylean "Holderness." In *Beau Brummell*, the actor was cast with Robert Morley, Henry Oscar, and Finlay Currie—a Mycroft, Holmes, and Watson.

Born in 1913, Granger made his stage debut in '35, and his first film was *So This is London* three years later. In the sword and dagger fight in *Romeo and Juliet*, with the Old Vic Company the next year, Robert Donat got a deep gash on the thumb when he failed to parry a blow delivered by Granger, who was cast as Tybalt. Like his fellow-Tybalt Basil Rathbone, Granger was to become one of the most outstanding of all film swordsmen. Granger's other plays for the Vic included *The Good-Natured Man* and *To Dream Again*.

In the 1950's Granger was listed in the Bernstein Poll as the next most popular film star in Great Britain (after James Mason). In a characteristic interview, Granger betrays a Holmesian affinity when, asked to name one of his indoor hobbies, replied, "arguing with inexperienced or inefficient producers!"

We would hope that perhaps with the renewed current interest in Sherlock Holmes, Granger's proposed series might be revived, for it promised to be the best moderately budgeted American effort in the genre since the Rathbone films—perhaps not surprising when it is considered that both were made by the same studio.

We have already mentioned in earlier chapters the magnificent British TV series *The Rivals of Sherlock Holmes*, which has also achieved great popular success in the United States. Based on the short story anthologies by Sir Hugh Greene, it deals, of course, not with Holmes himself, but with detective characters created by contemporaries of Doyle—the producers did, however, take the precaution of casting a generous selection of former portrayers of the roles of Holmes and Watson, as we have seen, to play the "rivals."

Set for the current American television season is a one-shot Holmes play starring Robert Shaw and Donald Pleasance, but, as we have said, no plans seem to be afoot for a regular series at the moment.

The Watson of this *Hound* pilot, Bernard Fox, is very

active on American television in such shows as *Anna and the King of Siam*, in which he played the very aristocratic British Ambassador. For a distinct switch, Fox essayed a Cockney policeman in the theatrical film *Arnold*, '74. Plumbing the depths of the ridiculous, he was not even unknown to the comedy-western travesty *F Troop*. Had this splendid character actor been in Hollywood in the '30's, he would no doubt have been as overworked as Reginald Owen.

A BBC television documentary devoted to *The Hound of the Baskervilles* was shown in the British Southwest region in 1964. It was made by Anthony Howlett and his fellow member of the Sherlock Holmes Society of London, Humphrey Morton—the latter also played Inspector Lestrade regularly on the Carleton Hobbs radio series.

Howlett also took part TV documentary in '71, *Mr. Sherlock Holmes of London*, together with the late illustrious Sherlockian Dr. Maurice Campbell and a number of other members of the Society.

And, finally, Dr. Campbell played the role of Dr. John H. Watson during the Society's visit to Switzerland in 1968 to reenact the Reichenbach Falls struggle, and the adventure was preserved in two theatrical documentaries, both in color: a *Pathe Pictorial* and *In the Footsteps of Sherlock Holmes*. Among the other cast members were the ubiquitous Mr. Howlett once again, impersonating the Immortal Detective; Lord Gore-Booth filled the deerstalker for part of the trip, but was not seen in the film; and Holmesian scriptwriters and historians Michael and Mollie Hardwicke, Michael Pointer, and the Marquis of Donegall were all on hand in various Conanical guises.

A last documentary, again theatrical, was *The Life of Sherlock Holmes*, made at the Slade School of Fine Art in London by Jeremy Marre in 1970. Clips from the Eille Norwood series were combined with other old film bits and pieces, such as old newsreel footage of London, to create a blending of fact and fiction in the vein of Jorge Luis Borges. For most viewers, however, there could be no such question involved of distinguishing the real from the imaginary, for the majority of people have long since accepted the invincible belief that Sherlock Holmes was indeed a real, flesh-and-blood human being.

Epilogue

Here at last we find ourselves at the point reached by Sir Arthur Conan Doyle in 1927 when he wrote, " . . . and so, reader, farewell to Sherlock Holmes!" Unlike Doyle, though, we are well aware that his immortal creation cannot be bid to his rest so easily.

There can never be a truly complete and absolutely up-to-date volume on Sherlock Holmes films, because there are new additions every day. By the time our manuscript reaches the bookstores, it will already be somewhat out of date. Even as we write these words, production is proceeding on *The West End Horror,* a sequel to the film *The Seven-Per-Cent Solution,* which unfortunately was released too late to assign it an entire chapter in this work, a chapter which it so rightly deserves.

The publishers of this book have graciously given us the opportunity to up-date the Epilogue, and pass on to you more information on the most recent additions to the films and television adventures of Sherlock Holmes.

Sherlock Holmes was the title of a British documentary film of 1975.

Donald Sutherland has been cast as Moriarty in a British film shooting now in England. The film is based on John Gardner's Moriarty books, in which Moriarty appears with hardly a mention of Holmes!

The Seven-Per-Cent Solution is the most important of the recent additions to our list of Sherlock Holmes films. The film is based on the novel of the same name, " . . . a posthumous memoir of John H. Watson, M.D., as edited by Nicholas Meyer." Meyer, an eminent Sherlockian scholar, also adapted his novel into screenplay form for this Universal release.

This marvelous film ran 113 minutes and was released in October of 1976 in New York. It was produced and directed by veteran Hollywood director Herbert Ross, and its cast included Alan Arkin as Dr. Sigmund Freud, Robert Duvall as Dr. Watson, Nicol Williamson as Sherlock Holmes, Vanessa Redgrave as Lola Deveraux, Laurence Olivier as the evil Professor Moriarty, who is really not so evil, Joel Gray as Lowenstein, Samantha Eggar as Mary Watson, Jeremy Kemp as Baron Von Leinsdorf (the real villain), Charles Gray as Mycroft Holmes, and Georgia Brown as Mrs. Freud.

Any true Holmes buff will of course recognize the title as referring to Holmes' unfortunate use of the hypodermic syringe and its contents when he is not involved in a case and feels the need of mental stimulation. In the original stories this vice is never spoken of as more than a harmless relaxation, but in *The Seven-Per-Cent Solution,* purported to be the story that Watson could never bring himself to tell, and which explains Holmes' Great Disappearance after the affair at the Reichenbach Falls, Holmes' addiction forces Watson, Freud, and (believe it or not) Moriarty, to conspire against Holmes, tricking him into traveling to Vienna to be cured of his drug dependence by Freud.

While there, and under Freud's care, he becomes involved in the kidnapping of Lola Deveraux by the nefarious Baron Von Leinsdorf, and together with Freud and Watson, solves the case and rescues the beauteous Miss Deveraux after a spectacular train chase borrowed largely from *Around the World in Eighty Days.*

Nicol Williamson does himself proud as Holmes, not only for his portrayal of The Great Detective, but even more so for his marvelous performance as the drug addict undergoing primitive withdrawal procedures. Williamson was quoted in *Playboy Magazine* shortly before the film's release as saying "What I want with *Seven-Per-Cent Solution* is to take people on The Great Adventure. None of your over-the-top outrageous foolery; we're leaving that sort of stuff to Gene Wilder. Of course, everybody considers Holmes a man of irony, wit, high intellect . . . but he's also sensitive, vulnerable, pained and anguished . . . with these last four qualities kept absolutely under wraps. A very complex man."

The other cast members all turn in performances that should be rated somewhere between Very Good and Superlative. Robert Duvall, seemingly miscast, very quickly proves to the contrary, presenting us with a Watson more than worthy of standing among the great Watsons Nigel Bruce, Andre Morell, Reginald Owen, Thorley Walters, and Donald Houston. Alan Arkin makes a credible Dr. Freud, although more than one reviewer commented that his German accent was "too Brooklyn."

Director of Photography Oswald Morris, B.S.C., Designer Ken Adam, and Musical Director John Addison, combined their talents most admirably to create the appropriately subtle beauty of atmosphere required to blend a good cast, a fine director, and an excellent script into an extraordinary motion picture, not exactly according to Doyle, but thoroughly enjoyable nonetheless.

We hope the sequel *The West End Horror,* in which Holmes battles The Plague in London, is handled as well.

Two television movies have paid homage to Sherlock Holmes in the past year in New York. The first was entitled *Return of the World's Greatest Detective,* which starred Larry Hagman as Holmes, and was inspired by (and to some extent copied) *They Might Be Giants.*

The second, aired on October 18, 1976 in New York, was called, appropriately enough, *Sherlock Holmes in New York,* and starred former *Saint* and *James Bond* Roger Moore, former *Avenger* Patrick Macnee as Watson, John Huston as Professor Moriarty (marvelous casting, that!), and Charlotte Rampling as Irene Adler. This TV movie, while giving Holmes a very Holmesian mystery to solve, unfortunately portrayed Holmes a little too closely to James Bond, having him openly flirt with a woman, surely something the real Holmes would never be caught doing (although, upon reflection, if Holmes ever were to become romantically attached to a woman, surely that woman must be *The Woman,* Irene Adler). Not only are they romantically linked in this film, but they have a son! (An eventuality explored and predicted by noted Sherlockian

William S. Baring-Gould—whose analysis of Rex Stout's neo-Holmes character Nero Wolfe suggests that Nero Wolfe might be the result of that union!) The part of the new lusty Holmes seemed written for Roger Moore, and Moore returned the favor, playing the part as if he had been born to play it, and play it well.

John Huston's Moriarty was equally as enchanting, and one cannot help but wonder why Huston was not cast in the role before this. It's a natural for Huston, and he looks as if he were enjoying himself in the role. The supporting players, Charlotte Rampling, Gig Young, David Huddleston, and Signe Hasso, played their roles with gusto, doing their best to help a weak script. Devoted Sherlockians will no doubt have been disappointed with Patrick Macnee's portrayal of the trusty Dr. Watson, but as a whole, it was quite an enjoyable and worthwhile effort.

A sequel to *Sherlock Holmes in New York* is planned, also to star Roger Moore as Sherlock Holmes.

In production as we go to press is *Sherlock Holmes' Adventure With the Golden Vampire,* directed by Frank R. Saletri and starring former Superman Kirk Alyn and with Keith McConnell as Sherlock Holmes. This information comes from a personal interview with Kirk Alyn. We await the premiere of this film with eagerness.

Also in the works is a Sherlock Holmes television special starring Robert Shaw and Donald Pleasance, and an ABC-TV *Short Story Special* for kids entitled *My Dear Uncle Sherlock* is scheduled for broadcast in February of 1977.

Christopher Plummer is Sherlock Holmes, and Thorley Walters recreates his Dr. Watson for a British television special this year. And Nigel Stock is the voice of Dr. Watson in a current British radio series.

And so we bid farewell not to Sherlock Holmes, nor to his film career, but to you, our readers.

Sherlock Holmes not only lives on, but he has long since joined the company of those archetypal legends who can never die.

As long as there are motion pictures, or books, or television, or radio, or theatre, there will be a Sherlock Holmes. And if, in the far, far distant future, all these are replaced by a new form of mass entertainment, someone will surely find a way to adapt the Sherlock Holmes characters to that new form.

There will always be a Sherlock Holmes.

Appendix A

The Sherlock Holmes Stories of Sir Arthur Conan Doyle
(* indicates those stories never filmed):

A Study in Scarlet
The Sign of Four
Adventures of Sherlock Holmes
    A Scandal in Bohemia
    The Red-Headed League
    A Case of Identity
    The Boscombe Valley Mystery
    The Five Orange Pips
    The Man With The Twisted Lip
    The Adventure of the Blue Carbuncle
    The Adventure of the Speckled Band
    The Adventure of the Engineer's Thumb
    The Adventure of the Noble Bachelor
    The Adventure of the Beryl Coronet
    The Adventure of the Copper Beeches
Memoirs of Sherlock Holmes
    Silver Blaze
    The Yellow Face
    The Stock-broker's Clerk
    The "Gloria Scott"
    The Musgrave Ritual
    The Reigate Puzzle
    The Crooked Man
    The Resident Patient
    The Greek Interpreter
    The Naval Treaty
    The Final Problem
The Hound of the Baskervilles
The Return of Sherlock Holmes
    The Adventure of the Empty House
    The Adventure of the Norwood Builder
    The Adventure of the Dancing Men
    The Adventure of the Solitary Cyclist
    The Adventure of the Priory School
    The Adventure of Black Peter

    The Adventure of Charles Augustus Milverton
    The Adventure of the Six Napoleons
    The Adventure of the Three Students
    The Adventure of the Golden Pince-Nez
    The Adventure of the Missing Three-Quarter
    The Adventure of the Abbey Grange
    The Adventure of the Second Stain
The Valley of Fear
His Last Bow
    The Adventure of Wisteria Lodge
    The Adventure of the Cardboard Box
    The Adventure of the Red Circle
    The Adventure of the Bruce-Partington Plans
    The Adventure of the Dying Detective
    The Disappearance of Lady Frances Carfax
    The Adventure of the Devil's Foot
    His Last Bow
The Case Book of Sherlock Holmes
    The Adventure of the Illustrious Client
    *The Adventure of the Blanched Soldier
    The Adventure of the Mazarin Stone
    *The Adventure of the Three Gables
    *The Adventure of the Sussex Vampire
    *The Adventure of the Three Garridebs
    The Problem of Thor Bridge
    *The Adventure of the Creeping Man
    *The Adventure of the Lion's Mane
    *The Adventure of the Veiled Lodger
    *The Adventure of Shoscombe Old Place
    *The Adventure of the Retired Colourman
*The Field Bazaar
*How Watson Learned the Trick
*The Crown Diamond (play)
  The Speckled Band (play)
*(One other unpublished play with Watson but without Holmes)

Appendix B

British Film Censors' Certificates:

"A" from January 1913 thru June 1970: *Adult*—
Children must be accompanied by an adult.
from July 1970 thru December 1970: *Adult*—
Unsuitable for children under fourteen
years of age.

"AA" Children under fourteen years of age not
admitted.

"H" *Horrific*: Children under sixteen years of age
not admitted.

"U" *Universal*: No restrictions

"X" *Adult*: until June 1970—No children under
sixteen
since July 1970—No children under
eighteen

Bibliography

BOOKS

American Film Institute Catalogue—Feature Films, 1921–1930

Arliss, George. *George Arliss By Himself*. London: John Murray, 1940.

————. *Up The Years From Bloomsbury: An Autobiography*. London: John Murray, 1927.

Balcon, Sir Michael. *Michael Balcon Presents: A Lifetime of Films*. London: Hutchinson, 1969.

————. *Twenty Years of British Film 1925–1945*. New York: Arno Press, 1972. (Originally published 1947)

Ball, Robert Hamilton. *Shakespeare on Silent Film*. New York: Theatre Arts Books, 1968.

Baring-Gould, William S. (ed. with intro., notes, and bibliography). *The Annotated Sherlock Holmes*. New York: Clarkson N. Potter, (Distributed by Crown Publishers), 1967.

Benson, Sir F. R., Foreword to *Telepathy And Spirit Communication* by L. Margery Bazett. London: Rider & Co., 1928.

Bergsten, Bebe. *The Great Dane and the Great Northern Film Company*. Los Angeles: Historical Films, 1973.

Blum, Daniel. *A Pictorial History of the Silent Screen*. New York: Grosset & Dunlap, 1953.

————. *A Pictorial History of the Talkies*. New York: Grosset & Dunlap, 1958.

Brault, Eustache. *Cine-Guide Perpetuel; Compilation de Plus de 10,000 Films par Ordre Alphabétique, avec Supplements à Date*. Montreal: Frides, 1942.

Carr, John Dickson. *The Life of Sir Arthur Conan Doyle*. New York: Harper, 1949.

Catalogue of Copyright Entries. Cumulative Series, Motion Pictures 1912–1939, Copyright Office. Library of Congress.

Catalogue of U.S. Copyright Entries: Motion Pictures 1894–1912.

Catalogo Generale dei Soggetti Cinematografici

Cowie, Peter. *A Concise History of the Cinema*, 1971.

Cushing, Peter and Hirst, Robert. *Three Men And a Gimmick*. The World's Work, (1913) Ltd., Kingswood Surrey, U.K. (Cedar Books), 1957.

Daisne, Johan. (pseudonym of Herman Thiery) *Filmographic Dictionary of World Literature*. Gand, E. Story-Scientia, 1971.

Davenport, Basil. *The Portable Roman Reader*. New York, Viking Press, 1951.

Dimmitt, Richard Bertrand. *A Title Guide to the Talkies*. New Jersey: Scarecrow Press, 1965.

Doyle, Sir Arthur Conan. (*see Appendix A*)

Druxman, Michael B. *Basil Rathbone; His Life and His Films*, South Brunswick and New York: A.S. Barnes & Co., 1975. London: Thomas Yoseloff, Ltd., 1975.

Durgnat, Raymond. *A Mirror for England; British Movies From Austerity to Affluence*. New York: Praeger, 1971.

Eisner, L. H. *L'écran démoniaque; influence de Max Reinhardt et de l'expressionisme*. Paris: A. Bonne, 1952. (Translated from the French by Roger Greaves—*The Haunted Screen; Expressionism in the German Cinema and the Influence of Max Reinhardt*.)

Everson, William K. *The Bad Guys; A Pictorial History of the Movie Villain*. New York: Citadel Press, 1964.

————. *The Detective in Films*. New York: Citadel Press, 1972.

The Film Index: A Bibliography/Volume I—The Film as Art. Writers Program: Museum of Modern Art Film Library. New York, 1941.

Frank, Alan G. *The Movie Treasury: Horror Movies: Tales of Terror in The Cinema*. New Jersey: Derbibooks, 1974.

Franklin, Joe. *Classics of the Silent Screen*. New York: Citadel Press, 1959.

Gaye, Freda. *Who's Who in the Theatre* (14th Edition), 1967.

Gertner, Richard (ed.) *International Television Almanac*, New York: Quigley Pub., 1971.

Gifford, Denis. *British Cinema: An Illustrated Guide*. New York: A.S. Barnes, 1968.

———. *The British Film Catalogue 1895–1970.* New York: McGraw-Hill, 1974.

Glut, Donald and Harmon, J. M. *Great Movie Serials.* Garden City, N.Y.:Doubleday & Co., Inc., 1972.

Granville-Barker, Harley. Preface to *Twelfth Night.* London: Heinmann, 1912.

Greene, Sir Hugh. (ed. and intro.) *Cosmopolitan Crimes: Foreign Rivals of Sherlock Holmes.* Harmondsworth, Middlesex, G.B.: Penguin Books, Ltd., 1972.

Griffith, Richard and Mayer, Arthur. *The Movies.* London: Spring Books, 1963.

Haining, Peter (ed.) *The Sherlock Holmes Scrapbook.* New York: Clarkson N. Potter, 1974.

Halliwell, Leslie. *The Filmgoer's Companion* (2nd, 3rd, & 4th Editions) New York: Hill & Wang, 1965–1975.

Hampton, Benjamin B. *History of the American Film Industry (From Its Beginnings to 1931).* New York: Dover, 1970.

Hardwicke, John Michael Drinkrow and Greenhalgh (afterwards Hardwicke), Mollie. *The Man Who Was Sherlock Holmes.* London: John Murray, 1964.

Harrison, Michael. *In the Footsteps of Sherlock Holmes.* New York: Drake Publishers, 1972.

Higham, Charles. *Films of Orson Welles.* London and Los Angeles: University of California, Berkeley.

Jacobs, Lewis. *The Rise of the American Film, A Critical History.* With an Essay: *Experimental Cinema in America, 1921–1947.* New York: Teachers College Press, 1968.

Joyce, James. *Ulysses.* Paris: Shakespeare & Co.; Sylvia Beach, 1922.

Kracauer, Siegfried. *From Caligari to Hitler; A Psychological History of the German Film.* Princeton University Press, 1947.

Lahue, Kalton C. *Clown Princes.* South Brunswick & New York: A.S. Barnes & Co.; London: Thomas Yoseloff, Ltd.

Le Jeune, C. A. *Thank You for Having Me.* London: Hutchinson, 1964.

Low, Rachael. *History of British Films, 1906–1918.* London: George Allen & Unwin, 1948.

Macqueen-Pope, W. *The Footlights Flickered.* London: Herbert-Jenkins, 1959.

Manchel, Frank. *When Pictures Began To Move.* New Jersey: Prentice-Hall.

Manvell, Arnold Roger, Dr. (ed.) *International Encyclopedia of Film.* New York: Crown Publishing, 1972.

———. (ed.) *Penguin Film Review, Nos. 1–9.* Penguin Books, 1946–1949.

Maude, Cyril. *Behind the Scenes with Cyril Maude.* London: John Murray, 1927.

Meyers, Warren B. *Who Is That? The Late Late Viewers Guide to the Old Old Movie Players.* New York: Personality Posters, 1967.

Michael, Paul (ed.) *The American Movies Reference Book.* New Jersey: Prentice-Hall, 1969.

Miller Maud M. (ed.) *Winchester's Screen Encyclopedia.* London: Winchester Publishing, 1948.

The New York Times Dictionary of the Film. Arno Press & Random House, 1970.

Niver, Kemp R. *Motion Pictures from the Library of Congress Paper Print Collection 1894–1912.* Berkeley: University of California Press, 1967.

Nordisk Films Kompagni; A.S. (includes Danish Film Index 1903–1956), Copenhagen, 1956.

Nordon, Pierre. *Conan Doyle, A Biography.* (English Translation) London: John Murray, 1966.

Norwood, Eille. *Hook and Eye.* London: Samuel French, 1937 (First Published 1887.)

Parker, John. *Who's Who In The Theatre: A Biographical Record of the Contemporary Stage.* London: 1930, 1936, 1939.

Parish, James Robert. *Actors' Television Credits 1950–1972.* New Jersey: Scarecrow Press, 1973.

———. *The Great Movie Series.* New York: A. S. Barnes, 1971.

Pathéscope Company of America, Inc.; Descriptive List of Pathéscope Films. New York, 1918.

Pearson, George. *Flashback.* London: George Allen & Unwin, 1957

Pearson, Hasketh. *Conan Doyle.* New York: Walker & Co., 1961.

Pirie, David. *A Heritage of Horror: The English Gothic Cinema 1946–1972.* New York: Avon Press (Equinox Books), 1973.

Planche, J. R. *The Jacobite* (with comments in this copy by Eille Norwood). London: Samuel French.

Powell, Dilys. *Films Since 1939.* London and New York: Longmans Green for the British Council, 1947.

Queen, Ellery. *Sherlock Holmes Versus Jack the Ripper* (U. S. Title: *A Study in Terror*). London: Gollancz, 1967.

Rathbone, Basil. *In And Out Of Character.* Garden City, New York: Doubleday, 1962.

Reed, Langford and Spiers, Hetty. *Who's Who in Filmland, 1928.* London: 1927–1931.

Rotha, Paul and Griffith, Richard. *The Film Till Now: A Survey of World Cinema.* New York: Twayne Publishers, 1960.

Saintsbury, H. A. (attributed). *Letters of an Unsuccessful Actor.* Boston: Small, Maynard & Co.

———. (coeditor). *We Saw Him Act.* London: Hurst & Blackett, 1939.

Starrett, Vincent (ed.) *221B: Studies in Sherlock Holmes by Various Hands.* New York: Biblio & Tannen, 1969.

———. *The Private Life of Sherlock Holmes.* New York: Pinnacle Books, 1975.

Thompson, H. Douglas. *Masters of Mystery: A Study of the Detective Story.* London: Collins, 1931.

Trewin, John Courtenay. *Benson and the Bensonians;* with a forward by Dorothy Green. London: Barrie & Rockliff, 1960.

Truitt, Evelyn Mack. *Who Was Who On The Screen.* R. R. Boulker: Xerox Corp., 1974.

Watson, John H., M.D. [sic—Watson was actually only a *Bachelor* of Medicine, as Holmes notes in *The Field Bazaar*] as Edited by Nicholas Meyer. *The Seven-Per-Cent Solution.* E. P. Dutton & Co., Inc., 1974.

Who's Who In The Motion Picture World. New York: Who's Who in Pictures Publishing Company, 1915.

Wilcox, Herbert. *Twenty-Five Thousand Sunsets: The Autobiography of Herbert Wilcox.* London, Sydney, & Toronto: The Bodley Mead, Ltd., 1967.

Winchester, Clarence (ed.) *The World Film Encyclopedia: A Universal Screen Guide.* London: Amalgamated Press, 1933.

MAGAZINES, NEWSPAPERS, PERIODICALS & OTHER SOURCES:

ABC Film Review, Nov. 1970.

American 8 May 1922; Barrymore Film Review
11 May 1922; Barrymore Film Review by Rose Pelswick

American Cinematographer Oct. 1975.

Baggott, King. Scrapbook at Lincoln Center Library for the Performing Arts.

Barter Street Theatrical Memorabilia Shop, London. 1972–1973.

Benham, Harry. Scrapbook at Lincoln Center Library for the Performing Arts.

British Film Institute, London: National Film Archives—Stills Collection, Microfilm, Motion Picture Collection.

British Theatrical Museum:
    Whatmore Collection—letters of Charles Frohman to Pauline Chase and Drawings of William Gillette by Charles Frohman
    Autographs and Letters donated by Brian Hill
    Walter Hudd Collection
    A. Harding Steerman Collection—Letters of Arthur Wontner
    Dick's Penny Plays
    Lillah McCarthy Collection
    Irene Mawer Memorial Library
    Ernest Short Collection
    Royal Court Photos
    Gielgud Collection—Haselden Drawings
    Sir Henry Irving Archive—Letters of Sir Arthur Conan Doyle & William Gillette
    Debenham Collection
    Denville Collection
    Cecil Madden Collection

Castle of Frankenstein, N.J. 1962, 1966, 1967, 1968

Chicago Tribune, 14 June 1916; Kitty Kelly's review of Gillette film.

Chiswick Post, 3 July 1964

Cine Fantastique, Vol. 4, No. 3, Fall 1975

Columbia Pictures Publicity Releases

Commonwealth

Compton Newsflash 6 October 1965

Compton Publicity Releases

Daily Express 1959, 1962, 1965

Daily Film Renter 1934–1936

Daily Herald 1956, 1959 (London)

Daily Mail 1959, 1960, 1965

Daily Mirror 1955, 1959

Daily News 1922

Daily Telegraph 1958–1960, 1965–1966, 1969

Daily Worker 1959, 1965

Der Kinematograph (Germany 1929)

Detroit Free Press 2 August 1916; Gillette Film Review

Dunham, Harold & Slide, Anthony, Notes for G. B. Samuelson Exhibition

Evening News (London) 1948, 1956, 1958–1959, 1965–1967

Evening Standard 1949, 1954, 1959, 1966, 1969, 1972

Famous Monsters Convention Souvenir Magazine (1975 Convention)

Famous Monsters of Filmland Philadelphia, 1961, 1964, 1966

Fashionable Dress, August 1922; Barrymore Film Review

Films and Filming. September 1965, May 1972, June 1972.

Film Daily Yearbook, 1930–1934, 1940–1947

Filmlexicon Degli Autori (Edelle Opere)

Film Fan Monthly No. 92 (February 1969)

Film Fun

Films Illustrated Vol. 1, No. 2, Aug. 1971.

Film Index, The, 5 December 1908; *Miss Sherlock Holmes Review*

Films In Review, VI—347, XII—409, cf 502—503, XIII—505, August–September 1961. New York 1960–1975

Film Pictorial 1932–1936

Focus on Film No. 8

For Monsters Only New York, 1967

Guardian 1959–1969

Hammer Films Publicity Releases

Henry, Arthur. *The Chaperon.* (A manuscript copy belonging to Eille Norwood.)

Herald Tribune 8 May 1922; Barrymore Film Review

Horror Monsters, Connecticut, 1964

International Motion Picture Almanac, 1945–1971

Journal

Kinematograph, The 1916

Kinematograph and Lantern Weekly 1933–1937

Kinematograph Weekly 1908, 1915–1916, 1922

Leader 1947

Library Journal

Life Magazine

London Sunday Times 1972

Mail 8 May 1922; Barrymore Film Review

Midi-Minuit Fantastique No. 14, June 1966

Midi-Minuit No. 1, May–June 1962; 1965, 1967

Modern Monsters Los Angeles, 1966

Monster Mania, New York, 1966–1967

Monthly Film Bulletin 1934–1936, December 1965, March 1970, April 1972. (British Film Institute)

Motion Picture Herald

Motion Picture News 1916

Moving Picture Stories 1913

Moving Picture World 1908; 15 July 1911; 6 December 1913; 6 May 1916; 27 May 1916.

National Film Archives, British Film Institute, London

National Film Theatre, British Film Institute, London (Program Notes)

New Outlook

New Republic

News Chronicle 1959

News of the World 1956–1959

New Statesman 1959

Newsweek 1959

New York Dramatic Mirror 1908–1916

New York Morning Telegraph 1916

New York Public Library

New York Times 1922–1970; Mar. 22, 1970; Pohle, Mae B., "A Connecticut Yankee's Real Life Castle In The Air"

Observer 1959–1966

People, The 5 May 1968; Kenneth Bailey's TV Insight

Philadelphia Free Library, Theatre Collection

Photoplay, June 1972; d'Arcy, Susan. "Peter Cushing and Christopher Lee"

Picturegoer

Picturegoer Weekly 1914–1936

Pictures and the Picturegoer 1914–1919

Playbill for *Sherlock Holmes* with John Neville, Broadway 1975

Playboy September 1975

Pulse 27 February 1972; Pohle, Robert. "Sherlock Holmes, Master Detective"

Punch 1915–1934

Radio Times 1 June 1972

Screen Thrills Illustrated 1964

Sherlock Holmes Journal 1962–1971

Shriek 1966

Spacemen 1961–1963

S.P.C. 1959

Spectator 1939–1965; 14 July 1939, Graham Greene Review

Star Mar. 26, 1959

Stoll's Editorial News 1922

Stoll Studios Publicity Releases

Strand Magazine July 1891–June 1892

Sun 1965

Sunday Dispatch 1957–1959

Sunday Express 1959–1971

Sunday Mirror 1968

Sunday Times (London) 1965

Sun Telegraph 1965

Sun Times 1959

Telegram 3 May 1922

Telegraph (New York) 1914–1922

Time 1965

Time & Tide 4 November 1959; MacLaren, Chas., Review of *Hound of the Baskervilles*

Times (London) 1958–1970

Times Literary Supplement 1975

Tribune

United Artists Publicity Releases

Universal City Studio Story—Souvenir Booklet

Van Name, Fred, "Gillette Castle State Park", 1956, Connecticut State Park & Forrest Commission

Variety 1960–1972

Views and Film Index 28 December 1907

Wessex Film Productions—British Lion Film Corporation, Publicity

William Gunning's Independent Reviews 1916

Woman's Own 22 October 1966; Beverley Nichols' interview with Douglas Wilmer.

Index

In our desire to make this work a truly authoritative and complete anthology of the motion picture and television adventures of Holmes, Watson, et al., we have attempted to make this index as complete as possible without crossing over the boundaries of absurdity. Toward that end, we have not included in this index certain character names and people names that occur very often in the text:

Sir Arthur Conan Doyle   Sherlock Holmes
Dr. John H. Watson, M.D.   Professor Moriarty
Inspector Lestrade   Mrs. Hudson

Billy   Sir Henry Baskerville
Stapleton   Mycroft
Other character names that occur less frequently are included in the index and appear in quotation marks.

Book and play titles, as well as the titles of radio shows and series, are identified as such in the index. Any other titles may be assumed to be the titles of motion pictures. Where more than one film exists with the same or similar title, the film's country of origin and date of manufacture appear in parentheses.

"Really, Mr. Holmes, this is a bit too much!"
"Mrs. Hudson" (Minnie Rayner)
The Sleeping Cardinal (GB '31)